The COMPLETE CUT & ENGRAVED GLASS of CORNING

The COMPLETE CUT & ENGRAVED GLASS of CORNING

by
Estelle Sinclaire Farrar
and
Jane Shadel Spillman

THE CORNING MUSEUM OF GLASS

CROWN PUBLISHERS, INC.
New York

A Corning Museum of Glass Monograph

Printed in the United States of America

Published simultaneously in Canada
by General Publishing Company Limited

Library of Congress Cataloging in Publication Data

Farrar, Estelle Sinclaire.
　　The complete cut & engraved glass of Corning.

　　(A Corning Museum of Glass monograph)
　　Bibliography: p.
　　Includes index.
　　1. Cut glass—New York (State)—Corning. 2. Engraved glass—New York (State)—Corning. 3. Glassware—New York (State)—Corning—History—19th century. 4. Glassware—New York (State)—Corning—History—20th century. 5. Corning Glass Works. 6. Corning, N.Y.—History. I. Spillman, Jane Shadel, joint author. II. Corning, N.Y. Museum of Glass. III. Title. IV. Series: Corning, N.Y. Museum of Glass. Monographs.
NK5203.F37 1978　　　　748.2′9147′83　　　　78-18514
ISBN 0-517-53432-0

To Corning's matchless craftsmen, past and present, we dedicate this book with admiration and affection, and offer one of Frederick Carder's favorite poems.

L'ENVOI

When Earth's last picture is painted, and the tubes are twisted and dried,
When the oldest colours have faded, and the youngest critic has died,
We shall rest, and, faith, we shall need it—lie down for an aeon or two,
Till the Master of All Good Workmen shall put us to work anew!
. . . .
And only the Master shall praise us, and only the Master shall blame;
And no one shall work for money, and no one shall work for fame;
But each for the joy of the working, and each, in his separate star,
Shall draw the Thing as he sees It for the God of Things as They Are!

—*Rudyard Kipling*

Acknowledgments

The tireless work of Otto W. Hilbert has been second only to that of the authors of this book. The records of Corning Glass Works and its predecessors have been open to us through Mr. Hilbert. No detail has been too tiny for him to check. His research into Corning Glass Works employment records has solved many a discrepancy in dates; his wide acquaintanceship with employees of the 1920s and 1930s elicited the answers to questions that seemed insoluble.

We are deeply indebted to many staff members of The Corning Museum of Glass, including Mrs. Jane Lanahan, who typed portions of the manuscript; Raymond Errett who took our cover photograph, and our librarians, Mrs. Norma Jenkins and Mrs. Virginia Wright. Mrs. Wright has time and again produced just the book or document that we needed. Priscilla Price, registrar, and Nicholas Williams, photographer, have spent countless hours arranging for and taking the majority of our photographs, often on very short notice.

Lois Janes and Thomas Dimitroff, as they researched their Bicentennial history of Corning, sent us a steady stream of information about Corning's cutting companies. They have also shared with us the photographs and documents that they unearthed. We are most grateful.

Mrs. Janet Dow Orr has most graciously lent documents pertaining to H. P. Sinclaire & Co., which she inherited from her father, the company superintendent. Mrs. Penrose Hawkes, widow of T. G. Hawkes & Co.'s last president, has helped with information and advice and lent valuable catalogs.

Master engraver Max Roland Erlacher has given us advice whenever asked and has lent us his vast knowledge of engraving. Steuben Glass engravers Peter Schelling and Kenneth Van Etten have shared their friendship with earlier Corning craftsmen.

Robert Rockwell, Jr., and Robert Rockwell III have put us on the track of informants and of unusual examples of cut or engraved glass. They have lent examples from their own collections. Equally important was their encyclopedic knowledge of who in Corning owned just the examples that we needed.

Corning residents—and Corning's children from the Altantic to the Pacific—have written and telephoned to provide information, have loaned us glass to be photographed, and generally added flesh and color to the skeleton of our story. The names of most will appear only as footnotes, but their contributions have been invaluable. It is clear that Corning's early relish for tackling tough jobs and doing them thoroughly is undiminished.

E. S. F.
J. S. S.

Contents

Chapters 4, 5, and 7 by Jane Shadel Spillman; all others by Estelle Sinclaire Farrar.

A Note on the Illustrations

The Corning Museum of Glass is fortunate in having extensive archives of local cut glass catalogs, including a large number from the Hawkes firm and one or two from each of several smaller and less-well-known glass factories. Unfortunately, all these catalogs were damaged in the June 1972 flood. Because the material they contain had never been published, the authors felt a selection of photographs from these catalogs should be reproduced in this book in spite of their condition. Accordingly, some of the illustrations are less than perfect in quality. However, we hope that the usefulness of the material will help the reader overlook its sometimes faded state. Except where noted, all the illustrations are from the collection of The Corning Museum of Glass, as are many of the documents quoted.

The Corning–Painted Post Historical Society, the owner of several important catalogs as well as some archival information, was kind enough to allow us to publish these as well. None of the catalogs is published here completely; rather, a selection was made from the contents of each one in order to show as many patterns and shapes as possible. Most of the catalogs are now on microfilm or microfiche, and in this form can be consulted at the museum by any interested researcher.

The careful reader will notice that different terms for the same thing are used by various glass companies, i.e., "pattern" and "design," "compote" and "comport." The authors have attempted to follow the style of each firm rather than to standardize throughout the book.

1
Background

Something of the ancient fascination with glass still lingers in the industry. New colors and secret formulas bear the touch of Egypt, where glass imitated gemstones, the gods' eyes into the world below. Glassmaking is a paradigm of classical atomic theory. Only its fires prevent water from returning silica to its natural crystalline state.

Glassmaking still has its mysteries, passed down from father to son, and through the nineteenth century, from Master to apprentice. A century ago the desire to transmute base elements into an imitation of the diamond approximated the alchemists' fervor.

Today's glass industry is called "close-knit." "Fraternal" is more accurate. Nineteenth-century American glassmakers knew and admired one another. They took pride in the industry's accomplishments, including those of their competitors. Rather than copy a fellow initiate's product, they regularly bought glass from one another.

It is not surprising, then, that Corning's cut-glass industry began with a group of glassmen who were friends and fellow enthusiasts, as well as relatives. They encouraged and helped one another. They had a common aim: quality products that would make a growing nation proud as well as self-sufficient. They fiercely resisted the inevitable progress of fine glass through popularization to mediocrity, but ultimately their grandsons prevailed.

Corning's dream was decades old. Briefly content with political freedom, America now hungered for economic and artistic independence. For these, her capitalists and mechanics—golden words in the nineteenth century—had only to strive together.

Trade fairs sprang up and prospered as early as the 1820s. Horace Greeley's *New York Daily Tribune* gave detailed coverage to the annual Fair of the American Institute, which opened for three weeks on October 6, 1845. Attendance topped 80,000; "the number of articles [exhibited]...exceeded by 500 those of any former year."

A "closing address" printed in Greeley's paper on October 27, 1845, stated the Fair's aims, and connected them with the Brooklyn Flint Glass Works, ancestor of Corning Glass Works.

> Gen. Tallmadge...[said] that this [fair] was designed to encourage Domestic industry; that the charges brought against it of being designed to keep up a high tariff were false; and that its main object was to give high wages to labor in this country; and to protect it against the pauper labor of Europe [*Applause*]....
>
> This Institution holds emphatically to the doctrine of self-preservation; that this country should create its own wealth—its own supplies—and hence its own happiness....
>
> He [Tallmadge] then alluded to the great improvement made in cut glass in this country, whereas a few years since and we had to import all our decanters and cut glass; now Mr. Curtis of the Glass Works, Brooklyn, produces glass of finer color and better cut than any imported glass; and we have no cause to pray for this article from foreign countries.

Superior American quality, self-sufficiency, and protection against "pauper labor"! Corning, New York, would still be fighting for them a century later. They seemed readily attainable after the Civil War. A recent book called the period "the Confident Years," and said of it:

> It was a period of exuberant growth, in population, industry, and world prestige. As the twentieth

century opened, American political pundits were convinced that the nation was on an ascending spiral of progress that could end only in something approaching perfection. Even those who saw the inequity between the bright world of privilege and the gray fact of poverty were quite sure that a time was very near when no one would go cold or hungry or ill-clothed. These were indeed the Confident Years.[1]

It is remarkable that the United States came close to realizing her dream. In Corning four generations of glass companies have pursued it. Most of the third succumbed by the 1930s to the competition of Europe's "pauper labor." Yet even as they died, a rebirth was taking place. Corning is still the Crystal City. The dream of American supremacy in fine glass has become a fact.

Fine cut glass requires brilliant lead-crystal cutting blanks as well as expert cutters. The mid-nineteenth century's uncertain transportation caused some cutters to set up shop in the factories of their suppliers. So it was with John Hoare and his partners and the Brooklyn Flint Glass Works.

That glassworks appeared on an 1827 map of Brooklyn,[2] but there is contradictory evidence about the identity of its founder. In 1864, according to Brooklyn and New York City directories, it was bankrupt and its furnaces were cold. John Hoare had left or soon did so, although he continued to operate his second cutting shop, which was in Greenpoint, in a glass factory founded by Christian Dorflinger.[3] At this critical point, a group whose active glassmen were Amory Houghton, Sr. and Jr., bought the Brooklyn Flint Glass Works.

The 1866 New York City directory indicated the furnaces were operating, but the company was still in receivership. A bill dated July 3, 1866, provides evidence that John Hoare was cutting and selling glass for Amory Houghton, Jr., in Hoare's Greenpoint shop at that time. Reorganization and fresh capital became imperative for the Houghtons.[4]

Corning's cut-glass industry was foreshadowed by a Brooklyn reorganization meeting in March 1866.[5] Stockholders included the two Houghtons, Josiah Oakes (brother of Mrs. Houghton, Sr.), and Charles H. Voorhees. Oakes was the chief stockholder, followed by the younger Houghton, who became president. Henry P. Sinclaire, married to another Oakes sister, was elected secretary although he was absent and owned no stock. The owners met again in April and voted to buy a Mr. Marrett's interest in a "Glass House property in Brooklyn" and "cutting shops in New York City and Boston, Mass."

Early in 1867 fire struck the Oakes-Houghton factory, but in that same year Amory Houghton, Jr., and two new stockholders reorganized the company,

filing incorporation papers on June 4. They retained Sinclaire as secretary and Houghton as president. Another and more pregnant development was already under way, however. A telegram (in Corning Glass Works archives) from Houghton to Elias Hungerford of Elmira and Corning ended with the words "the proposition looks favorable."

Hungerford's "proposition" epitomized the business fervor of the Confident Years. In February 1866, Hungerford had patented a glass shutter for indoor use. He called it a "window blind." Though the patent described a "slat composed of various colors," each extant blind is entirely amber, green, blue, or purple. Hungerford wrote:

> I am enabled to shade a room more or less by making the slats...more or less transparent, and... give the light which enters...any desired tint to correspond with...wallpaper, carpet or furniture, thus giving a most pleasing and harmonizing appearance. By this means...I...produce a very ornamental article, one that never needs painting... and can be produced at a very cheap rate.[6]

Hungerford's blind struck the glassmakers' imagination, and later Corning's. The *Corning Democrat* reported December 10, 1868:

> Mr. Hungerford has a valuable patent on window blinds made of glass which for three or four years he has been getting before the public. During this time he has thoroughly prospected all the localities where articles of glass are manufactured and...discovered that Corning was a point where glass works would meet with complete success. Mr. Hungerford set himself to this task and most successfully has he accomplished it. The Brooklyn Flint Glass Company was laboring under the very difficulties which could be obviated by a removal to Corning and concluded, if the capitalists of this village would contribute a portion of the capital stock, to come here.

The Glass Works minutes book entry of May 18, 1868, said only "Resolved to move."

What were the "difficulties that could be obviated"? Not the danger of fire, of course. But Corning "capitalists"—chief among them Quincy W. Wellington and George Spencer—offered $50,000. The village was free of the labor unrest that plagued Brooklyn. She was a transportation hub. Her Chemung Feeder Canal linked her to the Erie Canal system. The Corning & Blossburg and the Tioga railroads ran north from nearby Pennsylvania coalfields, promising cheap fuel. The Erie ran east to the coast, west to Lake Erie, and north to Rochester. In 1865 the Magee Switch connected the Corning & Blossburg with the Erie at Corning. Other small

1. Hoare & Dailey opened in Corning on the second floor of the Corning Glass Works's first building, completed in the fall of 1868. *Coll. Corning Glass Works*

railroads prospered and became part of larger systems.[7] Presumably Elias Hungerford neglected to mention that Corning's situation on the Chemung River, at its junction with the Tioga, made the village hopelessly, helplessly flood-prone.

One Amory Houghton (unspecified) and Henry Sinclaire moved to Corning early in 1868, according to the local directory. Construction of the new glassworks went quickly. It opened in October, and soon housed a Hoare & Dailey cutting shop run by a young man named Thomas Hawkes.[8] But John Hoare apparently sent only a few craftsmen to Corning. An 1869 Medina, Ohio, newspaper published an eyewitness report (reprinted in the *Corning Journal* of March 18, 1903) showing that there was an engraver among them.

Hoare & Dailey's success was crucial to that of the new glass works. "Best Metal" cutting blanks* were a major Glass Works product for decades, and the Houghtons agreed not to sell them to Hoare & Dailey's competitors.[9] The Corning Flint Glass Works also made molds for Hungerford's glass blind in 1869, but Corning Glass Works records suggest that production was small.

The company ran into trouble as quickly as it had in Brooklyn. A century later (*Corning Evening*

---

*A blank is an uncut bowl or vase that has been specially made of heavy, high-quality glass so that it can be cut. Glass chemists refer to their batches as "metal," a term that can be confusing for a layman. "Best metal" would signify the highest-quality glass made by a company—i.e., the one with the purest ingredients and the highest lead content. Most glass companies melted several grades of glass at varying prices; Corning Glass Works made at least two grades of glass blanks.

Leader, October 21, 1968), a spokesman called the Pennsylvania coal "ill fitted" to the needs of the glassworks. H.P. Sinclaire's explanation, according to Robert O. Sinclaire, was, "The coal was full of slate." In April 1879, Monkey Run Creek "went on a rampage." Erie trains were unable to reach Corning for three days, and the Blossburg coal railroad stopped service for a week. Part of the canal dam "went out." No waterborne freight entered or left Corning until July.[10] Meanwhile, American fine glass was in a period of decline. The number of cutters was dropping steadily; the revival would not begin until the Centennial Exposition of 1876.[11]

The Corning Flint Glass Works went into bankruptcy. A receiver was appointed in September 1870, the *Journal* reported on the fifteenth of that month. The 1870 census listed only five cutters in Corning— Hoare & Dailey's engraver had left; the Glass Works shut down.

A competitor to the southeast, however, was flourishing. Christian Dorflinger's glassworks in White Mills, Pennsylvania, prospered so mightily that he built a 36-room hotel with a ballroom. It is pleasant to imagine Corning's glassmakers among the guests at the opening ball May 25, 1870. The guest list included friends from New York and Europe.[12] Surely John Hoare, still living in Brooklyn and long associated with Dorflinger's Brooklyn factories, was among them. Later that year he used Brooklyn glass, probably from Dorflinger's factory, to cut a White House order.

A Bostonian bought Corning's glass works in 1871, and entrusted its management to Amory Houghton, Jr. A biographer later wrote that

the supply of ready capital was indeed meagre and the prospect of success...doubtful. However, Mr. Houghton started the smaller of two furnaces and soon put the works in running order, using every possible economy....Having introduced several specialties, and operating upon a very economical basis, the close of the year showed a profit for the owner. In 1872 the manager purchased the plant on credit.[13]

Corning read in the *Journal* May 9, 1872: "Mr. Emory [sic] Houghton is now the proprietor of the Glass Works." His brother Charles and their uncle Henry Sinclaire were working with him. And finally Corning's glassworks began to grow.

A week later a *Journal* story showed that former stockholders were good-humored about their losses. At Q.W. Wellington's fifteenth wedding anniversary party, most of the gifts were glass. One guest "had his joke by contributing ten shares of the original stock of the Corning Glass Works, costing...$1000, but now worth no more than a Confederate dollar."

The allusion to the Civil War reminded Corning that the joker had made a fortune in enlistment bounties by providing freed Southern slaves to fill Steuben County's quota.[14]

Elias Hungerford's glass blind was one of the specialties Amory Houghton, Jr., was introducing. Company records show that molds for it were made again in 1871. In January 1872, Hungerford formed a manufacturing company with capital reported as $50,000. The blinds would be "largely manufactured at the Glass Works," a news story in the *Journal* said on January 4. Again, few materialized.

Though summer usually meant poor business for glassmakers, the summer of 1872 seems to have been an exception in Corning. The combined Glass Works and Hoare & Dailey were reported as employing about 200 persons, including boys. The demand for glass was "very good," the *Journal* said on July 18. Even allowing for the incorrigible exaggeration of nineteenth-century businessmen and newspapers, things were looking up.

Prestigious orders began to arrive, and brought Corning her first permanent Bohemian engravers. Their arrival, unremarked at the time, led to many of the city's greatest triumphs. (Chapter 8 tells their story.) Meanwhile, Elias Hungerford had become superintendent of the Chemung Feeder Canal, on which millions of board feet of lumber left Corning, according to two reports in the *Journal* (March 14 and 21). Though his glass blind lay dormant, plans for it were not forgotten.

Fortune continued to smile on the Glass Works. On January 1, 1875, Amory Houghton, Jr., Charles F. Houghton, Henry Sinclaire, and an associate who later withdrew filed incorporation papers for Corning Glass Works. At about this time, according to company records, it had four to six shops (teams) of blowers making cutting blanks. (John Hoare had closed his Greenpoint cutting shop two years earlier and moved to Corning with his craftsmen.)

Yet there were clouds. A Corning bank failed early in 1875, and on October 5, 1876, the *Journal* reported on a fire of the day before that had done $35,000 worth of damage to the Glass Works and also damaged the Hoare & Dailey cutting shop.

However, Philadelphia's Centennial Exposition of 1876 revitalized the cut-glass industry by showing its products to more than 8 million visitors. Among the award winners were J. B. Dobleman of Greenpoint and Christian Dorflinger of White Mills, two former associates of John Hoare.[15] Hoare sent no exhibit, but may have worked for other exhibitors. One of Corning's founding craftsmen worked at the Exposition, according to his granddaughter, Mrs. Clarence Dencenburg. This was Bohemian engraver Joseph Haselbauer.

A 6-day, 60-hour work week exhausted neither Corning's energy nor its enthusiasm. The 1878 *Journal* wrote of a caricaturist at Washington Hall, birthday parties, and a cornet concert and "hop" by Pier's Corning Band. Then came a maple sugar and ice cream festival, a shooting match against nearby Painted Post, and a visit from General Tom Thumb and his wife. Mrs. Dencenburg says the General had relatives in town.

Relatives visited endlessly. Fraternal organizations were many and active. Charles Voorhees of Corning's Brooklyn contingent was an Odd Fellow, as was John Hoare. Hoare was also a thirty-second-degree Mason. The Saengerbund, a German singing club, met weekly. It gave annual balls and outings, as did the volunteer fire companies.

And business! It was the chief interest of the Confident Years. Manufacturers prided themselves on selling their own wares, and were often "on the road." What was good for business, clearly, was good for Corning. And so, as the population climbed toward 5,000, Corning rejoiced to read that G. S. Hastings had "a patent for putting glass handles upon knives," and that "he was here for some weeks to have moulds made at the Glass Works."

The Hungerford blind was in the news again in 1880. A dry-goods merchant sold his business to turn his attention to it. For several years "none of the owners of stock has [had] time to push it," the *Journal* mentioned on July 2, 1880. "It is intended to start manufacture immediately...." Fourteen years had passed since the patent was granted; its expiration may have been imminent.

It is perhaps from this period that extant glass blinds date. The "blue glass theory" that the *Journal*

2. Thomas Hawkes's Rich Cut-Glass Works opened in 1882 on the second floor of this brick building. Presumably the cart to the left is carrying a load of finished glass. The building still stands. *Coll. The Corning Museum of Glass*

referred to had become a health fad. Believers insisted that light filtered through blue glass cured illness in man and beast. Peddlers sold blue windowpanes door-to-door.[16] Their owners carried them from room to room.

The year 1880 provides a glimpse of Corning's heartfelt involvement in national politics. The presidential candidates were near-nonentities: Republican James Garfield opposed General Winfield Scott Hancock, called "the superb." The Democratic platform, the *Nation* wrote, suggested that "the conventions have now begun to treat the platform as a joke." The Republicans were against polygamy. The parties' stands on the question of protective tariffs, however, were clear. The Democrats wanted tariffs for revenue only, and none was needed. The Republicans stood for tariffs to protect American manufacturers and workers against Europe's low wages.[17] The issue was crucial for eastern cut-glass companies; they competed with Europe for the lucrative New York fine-glass market. Corning's newpapers carried scurrilous attacks and denials, but the glassmakers' Republican won.

The year was a Corning milestone for another reason: 1880 brought a second-generation cutting company, that of Thomas Hawkes. The following decade tightened the glassmen's close association with Corning cutting companies. Henry P. Sinclaire, Jr., became Hawkes's bookkeeper in 1883; George Abbott, Amory Houghton's brother-in-law, bought an interest in John Hoare's company.

On January 1, 1884, the *Journal* reported the annual meeting of the Corning Glass Blind Manu-

3. Hunt & Sullivan's Sixth Street factory about the turn of the century. *Coll. The Corning Museum of Glass*

facturing Co., and hoped that manufacturing would be revived. It wasn't. Inventor Hungerford had turned his attention to a railroad tie made of boiler iron that he was "getting patented," or so the *Journal* had said on June 8, 1882.

Late 1889 brought a stimulus to the American glass industry and especially to Corning. This was the Grand Prize that Hawkes's glass was awarded in Paris at the *Exposition Universelle*. Corning began to call herself "the Crystal City." Hawkes and Hoare adopted company trademarks. The Brilliant Period, made possible by the technological and artistic advances discussed in Chapter 2, was under way.

Change came more rapidly in the nineties, but cooperation rather than competition was the rule among the Crystal City's fine-glass companies. Hoare had not competed against Hawkes in Paris. Hawkes returned the favor at the 1893 Columbian

4. The O. F. Egginton Co. (misspelled) was shown on this postcard of the early twentieth century. *Coll. The Corning Museum of Glass*

5. H. P. Sinclaire & Co. about 1906, before its extensive plantings had matured. *Coll. Estelle Sinclaire Farrar*

Exposition. Hawkes & Co. was another jewel in Corning's crown; Corning Glass Works, which would not sell blanks to Hoare's competitors, sold to Thomas Hawkes from the first.

The short-lived Frank Wilson & Sons began the third generation of Corning cutting companies in 1894. Hunt & Sullivan followed in 1895, and the O.F. Egginton company in 1896. (Later companies will be discussed in subsequent chapters.) Wilson and Hunt had cut glass for the Hawkes company; Egginton had been its manager. Capital was readily available to men who knew their business. Typically, a group of local capitalists lent money for an initial period of three years. Blanks from Corning Glass Works were harder to come by; none of these companies used them.

If Corning had been cosmopolitan in 1870, when Thomas Hawkes played on the Glass Works cricket team, it was more so by 1900. Englishmen had arrived in the 1880s to work for Hawkes, and in the 1890s they came to work for Egginton. Several Bohemian engraving families lived and worked in Corning; the Saengerbund also had members from Alsace-Lorraine.[18] There was a small Italian colony too.[19]

A severe depression ended in the late 1890s, and a business boom began. The American Flint Glass Workers' Union president reported to the union's twenty-second convention in Pittsburgh in 1899: "General business conditions are good. There is a greater number of men employed than there has been for a long time, there is more money in circulation. What is true of business is also true of every department of the glass trade."

Business remained excellent for Corning cutting firms through 1903. Cut glass had long been the preferred gift of the wealthy, but now cost-cutting innovations had brought it within reach of middle incomes. For a brief euphoric moment American cut glass outsold the English. Grocers, blacksmiths, and bicycle manufacturers hastened into the cut-glass business in Corning. New firms grew up "like mushrooms in a night," to quote Thomas Hawkes. Their cheaper wares were destined for the department-store trade. Virtually all Hoare and Hawkes customers were jewelers.[20]

Thus the early twentieth century brought lower quality, increased sales, and more cutting companies to Corning. The Steuben Glass Works and H. P.

6. The second floor of this building belonging to the Corning Building Co. housed a J. Hoare & Co. cutting shop, H. P. Sinclaire & Co., and the Thomas Shotton Cut Glass Co. between 1900 and 1912. *Coll. The Corning Museum of Glass*

Sinclaire & Co. adhered to the old Corning standards of excellence, but many of the smaller firms did not. Corning's founding glass families viewed with apprehension the expansion shown in the following table.

Expansion in Corning, 1900-1905 (excluding engravers' and cutters' home shops)

Branch Shops	Founded
Hawkes shop 2	1901
J. Hoare branch	1901
Hawkes shop 3	1902
Elmira Cut Glass Co.	ca. 1903

New Companies	Established
George W. Drake & Co.	1901
Corning Cut Glass Co.	1901
Ernest Mulford	1901
Joseph Blackburn	1901
Arcadian Cut Glass Co.	1902 (possibly reported in error)
Crystal Mfg. Co.	1902
Giometti Brothers	1902
Ideal Cut Glass Co.	1902
Knickerbocker Cut Glass Co.	1902
Almy & Thomas	1903
Steuben Glass Works	1903
Ernest L. Bradley	1904
Painter Glass Cutting Shop	1904
H. P. Sinclaire & Co.	1904
J. J. Byrne	ca. 1905
Standard Cut Glass Co.	1905.

Trade journals reported several other companies opening in Corning during this period, but we have found no confirmation of them.

Corning's cut-glass industry reached its largest size in 1905, when the city had 490 cutters, according to the Corning directory. But James Hoare had testified in 1904 that "never was poorer glass sent out from Corning than is being sent out today...in order to meet the competition it has been necessary to cheapen to a considerable extent the cost of manufacture."[21] Corning's firms, in fact, continued to make superb hand-polished glass, but had added a cheaper line. Perhaps it was pride in Corning's reputation for quality that prompted Hoare to cut his pressed, figured blanks in Wellsboro, Pennsyl-

7. Detail of an Almy & Thomas nappy, cut between 1903 and 1907. Such slipshod cutting as in the points of these hobstars was unknown to Corning before the 1900-to-1910 proliferation of small cutting companies. *Coll. Frances Trachtenberg*

vania. We do not know that the company trademarked them.

Some of the newcomers brought dissension. James Sebring's use of the name Corning Cut Glass Co. provoked a lengthy lawsuit by Corning Glass Works. Thomas Hawkes's decision to manufacture blanks in his Steuben Glass Works alienated H. P. Sinclaire, Jr. Yet mutual respect continued strong among the industry's leaders. Their companies "borrowed" blanks and pay envelopes (later billed) from one another, helped one another out with large orders, entertained the same out-of-town buyers, shared designs, and generally respected agreements not to hire one another's craftsmen.

Corning's complexion changed again as Steuben Glass Works attracted blowers from C. Dorflinger & Sons. Former Dorflinger families, most of them of Scandinavian origin, still say that "half of Corning came from White Mills."[22]

8. J. Hoare & Co. operated an auxiliary shop that cut less expensive glass in this Wellsboro, Pennsylvania, building after 1906. Hoare & Millspaugh also used it. *Coll. Leon Swope*

9. The Hoare company passed its last five years, 1915 to 1920, in this Bridge Street building. G. W. Drake & Co. and the Thomas Shotton Cut Glass Works had used it earlier. *Coll. The Corning Museum of Glass*

Corning's small cutting companies came and went from 1900 to 1918, but the trend was downward after 1905. Trade directories show that cutting companies continued to increase through 1918, but that the industry's eastern center shifted south to the New York area.

The outbreak of war in Europe dealt the glass industry a double blow. It shut off supplies of both European blanks and raw materials for blank manufacture. According to Walter M. Allen, an August 19, 1916, article in the *Daily Tribune* of Johnstown, Pennsylvania, about the Allen Cut Glass Co. declared:

> It is not known with certainty where the potash now being used [in blanks] came from. It is believed, however, that a great deal was brought to this country by the Deutschland, the first German merchant submarine to enter an American port.

Corning Glass Works's oft-flooded records seem to show the company's last sales of Best Metal in 1910. We may wonder whether in fact that date was not a few years later.

Wartime restrictions on luxury goods followed America's entry into the war. Corning papers announced in January 1918 that Corning Glass Works had bought T. G. Hawkes & Co.'s Steuben Glass Works. It used the factory chiefly for commercial products until the war ended. Later in the year, the O. F. Egginton Co. closed.

A second catastrophe came in 1920, when a postwar economic readjustment turned into an unprecedented depression. An influx of cheap European glass followed. J. Hoare & Co. followed the Egginton Co. into bankruptcy. Steuben, however, with the financial resources of Corning Glass Works behind it, returned to the manufacture of its fine glasses and to cutting.

Prohibition was less of a blow than is often assumed. Corning salesmen's catalogs continued to show stemware of every sort. Those who could afford to were still drinking. The problem was that they were drinking from European glasses.

The twenties' fad for colored glass was no technical problem. Every conceivable color came from Steuben's furnaces, and between 1920 and 1927, from those of H. P. Sinclaire & Co. But neither company could match European prices.

The downtrend gained momentum. Perhaps even the industry's earliest leaders could not have reversed the trend away from quality that accelerated during the Great Depression. Home cutting and engraving shops abounded in Corning, but there was less and less work even for them.

Then taste changed again. Colored glass lost favor and was replaced again by crystal.

Virtually unnoticed in 1933, a courageous decision at Corning Glass Works enabled Corning to continue as America's Crystal City. This was the reorganization of the Glass Works's Steuben Division, long unprofitable. As Steuben Glass, with Arthur A. Houghton, Jr., as its president, it embarked on a new course. Following Houghton's vision of glass as a new art medium, the new Steuben aimed to make the finest crystal the world had ever seen.* This was a rededication, at a new level, to the founding principles of Corning's fine-glass industry.

Steuben's triumphant use of its new and utterly pure glass formula is not part of our story. Its cutting and engraving are. These brought hope to Corning's matchless craftsmen. By renewing Corning's faith in her glassmaking future, Steuben has been responsible for a renascence of creativity throughout the city. This story is told in our final chapter.

*Crystal is a colorless glass having a high lead content; half-crystal, also made in Corning, has a lower lead content. Paradoxically, the addition of lead makes the glass both brilliant and soft enough to cut and engrave readily. Less expensive glass formulas contain no lead.

10. The final home of T. G. Hawkes & Co. on West Market Street. This building is slightly to the west of the Hawkes building shown in Illustration 2. *Coll. The Corning Museum of Glass*

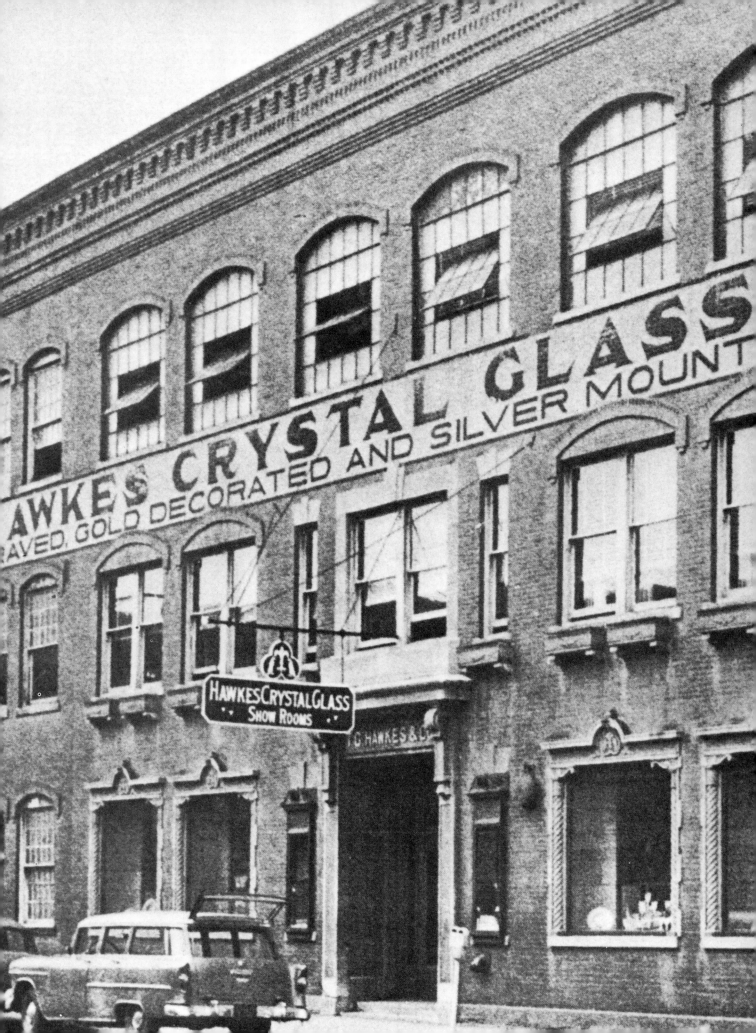

11. This stemware is part of a large set in a design engraved by both the Hoare and Sinclaire companies. Thirty pieces bear the Hoare trademark, forty-two pieces the Sinclaire one. The unsigned balance of the set may be the work of a third company. Height of tallest goblet, 14.7 cm. *Coll. Estelle Sinclaire Farrar*

2
The Cut-Glass Industry

The nineteenth century spotlighted both America's characteristic will to do great things and her equally characteristic tendency to ignore logical thought. Establishing her cut-glass industry depended on the second as surely as it required the first. Let us look at the handicaps that the Crystal City shared with other glass centers.

High American Wages

The making of fine cut glass is a handcraft. During its heyday, quality meant free-blown blanks, shaped and decorated by craftsmen who had learned their trade as apprentices. Many such craftsmen immigrated from Europe in search of higher wages. The 1880 census showed that 22 of Corning's 40 glass cutters had been born in Europe, 21 of them in England or Ireland.

Protective tariffs had been argued even before 1845. In 1888, a 45 percent tariff was failing to protect American glass from European competition, yet President Cleveland proposed to lower the tariff. On August 20 of that year the *Corning Journal* reprinted a *New York Tribune* story on its front page quoting C. H. Voorhees, speaking for J. Hoare & Co., and H. P. Sinclaire, Jr., spokesman for the Hawkes company. Voorhees said:

In our business labor is the largest item. We take a piece of glass...costing twenty cents and...in many cases put $36 of labor upon it. If this agitation of the Democrats [for lower tariffs] lasts five years, the weaker cut-glass firms will go into bankruptcy. Our best workmen in the glass-blowing works get $6 a day.... The glass cutters get $3.50 to $4 a day. We compete with Webb, of London...[who] pay their men far less.... Reduce the duty...and our men would suffer severely. Now [they] own their own homes, have cows and many of them have horses.

Sinclaire agreed, but cited lower wages:

A good workman in the cut-glass manufactures of England [makes] from $7 to $9 a week, while [here he earns] from $14 to $20 a week, and in Germany the glass cutters receive only $3 a week.... It is almost impossible for us, therefore, to compete....

Even if the duty were 100 percent, it would not protect us from...German cut-glass manufacturers. We now have keen foreign competition.... The only way we get a market for our goods...in New York and the cities which import this foreign cut-glassware is by inventing new styles and designs...as soon as we have a good run on one pattern the English and German manufacturers copy it and we have to get a new pattern. Then a foreign manufacturer steps in, copies the goods, and undersells us in the American market.

Though Harrison's election averted the threat of lowered tariffs, protection continued to be a sore point. When the duty on cutting blanks was raised in early 1904,[1] for instance, cutting firms that had economized by buying European blanks saw their savings vanish.

As late as election day of 1912 Corning's *Daily Journal* was reminding readers that "A PROTECTIVE TARIFF HELPS GLASS WORKERS. Wages Here Three and One-Half Times Higher than those Paid in Europe.... Do you Remember the Time Under a Democratic Low Tariff When Only Two Furnaces Were Running at the Corning Glass Works?" The headlines introduced a letter from the Republican

City Committee, which gave the following wage comparison:

	America	*Germany & Austria*
Good workmen, blowing		
...per hour	.55	.17
Good workmen, gathering	.40	.075
Glass cutters	.30	.10

The problem would not be solved. Implicit in America's high standard of living was the doom of handcrafts; America's economic future depended on mass production. The effects of these facts on the glass industry have been summed up as follows:

> The U.S., being a high-wage country, could not have been expected to produce competitively against foreign nations in any industry such as glassmaking where, one or two branches excepted, labor cost constituted a high percentage of total cost.... Until machinery transformed American glassmaking, manual processes, small-scale operation and little mechanical equipment more than offset any economies derived from cheap American fuel.[2]

During the 1920s American fine-glass lost the long battle. Trade journals traced an inexorable progress as foreign firms won an ever larger share of the market. In 1920 imports of cut and decorated glass almost tripled, reported *The Glassworker* on October 29, 1921. As the post-World War I depression ended, Europe's glassmakers expanded their markets in the United States.

Corning's cut-glass manufacturers adapted to the changing taste of the twenties. Painting, staining, gilding, and metal trims on crystal and colored glasses made up a larger share of production. But these too were handwork; the competitive gap remained.

Business Fluctuations

The cut-glass industry's second great weakness was the extreme variability of its sales. After an annual Christmas peak, Corning cutting firms closed for about two weeks. A second slow season came in summer; again cutting companies closed. Corning newspapers reported these "dull seasons" only when they were prolonged. They often were.

In 1879 most men in "the glass cutting department" of Corning Glass Works (i.e., Hoare & Dailey) had no work from January 1 to early February. They returned to work when "large orders" were received, the *Journal* reported on February 6. In 1885 Hawkes craftsmen worked three days a week—half time—from June to October, again according to the *Journal* (June 4 and October 1). Engraver Hiram Rouse's notebooks showed frequent shifts from "short time" to overtime.[3]

Because cut glass was a luxury, sales plummeted when the economy faltered. The Hawkes Cash Book showed a payroll drop of about 20 percent from 1903 to 1904.[4] A sharper business downturn came in 1907/8. One trade journal ran bankruptcy stories almost weekly.[5]

As already mentioned, the years from 1914 through 1922 were difficult ones for Corning. Glass-industry employees in New York State decreased 30.2 percent between May 1920 and May 1921, *Glass Industry* reported in August of 1921. The H. C. Fry and Libbey companies reduced their prices on some blanks. C. Dorflinger & Sons, a major supplier of blanks, closed permanently in May 1921.[6]

How did these ups and downs affect the craftsman? He expected far less security, even in 1900, than he does today. Farmers encircled Corning; the ravages of business cycles must have seemed much like those of flood and hail. Moreover, work as a carpenter, plumber, or mason was equally seasonal. With most workers in the same boat, the glass cutter wasted no time on self-pity. Perhaps he had a second trade: rural route mail carrier, post-office clerk, mason, or carpenter. Most engravers operated home engraving shops; one also managed a grocery store. Another was a machinist by day. Real estate was a favored investment. Building and selling a second house, or buying one and renting it, was not unusual.

As time went on, a few men left the industry for more secure and more highly paid work. Yet it is noteworthy that some of them continued to cut or engrave glass at home. Others "helped out" (Corning's expression) at small cutting companies in their spare time. Clearly, the industry's rewards went beyond the weekly pay envelope.

Labor Dissension

Though Corning's freedom from labor strife attracted out-of-town cutting firms as late as 1912, there were difficult moments. Corning's first strike began at the Hawkes company in late September 1886, and did not end until the following March.[7] The *Journal*'s stories were frequent—and favorable to Hawkes. During this period of labor activism, the ostensible cause was perhaps unimportant. The outcome was not: T. G. Hawkes & Co. continued its policy of employing no union men.

Corning glass cutters organized Local Union No. 60 on October 1, 1892. By 1897 it still had paid no regular assessments,[8] and presumably was disbanded.

The Hawkes victory of 1877 had not been without its price, however. When Thomas Hawkes opened his Steuben Glass Works in 1903, the smoldering antagonism of the American Flint Glass Workers' Union burst into flame.[9] (That story will be told in Chapter 13.) Another serious labor dispute came in 1912, when the AFGWU prevented Thomas Shotton from opening two cutting factories in Corning (see Chapter 16). The union threatened to establish a union cutting company in Corning immediately afterward. This never materialized, and a long peace followed. When the AFGWU finally organized Corning's cutting industry in the 1940s, the only remaining large companies were T. G. Hawkes & Co., the Hunt Glass Co., and the reorganized Steuben Glass. Relations between them and the union were cordial and marked by cooperation from the first.

The Struggle for Recognition

Though Corning's cut glass was of superlative quality, early manufacturers were unable to convince retailers of American supremacy. William Dorflinger, in a 1902 speech, described the situation as follows:

> In spite of the evident superiority of American glass and the originality and novelty of the cuttings ...prominent dealers were loath to confess that the ware was made here. American cut glass was sold as an English product; and when it became known that a fine quality of crystal was produced in this country and dealers were asked for it, they showed cheap German glass of poor color as the domestic effort. It became necessary to take a stand against one's own customers, and "American cut glass" was advertised and exploited and many thousands of dollars were spent in putting it before the public until the dealers were glad to advertise it themselves and sell it under its own name.

As Dorflinger spoke in 1902, the struggle for recognition had been won. Owning American cut glass had become such a mania that even a Corning blacksmith would soon try his hand at manufacturing it. It is ironic that, by the time American cut glass established itself as superior, its quality was already declining.

Untrained Owners

America's freedoms cut two ways in her fine-glass industry. Anyone with capital or access to it was free to manufacture or cut fine-glass; no law or guild required that he first learn the business. The nineteenth-century capitalists's enthusiasm seems to have been aroused by the marketable product more often than by the knowledgeable producer.

We have found no comparison between failures of American glass companies and those of Europe. Corning's story suggests, however, that American euphoria caused the founding of many cut-glass companies that inexperience soon destroyed. It is perhaps no accident that Corning's most successful and longest-lived cutting companies were founded by European-born or European-trained craftsmen.

* * *

Despite the cut-glass industry's economic vulnerability, American inventiveness enabled it to prosper until World War I. We have already mentioned the craftsman's love of his work, and of his adaptability. Let us consider the industry's other strengths.

Artistic and Technological Creativity

A distinctive American style of cut glass was born in the 1880s or slightly earlier. When William Dorflinger spoke of the "originality and novelty" of American cut glass, he probably had in mind the curved miter cut that made possible the ornate cuttings of the Brilliant Period. This is often dated to an 1886 design patent of John S. O'Connor, who headed the cutting department of Christian Dorflinger's Wayne County Glass Works (later C. Dorflinger & Sons).[10] T. G. Hawkes & Co. may have used the curved cut in its exhibit at the Universal Exposition in Paris in 1889. In fact, however, the curved miter cut appears on glass with impeccable credentials that show it was made in New England for the Centennial Exposition of 1876; we must suppose that O'Connor reintroduced the cut to the Corning-White Mills glassmaking centers. These had had friendly relationships since their predecessors' days in Brooklyn.

O'Connor's innovation may have reached Corning via the glass that his biographies say he cut for the 1889 Paris exposition. Inasmuch as Dorflinger did not exhibit there, we may suppose that his work was the two Dorflinger-made punch bowls that Hawkes admitted were in his exhibit.[11]

In any event, the curved cut freed American cuttings from dependence on straight-line cuts of the Anglo-Irish type. Though Corning continued to make them for decades, they became steadily less important. Another O'Connor introduction, according to his biography, was the hardwood polishing wheel. This too was used in Corning.

American firms also pioneered the use of more efficient sources of energy. Electricity came to Hoare & Dailey in 1886, though at first it lighted only the offices, the *Journal* said on November 4, 1886. One or two old craftsmen still remember their pleasure when its steady light replaced the flicker of gas lamps in the cutting rooms of smaller companies.

The American genius for efficiency helped the cut-glass industry compete against Europe's low-wage product, but also made possible lower quality. Mass production came to glass cutting when it was separated into the specialties of roughing, smoothing, and polishing. Though in 1904 Hawkes & Co.'s best workmen still began and completed his finest glass, changing wheels as necessary, the company's second line moved from hand to hand.[12] More cost-cutting innovations followed. Chief among them was acid-polishing, introduced in the early 1890s, as Dorflinger pointed out in his 1902 speech. Unless hand-polishing followed, however, acid was apt to leave wavy lines that the industry called "wrinkles"; acid also pitted the glass if it was not removed promptly. Finally, Thomas Hawkes asserted that the unbuffed acid polish was not permanent.[13]

Frederick Carder mentioned these and other American advantages in an interview given in England in 1903, and reported in the *Brierley Hill...Advertiser* on July 15. A few excerpts follow:

The vast extent of the country, and the wealth of the population, combined with their cultivated taste in artistic ware, were mentioned by Mr. Carder as amongst the advantages of the American glass trade; nor did he forget the tariff wall which has been erected....

"I could not help being struck [Carder said] with the American cut glass. We know that for some years they have been forging ahead...and where we used to sell them thousands of pounds worth of cut glass per annum, it has dwindled down to only a few pounds; in fact they are sending the cut goods over to Great Britain, instead of *vice versa.* The progress they have made...is abnormal. They have a metal which for brightness would be difficult to beat; and cutting their designs—some of which were very fine—deeply into the glass they get a brilliancy such as was once the exclusive pride of the Stourbridge district.... Following a characteristic American custom...their designs, both in form and cutting, are less numerous than ours. This enables them to get larger orders for separate designs, and sometimes the men will be engaged on one pattern for months, and, as a consequence, turn out more work.... As is well known, most of the polishing of cut designs [here] is done by means of wood wheels and brushes. This is partially done away with in the States, as...all their productions are polished by fluoric acid. Two points impressed me favourably: the immense size of the bowls—some of them 24 inches

in diameter—polished by this process, and the excellent way in which the work was done, leaving no smears or striated lines."...[11]

[To the question] Have the men a trade union over there? "Yes," was [Carder's] reply; "the Glassmakers' Union is stronger there than here; and it is conducted on lines less satisfactory tha[n] the union in this country. Many of the best American firms have blocked out the union men, and are employing only non-union men, solely because the rules and restrictions of the Society are so arbitrary."

Early in the twentieth century pressed figured blanks began to make headway. Their "figures" were the larger design elements such as hobstars and miter-cut-shaped leaves, which were pressed into the blanks. By eliminating much of the rougher's work, they lowered price and quality sharply.

The gang-cut wheel, which made several parallel incisions at once, dates from about 1913.[14] It made possible the rapid and inexpensive cutting of fine-line stripes. These are perhaps best known in T. G. Hawkes's *Millicent* and *Sheraton* designs. The gang-cut wheel also cut blunt-edged flower petals, cross-hatching, and other motifs.

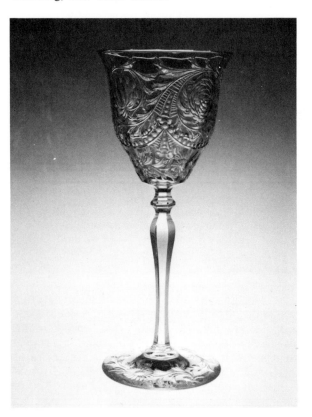

12. The design of this green-cased hock glass, signed by H. P. Sinclaire & Co., was also engraved by T. G. Hawkes & Co. Height, 17.2 cm. *Coll. Estelle Sinclaire Farrar; Frederic Farrar photograph*

The Glass Industry for August 1922 reported that the National Association of Cut Glass Manufacturers of America, in an effort to halt the use of figured blanks, had agreed to use a trademark on all cut glass produced by members of the association. This trademark, a star in a circle with "NACGM" between the points of the star, would distinguish genuine cut glass from glass cut on pressed figured blanks. A number in the center of the star would indicate the manufacturer. The number "3" was assigned to the Phillips Cut Glass Company of Montreal. Other manufacturers' numbers are not known. Unfortunately, this attempt to discourage the use of figured blanks was too late to stop the rising tide of imitations, and the industry continued to decline.

Cooperation

We have mentioned the close friendship among Corning's early glassmen, which permitted Thomas Hawkes to buy Corning Glass Works blanks despite a Glass Works-Hoare & Dailey agreement of exclusivity. There is no doubt that John Hoare and the Houghton family regarded the new Hawkes Rich Cut-Glass Works benevolently. The mention of it as a "cutting shop department" in the *Journal*, March 12, 1880, suggests that the Hawkes company may at first have been a subcontractor. This close connection is further emphasized by the signatures of two original Corning Flint Glass Works investors on the Hawkes company's first design patent.

When H. P. Sinclaire & Co. opened in 1904, it too was permitted to buy Corning Glass Works blanks. And there are several evidences also of close friendship between Corning and Christian Dorflinger.

But there was also an enlarged circle of friends after about 1895. This included the principals of the Drake, Hunt, and Egginton companies. As late as 1935 Corning's cutting companies "worked hand in hand," to quote a company officer, Mary Krebs, secretary of the Hunt Glass Co. from about 1915 to 1937. It was not unusual to escort a visiting buyer from one's own showroom to someone else's. And earlier we pointed out that cutting firms "borrowed" blanks and other supplies from each other when they ran short.

Borrowing also included craftsmen and the use of factory space. The *Daily Journal*, June 12, 1893, wrote that Corning's E. Jacobs, W. A. Langendorfer, and W. W. Winchester were "skilled cutters at work upon the World's Fair grounds." Inasmuch as Hoare, Corning's only exhibitor, showed no cutting operation, one assumes that the men were

working in the Libbey factory. In 1902 Libbey borrowed engraver H. W. Fritchie, who returned to T. G. Hawkes & Co. when the 1904 fair closed.

Cooperation extended to working together on large orders. The Hawkes and Hoare & Dailey companies both returned to full-time work when Hawkes received an order from the White House in 1885, the *Journal* reported on September 3 and October 1. Stemware sets signed in part by two or even three Corning companies confirm that they continued to work together. They could hardly have done otherwise; Corning manufacturers shared many of the same customers. Both Sinclaire and Hawkes made a design patented by Richard Briggs of Boston. Hawkes called it *Louis XIV*; at the Sinclaire company it was *Marie Antoinette*. Dozens of other shared designs are known.

But cooperation went still further. Walter Allen, son of the Corning-trained founder of the Allen Cut Glass Co. (see Chapter 19), remembers his surprise at finding that H. P. Sinclaire & Co. was cutting his father's patented *Pond Lily* design.[15] His mother assured him that it was done by agreement; the Allen company was also cutting Sinclaire designs. Sharing of designs doubtless explains a Steuben-signed but Sinclaire-designed goblet owned by the Corning Museum of Glass. Steuben "grotesque" vases bearing both the Steuben and Sinclaire trademarks are also known.

Nor did Corning cutting firms compete against one another in fairs and expositions. C. Dorflinger & Sons brought copper-wheel engraving work to Corning; they cut Hawkes's patented *Russian* design on White House orders. Hawkes licensed four companies to make its patented French-dressing bottle. Corning firms also bought and sold cut glass from and to out-of-town companies, as later chapters will show. Corning home shops specialized in "matchings."

Finally, the many small companies known to have subcontracted for Corning's giants demonstrate that even patented designs were legitimately cut in many places. In short, the "pirating" of designs that is often assumed was unknown in Corning and among its affiliated companies.

The Craftsman-Designer

Though the names of Thomas Hawkes, George Abbott, H. P. Sinclaire, Samuel Hawkes, and Walter Egginton appear on design patents assigned to their companies, cutting-firm proprietors also expected and encouraged their cutters and engravers to design. "Designing" is perhaps too modern a term to describe the craftsman's view of his more modest efforts. Two engravers have quoted their foremen as

13. H. P. Sinclaire & Co. tray, believed to have been designed and engraved by John Illig. When Illig went into business for himself, he made this design and the Sinclaire company discontinued it. Length, 36 cm. *Coll. Estelle Sinclaire Farrar*

14. Vase exhibited at the Universal Exposition in Paris in 1889 by the Hawkes Rich Cut-Glass Works. Designed by H. P. Sinclaire, Jr., the vase was made only at Sinclaire from 1904 to 1928 as design 3121 on blank 3121. This blank was made by Corning Glass Works and engraved by Joseph Haselbauer. Height, 33.8 cm. *Coll. The Corning Museum of Glass* (Gift of Mrs. John Sinclaire)

saying "Put something on there." Some craftsmen—perhaps most—created new motifs; the most talented produced complete engravings (or cuttings) that might occupy a shop for weeks.[16]

When a craftsman left a company to go into business for himself, he took his designs with him. His former employer discontinued them. This was true of H. P. Sinclaire when he left the Hawkes company, and of John Illig when he left Sinclaire. This custom is another explanation for the duplication of designs.

Corning's pool of talent partly explains the extraordinary number of designs that Corning's large firms made. Hawkes & Co. at one time offered more than 300; H. P. Sinclaire & Co. stocked about 475 in 1917, a depressed year. As might be expected, there was a correlation between a craftsman's ability to design and the likelihood that he would go into business for himself.

Blanks

Fine blanks are as important to quality glass as is fine cutting. We have explained that Corning Glass Works limited sales of its blanks to the Hoare, Hawkes, and Sinclaire companies. (Later chapters will discuss the occasional isolated exceptions to this rule.) Hoare and Hawkes used only these blanks until the late 1890s.[17] Because Hoare and Hawkes used no trademarks during this period, and made a high proportion of Anglo-Irish cuttings, Corning Glass Works blanks have long been unidentifiable. The catalog pages reproduced in Chapters 4 and 5 may help to end this anonymity.

The Hawkes and Hoare companies turned next to C. Dorflinger & Sons, buying chiefly tablewares that, Hawkes said, "we couldn't get of the Corning Glass Works."[18] Presumably the Glass Works had discontinued stemware blanks in their best-quality glass. By 1904 the Steuben Glass Works began to supply blanks; Hawkes and Hoare discontinued their use of Dorflinger blanks, but Sinclaire continued to buy them. Shortly thereafter the necessity of making a cheaper grade of cut glass prompted all three to buy at least small quantities from a number of firms; Corning Glass Works discontinued blank-making altogether about 1910–12 and resumed it after World War I in the newly purchased Steuben factory.[19]

Corning Glass Works, C. Dorflinger, and Steuben made special blanks for the Hawkes and Sinclaire companies, and presumably for Hoare as well.[20] Hawkes records show that Dorflinger took over production of several stemware shapes discontinued by Corning Glass Works. The Glass Work's later production was of heavy vases, bowls, jugs, and the like. Some were so thick that they had to be annealed in a kiln rather than a lehr. These are designated "K.M." for "Kiln Metal" in the Hawkes

& Co. suppliers' book, though their glass was in fact "Best Metal," the designation given by the Glass Works to its highest-quality blanks.

Both these companies believed that their glass was probably unmatched and certainly unexcelled. T. G. Hawkes testified in 1904 that Dorflinger blanks were of "half crystal."[21] An extant Dorflinger formula, however, has a lead content of about 29 percent and no decolorizing agent. Perhaps future identification of Corning Glass Works and Dorflinger blanks will enable collectors to compare the brilliance of the two companies' glass.

* * *

Let us look now at some characteristics of Corning's cut-glass industry.

The Size of the Industry

Corning was a village of about 4,000 persons when its glass industry began in 1868. When cutting reached its height in 1905, the population was about 13,500. Though cutting was an important trade, Corning newspapers regularly exaggerated the number of cutting craftsmen. The table below, compiled chiefly from census figures of 1870 and 1880 and city directories from 1873 to 1909, gives more accurate totals.

Cutters and Engravers in Corning 1869-1909

Year	Cutters	Engravers
1869	unavailable	1 or 2
1870	5	0
1873	15*	1
1875	23	2
1880	40	2
1889	119	3
1891	118	4
1893	181	5**
1895	212	4
1897	176	3
1899	372	5
1901	383	16
1903	471	32***
1905	490	33
1907	unavailable	unavailable
1909	340	45

*Includes Joseph Haselbauer, an engraver by 1876.
** Includes one "glass carver," who returned to England later in the year.
*** The doubling of Corning's engravers between 1901 and 1903 was caused by the introduction of Hawkes Gravic glass.

These figures are far lower than contemporary reports. T. G. Hawkes testified in 1904, "At the time I...severed my relations with John Hoare [in 1880], I should say that he had maybe 200 employees."[22] If Hawkes was correct, the proportion of other employees to cutters was about four to one.

Frederick Carder told his English interviewer in 1903: "In one [Corning cutting] factory 400 men are employed, in another 200, in another 80, and there are several smaller factories with 60 to 30 men...." The total is 800 or more, perhaps accurate if we note that he said "men," not "cutters." Yet there is reason to suspect exaggeration: the *Commoner and Glassworker,* November 11, 1905, printed a plea to glassmen to tell the truth to their trade journals.

We have sales figures earlier than the 1940s only for H. P. Sinclaire & Co. These are small indeed by today's standards, and meaningless without a basis for comparison. The following table, however, compiled from the 1912 *Thomas' Register of American Manufacturers,* suggests the relative size of some Corning and Corning-related companies.

Capital Of Corning and Corning-Related Cut-Glass Companies

T. G. Hawkes & Co.	over $100,000
J. Hoare & Co.	over $100,000
H. P. Sinclaire & Co.	over $100,000
Thomas Shotton Cut Glass Works (Brooklyn)	over $50,000
Enterprise Cut Glass Co. (Elmira Heights)	over $10,000
Eygabroat-Ryon (Lawrenceville, Pa.)	over $10,000
Hunt Glass Co.	over $10,000
Corning Cut Glass Co.	over $5,000
O. F. Egginton	over $5,000
Elmira Glass Cutting Co.	over $5,000
Ideal Cut Glass Co. (Canastota)	over $5,000
Giometti Brothers	not reported

Women in the Industry

Corning's women were self-reliant and influential. Some were capitalists, pure and simple. Mrs. Amory Houghton, Sr., was the chief investor in the Brooklyn Flint Glass Works.[23] The Hawkes Cash Book shows the repayment of a $17,000 loan from "Mrs. C.H.V.," wife of the company's bookkeeper. These women may have been exceptional. Yet Susan B. Anthony's 1870 talk in Corning, "Equal Rights Regardless of Sex," was well attended.[24]

Though women moved and worked from the shelter of their husbands' names earlier in the century, their activities came into the open during the 1890s. Three of Corning's nine cigar manufacturers in 1895 were women, according to the local directory.

By the turn of the century many of Corning's young women held jobs, though they usually stopped working when they married. Cut-glass factories were the preferred employers. Girls loved to "help out" there during busy seasons; many later moved into full-time jobs. Those who have reminisced about their work call Corning's cut-glass firms "a wonderful place to work," and remember their product as looking like "a mass of diamonds."

The cut-glass industry kept some of its nineteenth-century lack of specialization to the end. Women worked wherever they were needed, beginning by dusting the glass in their employers' salesrooms. They went on to distributing glass to cutters, keeping catalogs up-to-date, making drawings of new blanks, waxing the glass before its acid bath, washing, drying, and packing it, and a dozen other jobs. Some girls became saleswomen.

Women were painting and gilding Hawkes & Co. glass about 1913, and later did the same work at H. P. Sinclaire & Co. The head of the Hawkes silver department had as his assistant a woman silversmith.

If the Corning directory's spelling of "Bernice Johnson" is correct, Corning probably had a woman cutter as early as 1905. Corning directories also list a number of "foreladies." Their duties varied from company to company, but the position was always a responsible one. Where the forelady was chief inspector, her judgment determined acceptable work. She might also manage all the female help; at least one did so with an iron hand.

The Hunt Glass Co.'s woman business manager left to found her own company about 1917. Hunt was employing a number of female cutters by the 1930s; the company's secretary from about 1915 to 1937 was a woman, the Mary Krebs referred to earlier.

Women were among the incorporators of the Knickerbocker, Corning Cut Glass, and Signet companies, founded 1901 through 1913. Women's interest in glass continues. Half a dozen or more are cutting glass in Corning today.

Pay and Advancement

Though glass cutters earned less than blowers or engravers, cutting provided a comfortable standard of living: usually a house and cow, often also a horse. The workmen who made $24 a week in 1888, however, were doubtless foremen. The more common wage was about $14, with $20 "good pay for

those times," as Corningites put it. H. P. Sinclaire, Jr., began work as the Hawkes company's bookkeeper in 1883 at a salary of $600 a year. This was so munificent that T. G. Hawkes explained its size even as he offered it.

How do these figures compare with owners' and officers' salaries? We have data only for the Hawkes company. Hawkes and Sinclaire each earned $1,800 as president and secretary in 1890.[25] In good years owners also earned dividends; in bad years they did not. They might also earn commissions on sales. The dismal record of Corning bankruptcies shows that ownership was no guaranteed road to riches. No Corning cutting-company proprietor made a fortune in that business, though other investments might provide one. On a smaller scale this was true also of craftsmen.

Yet the best craftsmen were able to advance in the industry. Each large company had several foremen, a manager, and/or a superintendent. These men were in demand elsewhere; a number of them founded their own companies.

Why Corning?

Inasmuch as Corning Glass Works sharply restricted the sales of its blanks, what attracted scores of cutting and engraving companies to the Corning area? James O. Sebring, when he was president of Corning Cut Glass Co., gave the following reasons.

Corning has several facilities over other places for the manufacture of cut glass;...it...has been for many years a cut glass center...and the public trade knew [it]...further...it is not a union city in so far as cut glass is concerned... [and finally] there are many hundreds of men here...who are experienced and expert workmen...and the availability of employees is one of the very important things that enter into the desirability of [locating] a cut glass plant in Corning. It is not possible to...manufacture...cut glass...[where] there are wanting these men... without importing...the skilled labor to begin with. It takes a long time to educate...expert workmen....[26]

Sebring was an astute lawyer and businessman; we may assume that his analysis was sound. Corning attracted cutting companies because it was a non-union city, was known in the trade as a cut-glass center, and had plenty of skilled craftsmen. For all these advantages, latecomers were indebted to Corning Glass Works, J. Hoare & Co., and T. G. Hawkes & Co.

3
The Cutting and Engraving of Glass

Cutting or engraving decorated Corning's costliest glass; silver mountings were sometimes added. Hand-painting and silver trims were in use before World War I, and their use increased after it ended. During the 1920s the Hawkes, Steuben, and Sinclaire companies (and perhaps others) were collectively using handpainting, acid-etching and acid-cutback, staining, gilding, silver-deposit, sand-blasting, and gold, silver, and enamel trims of various sorts. Some of these will be mentioned briefly in appropriate chapters.

Our subject, however, is Corning's cutting and engraving. The two differ in style, technique, and cost; it is essential to understand their differences.

The cutter's wheel is below his cutting blank. He must look through the blank and work on its bottom surface. The engraver, on the contrary, brings the blank up under his wheel. Illustration 15 shows a cutter at his frame, as it is called. Illustration 19 shows an engraver at his lathe.

Glass-Cutting

Thomas Hawkes was asked in 1904 to describe glass cutting. His answer was as follows:[1]

Cut glass is...done by steel or iron wheels revolving in a trough with a stream of [abrasive] and water dripping on the...wheel, which makes the first cut or roughing....[In] the next process [the glass] goes to a hard stone wheel with a small stream of water dripping on it. [The second] workman smooths the rough cut...then it goes to a polisher who polishes it on a wooden wheel, and then it goes to a buffer, who buffs it on a buffing wheel. These are the principal operations in the process of manufacturing cut glass.

The workmen are today divided into roughers and smoothers and possibly a third sub-division of polishers, but not the best workmen. The best workmen can take a piece of glass and commence and finish it out.

Roughing

The first thing...done with a blank is for the rougher to take it and with a brush or some other instrument roughly mark...the main outline of the pattern....Then with this steel wheel, called a mill, with a sharpened edge with [abrasive] and water dripping down on it, the wheel revolving [over] a trough, he holds the blank over the wheel. The wheel with the [abrasive] and water cuts out the glass where he has made these marks. That process will leave the blank with deep...cuts in it with rough surfaces.

Smoothing

That [rough-cut] blank...is then passed on to a man with a stone wheel of some kind and...[he] smooths out or grinds out these rough cuts....In addition...[he] cuts the smaller and finer lines.... (In some cases, as I remarked before, the best workmen commence and finish their work. If it is the same workman, that is practically the process.) That is called smoothing of the blank.

Polishing

The [next] workman then takes this blank and on a wooden or felt wheel or some wheel of that character smooths it all over. In the early process of manufacture the workmen completed the polishing....

Some years ago there was introduced...what is known as acid polishing.[2] [It] was introduced largely by glass cutters who made an inferior quality of glass. That is, after the glass [is] roughed and smoothed it is dipped into an acid bath which polishes the glass to a certain extent. These people ...send it to market in that form. That eliminated the process I call buffing, and so they could sell the glass a great deal cheaper than we could.

This matter of acid polishing has been one of the

15.   Leonard Dow roughing a goblet at Steuben Glass Works in the late 1920s. Dow and his brothers, William Thomas and Oliver, were half nephews of Oliver Egginton and ranked among Corning's greatest cutters. *Coll. Mrs. Marilyn Dow Zaludny*

causes of lowering the price of cut glass with certain manufacturers who sell to...department stores, but not with reputable manufacturers. After dipping... in acid, the better grade of cut glass in order to properly complete [it] requires considerable buffing and wooding.

I can't say whether there are any...manufacturers now who do not use acid polishing...but I think they all use it to a more or less extent for a cheaper grade of goods. For a finer grade of goods, such as we sell to Gorham, Tiffany, Theodore Starr & Co., and these people who put expensive silver mountings on the glass, we finish all our glass by hand....

Where we dip our glass in acid, it costs us more to cut our glass today than it ever did. Where these people have to compete in the department store business they send their glass to the market right from the acid bath. We have to go all over that three times and repolish it and buff it. So that with considerable of our expensive glass we...use acid polish, completing the work by wooding and buffing....

Where they send the glass to the market [from] the acid bath, the polish is not permanent....

The only object to the manufacturers [of] good glass in using an acid bath is that the acid would get into...fine cuts in certain patterns that wood cannot get into.

T. G. Hawkes's emphasis on the final hand-polishing was entirely justified, for reasons that we have already mentioned. His statement that an unbuffed acid polish "is not permanent" is one key to the lasting beauty of Corning's best cut glass. Michael Grady, manager of Corning Cut Glass Co., explained the fine color of Hawkes cut glass this way:

> You may take...an ordinary good blank, and after it is [smoothed] if you do not wood it...it will be dark in color. If you wood that and brush it and get all...stone mark of gray off and then brush it with the fiber wheel it will come out perfectly white. I believe Mr. Hawkes does something like that; he woods [his glass] more than some people and that gives largely the matter of color.[3]

The cutting frame that Thomas Hawkes described includes a shaft on which a wheel rotates, a wooden trough beneath it, and a hopper from which abrasive and water drip along a wick onto the cutting wheel. Behind the frame runs a shelf that holds the day's work (Ill. 16). The number of frames in a factory corresponded roughly to the number of cutters employed during peak periods. New factories, however, usually allowed for growth by installing more frames than were needed immediately.

The Training of Cutters

J. Hoare & Co. and T. G. Hawkes & Co. operated formal apprenticeship programs of substantial size. The Hawkes graduates and probably those from Hoare received diplomas when they completed their training.[4]

Apprenticeship was the vocational high school of its era. It began after the eight grades of public

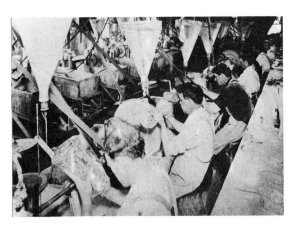

16.   H. P. Sinclaire & Co. upstairs cutting and engraving room before World War I. James Hanley is the cutter in the foreground. *Coll. Mrs. Edna Hanley Rotsell*

school—i.e., when the apprentice was about fourteen. He usually "got his trade" in three years. Unlike many European apprentices, he received a small salary. This could increase with his skill to about half the journeyman's wages. He paid nothing for his training.

Hoare and Hawkes apprentices had their own foremen, and their own sections of the factories, "the apprentice shop." A ratio of one apprentice to five cutters seems to have been customary in the late 1880s.

Young men who worked at smaller or later companies learned to cut glass more informally. Foremen, usually the companies' best cutters, were generous with their time and interest. The novice might begin by polishing bases, and work into more difficult assignments, called "jobs." Cutting firms always had imperfect or broken blanks on hand; these seem to have been available to learners for the asking. Judging from pieces that appear on the market from time to time, a customary exercise was to copy the employers' simpler designs.

Young cutters who lacked formal training sometimes were ambitious and talented enough to be dissatisfied with a single foreman's instruction. They were apt to move from company to company in order to learn the specialties of each.

Kinds of Cutting

The chief aim of modern cutting was originally to admit light into dull glass and to remove imperfections. Cutting imparts facets, and hence prismatic effects, to uncolored glass. When glass color improved in the nineteenth century, and cut designs became an end in themselves, the goal of brilliance endured. Former employees usually described the cut glass they worked with as resembling "a mass of diamonds."

Cutting that aimed for brilliance was geometric in design. But cutting might also be representational. Floral designs, which date from before 1910 in Corning, became more important as time went on.

A third type of cutting shaped the blank, rather than decorated it. This function became important during the 1930s.

Decorative Cutting

Though the bolder geometric cuts impart light, fine cuttings such as cross-hatching do not. Present-day mid-European cut glass exploits the contrast of polished and unpolished geometric motifs. Early Corning cut glass did not. H. P. Sinclaire & Co. began to use unpolished cross-hatching ("silver diamonds") in 1912. The introduction of the gang-

17. The Corning area called this kind of cutting "intaglio" when Enterprise Cut Glass Co. ran this ad in 1910. *Coll. The Corning Museum of Glass*

cut wheel about 1913 made possible the quick, inexpensive cutting of stripes composed of several parallel lines, which were cut simultaneously.

Pictorial cutting was sometimes called "intaglio cutting" (see Ill. 17) in the Corning area. England used the term intaglio cutting to describe stone engraving—and, at present, it is often used all over the United States to describe both copper-wheel and stone engraving. However, the term has been used and misused in so many connotations that we shall avoid it in this book.

Because the cutter must look through his blank, and his wheel is large, pictorial cutting is relatively undetailed. Often it attempts little more than a silhouette. It is the cheapest way to put a picture on glass by means of a revolving wheel.

In the hands of an expert cutter, however, pictorial cutting can produce some detail, for example the lines of rigging of a sailing ship. Cork or wooden wheels can add bloom to a bunch of grapes. Pictorial cutting cannot be mistaken for copper-wheel engraving; it is unfortunate and confusing that Corning has called it "engraving" or "stone engraving" since it began to be used on Pyrex-brand glass.

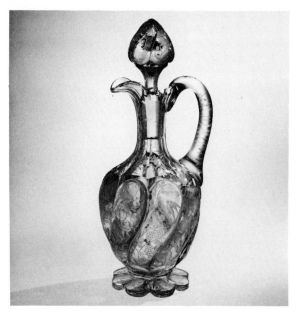

18. This H. P. Sinclair & Co. quart decanter in *Birds, Bees & Flowers* design has the cut pillars characteristic of Corning's best rock crystal. The piece wholesaled for $350 in 1927. Height, 33.7 cm. *Coll. The Corning Museum of Glass* (Gift of Mrs. John Sinclaire)

Shaping Glass on the Cutting Frame

Cutting may also reshape the cutting blank. The scalloped feet on stemware cut in England, Corning, and elsewhere are an example, as are the pillars of rock crystal (Ill. 18). Such cutting was often combined with decorative cutting or engraving. As changing taste and rising costs diminished sales of rich-cut glass, however, cutting-as-shaping became more important. It is virtually the only kind of cutting used in today's Steuben glass.

Glass Engraving

Unlike glass cutting, glass engraving is chiefly a representational art. When the engraver carves his glass—and this has been extremely rare in Corning—his aim is sculptural. Corning's copper-wheel and stone engravings have always been outstanding. In both, the lathe's spindle and wheel project laterally over the cutting blank; the design is engraved on the blank's top surface. As with cutting, the design may be marked on the glass before the first incision is made. Often, however, a copper-wheel engraver works directly on the unmarked oiled glass, referring frequently to the design he follows.

A visitor to the Philadelphia Centennial Exposition of 1876 was delighted with the demonstration of engraving in the Gillinder Brothers glass factory. He described the process as follows:

The [copper-wheel] engraving on glass was one of the most curious and attractive departments in this building....The operator carried the pattern in his mind, and did not outline it upon the glass, but depended entirely upon his eye and hand. He held the glass to the wheel, which instantly cut through or roughened the surface, he rubbed off the oil with his thumb or finger to see the result, alternating this movement with pressing the glass to the wheel, and these movements were so rapid that the glass seemed to be almost continuously upon the wheel. Flowers, birds, leaves, fruit, and in fact any object was thus cut upon glass by the skilled workman.[5]

It has been said that "copper wheel engraving is to...glass cutting what watchmaking is to riveting."[6] It is more delicate, time-consuming, and costly than cutting or even true stone-engraving. Let us look more closely at the process.

Copper-wheel Engraving

Paul Perrot, former director of the Corning Museum of Glass, describes copper-wheel engraving as follows:

Copper wheel engraving was the last refinement in the abrasive techniques: copper discs of various thicknesses, diameters, and rim profiles were rotated individually on a spindle; from time to time, an abrasive such as emory (now carborundum) mixed with oil was applied to the face of the wheel. Pressed against the vessel...by the rotating wheel, the abrasive ground its way into the surface, the roughness of the cut being determined by the coarseness of the abrasive, the depth and width of the cut by the size of the wheel.[7]

The copper-wheel engraver uses up to 150 wheels. The smallest is the diameter of a pinhead. In earlier days, when his lathe was operated by a foot-powered treadle, he might entrust early, deep incisions to a talented rougher or do them himself on a cutting frame. The power-operated lathe, however, made possible his use of larger stone wheels, including the so-called "diamond wheel." As a result, today's engraver usually begins and completes each piece—as did Corning's best cutters. This progress reverses that of cutting in the United States, where for economy's sake cutting was divided into the specialties of roughing, smoothing, and polishing.

In addition to his thin copper wheels and coarser stone ones, the copper-wheel engraver uses polishing wheels of various sorts: brush wheels, wooden ones, or tiny lead ones to brighten accents in an unpolished design.

The time expended on a fine copper-wheel engraving may be measured in weeks, months, or

19. Master engraver Joseph Libisch working at Steuben Glass in 1947 on the *Merry-Go-Round Bowl. Coll. Steuben Glass, Steuben Glass photograph*

years. Its detail surpasses that of the finest drawing in that engraving adds the third dimension of depth. On the other hand, the copper-wheel engraver can execute shallow but detailed monograms, pictures, or coats of arms on blanks too thin for the cutter's wheel. Such work is sometimes called "surface engraving."

Stone Engraving

The familiar description of stone engraving as a technique midway between cutting and engraving is more confusing than helpful. This is simply a coarser type of engraving; it uses a lathe fitted with stone wheels. The smallest we have seen is a gang-cut wheel ⅜ inch in diameter, used for adding the scales to a two-inch fish.

Stone wheels were used for depth; they are incapable of the fine detail achieved with copper wheels, though leaf-veinings are not beyond their range. They are incapable of portraiture, but can add small floral motifs to designs that combine cutting and engraving.

Perhaps the most common use of stone engraving was to add names and addresses to flashed souvenir wares. The fruits and flowers of the Tuthill company

and the Hawkes Gravic glass of the middle period illustrate stone engraving at its best. The technique is quicker than copper-wheel engraving; the product is less expensive. It too may be shaded or polished.

The copper-wheel engraver may be an artist; the stone engraver is a craftsman. The copper-wheel engraver uses stone wheels, but the stone engraver is incapable of the fine draftsmanship of copper-wheel work.

The copper-wheel engraver was the aristocrat of glass decorators and the product of a long apprenticeship. His pay was higher than the cutter's. The only exception to this rule in Corning seems to have been at T. G. Hawkes & Co. during the 1940s and 1950s. There, the Hawkes payroll book shows, several cutters were more highly paid than the engravers.[8]

The Copper-Wheel Engraver's Training

Corning's early copper-wheel engravers came from Central Europe. Most were Bohemian. They immigrated as journeymen or Masters, and trained Corning's American engravers in European methods. Though the modern Steuben Glass has operated engraving apprenticeships, it also continues to employ Central European engravers. Because of this century-long tradition, we shall describe today's Austrian engraving apprenticeship in some detail.[9]

The apprentice begins his training at the age of about fourteen. Unlike his American counterpart, he pays for his studies and receives no wages. Since about 1870 there have been state schools for glass studies, or *Glasfachschulen,* though students may still elect to do their practical work in the shop of an engraving Master. Training has changed very little since the nineteenth century.

The applicant must prove by examination that he is qualified in German, mathematics, bookkeeping, and drawing. Once accepted, he studies seven or eight theoretical subjects a year. They include German, mathematics, calligraphy, glassmaking technology, glass chemistry, design, technical drawing, and drawing from nature. In the last named, Bohemians (now Czechoslovakians) have always been peculiarly apt, perhaps because many early Bohemian engravers were also painters.[10] Meanwhile, practical engraving increases yearly, reaching twenty hours a week in the third year. At its end the apprentice may have mastered the use of 100 or more engraving wheels.

The journeyman's certificate requires the student to pass a comprehensive examination on the three years' theoretical subjects. His engraving and design skills are judged from a work of his own design, which must incorporate all he has learned.

Though the graduate may elect to study further under one of his teachers, he must also engrave for a minimum of three years under the supervision of an engraving "Master."[11] He may neither teach nor open his own engraving shop. After this period, if his skill, probity, and demeanor warrant, the Master may recommend him for Master's training.

Master's studies require another year of work at the journeyman's expense. He studies the economic and other aspects of setting up an engraving shop, including applicable tax laws. He learns to teach. He studies the design of blanks as well as of engraving. At year's end he must pass a written examination.

Practical work culminates in the "Masterpiece." The candidate designs its blank, designs and executes its engraving, and estimates total cost. He must also engrave for three hours under the watchful eyes of visiting Masters. They return to put him through his paces again as part of his Master's examination. They inspect the Masterpiece at that time, asking how many cuts it required so that they can judge the cost estimate.

The candidate who fails may try for his certificate again, but a third failure is final. He may never teach or open a shop, as a Master is privileged to do.

The moral standards and dignity required of Master's candidates cannot be overemphasized.

Corning's engraving Masters shared other characteristics. They insisted on operating their own shops, though they also engraved in Corning's factories. They lived with a style that approached elegance. They were eager to teach their craft, especially to their sons, and were skilled at doing so. They were "fine gentlemen," as tradition required them to be, and Corning remembers them warmly.

The Mid-European apprenticeship provides an interesting comparison with American ones. The American freedom to open one's own glass business regardless of training simultaneously provided a large measure of freedom to go bankrupt.

Cameo and Rock Crystal Engraving

Cameo engraving, in which the background of a design is carved away, was virtually non-existent in Corning. A few simple cameo designs were made during the 1920s, notably by H. P. Sinclaire & Co. on black glass; in general, however, cameo effects were limited to the acid cutbacks of the Steuben Glass Works.

Rock crystal, on the other hand, was immensely important. This engraving style (usually spelled with capitals in Corning) was introduced by Thomas Webb & Sons of England in the 1870s. It was a

20. Two-piece cut and engraved punch bowl from H. P. Sinclaire & Co., ca. 1912, made also in the polished rock-crystal finish. Height, 38.7 cm. *Coll. Harry Kraut; Taylor & Dull photograph*

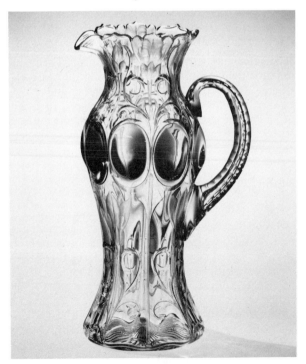

21. Cut and stone-engraved Steuben Glass Works ewer, ca. 1910, used a molded blank that imitated the cut medallions of costlier rock-crystal designs. Height, 26.4 cm. *Coll. The Corning Museum of Glass* (Gift of Mr. and Mrs. Gillett Welles)

specialty of Bohemian engravers. The name suggests earlier objects carved from natural crystals. Rock crystal was always polished. It added to copper-wheel representational engraving something of the third dimension of the Bohemian *Hochschnitt* (high-relief engraving). The archetype of rock crystal is the Fritsche ewer shown in Illustration 479. (The electrifying effect on Corning of this Webb piece is described in Chapter 8.)

Corning's rock crystal went through three phases. Though Corning never equaled the high relief of the ewer, the rock crystal of 1890 to perhaps 1915 combined three-dimensional wheel shaping with representational copper-wheel engraving. Typically, medallions or curved areas called "pillars" were cut in a thick blank. These were engraved and polished, though many might also be ordered in the un-polished "engraved" finish. H. P. Sinclaire & Co. specialized in this work, and continued it after other companies began to produce cheaper interpretations of rock crystal.

One of these is the ewer in Illustration 21. Its raised areas were molded in the blowing rooms; its decoration is stone engraved. The Steuben Glass Works was one of several American companies that made such blanks.

Corning was highly successful with its rock crystal. By the 1920s the term was used to describe the polished finish on engraved glass of any sort. Rock crystal was no longer necessarily the top line of the companies that made it, though often it was.

Hochschnitt (High-Relief Engraving)

Hochschnitt was even rarer in Corning than was cameo engraving. J. Hoare & Co. hired a glass carver from Webb of England about 1892. He was in Corning only during the period when Hoare was preparing an exhibit for the Columbian Exposition of 1893. We assume that the rock-crystal engraving cited in Hoare & Co.'s award was the work of this man. The present whereabouts of these pieces is unknown.

At present we know of no other *Hochschnitt* in Corning before Steuben Glass's *Hull,* Illustration 744 (Chapter 20).

Engraved by J.K.Campbell. N.Y.

4
J. Hoare & Co.

J. Hoare & Company was the first of Corning's many cutting companies and one of the longest lived. It had its origin in a cutting firm that started in Brooklyn in 1853; hence the date in their trademark, which is often confusing to collectors. The founder of the firm was John Hoare, who was born in Cork, Ireland, on April 12, 1822. He learned the trade of glass cutter, probably from his father James Hoare, and worked in Belfast before he went to England, where he worked for several different cutting firms in the Birmingham area, including Thomas Webb & Sons. It was in England that he married Catherine Dailey, probably in 1845.[1] When Hoare and his family came to the United States in 1848, he was already an accomplished glass cutter. (He had one son, James, who was born before the Hoares left England.) In fact, Hoare came to New York to ply his trade, and in 1853 he started his own business, probably with one or more partners.

The first evidence found of Hoare's company is a printed announcement of the cutting firm of Hoare, Burns and Dailey, tenants at 44 State Street, Brooklyn. Dated August 1857, it said in part:

> Having purchased from the "Brooklyn Flint Glass Company" their entire cutting department, we are now prepared (more particularly from the extended facilities which we now have under our control) to execute orders more promptly and on a larger scale than we did at our late factory in 18th Street, which establishment, we beg to inform you, we are no longer connected with, having transferred our machinery, and &, as above mentioned.

A line of dots where the street address was to be filled in by hand may show that the company had more than one location. In 1864, however, Hoare's were still tenants of the Brooklyn Flint Glass Company, but a letterhead of July 3, 1866, indicated they must be occupying part of Dorflinger's factory on Commercial Street in the Greenpoint section.

The Brooklyn Directory of 1860 listed Joseph Dailey and John Burns as living with the Hoares in Brooklyn. It is probable that Joseph Dailey was a brother or a relative of Catherine Dailey, Hoare's wife, and that he and John Burns were cutters. In spite of the mention of a previous shop on 18th Street, none was ever listed in the directory.

As described in Chapter 1, Hoare, Burns, and Dailey were tenants when the Houghtons bought the bankrupt Brooklyn Flint Glass Company in 1864. When the Houghtons decided to move to Corning, they were able to persuade Hoare & Dailey to open a branch shop there. Previously, Hoare & Dailey had experimented with a branch shop in Rochester, which engraved lamp chimneys, but it was a short-lived venture.[2]

Corning Glass Works began manufacturing glass on October 22, 1868, in Corning. In 1869 a newspaper report said:

> Cutting glass is a distinct branch of the business. ...Messrs. Hoare and Daley [sic] of Brooklyn, have perfected an arrangement with the glass company to do this kind of work and are putting it in complete order for cutting glass of all descriptions. ...there are articles lettered and most beautifully ornamented with flowers....

Doubtless the cutting went on in only a small way for the first couple of years,[3] as obviously not much could be done until the Glass Works had completed a large supply of blanks. On December 22, 1870, the Corning newspaper reported that the Glass Works

22. *Opposite:* Portrait of John Hoare from Harlo Hake's *Landmarks of Steuben County,* 1896.

had received an order from President Grant for $1,000 worth of glass. This must have been cut glass, to have been produced by Hoare & Dailey. Since Corning Glass Works was in receivership at this time, Hoare & Dailey probably cut the set at their main shop in Brooklyn, on Dorflinger's blanks.

23. Goblet engraved with "Mr. and Mrs. J. Hoare/Nov. 29th 1869." Probably made at Hoare & Dailey's cutting shop in Greenpoint, Brooklyn, for the Hoares' 25th wedding anniversary. Height, 14 cm. *Coll. The Corning Museum of Glass* (Gift of Mrs. P. M. Chamberlain)

Incidentally, by June 9, 1870, according to the *Corning Weekly Journal*, Thomas G. Hawkes, an Irishman of twenty-four, was foreman of J. Hoare's Corning shop.

On May 23, 1872, the *Journal* reported that John Hoare had bought a house in Corning; in 1873 he moved his entire business from Brooklyn, closing the Greenpoint shop. This move may have been occasioned by C. Dorflinger's leasing of his plant to another firm. In any event, on March 28, 1873, Hoare was advertising for a dozen dwellings for the use of his glass cutters from Long Island. In August of that year another order for glass for the White House was received. This took three months to blow and cut, and when it was finished, so many Corningites wanted to see it that the ladies of the Episcopal Church arranged an exhibition. Charging a two-shilling [sic] fee, they raised $215.[4] (Unfortunately, no records exist to show what these 1870 and 1873 presidential orders looked like.)

Although the Corning Glass Works never owned Hoare & Dailey, neither firm made the slightest effort in the early years to indicate separate ownership. Hoare's company was called the "Glass Works cutting shop" more often than not, and the earliest J. Hoare & Co. price list, published around 1890, advertised "CORNING RICH CUT GLASSWARE" on the title page. As late as 1909, *Thomas' Register of American Manufacturers* listed the Corning Glass Works as a cut-glass manufacturer.

24. John Hoare's house, 83 E. First Street, Corning, from a city map of 1882.

An article in the *Corning Journal's* "Special Trade Edition" of September 4, 1895, epitomized the confusion of ownership. It said that "before coming here [Corning Glass Works] made for President Lincoln a set of tableware of flint glass in various colors." The Lincoln set was, in fact, produced at Christian Dorflinger's factory in 1861. It was, however, cut by John Hoare's shop, which was then occupying space in the factory. A lawsuit of the early twentieth century explains in part why Hoare came to Corning and why this confusion existed. According to testimony of a Glass Works executive, "J. Hoare [had] always occupied a part of plaintiff's building...an understanding existed... that plaintiff would not sell blanks...to [Hoare's] competitors ...we rented them room and steam power."[5]

In 1873 another exciting order came to Corning. The *Philadelphia Public Ledger* required for its editorial rooms twelve large globes for burners. "Likenesses are to be engraved on the bowls," the *Corning Journal* reported on May 23. The cost was to be $80 each, which was several weeks' wages for a glass cutter; thus, for that day, the order represented a tremendous sum.

25. Canoe Centerpiece in the *Hobnail* pattern, J. Hoare & Co., ca. 1890. Length, 31.8 cm. *Coll. The Corning Museum of Glass* (Gift of Mrs. P. M. Chamberlain). This piece is illustrated in the earliest known Hoare catalog.

On October 5, 1876, a bad fire occurred in the Corning Glass Works building. The works suffered a considerable amount of damage, and John Hoare's stock was burned out. He had a loss of almost $20,000, probably in stock being accumulated for Christmas sale. However, by the next week, the *Journal* reported on the nineteenth, Hoare had set up a cutting and engraving room in the south storeroom of the factory—he was now employing between 30 and 40 men—and by December, Corning Glass Works had rebuilt the building. There was more room on the third floor of the new building, and all the glass cutting was done there with new cutting equipment.

A *Journal* report on January 4, 1877, describing the Glass Works listed John Hoare, Thomas Hawkes, and John Earle as proprietors of the "cutting shop department." Hawkes was still foreman, and he and Earle each owned a small percentage of the business.[6] Clayton's *History of Steuben County* (1877) reported:

In this establishment from 80–100 skilled hands are employed, and all the finer work is done for the britannia, silver, and silver-plated ware manufacturers. Also the fine cut glass for the Executive Mansion in Washington. The manufactured glass for cutting and engraving is purchased of the Corning Glass-Works. The cutting and engraving done here amounts to $100,000 annually.

This figure was probably an exaggeration.

John Hoare had two sons whom he introduced into the cut-glass business, John Hoare, Jr., and James, who later took over the business from his father.[7] James Hoare was a salesman, but John, Jr., trained as a glass cutter both in Brooklyn and in Corning, was a foreman of the shop until his death in the 1890s.

Judging by a letter in the *Corning Journal* of October 14, 1880, signed by all Corning Glass Works and Hoare employees of voting age, Hoare employed 58 men of voting age and Corning Glass Works employed only 60. The letter placed Bohemian engraver Augustus Haselbauer at the firm in 1880; Charles Voorhees of Brooklyn was bookkeeper, James Hoare, agent (sales manager), and John Earle, still foreman. Superintendent Thomas Hawkes had left to found his own firm.

Labor troubles were rife in the 1880s. There was a strike and walkout at T. G. Hawkes and Company in 1886, which spread to Hoare's shop. There, one man declined to finish some champagne glasses because they had been sent over from Hawkes. The employees and the foreman discussed the matter; the champagne glasses remained untouched, and so the machinery was stopped and the employees left the shop. After Hoare returned from his Hammondsport summer home, he is said to have told his men:

Our relations have always been pleasant and there is no reason why they should not continue so. You say you are willing to do any work I may ask of you. I reserve to myself the right to employ as many apprentices as I need and to do the kind of work I want. Prove our pleasant relationship by returning to work.

The glass cutters received his remarks with applause, and promptly decided to resume their duties, after which Hoare said to them, "You know I shall not ask you to do any work I myself would not do," the *Journal* reported on October 7. Local tradition has it that John Hoare was the most popular of Corning's many cutting-shop proprietors and that his men would do anything for him.

In 1887, John Earle, who had been foreman at Hoare's for about a dozen years, resigned to become a partner in a cutting firm in New York City. John Hoare, Jr., returned to Corning after three years at Hoare's New York City sales office, to become foreman of the cutting shop. Around the same time George M. Abbott, a son-in-law of Amory Houghton, became a partner, and it was then that the name of the company was changed to J. Hoare & Co.

The officers of Corning Glass Works moved, in 1889, to new quarters giving themselves offices to "rank among the most magnificent and luxurious of any between New York and Buffalo." The *Weekly Journal* wrote on July 18:

> The late quarters of the Glass Company will be occupied by J. Hoare and Company as an office and for the much ampler display of cut glass. . . . In the new offices there will be five times the space for the display of the goods manufactured in their cutting shop. The engraved or cut glass makes a brilliant exhibition, and has no superior in elegance or finish anywhere.

About three years later, on June 3, 1893, a reporter for the *Corning Daily Journal* wrote of seeing, at J. Hoare & Co., a magnificent exhibit of cut glass with a "mammoth and beautiful" punch bowl for exhibition at the Chicago World's Fair. The bowl was 24 inches in diameter, 18 inches high, and weighed about 70 pounds. It had taken the best employees of the shop about two months to produce, and could not be duplicated short of $800. However, another story later in June mentioned that Hoare was duplicating the punch bowl, which broke while on exhibition at the Fair. The Special Trade Edition of the *Journal* published in 1895 carried a picture of the bowl and a story about the prize Hoare won at the World's Columbian Exhibition in Chicago in 1893, a bronze medal awarded for Quality of Glassware, Artistic Design, Perfection of Finish, Depth of Cutting, and Symmetrical Shape. (Oddly enough, the medal was not received in Corning until June 11, 1896.) *The Report of the Board of General Managers of the Exhibit of the State of New York* (Albany, 1894) listed the award as being for 1) glassware, 2) rock-crystal cutting, 3) cut glass, 4) engraved glass. At most of these fairs, prizes were given fairly freely, and more than one prize was given for the same thing. Thus, it would be wrong to imply that J. Hoare & Co. received awards for being the best cut-glass company in competition with many others. The only other entrants in Hoare's category were L. Straus & Sons and the Tiffany Glass and Decorating Co., both of New York City, and both companies also won awards for excellence. In all, 36 percent of the exhibitors

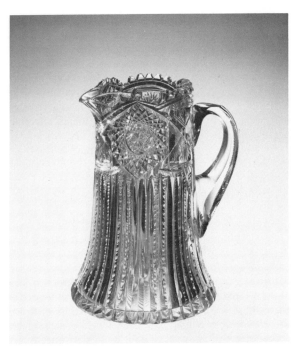

26. Pitcher in the *Hindoo* pattern, J. Hoare & Co. ca. 1903. Height, 22.8 cm. *Coll. The Corning Museum of Glass* (Gift of Mrs. H. J. Wilson). This pitcher was a wedding present from the Houghton family to a relative of George Abbott.

27. Cut punch bowl in a pattern similar to the one exhibited at the World's Columbian Exposition, Chicago, 1893. J. Hoare & Co., ca. 1900. Diam., 53.5 cm. *Coll. The Corning Museum of Glass* (Gift of Mr. and Mrs. M. T. Allen)

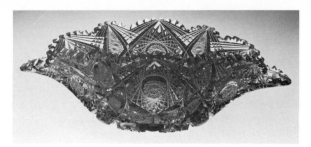

28. Bowl cut by Andrew Callahan in 1893 for the World's Columbian Exposition, Chicago. Not exhibited because of a crack, although a duplicate, also cut by Mr. Callahan, was in Hoare's exhibit. Length, 35.5 cm. *Coll. Miss Frances Barrett*

30. Cut bowl in an unknown pattern by J. Hoare & Co., ca. 1900–1910. Diam., 20.3 cm. *Coll. The Corning Museum of Glass* (Gift of R. Lee Waterman)

29. Bowl in an unknown pattern. J. Hoare & Co., ca. 1902. Diam., 17.7 cm. *Coll. The Corning Museum of Glass*

31. Engraved pane from John S. Hoare's office door in Wellsboro, Pennsylvania, ca. 1906. Height, 132.2 cm. *Coll. Mr. and Mrs. Edward Owlett*

received awards, and the Board of General Managers noted that this was a smaller number than usual at such fairs. In Paris, in 1889, 55 percent of the exhibitors won awards; but this is not to imply that the glass exhibited was not of high quality. Unfortunately, the mammoth punch bowl is no longer in existence, so far as is known.

In 1896 John Hoare died, and the affairs of the company passed into the hands of his son, James, and George L. Abbott. On March 21, 1901, the *Corning Weekly Journal* reported that the Hoare firm wished to enlarge, and was looking for a suitable location. In 1902 they did so, by opening an apprentice or branch shop in a building at the corner of Cedar and Tioga in Corning. The building belonged to the Drake family and was usually referred to as Drake's Mill.[8] This shop had some labor difficulties and apparently felt a spirit of competition with the cutters in the main shop. The *Journal* reported on April 1, 1903, that the men at the branch shop had quit work rather than "cut glassware the pattern of which had been marked in the main shop." Edward Mayer was the first foreman of this shop, succeeded in August 1902 by Albert L. Sullivan. On November 12, 1904, a *Journal* story reported that the employees in the branch shop had all been laid off. In view of the approaching Christmas season, this seems surprising. (The *New York Sunday Tribune* of November 23, 1902, had carried a lengthy story on glassmaking in Corning, illustrated by pictures of the Hoare cutting room, an engraver at work, and several other photographs. Unfortunately, they are not of good-enough quality to reproduce here.)

By 1906, Hoare was again expanding, and it is probably not a coincidence that this was the same year in which John S. Hoare, the son of James and the third generation to cut glass, entered the firm. The Wellsboro, Pennsylvania, Board of Trade raised the funds to erect a factory on the "Industrial Grounds," and J. Hoare & Co. set up a branch plant there with 50 to 75 frames,[9] shipping the equipment from the Drake's Mill building to Wellsboro. John S. Hoare became the manager of the new factory, according to the *Daily Journal* of June 26. This factory operated until early in 1914, when John S. Hoare, in partnership with Harrie Millspaugh, opened his own glass-cutting firm on the same premises.[10]

This separate company probably came into existence because of changes in the parent firm. James Hoare and George Abbott had incorporated in 1908, with Abbott owning one third of the company and Hoare two thirds. Later the same year, they granted a share to Hasell Baldwin, the firm's treasurer, and when Abbott died in 1911 Baldwin acquired more shares.[11] Around 1913, Baldwin took over a majority interest in the firm, although James Hoare remained president.

The cut-glass business was beginning to go downhill at this point, and Hoare started advertising—something Hawkes, Libbey, and other large firms had done for some time. The Hoare trademark, concentric circles with "J. Hoare & Co., Corning 1853," had been adopted in 1895, a few years after T. G. Hawkes started making great use of his mark. Hoare's trademark was not registered until 1914, but according to the Patent Office it had been in use since 1895. Testimony given in a suit in Corning in 1904 claimed that J. Hoare & Co. acid-stamped all its products except when a customer such as Gorham requested the mark be omitted. In advertising copy in the *Corning Leader* in December 1910 and 1911, Hoare's was using the slogans "The Pioneers in Cut Glass" and "The Oldest Cut Glass Factory in America" to promote their position against larger rivals.

In 1912, an article in the *Leader* stated that Hoare's business was picking up and the men would go back on a 5½-day schedule and get 10 percent pay increases. However, the decreasing importance of cut glass by 1915 is indicated by the fact that Corning Glass Works requested J. Hoare & Co. to move—the space the cutting shop occupied was needed for other purposes. Hoare moved to the building on Bridge Street formerly occupied by George W. Drake's Cut Glass Company. The

number of Hoare employees had by then fallen to about 50. Two years later Hasell W. Baldwin sold his interest back to the Hoares; Jack (John S.) Hoare closed his factory in Wellsboro and came home to Corning to run the Bridge Street plant. Although James Hoare remained titular head of the firm, he had been injured in an automobile accident and was not in good health. In spite of the change in management, the cut glass industry continued to decline and J. Hoare & Co.'s fortunes fell with it. The *Leader* of October 29, 1920, reported that the company was bankrupt. James Hoare died the following year, and John S. Hoare in 1926.

* * *

In the 1870s and early 1880s, John Hoare's company was one of the largest cut glass concerns in the country—C. Dorflinger & Sons in White Mills, Pennsylvania, was its chief rival. Factory records from that period mention the following products: engraved castor bottles, bay rum bottles, colognes, vinegar bottles, oil bottles, bar bottles, bitters bottles, cut wines and tumblers, cut stem goblets, nappies, glass lining for sugar dishes, inkstands, covered pickle jars, epergnes, vases, preserve dishes, and butter dishes. Customers in these early days included J. N. Johnson, Henry Allen & Co., Stearne Son & Hall, Chamberlin, Whitmore & Co., and Ovington Bros., all in New York City, and retail stores in Philadelphia, Utica, Albany, Cincinnati, Pittsburgh, Rochester, Baltimore, St. Louis, Chicago, Helena (Montana), and other cities. The Gorham Manufacturing Company bought from Hoare, as did Simpson, Hall, Miller & Co., a manufacturer of electroplated ware, the Derby Silver Company, the Racine Silver Plate Company, the Wilcox Silver Plate Company, and the Aurora Silver Plate Manufacturing Company. Several perfumers were also customers, as were Hagerty Brothers, the large producer and seller of druggists' wares.

In 1887, J. Hoare & Co. perfected an "Electric Light Radiator" made of rich-cut flint glass. This two-part cover for diffusing the glare of an ordinary electric light bulb was probably inspired by the recent (November 1886) electrification of the buildings of Corning Glass Works, a modernization of which the company was very proud.

Although the Hoare firm cut a variety of patterns, they patented very few of them. In February 1887, George Abbott was granted a patent for a simple "brilliant" pattern; and in February 1891 John Hoare patented an unusual design of interlocking circles, which appears in his catalog as "Crystal City" (Ill. 75). It would be interesting to know if the actual designer of the pattern was the elder John

32. Powder box, J. Hoare & Co., ca. 1900–1905. Height, 8.8 cm. *Coll. The Corning Museum of Glass* (Gift of Mrs. P. M. Chamberlain)

33. Group of cut and engraved pieces, J. Hoare & Co., ca. 1900-1918. *Coll. The Corning Museum of Glass* (Gift of Mr. and Mrs. F. Blake; gift of Mrs. P. M. Chamberlain)

34A. Cut light radiator, J. Hoare & Co., ca. 1887. Length, 15.6 cm. *Coll. The Corning Museum of Glass*

35. Goblet cut in a pineapple-like pattern. J. Hoare & Co., ca. 1910. Height, 14.6 cm. *Coll. The Corning Museum of Glass* (Gift of Mrs. P. M. Chamberlain)

36. Decanter engraved in the "rock crystal" style. J. Hoare & Co., ca. 1910-15. Height, 28.3 cm. *Coll. The Corning Museum of Glass* (Gift of Mrs. John S. Hoare)

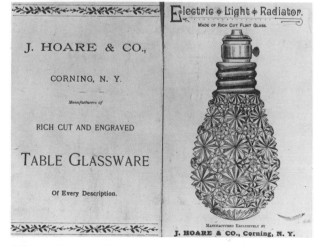

34B. Advertising brochure for the cut light radiator. The inside of the brochure demonstrated how the "radiator" fit over a light bulb to diffuse glare. *Coll. The Corning Museum of Glass*

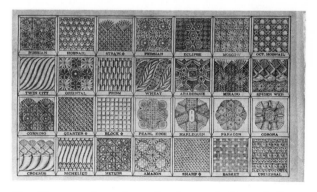

37. First page from the earliest known J. Hoare & Co. catalog, ca. 1890, showing their 28 patterns. In this catalog prices are given for only a few of the patterns. By the dozen, tumblers were: *Russian,* $27.00; *Hobnail,* $21.00; *Strawberry Diamond,* $19.50; *Mikado,* $30.00; *Block Diamond,* $15.00; *Persian,* $37.50. *Coll. Corning–Painted Post Historical Society*

Hoare, then in his seventies, or his son. A catalog of about 1890 listed ,*Russian, Hobnail, Strawberry Diamond, Block Diamond, Quarter Diamond, Sharp Diamond, Moscow, Chair Bot.* [tom] *Hobnail, Persian,* and *Wheat* as "Old Patterns" and *Spider Web, Prism, Mikado, Twin City, Corning, Arabesque, Richelieu, Oriental, Pearl Edge, Paragon, Harlequin, Eclipse, Corona, Amazon, Meteor, Croesus, Basket,* and *Universal* as "New Patterns." (See Ills. 37–68.)

Another early catalog added *Strawberry Diamond and Fan; Strawberry Diamond and Pillars; Russian and Fan; Russian and Pillars; Russian, Prism and Fan; Strawberry Diamond and Prism; Hobnail and Fan; Russian, Pillars and Fan; Cleveland; Grecian; Keystone; Stella; Crystal City,* and a variety of numbered patterns. (See Ills. 69-79.) It is likely that few pieces cut in these patterns were signed, as the Hoare signature was not adopted until about 1895.

Several catalogs of the 1910 to 1913 period had an entirely new series of patterns (Ills. 80-94). The names were *Bolo, Carolyn, Carlyle, Crosby, Comet, Cleary, Erie, Fleuron, Gotham, Hindoo, Iola, Jappy, Jersey, Kohinoor, Leo, Lily, Limoge, London, Marquise, Monarch, Nassau, Niagara, Newport, Oxford, Pluto, Princeton, Prism, Quincy, Saturn, Sparkler, St. James, Steuben, Tokio, Versailles, Venice,* and *Victoria,* as well as several series of numbered patterns.

An undated catalog that seems to fall between the pre-1900 catalogs and the 1910-to-1913 series included *Croesus* from the 1890s and *Argand, Champion, Crystal, Delft, Eleanor, Elfin, Golf, Lenox, Manitoo, Monarch* (a different pattern from the later one), *New York, Pebble, Signora, Tokio, X-ray, Yquem, Yucatan,* and *Zenda.* These patterns, like those of 1910 to 1912, should all have been trademarked. (Ills. 95-109.)

In the early catalogs no engraved ware was shown, although it undoubtedly could have been made, since Augustus Haselbauer is known to have been employed at Hoare and a few samples of his special-order work are known. Notable among these is the pair of colognes first pictured in a book by George S. and Helen McKearin in 1941,[12] and the pair of decanters shown here in Illustration 478. In the later series are very few engraved patterns. Nos. 2141, 2142, and 2143 represent a series of engraved flower designs similar to Hawkes Gravic wares.

The Hoares introduced a few of the late "flower" patterns, but in general their wares remained the same from 1890 on. *Kohinoor*—a very elaborate lattice-like pattern—was the most expensive in 1910. A 9-inch bowl in that pattern was priced at $35, compared to about $10 for the same bowl in most of the other patterns.

NOTE: Illustrations 38 to 68 are pages from a Hoare catalog of ca. 1890. They show a variety of shapes, but the patterns are nearly all variations of *Russian* and *Hobnail.*

Ill. 43 shows the usual shapes of a champagne pitcher, claret jug, and decanter; a claret pitcher is shown in Ill. 51. A whiskey set is pictured in Ill. 59.

A *Mikado* pattern bowl appears in Ill. 48. Other pages from this catalog illustrate a wide variety of bowl shapes: oval, octagon, and square as well as round, and both deep and shallow.

38

39

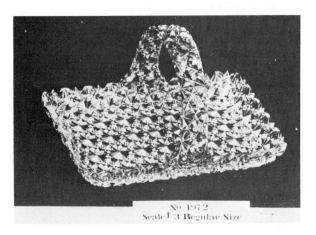

40

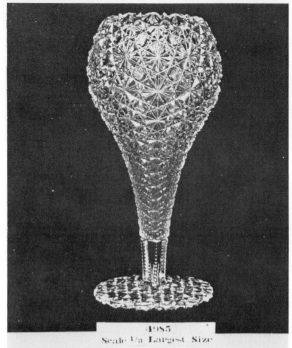

4985
Scale ⅓ Largest Size
Large Medium Small

41

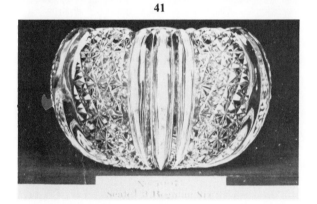

42

43

44

5105 Scale ⅓ Regular Size

45

Scale ⅓ Regular Size

46

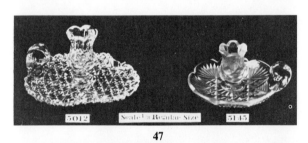

5012   Scale ⅓ Regular Size   5145

47

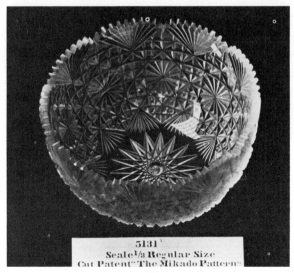

5131
Scale ⅓ Regular Size
Cut Patent "The Mikado Pattern"

48

49

Decanter   5160   Cruet
Scale 1/4 Regular Size

52

5142
Scale 1/4 Regular Size

50

5165
Scale 1/3 Regular Size

53

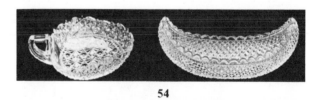

54

5168
Claret Pitcher
Scale 1/4 Regular Size

51

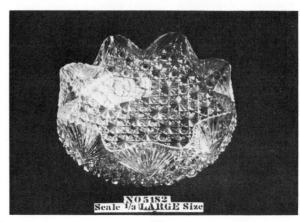

NO 5182
Scale 1/3 LARGE Size

55

56

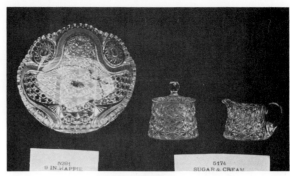

58

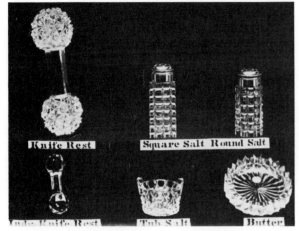

57

60

59

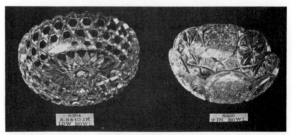

62

61

63

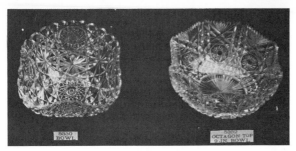

64

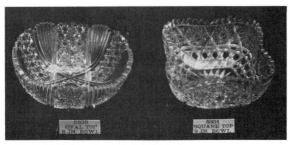

65

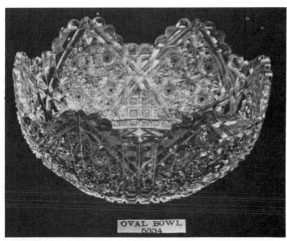

OVAL BOWL
5334

66

67

68

NOTE: Illustrations 69 to 79, pages from a Hoare catalog of ca. 1895, show mostly bowls. The pattern listed as *Crystal City* in Illustration 75 was one of Hoare's only two patented patterns. Patented in 1891, it has been miscalled *Wedding Ring.*

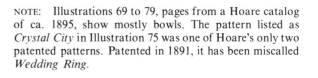

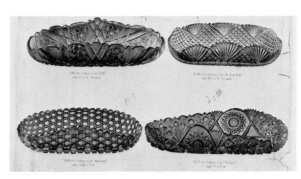

69. These celery trays varied in length from 9½ inches to 11 inches. The patterns are (top row): *5290* and *Strawberry Diamond & Fan;* (bottom row): *Hobnail* and *Eclipse.*

70. Bowls (top row) cut in *Cleveland* and *5468* and (bottom row) *5542* and *5417.*

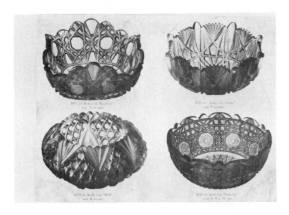

71. Patterns at top are *Keystone* and *Stella*. At bottom are *5418* and *Corning*.

72. Oval dish at top left is *Wheat* pattern; at top right, pattern is identified as *5278*. Dishes in the bottom row are *Strawberry Diamond & Fan* and *Hobnail & Fan*.

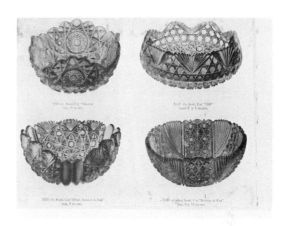

73. This oval punch bowl was very large: 20 inches long and 13 inches wide.

74. The bowl at top left is *Oriental* pattern; the one at top right is identified as *5288*. The two at bottom are *Pillar, Russian & Fan,* and *Russian & Fan.*

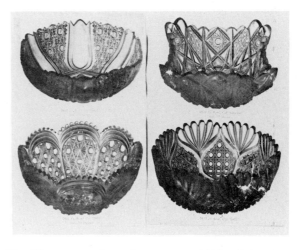

75. These bowls are, top, *5595* and *Strawberry Diamond & Fan;* bottom, *5601* and *Crystal City.*

76. The patterns shown here are, top, *5401* and *Grecian;* bottom, *5408* and *5413.*

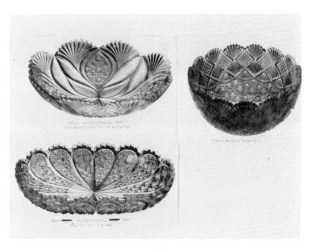

77. Like many other bowls, these were available in a variety of sizes—in this instance, 7, 8, 9, 10, and 10½ inches. The patterns illustrated are *5360, 5417, 5507,* and *5409.*

78. The bowl here at top left is also *5417,* but this one is oval. At top right is *Spider Web;* at lower left, an oval bowl in *5032.*

79. The bowls here are, top, *Russian & Pillars* and *Russian & Fan;* bottom, *Persian* and *Paragon.*

80. Page of "jugs" from an undated Hoare catalog of about 1912. The patterns are *St. James, Fleuron, Oxford,* and *1767.* Tumblers to match were available for all these. The least expensive (both jug and tumblers) was *St. James* pattern.

NOTE: Illustrations 81 to 94 show various pieces cut from an August 1910 Hoare catalog. They are presented here as found—pasted in a scrapbook.

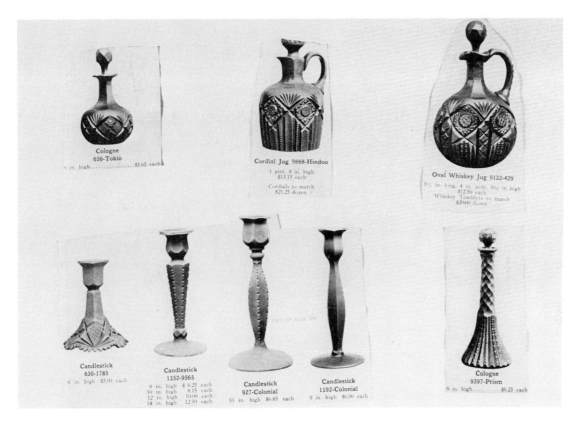

81. The two colognes (top left and bottom right) are in *Tokio* and *Prism* patterns. Both the cordial and the whiskey jugs (at top) are in *Hindoo* pattern.

82. Also from the 1910 catalog are the pieces shown here. Bowl at top left is *Kohinoor;* punch bowl and comport (bottom) are *Marquise.*

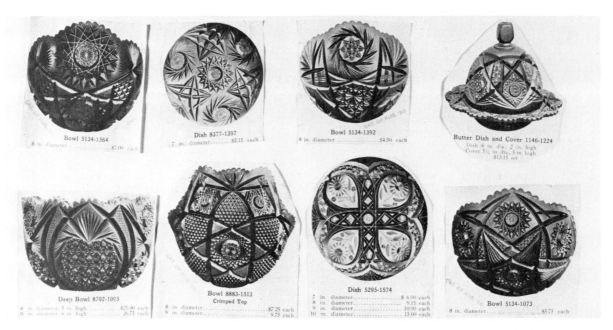

83. These pieces from the Hoare 1910 catalog are in patterns identified only by number: *1546, 1397, 1392, 1224, 1095, 1513, 1574,* and *1073.*

84. Here the top and middle rows show an oval fruit bowl and four celery dishes offered by Hoare in 1910. At bottom are four mayonnaise sets. The only "named" pattern is that of the celery at center left: *Victoria;* others are identified only by numbers.

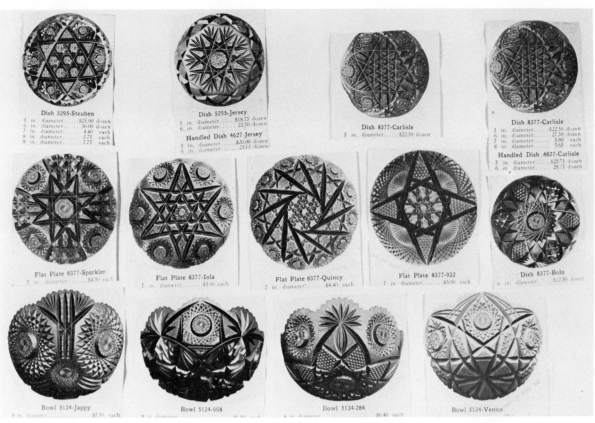

Dish 5295-Steuben
5 in. diameter.....$25.00 dozen
6 in. diameter.....30.00 dozen
7 in. diameter..... 4.40 each
8 in. diameter..... 5.75 each
9 in. diameter..... 7.75 each

Dish 5295-Jersey
5 in. diameter.....$18.75 dozen
6 in. diameter.....22.50 dozen

Handled Dish 4627-Jersey
5 in. diameter.....$20.00 dozen
6 in. diameter.....23.75 dozen

Dish 8377-Carlisle
5 in. diameter.....$22.50 dozen

Dish 8377-Carlisle
5 in. diameter.....$22.50 dozen
6 in. diameter.....27.50 dozen
7 in. diameter..... 3.80 each
8 in. diameter..... 5.65 each

Handled Dish 4627-Carlisle
5 in. diameter.....$23.75 dozen
6 in. diameter.....28.75 dozen

Flat Plate 8377-Sparkler
7 in. diameter.....$4.50 each

Flat Plate 8377-Iola
7 in. diameter.....$3.50 each

Flat Plate 8377-Quincy
7 in. diameter.....$4.40 each

Flat Plate 8377-932
7 in. diameter.....$3.90 each

Dish 8377-Bolo
6 in. diameter.....$22.50 dozen

Bowl 5134-Jappy
8 in. diameter.....$5.50 each

Bowl 5134-998
8 in. diameter.....

Bowl 5134-284
8 in. diameter.....$6.40 each

Bowl 5134-Venice

85. Most of these plates, dishes, and bowls from the Hoare 1910 catalog are identified by pattern names. TOP ROW: *Steuben, Jersey,* and two pieces in *Carlisle.* MIDDLE ROW: *Sparkler, Iola, Quincy, 932,* and *Bolo.* BOTTOM ROW: *Jappy, 998, 284,* and *Venice.*

Decanter 1652-1774
2 pt. 11 in. high $18.75 each
Whiskey Tumblers to match 38.00 dozen
Whiskey Tumblers to match
(without upper border).....28.00 dozen

Decanter 910-St. James
2 pt. 12 in. high $15.25 each
Whiskey Tumblers to match
$17.50 dozen

Decanter 1043-Monarch
13¾ in. high
With handle.....$35.00 each
Without handle.....31.25 each
Clarets to match.....27.50 dozen
Whiskey Tumblers to match 20.00 dozen

Decanter 1653-1775
2 qt. 12 in. high $12.50 each
Whiskey Tumblers to match.....25.75 doz.

Demijohn 9658-Monarch
2 pt. 4 in. dia. 13 in. high $23.00 each
4 pt. 5 in. dia. 14 in. high 30.00 each
8 pt. 6 in. dia. 15 in. high 40.00 each
Whiskey Tum. to match.....20.00 doz.

Squat Carafe
1791-1425

Carafe
8763-Pluto

Globe Carafe
1792-Monarch

Carafe
9810-Carolyn

86. Decanters, carafes, and a demijohn, Hoare 1910. In the top row, second from left, is *St. James* pattern. The decanter next to it and the demijohn at far right are both in *Monarch.* In the lower row the first carafe is unnamed; the other three are *Pluto, Monarch,* and *Carolyn.*

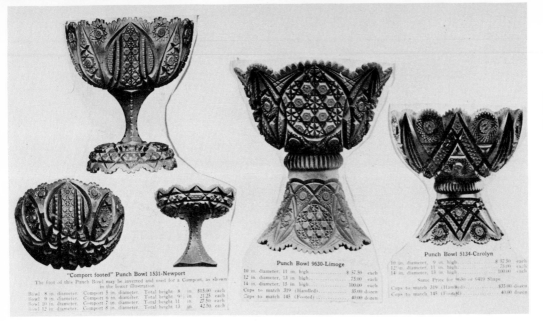

"Comport footed" Punch Bowl 1531-Newport
The foot of this Punch Bowl may be inverted and used for a Comport, as shown in the lower illustration.
Bowl 8 in. diameter. Comport 5 in. diameter. Total height 8 in. $15.00 each
Bowl 9 in. diameter. Comport 6 in. diameter. Total height 9½ in. 21.25 each
Bowl 10 in. diameter. Comport 7 in. diameter. Total height 11 in. 27.50 each
Bowl 12 in. diameter. Comport 8 in. diameter. Total height 13 in. 42.50 each

Punch Bowl 9630-Limoge
10 in. diameter, 11 in. high............ $ 57.50 each
12 in. diameter, 13 in. high............ 75.00 each
14 in. diameter, 15 in. high............ 100.00 each
Cups to match 319 (Handled)............ 35.00 dozen
Cups to match 145 (Footed)............ 40.00 dozen

Punch Bowl 5134-Carolyn
10 in. diameter, 9 in. high............ $ 57.50 each
12 in. diameter, 11 in. high............ 75.00 each
14 in. diameter, 13 in. high............ 100.00 each
Same Price for 9630 or 9419 Shape
Cups to match 319 (Handled)............ $35.00 dozen
Cups to match 145 (Footed)............ 40.00 dozen

87. *Left:* Three punch bowls, Hoare 1910: *Newport, Limoge, Carolyn.*

88. *Right:* These varied items were also cut from the Hoare 1910 catalog. Top left is a celery vase; right is a puff box. In the bottom row is a globe-shaped cologne, a small basket in *Crosby* pattern, and another puff box.

Celery 1274-770
8 in. high $8.50 each

Puff Box 9916-Regular
4 in. high, 4 in. square $9.50 ea

Globe Cologne
1793-1329
4 oz., 5 in. high $5.75 each
6 oz., 5½ in. high 7.00 each
10 oz., 6 in. high 8.40 each
12 oz., 6½ in. high 9.75 each

Basket 306-Crosby
2½ in. diameter, 5 in. high $3.95 each

Puff Box 1019-Regular
5 in. diameter, 4 in. high $11.50 ea.

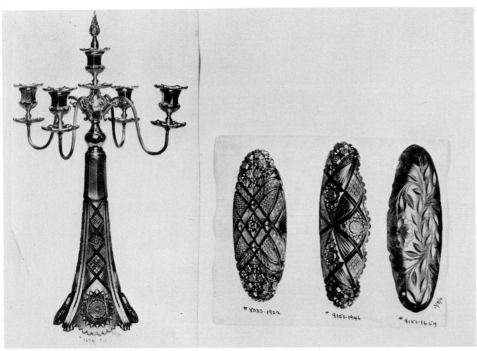

8033-1922   # 9151-1946   # 9151-1654

89. *Left:* A candelabrum and three celery trays, patterns unidentified, cut from a 1911 Hoare catalog.

90. *Right:* Most of this group, clipped from the 1911 Hoare catalog, are unnamed. The decanter at far right is *Nassau* pattern; the one next to it appears to be *Oxford*.

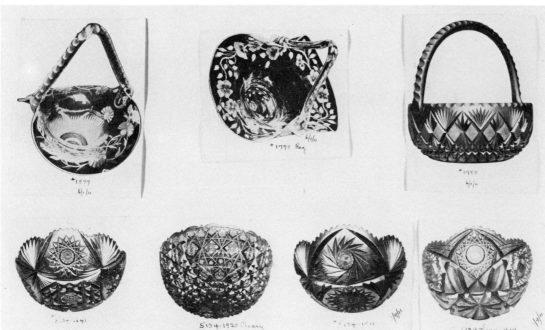

91. *Left:* Baskets and bowls from the Hoare 1911 catalog. Only the second and fourth in the bottom row are named: *Cleary* and *Venice,* respectively.

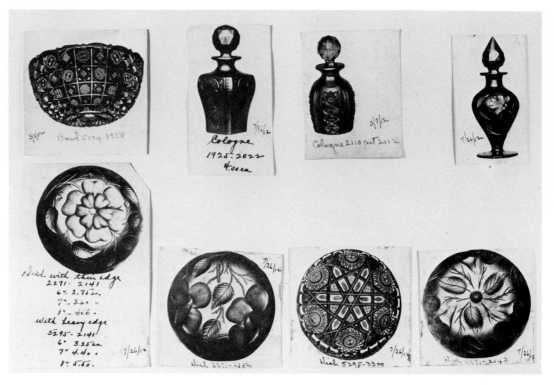

92. This selection of items came from a 1912 Hoare catalog. None of the patterns is named.

93. From a 1913 Hoare catalog. Handwritten below the first piece in the top row is "Figured / Limoge Mould Used." Third piece in top row is *Niagara* pattern. "Figured Mould Fry" (probably H. C. Fry, Rochester, Pa.) is penned beneath the first piece in the lower row. Piece at bottom center is identified as *Saturn*. It is rare to find the blank supplier listed in a catalog—even rarer to find evidence of a mold-blown blank.

94. The only clearly identified patterns in this group taken from the pages of a 1913 Hoare catalog are *London* (fourth in the top row) and *Gotham* (first in the lower row).

NOTE: Illustrations 95 to 109 are pages from a Hoare catalog of ca. 1905–10.

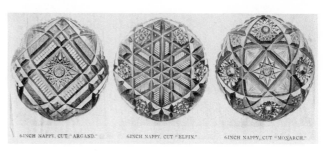

96. Nappies in *Argand, Elfin,* and *Monarch* (Hoare, 1905–10).

SALAD BOWL, (No. 8702. CUT "NEW YORK.") IN CASE.

WITH FORK AND SPOON.

95. *New York* pattern salad bowl with matching fork and spoon came as a boxed set.

97. The pattern on this "triangular top" bowl was called *Golf* (Hoare, ca. 1905–10).

No. 5134. BOWL, CUT "LENOX."

Sizes 7, 8, 9, 10 and 12 Inches.

No. 5134. BOWL, CUT "YQUEM."

98. These two bowls—*Lenox* pattern and *Yquem*—were available in several sizes.

No. 8010. BOWL AND PLATE.

Size. Bowl 9 in. Plate 12 in.

No. 8702. BOWL AND PLATE, CUT "ELEANOR."

Size. Bowl 10 in. Plate 12 in.

99. The bowl and plate at top were not identified in the Hoare catalog. The set at bottom was *Eleanor*.

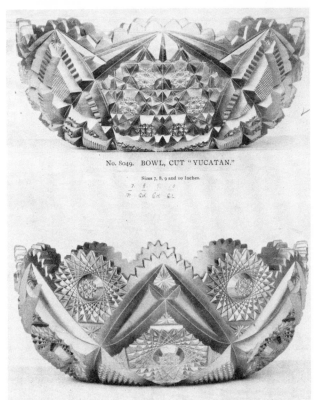

No. 8049. BOWL, CUT "YUCATAN."

Sizes 7, 8, 9 and 10 Inches.

100. *Yucatan* (top) and *Manitou* were both available in four sizes.

101. Three Hoare celery trays from ca. 1905 to 1910.

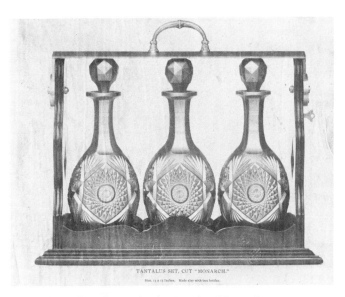

TANTALUS SET, CUT "MONARCH."

Size, 13 x 17 Inches. Made also with two bottles.

102. Tantalus set in the popular *Monarch* pattern.

No. 5354. DECANTER, CUT "CRYSTAL."   No. 5160. DECANTER, CUT "CROESUS."

Size 1 Quart.   Size 1 Quart.

104. Quart decanters in *Crystal* and *Croesus* (Hoare, ca. 1905–10).

No. 8577. NAPPY, CUT "ELEANOR."   No. 8577. NAPPY, CUT "PEBBLE."

Sizes 6, 7, 8, 9 and 10 Inches.   Sizes 6, 7, 8, 9 and 10 Inches.

103. These nappies—*Eleanor* and *Pebble*—were available in four sizes.

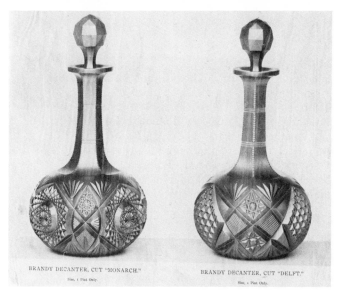

BRANDY DECANTER, CUT "MONARCH."
Size, 1 Pint Only.

BRANDY DECANTER, CUT "DELFT."
Size, 1 Pint Only.

105. These two brandy decanters came only in pint size: *Monarch* and *Delft.*

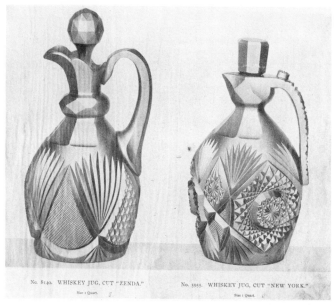

No. 8140. WHISKEY JUG, CUT "ZENDA."
Size 1 Quart.

No. 5955. WHISKEY JUG, CUT "NEW YORK."
Size 1 Quart.

106. Quart whiskey jugs: *Zenda* and *New York.*

No. 8377. NAPPY, CUT "ZENDA."
Size 7 inches.

No. 8377. NAPPY, CUT "X-RAY."
Size 7 inches.

No. 8377. NAPPY, CUT "YUCATAN."
Size 7 inches.

No. 8377. NAPPY, CUT "TOKIO."
Size 7 inches.

107. *Left:* Nappies in *Zenda, X-Ray, Yucatan,* and *Tokio.* All were seven inches in diameter.

109. *Below:* Decanter in *American* pattern.

No. 5606. DECANTER, CUT "AMERICAN."

No. 8237. COLOGNE,
CUT "ELEANOR."
No. 1 and 2.

CYLINDER SHAPE COLOGNE,
CUT "CHAMPION."
No. 1 and 2.

CYLINDER SHAPE COLOGNE,
CUT "SIGNORA."
No. 1 and 2.

108. *Left:* Colognes in *Eleanor, Champion,* and *Signora.*

Around 1918, J. Hoare & Co. began to advertise "engraved" PYREX Brand Baking Ware, although this was actually cut. The shapes and the cut patterns shown in Hoare's advertising circular are identical to those in Corning Glass Works brochures of 1918 to 1920, so it seems likely that for several years Hoare did the cutting for both companies. Corning Glass Works began its own cutting in 1921 after Hoare closed, but ceased in 1926 because of low profits. (From 1932 to 1941, cut Pyrex was produced again.)

According to James Hoare, the firm began buying blanks from other suppliers besides Corning Glass Works in about 1896. At that time they bought primarily from C. Dorflinger & Sons in White Mills. Dorflinger's record books indicate that Hoare purchased all types of blanks from them: Vases, olive dishes, colognes, stemware, salts, tumblers, bowls, finger bowls, celeries, carafes, sugar and creamers, ice tubs, and punch bowls are among the items listed.

Information from Corning Glass Works in 1904 stated that "the firm of J. Hoare & Co. prepared and supplied molds for [CGW] to use—about 75% of the entire output of cut glass manufactured by J. Hoare & Co. was manufactured from their blanks." It seems likely then that Hoare obtained his mold-blown blanks from Corning and his free-blown ones from Dorflinger. Blanks from the Union Glass Company of Somerville, Massachusetts, were also used from about 1903.[13] James Hoare experimented with blanks from Baccarat in France at about this time too, but found them no better than the American ones. He imported lapidary cut stoppers as well, and considered them quite successful.[14]

Records of this period make it apparent that Corning Glass Works, C. Dorflinger & Sons, and other manufacturers of blanks did not compete with each other in regard to shapes. For that reason, most cutting shops bought blanks from more than one supplier. Hoare bought some from Steuben Glass Works shortly after it started, and probably bought from other suppliers in addition to those mentioned. Blanks were less than 10 percent of the business of Corning Glass Works in 1905.

By the turn of the century, J. Hoare & Co.'s chief customers were silver manufacturers, jewelry stores such as J. E. Caldwell, Philadelphia, Bigelow & Kennerd in Boston, and Burley & Co. in Chicago, and one department store, John Wanamaker, in Philadelphia.[15] Hoare had its period of greatest prosperity at this time. They employed 265 men—increasing the work force to 300 every fall. Fifty-four men were located in the Drake's Mill shop.[16]

This was a substantial growth, as the following statistics show. The 1870 census had listed just five cutters in Corning: John Hoare, Henry Hawks,

Charles Kelly, Alfred Daybill, and E. McConnell. Area directories of 1872/73 gave 16 cutters, 16 blowers, and 6 "glassmakers," and a 1874/75 directory listed 23 cutters, 2 engravers, 19 blowers, and one "glassmaker." The figures probably reflect the effect of Hoare's moving his principal shop to Corning in 1873. In the 1880 census, the number of cutters had risen to 41 and two engravers had been added, Augustus and Joseph Haselbauer. Nineteen of the cutters had been born in England or Ireland, 18 in the United States; the two engravers came from Bohemia. In that same year, as already mentioned, 58 employees of John Hoare—all those of voting age—signed an open letter to the *Corning Daily Journal* (October 14, 1880). Their names follow:

Campbell, Daniel	Coakley, Thos.	Casey, J. O.
Callahan, Andrew	Osborn, Joseph	McGeorge, W. L.
Harrison, George	Walker, John	Quill, Daniel
Lunford, Wm.	Kennedy, John	Lanigan, Daniel
Mulford, Ernest	Hoare, Richard	McMahon, Michael
Osborn, Reuben	McConnell, A. J.	Genung, Frank
Stretch, James	McGeorge, F. M.	Rowe, John
Fleming, John T.	Moloney, Thos. E.	Drake, John
Lear, Henry	Sheehan, Wm. F.	Earl, Wm.
Fleming, John	Bergstrum, C. H.	Hoare, John, Jr.
Weller, George H.	Ray, John	Speake, Samuel
C. A. Ricker, J. P.	Lyons, Robert	Sullivan, Albert L.
Walker, Richard	Barenthaler, Wm.	Smyth, John M.
Eich, Joseph	Donovan, W. J.	Howard, John
Leddy, John	Dee, Thomas	Pender, John
Nunan, Wm. F.	Phillips, James	Pender, James
Tanner, Chas. H.	Davis, Joseph	Quill, Dennis
Hazelbauer, Aug. W.	Barnes, George	Hoare, T. D.
Perks, Henry I.	Day, E.	
Killian, Edward	Warner, Edward	

The letter they signed as "the workmen" declared that John Hoare had not pressured them to vote for
the Republican candidates.

By 1890, the total number of cutters in Corning was 119, plus 3 engravers employed by Hoare and Hawkes; by 1900 the number had soared to 390 cutters and 9 engravers, employed by Hoare, Hawkes, Egginton, and Hunt.

By the time the Hoares had moved to Bridge Street, however, the number of employees was below 50 again, with only 3 engravers, George McQuade, Wilmot Putnam, and Joseph Sidot, left. The decline of John Hoare & Co. from 1905 on was part of the general decline of the cut glass business, a slide accelerated by the First World War.

SUMMARY

Dates: 1868-1920
Location: 1868-1915—2nd floor of Corning Glass Works Main Plant at the foot of Walnut Street
1902-1904—Branch shop, corner of Cedar and Tioga Streets, Corning

1906-1914—Industrial Grounds, Wellsboro, Pennsylvania (branch shop)

1915-20—Bridge Street, Corning

Blanks: 1868-1896—Corning Glass Works

1896-1920—Corning Glass Works, C. Dorflinger & Sons, Union Glass Company, Baccarat, Steuben Glass Works

Trademark: 1868-1895—none

1895-1920—"J. HOARE & CO/1853/CORNING" in a circle acid-stamped on each piece

ca. 1900-1920—"HOARE" acid-stamped on stemware

Products: Brilliant cut glass and fine engraved wares until 1920. Stone-engraved Pyrex ware from about 1918 to 1920. Some lighter ware probably made ca. 1910-20

Employees: Several hundred over the 50-year life of the firm. See text for partial list.

Customers: Silver manufacturers such as the Gorham Manufacturing Company; leading jewelry stores all over the United States and Canada, and some department stores, particularly John Wanamaker in Philadelphia

Engraved by J K Campbell NY

Thomas G Hawkes

5
T. G. Hawkes & Co.

Thomas Gibbons Hawkes was an Anglo-Irish-man, born in 1846 at Surmount, his father's estate outside Cork. The Hawkes family had come from England to Ireland in 1726, and although branches of the family had been glass cutters in England (the Hawkes brothers of Dudley in the 1820s), and his maternal grandmother was a Penrose of Waterford, one of the first glassmaking families in Ireland, his immediate forebears were not glassmen. Thomas himself studied civil engineering for two years at Queens College, Cork, but in 1863, at the age of seventeen, he left school and came to New York, on his way to "see the world."[1]

In order to support himself in New York, young Hawkes found a job as a draftsman with the firm of Hoare & Dailey, a cutting shop in Brooklyn, where he also learned glass cutting and worked at selling as well. Next, he worked briefly as a glass cutter in Rochester, New York (running a Hoare & Dailey branch shop that engraved lamp chimneys),[2] but by 1870 he was in Corning supervising their branch shop on the second floor of the Corning Glass Works building. In 1876, he married a local girl, Charlotte Bissell, and the following year they had a son, Samuel.[3] Daughters Alice and Charlotte completed the family within a few years.

In March 1880, the *Corning Journal* reported that Hawkes, "for many years foreman of Corning Glass Works cutting shop [sic]," was about to open his own shop on West Market Street over L. Field's marble works. According to Hawkes's later recollection, he started with "little capital and in a small and tentative way" with about seven or eight employees.[4] Hawkes's and Hoare's parting was apparently friendly, since T. G. Hawkes was allowed to buy glass blanks from Corning Glass Works, which, by

agreement, had previously restricted its output to Hoare's firm.

His first notable order was for a pair of "elegant toilet bottles" ordered by Austin Lathrop, Jr., a local businessman, for W. H. Vanderbilt for his sixtieth birthday in June 1881. The bottles carried engraving worth $100, the *Journal* reported on May 2 and June 6 of that year, and showed a steamer, the telegraph, and a railroad scene.

In 1882, Hawkes was granted his first design patent, No. 12,982, for the pattern later called *Russian,* which was designed by Philip MacDonald, a Hawkes cutter. The patent was signed by Q. W. Wellington, a local banker, and George T. Spencer, both of whom had been original Corning Glass Works investors. It is quite possible that they were T. G. Hawkes's financial backers, along with a brother in the real estate business in New York City.

That same year, Stephen Hayt put up another building just west of his flour mills, at Market and Walnut, and fitted up the top two floors for T. G. Hawkes's use, and in October Hawkes moved across the street to Hayt's new building, where the firm was to remain, renting space and steam power, until 1916. Hawkes could now expand his business from 50 to 62 frames, the *Journal* announced in its October 2 issue. It is doubtful, however, if this meant 62 cutters, as the census of 1880 had listed only 40 cutters in town, and more than half of them probably worked for John Hoare, who employed 60-odd men of voting age, at least half of whom must have been cutting.

Also in 1882, Henry P. Sinclaire, Jr., finished a six-month course at Rochester Business University and became Thomas Hawkes's bookkeeper. Sinclaire was the son of the Corning Glass Works

110. *Opposite:* Thomas G. Hawkes from Harlo Hakes, *Landmarks of Steuben County,* 1896.

corporate secretary, who was a good friend of Thomas Hawkes.

In 1883, a local railroad entrepreneur, John Magee, presented a Hawkes-engraved punch bowl to W. H. Vanderbilt. This gift, which cost $500, was decorated with industrial scenes copied from photographs, including railroads and coke ovens—it must have been truly remarkable. Two years later, in August, T. G. Hawkes received his first White House order, for 50 dozen pieces in the *Russian* pattern for President Grover Cleveland, a service that with replacements and additions by Hawkes and by C. Dorflinger & Sons, was used in the White House until 1938. Since Hawkes's firm was only five years old, and previous orders had gone to his former employer, John Hoare, such a coup seems quite remarkable. Two large services in the *Russian* pattern had already been ordered, however, for the American Embassy in St. Petersburg and the Russian Embassy in Washington, and these probably led to the White House order. The blanks were manufactured by Corning Glass Works.

Oliver Egginton had left Hoare's employment to supervise Hawkes's shop either in 1880 or shortly after; his son, Walter, joined the company as a cutter and later a designer.

From 1886 to 1888, the only local newspaper stories mentioning Hawkes were concerned with the ups and downs of his business. On December 2, 1886, the *Journal* noted that his payroll had increased to 50 or 60; on January 5, 1888, it reported

111. Plate cut in *Chrysanthemum* pattern and exhibited in Paris, T. G. Hawkes Rich Cut-Glass, 1889. Diam., 30.5 cm. *Coll. Lightner Museum of Hobbies* (Gift of Samuel Hawkes)

that he had laid off 17 men. However, in 1889, T. G. Hawkes Rich Cut-Glass decided to enter the Universal Exposition in Paris. In July, 612 pieces valued at $6,000 were shipped to Paris, and T. G. Hawkes won an award. The local newspaper story (*Journal*, October 3) exaggerated the number of competitors, but not the importance to American industry of the prestigious award.

On Monday, Thomas G. Hawkes had a cablegram saying that his exhibit of cut glass-ware at the Paris Exposition had taken the Grand Prize, against twenty competitors. This is a great compliment to the excellence of the work done at their cutting shop, and is a good advertisement for Corning. It will doubtless lead to largely increased orders for cut-glass and thus add to the number of employees. On Monday evening Mr. Hawkes was serenaded at his residence by the Fall Brook Band and there were several hundred people present. Thomas S. Pritchard introduced Mr. Hawkes who heartily thanked his friends for their congratulations. Remarks were made by C. F. Houghton, John Hoare, and A. Gaylord Slocum. There was much cheering throughout.

Unfortunately, no records identify all the pieces sent to Paris, but doubtless some were in the *Russian* pattern. A *Chrysanthemum* pattern plate (Ill. 111) was one entry. An engraved vase (Ill. 14) designed by H. P. Sinclaire and engraved by Joseph Haselbauer was another. Egginton family tradition claims that Walter Egginton also designed some of the Paris pieces. Hawkes later testified that two large punch bowls in the exhibit were cut on Dorflinger blanks, the remainder being from Corning Glass Works. One of Sinclaire's chief contributions to the success of T. G. Hawkes & Co. in the 20 years he worked there was the encouragement he gave to engraving, which had previously taken a back seat to brilliant cutting. Sinclaire preferred engraving, and he hired a number of European engravers for Hawkes.

In June 1890, Thomas Hawkes incorporated his business as T. G. Hawkes & Co. and gave single shares to Oliver Egginton, his manager, Ellsworth Mills, Charles Voorhees, and H. P. Sinclaire.[5] Soon after that, Sinclaire was allowed to buy 62 additional shares at preferred rates.

In August 1898, the *Journal* reported that Hawkes was "for the third time filling an order for cut glass for use in the White House." He had, by this time, purchased and expanded into the adjacent building on the west, and in 1899 he erected a two-story brick building farther down the block, which was called "Factory No. 2." Also in the 1890s, T. G. Hawkes purchased Inniscarra House, an estate in Ireland near his father's home—until his death, he and his

112. Showroom full of glass from the Paris Exposition. T. G. Hawkes Rich Cut-Glass, 1889. *Courtesy Mrs. Penrose Hawkes*

wife spent every other summer there. Hawkes's increasing business success was accompanied by his change of residence, from the house of his wife's parents in the early years of their marriage to the large house at 24 East Second Street, which he bought or built before 1889 and occupied until his death. That house is still standing in Corning.

Local newspapers of the 1880s and 1890s are full of small notices about the working time and layoffs. The work week usually dropped from 6½ to 5½ or 5 days in January and February and again in May; the men's shifts dropped from 10 to 8 hours. In the fall the time would increase again. One serious labor dispute also occurred in the 1880s. This was a six-month strike, which was extensively reported in the local papers. It began in October of 1886, when about 50 men and 2 boys from Hawkes walked out. The union involved was the Knights of Labor. The main issue seems to have been Hawkes's excessive use of apprentices, who worked at lower pay and thus saved money for management, the *Corning Democrat* said on September 27. Hawkes's position, as presented in the *Corning Journal* three days later, was that his men worked full-time eight months a year and four days a week during the summer months, got the going wages, and should be satisfied. The men claimed that Hawkes had 47 cutters and 32 apprentices in spite of the four-day week. They felt that Hawkes, in addition to cutting short their work, was oversupplying the demand for cutters by training so many apprentices, and that future wages would fall. The strike spread briefly to Hoare when some unfinished Hawkes work was sent over there, but John Hoare was able to persuade his men to return to work.

Throughout October and November Hawkes advertised for cutting apprentices in the *Corning Weekly Journal*. Meanwhile, the mood of the striking cutters was such that the few remaining at work were in danger of being "roughed up" while going to and from the shop. John Cruxton[6] was pelted with rotten eggs and fruit in September, and on February 5 of the following year a small riot led to the arrest of Allen Griffiths, Neil Dougherty, John McGivern, Jacob Underiner, Frank Scheb, Patrick Walker, John Roberts, and Walter Jenkins. Finally, on March 24, 1887, the *Journal* reported that the strike was "amicably settled" following a conference between four of the men and Oliver Egginton, foreman.

Hawkes's victory in this dispute not only earned him the permanent dislike of the fledgling labor movement, but also caused the American Flint Glass Workers' Union to go to great lengths to stop his importation of English blowers for Steuben Glass Works in 1903. The AFGWU said then, "We were particularly opposed to their contracting to work...with such an oppressor of humanity as T. G. Hawkes."[7]

However, the Hawkes firm continued to prosper in spite of these problems. In 1898 Chauncey Depew made a speech in Corning while campaigning for Theodore Roosevelt, and T. G. Hawkes sent his 250 employees during their paid working hours. Mr. Depew "paid a high compliment to the glass industry of [Corning]" and discussed "the result of disillusioning the American people as to the merits of foreign cut glass over the production of this country," the *Journal* reported on October 26.

On March 13, 1901, the *Corning Journal* reported an "Important Real Estate Transfer" when T. G. Hawkes bought the old Payne Foundry on West

113. "Clinger on The Firing Line, 1905"—H. H. Clinger, Hawkes, salesman, displaying his wares in a hotel room. Both cut glass and the newly introduced Steuben Aurene are in his stock. *Courtesy Mrs. Penrose Hawkes*

Erie Avenue. Mr. Hawkes would not say *why* he had bought it, but the paper speculated on a doubling of his glass-cutting force. By July 16 of the following year—16 months later—he had, indeed, opened two large cutting shops in the building.[8] Only two weeks after he bought the foundry, Hawkes announced plans to erect an annex behind his building on Market Street across the alley. This building, two stories high and shaped like a flatiron, contained showrooms and storage space. It was reached by a bridge across the alley.[9]

The year 1901 also saw a Hawkes tour de force exhibited at the Pan-American Exposition in Buffalo. Described in the *Corning Journal* of June 12 was

> ...a cut glass bedstead valued at $3,000. The glass...was made and cut by T. G. Hawkes & Co. of Corning for the exhibition, for Oliver Bros. Co. of Lockport, N.Y. Critics who have seen this novel piece of furniture pronounce it to be magnificent and by far the finest work of its kind ever produced and put on exhibit in this or any other country.

Local interest, naturally, was rather partisan. Unfortunately, the official program of the exposition does not mention the bed.

In 1903, citizens of Corning were astonished to learn that T. G. Hawkes planned a glass factory, rather than a cutting shop, on the Erie Avenue property. Frederick Carder, formerly second-in-command at Stevens & Williams in Stourbridge, England, was coming to Corning to run the newly founded Steuben Glass Works, which was completely financed by T. G. Hawkes. It seems likely that

Hawkes founded Steuben to ensure himself a continuous supply of blanks under his own control. In any event, by the end of the first quarter of 1904, Steuben Glass Works had replaced Dorflinger as Hawkes's major supplier of blanks, and the monthly payments to Corning Glass Works for blanks dropped sharply.[10]

In 1906, Hawkes made headlines again by making a wedding present for Alice Roosevelt, "a magnificent specimen of their celebrated Rock Crystal," according to the *Journal*. The vase was decorated with Japanese chrysanthemums. A list of other Hawkes customers around the turn of the century is impressive. Astors, Vanderbilts, and Whitneys jostle each other; H. C. Frick, Sir Thomas Lipton, and the Presidents of Cuba and Mexico are also on the list.

One of T. G. Hawkes's last business decisions was to institute a silver-mounting department, a business he started in 1912.[11] Until then, he had purchased mounts from Gorham and similar companies. Edwin G. Jackson was the first foreman of this department, but he was succeeded by Orlando Dunn, who worked there until nearly the end. Silver-mounted ware never became a major part of the Hawkes business, but they did mark their product "HAWKES STERLING."

T. G. Hawkes died rather suddenly in 1913, leaving an estate of nearly half a million dollars, according to local newspapers, and his business in the hands of his only son, Samuel Hawkes. Townsend deMoleyns Hawkes, a first cousin of T. G.'s, was secretary of the firm, a position to which he had succeeded when H. P. Sinclaire, Jr., left. Like James Hoare, who had succeeded his father in 1896, Samuel Hawkes had been trained in the business end and was not a glass cutter. Neither was Townsend, nor Penrose Hawkes, a nephew of T. G.'s who came from Ireland to join the firm in 1916, when he was scarcely twenty.

In January 1915, the directors of T. G. Hawkes & Co. voted to spend $10,000 to $15,000 to modernize the existing plant. The four frame buildings at 73-79 West Market Street were to be combined into a "single modern factory" with a unifying brick facade. Pierce & Bickford of Elmira were the architects. Packing, shipping, and storage were on the first floor; "handsomely appointed offices," stockrooms, and assembly rooms were on the second floor, and cutting rooms on the third, the *Evening Leader* announced on January 21. The remodeling operation took several months, and because of the press of Christmas orders, the workmen were not able to transfer to their new quarters when they were finished in the fall. The move into the new building was finally reported in a *Leader* story of December 24, 1915. At that time T. G. Hawkes & Co. moved completely out of the Hayt building, which they had occupied since 1882.

On January 15, 1924, a fire caused $30,000 worth of damage to the Hawkes plant, but by May 22 of that year the newspaper could report that elaborate new display rooms decorated with gold satin, black velvet, and ivory woodwork had been installed in the former shipping rooms at the head of the main-entrance stairway. A designer from the Tiffany firm in New York created the rooms. It was probably at this time or shortly thereafter that the ornamented doors leading to Samuel Hawkes's office (Ill. 115) and the elaborate show windows on Market Street were installed. The doors were engraved with the lineage of the Hawkes family as glass cutters and the names of Hawkes's most famous customers; in the 1930s the panes were still periodically removed so that new names could be added. The "White House," squeezed into the bottom of a diamond pane, may mark a 1938 order (when the doors were first designed the White House orders of the 1880s must have been forgotten). The large copper trade-mark sign was added in 1924, according to a piece in the *Evening Leader* on January 3 of that year.

The production of "brilliant" cut glass had, by this time, practically ceased. During World War I, Steuben had had such difficulty getting raw materials that it nearly closed—in the end, only the sale of the business to Corning Glass Works saved it.[12]

T. G. Hawkes & Co. survived this loss and turned to making lighter-weight cut and engraved wares. In 1938, when the Roosevelts decided to order new glass for the White House before the visit of the King and Queen of England, they wrote to Hawkes to find out about replacements for the *Russian* pattern. Prices were so high that Mrs. Roosevelt asked for samples of less expensive patterns, and finally selected one called *Venetian* (Ill. 117). A

114. Showroom at 73–79 W. Market Street, newly redecorated after the 1924 fire.

complete service was ordered. (This is not the same *Venetian* as the design patented earlier.) In 1941, the Roosevelts ordered sherries and more wines in the same pattern.[13]

In the thirties, when the cut and engraved glass business nearly went under, Hawkes turned to gold-decorated and fancy enameled wares as well as a line of Stiegel reproductions. These pieces were signed (Ills. 118, 119), but without the signatures they could easily be mistaken for European imports.[14]

After World War II, T. G. Hawkes & Co. did a booming business for a while, according to Penrose Hawkes's later recollection, but the Hawkes catalog for this period shows few new designs. Hawkes was cutting the patterns of the 1920s and 1930s up until 1962. It was also possible to "special order" replacement pieces for old sets of both Hawkes and non-Hawkes glass. However, the Hawkes cutters were growing older and no new ones were being trained. President and Mrs. Truman ordered additional glass for the White House in 1947, but without the crest, another cost-saving measure.[15]

Samuel Hawkes retired to Florida during the early 1940s, leaving the business in the hands of

Bradley Lindsley, a manager who was unable to adapt to the changing conditions of the fine-glass business. Penrose Hawkes, who was vice-president and had managed the New York sales office on Fifth Avenue for a quarter century, closed that office in 1949 and came home to Corning as the Hawkes business shrank. After 1956, the company operated at a loss. Samuel Hawkes died in 1959, and by that time the downward momentum was too great for Penrose Hawkes to stop it. In July 1962, the remaining stockholders, all Hawkes family members, decided to liquidate. The Tiffin Glass Company of Tiffin, Ohio, bought the Hawkes name, trademark, and patterns, and subsequently produced a few of them. However, Tiffin was itself in financial difficulties and paid scant attention to the Hawkes line.

Penrose Hawkes operated a retail store in the old showrooms until his death in 1972. He had glass locally cut, primarily by Floyd Manwarren, who had been one of the last of the Hawkes cutters. This glass was marked "Hawkes" in diamond-point script to avoid confusion with former Hawkes products. Mr. Hawkes also sold Waterford glass and fine-quality gifts. After he died, his business was carried on by his widow until 1975, when Corning Glass Works bought the building from the heirs of Samuel Hawkes.

116. Samuel Hawkes, second president of T. G. Hawkes & Co.

T. G. Hawkes & Co. was Corning's second cutting firm, and the next to last to go out of business. Its 82 years were a record in Corning and probably in the United States. In its heydey, Hawkes was one of the two or three most important and largest cutting companies in the country, producing wares of the highest quality. It was also the only firm whose founder started in a small way and died a wealthy man—T. G. Hawkes invested in other businesses in the area, and was a shrewd manager and an early believer in the value of advertising.

* * *

The glassware produced by Hawkes varied in quality over the years, as did that of most firms, but it was, generally speaking, quite good. Hawkes adopted his trademark after the Paris exposition and used it on a paper label until about 1900, although he did not register it until March 3, 1903. On December 26, 1905, he registered a slightly modernized version of the same trademark with "HAWKES" underneath. Both these marks are found acid-stamped on glass, but a label has not so far turned up. Hawkes registered an additional trademark on March 3, 1903—the usual Hawkes shamrock with "GRAVIC GLASS PAT'D." below. This was said to have been in use since December 13, 1902. Somewhat later, a simple "HAWKES" was

115. Doors to Samuel Hawkes's office, Market Street, late 1920s (as installed at The Corning Museum of Glass in 1977).

used for stemware but never registered as a trademark. Hoare and Sinclaire used a similar block-letter mark on stemware.

T. G. Hawkes, along with C. Dorflinger and the Libbey Glass Co., began heavy advertising at this time. None of the other Corning firms advertised as widely as Hawkes, whose ads—with the words, "No piece is genuine without this trademark"—can be found in every women's magazine of the period. Some early Hawkes patterns can probably be identified from such ads.

Except in the case of sets of tableware, it is rare to find unmarked glass that can be positively identified as Hawkes.

Hawkes patented at least 22 designs between 1882 and 1914. Most of them have been illustrated in other books, but a list follows here:

No.		
12,982	1882	*Russian,* des. by Philip MacDonald
——	Oct. 25, 1887	*Russian and Pillar*
17,837	Oct. 25, 1887	*Grecian*
——	Apr. 24, 1888	*Old-Fashioned Hobnail*
——	Apr. 24, 1888	*Star Rosette*
——	May 8, 1888	*Devonshire*
——	May 28, 1889	*Brazilian*
19,865	June 3, 1890	*Venetian*
20,132	Sept. 2, 1890	*Maltese Cross*
20,257	Nov. 4, 1890	*Chrysanthemum*
21,705	July 12, 1892	*Coronet*
——	Jan. 17, 1893	*Valencian,* des. by Walter Egginton
25,386	Apr. 14, 1896	*Aberdeen*
25,944	Aug. 18, 1896	*Nautilus*
26,730	Mar. 9, 1897	*Festoon*
26,731	Mar. 9, 1897	*Nelson*
40,195	Aug. 3, 1909	*Panel*
40,325	Nov. 2, 1909	*Gravic Carnation,* des. by Samuel Hawkes
——	Nov. 29, 1909	*Gravic Floral,* des. by Samuel Hawkes
41,000	Nov. 29, 1910	*Tiger Flower*
41,153	Feb. 7, 1911	*Latticed Rosette and Ribbons*
46,500	Oct. 6, 1914	*French Dressing Bottle,* des. by Townsend d'M. Hawkes

The earliest catalog material in the Hawkes archives at The Corning Museum of Glass are several sets of salesmen's sample cards stamped "T. G. Hawkes Rich Cut Glass." The use of this pre-1890 name dates them in the 1880s. Few patterns are

117. Goblet in the pattern ordered by Franklin and Eleanor Roosevelt for the White House in 1938 and 1941. Height, 15.5 cm. *The Corning Museum of Glass* (Gift of T. G. Hawkes & Co.)

illustrated: *Strawberry Diamond, Hobnail,* and *Russian* are the most numerous; they occur in a great variety of shapes, all probably on Corning Glass Works blanks. Hoare (q.v.) was cutting similar patterns and using the same names, including *Russian.* One assumes he must have had Hawkes's permission to do so. Likewise, much of the famous *Russian* set at the White House was ordered from C. Dorflinger & Sons of White Mills. They, too, probably had permission from Hawkes to cut this design, since Presidents Harrison (1889), Theodore Roosevelt (1906), and Woodrow Wilson ordered it from them. It is also possible that Dorflinger accepted the order, made the blanks, and sent them to Corning to be cut and engraved by T. G. Hawkes & Co. (see Joseph Haselbauer Chapter 8).

Correspondence between Hawkes and Fostoria in September 1916 in regard to the licensing of Hawkes's famous French dressing bottle design perhaps indicates the procedure usually followed. Fostoria manufactured the bottles and had permission to decorate them with gold or enamel. They paid 50 cents a dozen to Hawkes for the privilege, and undertook not to sell blanks to other decorators without the express permission of T. G. Hawkes & Co.[16] The bottles were still in Fostoria's 1932 catalog, and so the agreement was in effect for at least sixteen years.

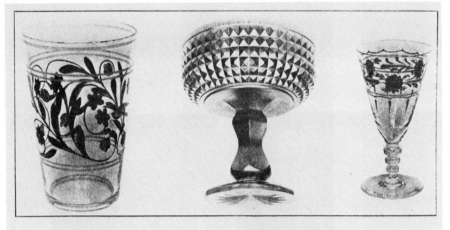

EXCELLENT REPRODUCTIONS OF FAMOUS STIEGEL AND WATERFORD GLASSWARE

118. Illustration of Hawkes "Stiegel-type" glassware, *Jewelers' Circular,* Dec. 8, 1926.

119. *Right:* Enameled vase. T. G. Hawkes & Co., ca. 1925–35. Height, 13.5 cm. *The Corning Museum of Glass*

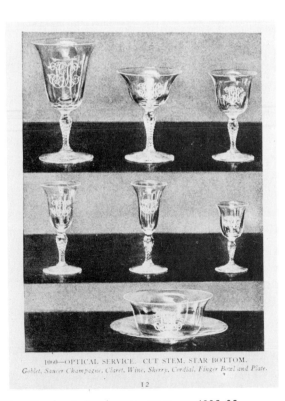

1044—OPTICAL SERVICE. CUT STEM, STAR BOTTOM.
Goblet, Saucer Champagne, Claret, Wine, Sherry, Cordial, Finger Bowl and Plate.
13

1060—OPTICAL SERVICE. CUT STEM, STAR BOTTOM.
Goblet, Saucer Champagne, Claret, Wine, Sherry, Cordial, Finger Bowl and Plate.
12

120–121. Two pages from a brochure "Hawkes Glass Services" showing stemware, ca. 1925–35.

122. Penrose Hawkes, vice-president of T. G. Hawkes & Co. *Courtesy Mrs. Penrose Hawkes*

By no means can all Hawkes patterns be found in the various catalogs. The outsize tray shown in Ill. 170 is cut on a very thick blank and is a striking variation on the usual brilliant cutting. It bears a Hawkes mark; an 11-inch plate in the same pattern has been illustrated elsewhere.[17] It probably dates from around 1908 to 1912, when there was a revival of interest in very detailed patterns that could not be imitated by pressing and when Sinclaire's *Assyrian* and Egginton's *Trellis* were developed. The bowl, flowerpot, and plate (Ills. 171-173) are pieces that cannot be found in any Hawkes catalog. The bowl and flowerpot were wedding gifts in 1909, and so can be dated; the smaller plate has the older Hawkes mark, used ca. 1890 to 1900.

A catalog of ca. 1897 to 1903 in the collection of Mrs. Penrose Hawkes contains most of the previously shown patterns, along with the Hawkes patented patterns of the 1880s and 1890s and the following newly discovered patterns, illustrated here:

Brazilian & Lapidary, Cobweb, Cut No. 1, Cut No. 2, Cut No. 7, Cut No. 8, Cut No. 9, Feather & Diamond, Grecian & Hobnail, Imperial, New Princess, Penrose, Pillars, Pillars & Diamonds, Prisms, Rock Crystal Engraved, Stars, Stars & Prisms, Thistle, Venetian & Lapidary, Windsor, Yadoo, No. 6424, and a number of kerosene lamps, plus these

patterns: *Florence, Norwood, Pillars & Stars, Savoy, Table Diamond* illustrated in the next catalog. This was before the period of acid-stamped trademarks. (See Ills. 174-206.)

The catalog next in date in The Corning Museum of Glass archives has dropped all but seven of the preceding patterns, including most of the patented ones. Patterns illustrated from this catalog are probably from ca. 1900 to 1910 and will bear Hawkes trademarks:

Albion, Brunswick (not illus.), *Colonial, Constellation, Coronet, Fancy Star, Festoon* (not illus.), *Florence, Flutes, Flutes & Prisms, Franklin, George III, Gladys* (not illus.), *Harvard, Holland, Jubilee, Kensington, Lorraine, Madeline, Marion, Marquis, Melrose, Monroe, Navarre, Norwood, Pillars & Stars, Premier, Queens, Regent, Rouen, St. James, Savoy, Table Diamond, Teutonic, Tokio, Triumph.* (See Ills. 207-239.)

The next catalog also probably dates from before 1914. It includes a *Kaiser* pattern, which would have been an unpopular name after that date, and an entirely new set of patterns except for *Jubilee* from the previous catalog. The list follows:

Alberta, Brighton, Canton, Caroline, Celeste, Cordova, Cut and Rye, Delhi, Dundee, Flutes & Greek Border, Harold, Herald, Isis, Jersey, Juno, Kaiser, Milton, Minerva, Mirage, Ormond, Palmyra, Panama, Tyrone, Weston, Willow (pat. appl. for), *York.* The *"Willow"* pattern is the one called "Latticed Rosettes and Ribbons" and patented in 1911. (See Ills. 240-279.)

123. Bowl in a slightly greenish glass cut for Hawkes Crystal in 1973, probably by Floyd Manwarren; signed in diamond point: "HAWKES CORNING N.Y." Height, 16 cm. *Coll. Mr. & Mrs. Marvin Ashburn*

NOTE: Illustrations 124 to 169 are taken from salesmen's cards for T. G. Hawkes Rich Cut-Glass, ca. 1885. They represent the earliest Hawkes catalog.

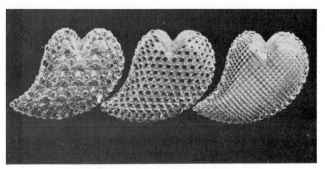

125. Leaf-shaped olive or bonbon dishes—from right to left: *Strawberry Diamond, Hobnail,* and *Russian.*

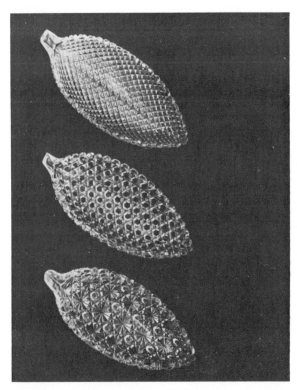

124. Olive or bonbon dishes. Patterns, from the top, are *Strawberry Diamond, Hobnail,* and *Russian.*

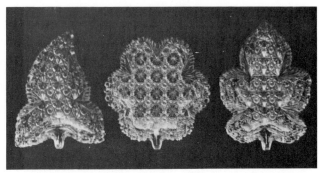

126. *Russian* bonbon or olive dishes. Hawkes offered these dishes also in *Strawberry Diamond* and *Hobnail.*

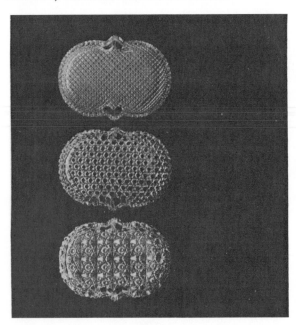

127. Still another style of bonbon dish by Hawkes in *Strawberry Diamond, Hobnail,* and *Russian.*

128. Quart water bottles made by Hawkes in *Hobnail*, ca. 1885.

Right:
129. *Russian, Hobnail,* and *Strawberry Diamond* sugar bowls by Hawkes.

130. Hawkes naturally made creamers in the same three patterns.

132. Hawkes tableware in *Hobnail* pattern: cordial, ½-pint tumbler, champagne tumbler, and finger bowl. These pieces ranged in price from $12.50 to $24 a dozen.

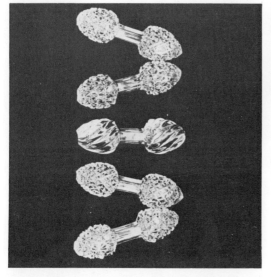

131. Knife rests from Hawkes, ca. 1885 (from the top): *Lace Hobnail, Hobnail, Pillars, Strawberry Diamond,* and *Star & Hobnail.*

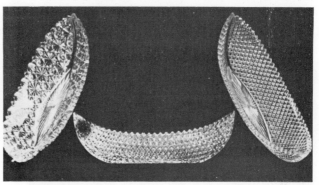

133. Celery dishes in *Russian, Hobnail,* and *Strawberry Diamond.*

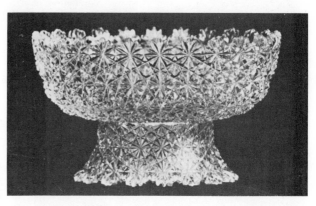

135. *Russian* punch bowl and stand; 16-inch height cost $75.

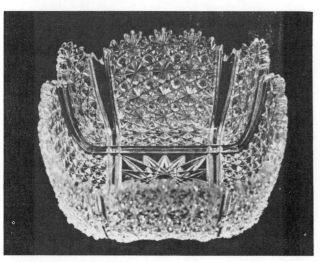

134. Salad or fruit bowl in *Russian:* 10-inch size was $26.50; 9-inch, $23.25; 8-inch, $19.75.

136. *Right: Russian* pattern "jug." The 2-pint size was $12.25; the single pint, $6.75.

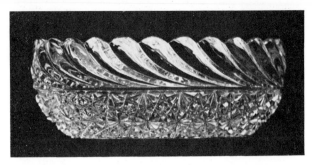

137. Salad or fruit bowl in *Russian & Pillars*. Pattern was listed in three sizes; prices ranged from $13 to $20.

138. Oval dish in *Persian & Pillars* came in five sizes.

139. Flower vase in *Russian,* 13 inches tall, was priced at $25. It also came in 11-inch height.

140. Hawkes quart decanter in *Russian* listed at $16. Ca. 1885.

141. Four-pint *Russian*-pattern champagne jug has the neck cut in hollow diamonds. Price was $18.

142. *Right:* Candelabrum, height 17 inches. With four lights, price was $45; with three, $35.

143. Quart *Hobnail* decanter listed at $9.50 and claret jug at $11.

144. The footed claret jug and decanter here were priced at $16.50 and $14.75, respectively.

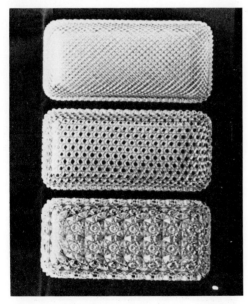

145. Celery trays: *Strawberry Diamond* ($5.50), *Hobnail* ($7.75), and *Russian* ($10).

146. Low, footed bowl in *Russian*. Sizes ranged from 8 to 10 inches; prices, $13 to $18.50.

Right:
147. *Strawberry Diamond* "jug"—more often called a pitcher today. It was available in six sizes, ranging in price from $4.75 to $13 each.

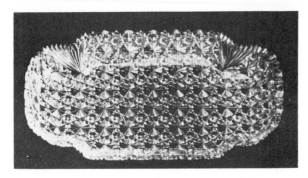

148. The *Russian* pattern ice cream tray was 14 inches long and cost $16.

149. Quart decanter; Hawkes, ca. 1885.

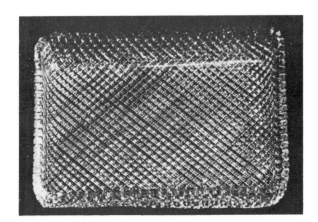

150. Shallow bowl in *Strawberry Diamond* came in seven sizes. Prices ranged from $4.50 to $15.

152. Fruit or flower basket in *Russian* by Hawkes. The 10-inch diameter size was $33. It also came in 8- and 9-inch sizes.

151. Footed quart decanter that was listed at $20.

153. *Russian* pattern flower vase, 10 inches high, was listed at $28.

154. *Strawberry Diamond* stemware. The three hock glasses pictured were in different colors (rose, amber, and green). All were marked $15.50 a dozen. The sherry at far right was listed at $10.50 a dozen.

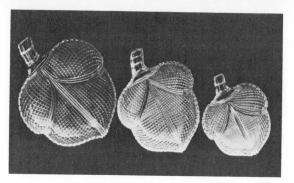

156. Leaf-shaped olive or bonbon dishes in *Strawberry Diamond*. They were available in three sizes. The largest (9 inches) was listed at $8.25.

157. Hawkes salad or fruit bowl that came in three sizes—10, 9, and 8 inches. Prices were $25, $20, and $15.

155. The tall candlestick was available in either 9- or 11-inch height ($15 or $18); the low stick was $8.50.

159. Fruit or salad bowl and stand in *Persian* pattern. The 12-inch size was $40.

158. This fruit bowl in *Lustre* pattern came in the same three sizes, which were priced the same as those in Illustration 157.

160. Sugar bowls in *Russian* and *Star & Hobnail*. Prices were $9 and $13.

161. *Russian* pattern salad or fruit bowl. The 11-inch size was $26.50.

162. Another *Russian* pattern salad bowl by Hawkes. This 12-inch bowl was $29.75.

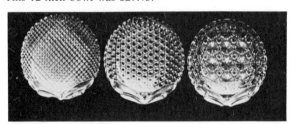

163. Ice cream saucers were available in *Strawberry Diamond*, *Hobnail*, and *Russian*. In *Russian*, they were $49.50 a dozen; in *Hobnail*, $30.75; in *Strawberry Diamond*, $23.

166. *Star & Hobnail* stemware. As in Illustration 154, the three hock glasses were available in rose, green, or amber; all were $24.25 a dozen. Sherry glasses were $18 a dozen.

168. This stemware in *Russian* pattern had the foot cut to match the bowl. As before, the hock glasses were available in rose, green, and amber—all at $34.25 a dozen. The sherry glasses were $27.50.

164. *Russian* pattern ice cream tray.

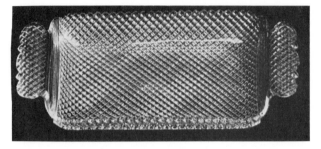

165. *Strawberry Diamond* ice cream tray. This one was $10.50, whereas the *Russian* tray in Ill. 164 was listed at $20.

167. Additional Hawkes stemware in *Star & Hobnail*: Goblet, $22 a dozen; saucer champagne, $19 a dozen; claret, $16 a dozen; wine, $13.50 a dozen.

169. Round salad bowl in *Star & Hobnail* with matching spoon and fork. The 10½-inch size was listed at $30, the 9-inch at $25.

The next catalog seems to date from the period of World War I, to judge from the inclusion of the *Servia* pattern. It also lists *Jubilee, Albion, Alberta, St. Regis, Queens,* and *Priscilla,* but otherwise contains a new set of patterns, including several Gravic ones:

Alpine, Albany, Argo, Adam No. 2, Anson, Albion, Bengal, Belmont, Cecil, Chippendale, Crete, Conquest, Colonial, Dallas, Doris, Empire, Flora, Gravic Meadow Rose, Gravic Strawberry, Geneva, Harmony, Hebe, Isabelle, Josephine, Lamont, Lawrence, Manlius, Naples, Old Colony, Oxford, Pacific, Patrician, Paul Revere, Persian, Pilgrim, Princess, Satin Iris, Satin Strawberry, Servia, Trellis, Viking, Virginia, Wild Rose. (See Ills. 280-330.)

170. T. G. Hawkes & Co. tray, ca. 1908–12. Diam., 38.1 cm. *Coll. Harry Kraut*

Hawkes introduced his "Gravic" engraved wares in 1903 and, as already mentioned, registered that word as a separate trademark. The *Gravic* designs are usually fruits and flowers, which were copper-wheel engraved in the beginning and were later stone-engraved, as that was a less expensive process. The engraved flowers usually had miter-cut leaves and stems. At this time, T. G. Hawkes & Co. trained three new engravers, Hiram Rouse, Wilmot Putnam, and William Morse, and hired three from Europe, John Illig, Nicolas Underiner, and Emil Walter. Obviously, Hawkes expected the line to be a success.

An advertising brochure of ca. 1900-1903 titled "HAWKES CUT GLASS" shows an engraver at work,

probably Joseph Haselbauer, and pictures several patterns from the 1890s. The only engraving shown is labeled "Rock Crystal."

171. T. G. Hawkes & Co. bowl, ca. 1909. Height, 8.4 cm. *Coll. Misses Evelyn and Mildred Durkin*

Engraved designs listed chronologically in an engraver's notebook between August 1902 and July 1905 were mostly flowers—either Gravic[18] or Hawkes's more expensive copper-wheel designs:

Silver Diamond	*Clematis*
Alhambra	*Berry pattern*
Empress	*Diamond*
Waterlilies	*16-point daisy star*
Colamore	*filling*
Forget-me-not	*Barley*
Queen Louise	*Viola*
Princess	*King Edward*
Butterflies	*Curl*
Carnations	*Swing horn*
Grapevines	*Rose buds*
Grape wishbone	*Miniature spiders*
Louis SIV (1/11/04)	*Fish, crabs &*
St. Cloud	*seaweeds*
Corn	*Olive,* Fritchie's first
New St. Cloud	pattern after he
Rye	came back
Rudolph's 3 flower	*Shells-fan*
pattern	*Alexandria*
S C O T C H	*Lily of the Valley*
Poppy	*Thistle*
Chrysanthemum	*Beddell*

After the sale of Steuben, the Hawkes designs were to some extent dependent upon the supply of available blanks. Colored cased wares, lightly engraved, were popular in the 1920s, as were plain monogrammed or crested table sets (Ills. 120, 121).

The "rock crystal" of this and later periods is a far cry from the heavy sculptured rock-crystal designs of the 1890s and early 1900s. Rock-crystal wares after World War I were delicate, and decorated with shallow continuous engraving (Ill. 332). Better-quality engraved wares can sometimes be found signed by individual engravers such as William Morse or Joseph Sidot. It was Penrose Hawkes's recollection, in later years, that these were mostly produced in the late 1920s and 1930s when business was very slow and Hawkes had scarcely enough orders to occupy the engravers. The men were free to use their time and Hawkes's blanks to work on special pieces, which they designed and signed. A bowl (Ill. 505) signed by William Morse is such a piece, as is the famous Edenhall goblet that Morse designed and engraved after Sir Walter Scott's poem "The Luck of Edenhall," in 1920. The pitcher "Before the Storm" (Ill. 499) by Edward Palme is a similar effort; other pieces by Morse and Sidot are also known.

During the 1920s, Samuel Hawkes introduced a line called "Old Singing Waterford," which included both copies of and adaptations from Anglo-Irish designs of ca. 1800. Several catalogs of that period exist showing *Georgian, Old English,* and *Waterford* patterns. Engraved wares of the same period are usually simple and make much use of stone-wheel work and gang cutting.

The designs introduced in this period stayed in the Hawkes line until the end. With few exceptions, they are lighter in weight and are simpler compared with pre-World War I patterns (Ills. 426-442). *Kohinoor & Panel* (Ill. 440) was Hawkes's most expensive cut at this time, and so was rarely ordered—pieces are comparatively scarce. *Queens* pattern (Ill. 441) and *Kensington* (Ill. 424) were holdovers in the Brilliant style. Special designs such as cocktail sets were introduced from time to time, and in the 1930s Hawkes did some cutting on cheap pressed glass, as that was all that was available for a while. In the later 1930s Samuel Hawkes created a special traveling exhibit of old Hawkes glass and new designs, which circulated to department stores throughout the country, accompanied by a small catalog. These designs—many of which were engraved birds and animals—do not appear in other Hawkes catalogs.

During the 82-year life of the Hawkes firm a number of different blank suppliers were used—some well known and some less so. In the 1880s Corning Glass Works blanks were used for most things, but stemware began to be ordered primarily from C. Dorflinger & Sons of White Mills before 1900. In his testimony in a Corning Glass Works suit of 1902 (against Corning Cut Glass Company; see Chapter 11), Hawkes said that he had tried Baccarat, Val St. Lambert, Webb, Stevens and Williams, and F. & C. Osler of Birmingham, and found Osler the best of these but no better than Corning Glass Works. He stated on June 8, 1904,

We have never found on the average anything as good as the glass made by Corning Glass Works in the way of brilliancy and the luster;[19] we are paying today to the Corning Glass Works 35 cents per pound for blanks which we can buy in this country ...for 17 cents per pound, and we can buy them from St. Lambert [*sic*] and Baccarat for 17 cents a pound. These are the two largest factories in Europe.

At this time the Glass Works was supplying three grades of blanks: Best Metal, Best Kiln (very heavy), and Batch. According to testimony from both Hawkes and Amory Houghton, French and Belgian blanks flooded the country from about 1900 until 1905, causing the production of Corning Glass Works blanks to drop from 10 percent to 5 or 6 percent of its business. Hawkes also mentioned that he bought blanks for his "cheaper grade of goods" from factories other than Corning Glass Works, and spoke of cut stoppers from Baccarat and water bottles and 8-, 9-, and 10-inch salad bowls from "St. Lambert." Twenty percent of his blanks came from Europe in the period between 1900 and 1905; 5 percent came from the Union Glass Company, mostly punch bowls and vases; a few cream and sugar sets came from Pairpoint; 3 or 4 percent was bought from Libbey, and another 3 or 4 percent from Fry, leaving about 30 to 35 percent each from Corning Glass Works and Dorflinger. These factories were the only ones making blanks for cutting in the United States.

A few Union blanks can be identified from Hawkes's ledgers for 1897 to 1903: No. 931, a 14-inch bowl; No. 788, a round three-footed bowl; No. 1102, a 9-inch octagonal bowl; No. 1463, a "derby hat"-shaped bowl, which came in four sizes; No. 1457, another footed bowl; and No. 528, a squat pitcher.[20]

An examination of the Hawkes Cash Book for October 1902, a typical month, shows payments of $3,032.79 to Dorflinger for blanks and $2,178.81 to Corning Glass Works; $180.42 went to Libbey to balance the account, and $306.77 to Fry. In Novem-

172. Flowerpot and liner, T. G. Hawkes & Co., 1909. Height, 14.1 cm. *Coll. Misses Evelyn and Mildred Durkin*

ber $53.05 went to Pairpoint. In April of 1903 Hawkes balanced his account with Union for $1,462.16 and paid B. Gunthel of New York City, a supplier of Val St. Lambert blanks, $1,976.68. In 1902, Dorflinger sold Hawkes $40,404 worth of blanks, Corning Glass Works, $20,948. In 1903 the figures were Dorflinger, $33,655; Corning, $15,746. By 1905, when Steuben was in full blast, payments for Dorflinger had disappeared.

During the years in which T. G. Hawkes was a heavy user of Dorflinger blanks, he bought stemware in nearly 20 different designs, identified only by number, and miscellaneous pieces of decorative and table ware such as match safes, spoon holders, miscellaneous doorknobs, rose glasses, blue and green honeypots, inkwells, candelabra arms and centers, handled oils, colognes, lamps, optical vases, paperweights, napkin rings, darners, ring trays, decanters, and loving cups. By 1909 Hawkes was again buying some blanks from Dorflinger, according to Dorflinger records,[21] but never again in the pre-1903 quantities. Some of the Dorflinger shape numbers are the same as those purchased from Corning Glass Works, so it may be assumed that Hawkes went back to C. Dorflinger & Son when Corning Glass Works stopped the production of stemware blanks.

During the early years of the Hawkes firm, few colored pieces appeared in the catalogs, although colored hock glasses were routine in stemware sets. After 1903, Hawkes used more colored blanks; however, colored cut or engraved glass was not really fashionable until the 1920s.

In 1918 Hawkes was forced to sell Steuben to Corning Glass Works, and after that he once again bought blanks more widely. He still bought colored blanks from Steuben and also what were called "cased-band" blanks from H. P. Sinclaire's Bath plant (Ill. 430; compare with Ill. 559, Chapter 14).

In the early 1920s, Hawkes used primarily Sinclaire and Steuben blanks. By late in that decade, the firm had come to an arrangement with Tiffin in Ohio whereby Tiffin would manufacture blanks using a formula supplied by Hawkes. Tiffin guaranteed not to sell these blanks elsewhere. Pairpoint and Libbey blanks were also used in the late 1920s and the 1930s. When enameled and gold-decorated wares were popular in the 1920s and 1930s (and much cheaper than cut glass), Hawkes used amber and pink Heisey blanks and occasionally Duncan & Miller glass.[22]

The Silver Department did its sterling mountings mostly on the "rock crystal engraved" wares. The enamel work was done by the "Decorating Department," headed by a Mr. Hille, who had about eight women working for him. One method of decoration

173. Plate by T. G. Hawkes & Co., ca. 1890–1900. Diam., 25.5 cm. *The Corning Museum of Glass*

was to apply a thick gold band above acid-etched decoration. Enameled flowers over gold bands and enameled fruits and flowers were also used, especially deep yellow roses or daffodils. All these wares were fired in kilns in the basement of the Hawkes factory. Some pieces were stained blue, green, or violet, and engraved with flowers. These were usually candy boxes, candlesticks, or vases, and not stemware. Black glass console sets were etched and hand-painted.[23] Mr. Hille died in the late 1920s, but the department continued for several years without him. Around 1929, Joseph Lalonde, Townsend d'M. Hawkes's son-in-law, joined the firm as a designer and decorator. Lalonde was primarily a painter, but he apparently both designed and did actual enameling during the 1930s. At least one piece has been found with his signature as well as the usual Hawkes mark.[24] Lalonde also designed a line of "Stiegel-type" reproductions and a game bird and animal series enameled in natural colors.

After World War II, Hawkes enjoyed a "boomlet" in cut glass, and was able to drop the other lines and concentrate on the old patterns cut on the "Hawkes formula" blanks from Tiffin. German cut pieces were also bought in the 1950s, recut slightly, and mounted in silver.[25] Since T. G. Hawkes & Co., like Dorflinger and other reputable firms, was always willing to "special-order" or match glass—and was still cutting their 1920s designs in 1962 when they closed—it is difficult to tell 1920s Hawkes glass from that of the 1950s.

Hawkes glass was always sold at the company

showrooms in Corning and New York, and individually to such customers as Marjorie Merriweather Post (who ordered a set of Hawkes stemware for her yacht, the *Sea Cloud,* in 1938 when she was Mrs. Joseph B. Davies). Their principal trade in the early years was to silver manufacturers, such as Gorham, and to fine jewelry outlets, like Theodore Starr and Tiffany in New York, J. E. Caldwell in Philadelphia, and Emmet, Burley & Co., Chicago. Their New York agent was Davis Collamore & Co. A cheaper line was sold to John Wanamaker's department store in Philadelphia, Frederick Loesser & Co. of Brooklyn, and later to other department stores. According to T. G. Hawkes's testimony, their trade in 1904 "covered the whole of the United States... reaching into Canada and other foreign countries." Hawkes had a number of salesmen on the road, some of whom may also have sold for other companies, such as J. Hoare. T. G. Hawkes & Co. continued to employ salesmen throughout its career, dropping to a force of six in the last years and, finally, to about four. Hawkes outlets shrank in these years but Hawkes maintained its reputation to the end and was still selling to Tiffany's—and advertising extensively in women's magazines at Christmas and in June.

* * *

During the 82 years that the Hawkes firm was in business several hundred workmen were employed there. Hawkes grew from six or seven at the beginning to a peak of 250 to 300 (depending on the season) in the 1900-1910 period, fell slowly to around 50 employees in the 1930s, picked up to 60 in the 1940s and 1950s, and closed in 1962 with a couple of dozen.

The names of Thomas Hawkes's first few cutters are unknown, but he must have hired Oliver Egginton and Thomas Hunt in the early 1880s. He also employed Joseph Haselbauer, one of Corning's earliest engravers, and various members of the Dow and Share families, all of whom were English. Hawkes was in the habit of sending experienced workmen to Europe as recruiters.[26] Samuel J. Share went to England more than once for this purpose. Nicholas and Fred Bach also recruited for the company. A large Cash Book payment in July 1902 confirms the Illig family tradition that Nick Bach brought John Illig to Hawkes from Alsace-Lorraine.

The earliest list of workmen at Hawkes can be compiled from a comparison of the 43 cutters listed in the 1880 census with the list of Hoare's employees over 21, given in the newspaper in 1880. The "leftovers" must be Hawkes cutters. The list—with the men's ages in 1880 and birthplaces—is as follows:

Joe Krebs	22	b. New York
Hilling Henner (?)	25	New York
Ed Henner (?)	23	New York
Chas. Peters	31	Ireland
Michael Maloney	54	New York
Pat Callahan	27	New York
Philip McDonnell [sic]	32	England
John Garty	24	Pennsylvania
Wm. Elwell	29	England
Jim Hifeles (?)	27	England
Mike Fitzgerald	30	Ireland
Joseph Haselbauer	28	Bohemia

Additional names compiled from newspaper accounts include George Haar, Fred Nichols, John Albright, and Samuel Share, all mentioned in Corning newspapers between 1886 and 1893 as Hawkes cutters. A list compiled by comparing Hawkes's Cash Book entries for 1903 to 1905 with the Corning directories for those years added 130 names, among which were Thomas Dow, cutting foreman, a mainstay later of H. P. Sinclaire; H. Fritchie, engraver; John S. Garty, who designed at least one pattern (Ill. 441); Joseph Haselbauer, engraving foreman; and a number of others who are discussed elsewhere in this book as home-shop proprietors or founders of small firms. There was a total of 15 engravers during these years; most of the remaining names represented cutters: G. Abbey, Bert Abbey, William Allen, Fred Balcom, John Barenthaler, J. Batchelor, Floyd Berleue, Norman Bigart, Asher Bishop, Joseph Blinco, August Blomberg, G. Bronson, Raymond Brooder, Charles Brown, Fred Bucher, F. Burweiler, Matthew Candelina (polisher), M. Casey, Frank Clark, James Clark, Charles Coats, J. Crannage, G. Cuneen (glass stopperer), W. Custer, J. L. Deats, E. W. Dimmick (foreman), Nelson Doane, Leonard and Oliver Dow, John Dunigan, Joseph Egginton (glass decorator), Joseph Eick, David Everson, Earl Farrell, Claude Fassett, Charles Feagles (engraver), John Green, Charles Greiner, G. Leon Haradon, William Haradon, August Hartman, O. Heigle, Herman Hockie, William Horton, C. Hotalen, Daniel Hotalen, Gilbert Hotalen, Clair Hoyt, Anton Keller (engraver), Preston Kelly, George Kennedy (engraver), John Kidder, John Klang, Chauncey Knowlton, William Kretchman, Harry Kretschman, C. Lagerburn, S. McCormick (glassworker), William McCrannels, J. McLaughlin, Judson Madison, C. Manning (engraver), Matthew Mitchell, Patrick Morgan, William Morse (engraver), Clement Nitsche (engraver), George O'Brien, Arthur O'Dell (or Odell), Gunnar Olson, Sidney Perkins (engraver), V. Peterson, Simeon Powers, Nathan Pound, A. Preston, John Purcell, Francis Quinn (engraver), Franklin Rasch, Peter Rogers, James Rooney, William Rooney, Augustus and Benjamin Rose, Hiram Rouse (engraver), W. Sensabaugh (engraver), Henry Shannon, Frank Shay, ? Sheppard (engraver), Fred

Sherman, Francis Smith, E. Snover, Charles Sparks, Lee Stage, Hugh Stephens, Jay C. Stephens, Henry Sullivan, Lavern Terwilliger, Chauncey Tobias, Arthur Underwood, Jesse Underwood, Archie Van Etten, A. F. Van Gorder, Otto Vollgraff, Richard E. Walker, Walter Walker, Emil Walter (engraver), William Warner, Frank Weber (glassworker), Clyde and Daniel Welch, Fred Wescot, Harry Wheeler, Edward White, R. Whitney, Arthur and Walter Wilson, Clarence Wixson, Frank Wood, ? Worth, James and Thomas Young.

Traveling salesmen for the company in the early years included Harrie Millspaugh, who later worked with Jack Hoare in Wellsboro and for Steuben, H. H. Clinger, Miles Evans, and J. A. Watts.

The lengthy list above covers the years of the company's greatest prosperity and largest production. In 1900, the census showed nearly 400 cutters and engravers in Corning; by 1905 there were over 500. The number declined yearly after that.

During the period from 1902 to 1910, Hawkes was also paying several subcontractors for cutting work. Ernest Mulford was listed in the cash books in this way from 1902 to 1910; Joseph Blackburn was paid for cutting at home from 1902 until his death in 1905. "American Cut Glass" was listed as a subcontractor in 1905 and 1906, and the Standard Cut Glass Company was listed in those same years. J. F. Haselbauer & Sons was listed in 1910—about a year before it was listed in the city directories.

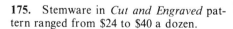

NOTE: Illustrations 174 to 206 are pages from a Hawkes catalog of about 1900. *Courtesy of Mrs. Penrose Hawkes*

174. Stemware in *Thistle* pattern ranged in price from $22 to $46 a dozen.

175. Stemware in *Cut and Engraved* pattern ranged from $24 to $40 a dozen.

176. In the *Rock Crystal* pattern, stemware prices were $106 to $160 a dozen.

179. Quart water bottles (with different cutting on neck) in *Chrysanthemum,* $18, and *New Princess,* $9.

177. Quart water bottles in *Strawberry Diamond and Fan* and in *6424* were both $7. *Brazilian* pattern cost $12.

178. Quart water bottles in *Venetian* and in *Cobweb,* both $12; in *Chrysanthemum,* $18.

180. Quart water bottles in *Windsor* and in *Penrose* were, respectively, $9 and $8.

181. Decanters: *Large Hobnail* pattern, $30 a dozen; *Imperial,* $44 a dozen.

182. Decanters: *Cut No. 1* was $70 a dozen, as was *Cut No. 2.*

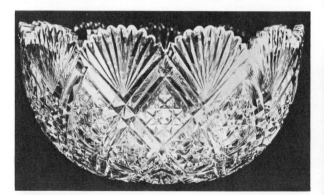

183. A 14-inch punch bowl cut in pattern *No. 2* was $54.

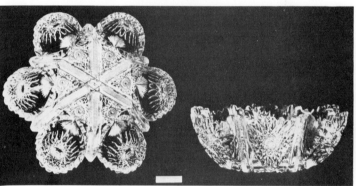

186. A 13-inch bowl in *Stars and Prisms* pattern was listed at $70.

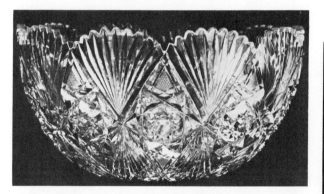

184. A punch bowl of the same size cut in pattern *No. 3* was $48.

187. Bonbons in (left) *Pillars & Diamonds* and (right) *Feather & Diamonds* were $9.

185. *Left:* A 14-inch punch bowl cut in pattern *No. 1* was also $48.

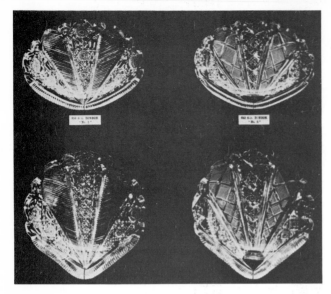

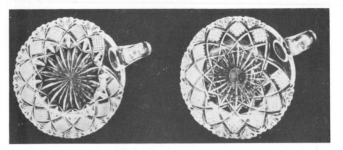

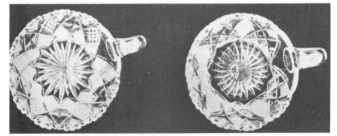

189. These 5- and 6-inch nappies cut in *No. 1* and *No. 2* patterns ranged from $30 to $36 a dozen.

188. Bonbons cut in (left) *No. 1* and (right) *No. 2* patterns were listed at $9.

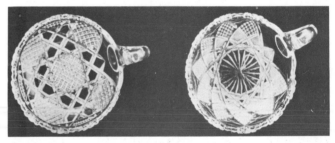

190. Slightly more expensive were 5- and 6-inch nappies in *No. 3* and *No. 4* patterns—$36 to $42 a dozen.

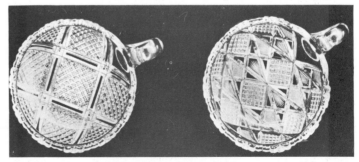

191. Nappies of the same size cut in *No. 5* and *No. 6* patterns were $42 to $48 a dozen.

193. Jugs in (top) *Princess*, (bottom) *Chrysanthemum*, and *Brazilian*.

192. Cut in *No. 7* and *No. 8* patterns, 5- and 6-inch nappies were $48 to $54 a dozen.

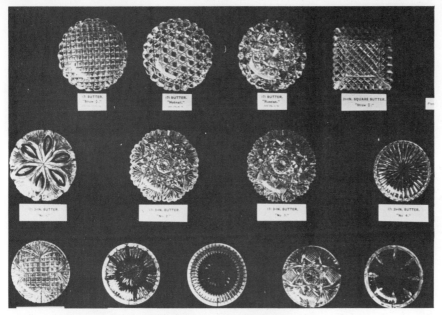

194. Individual butters ranging in price from $7 to $24 a dozen.

195. Table bells. *Left: Flint,* $4.50 to $6.00 each; colored, $6.00 to $6.50 each. *Right* (with silver-plated handle): $4.00.

196. Colognes. Top: *Prisms,* $9; *Table Diamond,* $9; *Pillars,* $12. Bottom: *Brazilian,* $12; *Venetian,* $12; *Chrysanthemum,* $20. The prices were for the 18-ounce size.

197. Hawkes vases in *Brazilian* pattern, $14.00 to $30.00; *Venetian & Lapidary,* $7.50 to $16.00; *Strawberry Diamond and Fan,* $3.50 to $4.00.

198. Vases by Hawkes in *Chrysanthemum,* $80, and *Russian & Pillars,* $70.

199. Candelabrum, $72.

200. Candelabrum, $250.

201. Candlesticks. *Left:* No. 641, $15 to $23. *Center* (with extinguisher): No. 636, $13. *Right:* No. 756½, $14 to $46.

202. *Left:* Small three-light candelabrum with silver-plated arms, $50.

203. Ice tubs. *Strawberry Diamond and Fan,* $15; *Stars,* $22.

204. Kerosene lamp with cut chimney, $100.

205. Kerosene lamp with cut chimney, $130.

206. Kerosene lamp with cut chimney, $110.

Hawkes also operated two branch shops on Market Street at various times and two in the Payne Foundry Building (Steuben Glass Works) on Erie Avenue from 1901 at least through 1910, when the records end.

A typical month's payroll (December 1910) shows the following salaries:

T. G. Hawkes, Pres.	$515.67 (monthly)
Samuel Hawkes	$125.00 (& pocket money in cash)
Townsend Hawkes	$100.00 (& pocket money in cash)
Frederick Carder	$25.00, as consultant
Five salesmen	$726.66
Office staff	$825.00
Weekly payrolls for workers	Ranging from $2,788 to $3,379 (this was a peak period)
"Special payroll"	Paid weekly, ranging from $5.50 to $10.60 to especially talented craftsmen

A list of Hawkes employees compiled from the 1921 and 1923 city directories had only 47 names. It doubtless was incomplete, since women employees were not given. Notable additions were two silversmiths; Jacques Hille, decorating foreman; and a "gold decorator." Thirteen engravers were listed, a much larger percentage than before.

In 1936 the Hawkes payroll stood at 54:

Cutting Dept.
H. A. Jacoby, foreman
18 cutters

Engraving Dept.
J. Sidot, foreman
7 engravers

Office
Samuel Hawkes
Townsend Hawkes
Penrose Hawkes
Joseph Lalonde
4 others

Decorating Dept.
Orlando Dunn, foreman
8 workers, including 2 silversmiths

Miscellaneous
Wm. LeBrantz, photographer and designer
6 others

Shipping
3 people

Only the foreman in each department and the office staff worked full time; the others were working 16 to 24 hours a week.

By 1949, the payroll figures had risen substantially with postwar prosperity, but it included only 51 names. The Decorating Department, except for Orlando Dunn, was gone by this time, but the cutting department was considerably expanded so that the total of employees was about the same, with everyone working full time or even overtime. After 1949 few new names were added, and attrition decreased the work force. Most of the cutters were older men and no new ones were interested in being trained. By the time Hawkes closed in 1962, only a handful were left.

NOTE: Illustrations 207 to 239 are pages from a Hawkes catalog of ca. 1905 in The Corning Museum of Glass. This catalog seems to have been made up from two or more sources, as the pages vary in format. Four of the pages are from the ca. 1900 catalog, but they have lower prices.

208. Tumbler and water bottle in *Monroe* pattern. Tumblers were $11 a dozen; bottle was $4.

207. Three-bottle tantalus stand in *Florence* pattern; $70.

209. Tumbler and water bottle in *Jubilee*. Tumblers were $18 a dozen; bottle was $7.

210. Tumbler and water bottle in *Madeline*. Tumblers were $24 a dozen; bottle was $8.

211. Tumbler and water bottle in *Teutonic*. Tumblers were $30 a dozen; bottle was $11.

212. Claret glass and decanter in *Melrose*. Clarets were $24 a dozen; decanter was $12.

213. Quart decanter in *Recent*, $15.

214. Quart decanter in *St. James* pattern, $15.

215. Quart decanter in *Table Diamond*, $16.

216. Quart decanter in *George III*, $16.

217. Quart decanter in *Colonial*, $16.

218. Quart decanters in *Rouen,* $21.

219. Quart decanters in *Navarre* and in *Flutes.*

220. Wine bottle, 18 inches tall, in *Colonial,* $9.

221. Oval whiskey bottle cut in *Flutes & Prisms* pattern, $10.

222. "Eye opener set" (water bottle and tumbler), $10.

223. Beer mugs in (left) *Marion,* $6; in (right) *Queens,* $9.

224. Stem punch cups: *Holland,* $27.50 a dozen; *Brunswick,* $33 a dozen; *Kensington,* $72 a dozen.

226. *Lorraine* pattern sugar and cream pitcher.

225. Highball tumblers (top): *Marion,* $22 a dozen; *Queens,* $42 a dozen; (bottom): *Teutonic,* $42 a dozen; *Marquis,* $42 a dozen.

227. *Triumph* pattern bowl came in four different diameters.

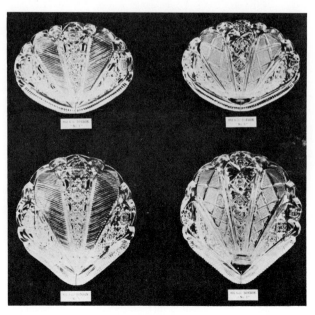

228. *Premier* pattern bowl came in only one size, 8 inches in diameter.

229. Bonbons in two sizes, in *No. 1* and *No. 2* patterns. Smaller ones were $5.25; larger, $6.75.

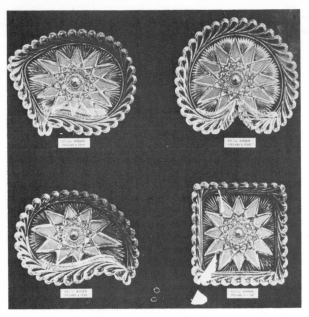

230. Four bonbons in *Pillar & Star* pattern. Prices ranged from $7.50 to $9.00.

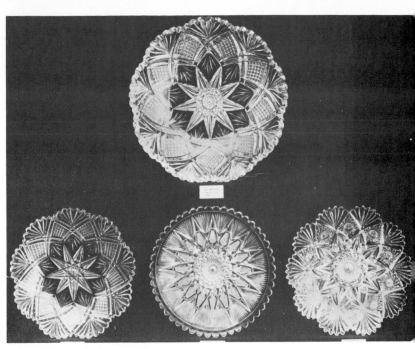

231. Ten-inch nappy in *Norwood* (at top); 7-inch plates are in *No. 4*, *Fancy Star* and *No. 2* patterns.

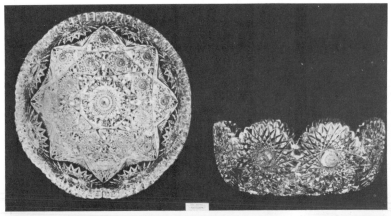

232. Bowl in the elaborate *Festoon* pattern came in four sizes.

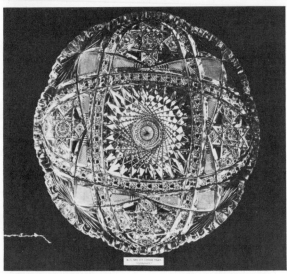

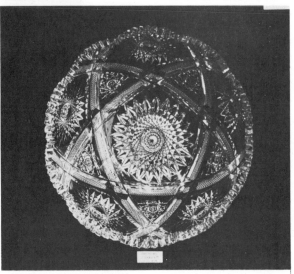

233. Ice cream tray in *Coronet* pattern was listed at $45.

234. Bowl in *Savoy* pattern.

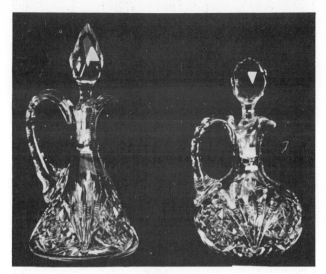

235. Two oil cruets in *Harvard* pattern.

236. Vase, 12 inches in height, in *Franklin* pattern.

237. Tumbler and two-pint jug in *Albion*.

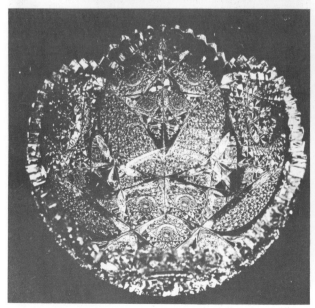

238. *Tokio* pattern bowl came in three sizes.

239. Plate in *Constellation* pattern was available in 16-, 14-, 12-, and 10-inch sizes.

NOTE: Illustrations 240 to 279 are pages from a Hawkes catalog of ca. 1911.

240. *Willow* pattern bowl, which came in three sizes.

242. *Brighton* pattern vase 14 inches in height.

241. This 9-inch bowl is in *Alberta* pattern.

243. Berry set in *Canton*.

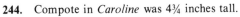

245. Colognes in *Kaiser* and *Celeste*. Each held two ounces.

244. Compote in *Caroline* was 4¾ inches tall.

246. *Cordova* bowl.

247. Tumbler and quart jug in *Cut & Rye.*

248. Three-pint pitcher or "jug" in *Delhi.*

249. *Right: Dundee* oil bottle was 9 inches in height.

250. This 5-inch ice tub was patterned in *Flutes & Greek Border.*

251. Sugar and cream pitcher in *Harold.*

252. *Right:* Tumbler and "jug" in *Herald.* Jug came in either 3- or 4-pint capacity.

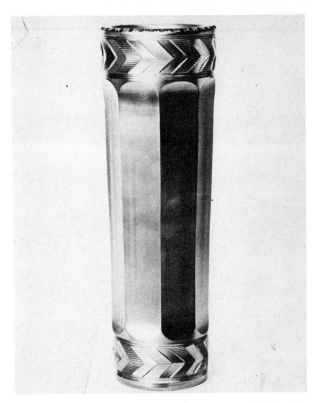

253. *Isis* pattern vase was available in three heights, the tallest being 12 inches.

255. *Juno* pattern tumbler and quart water bottle.

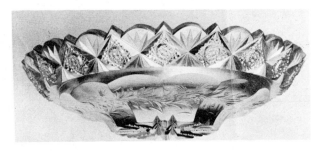

258. The cut and engraved *Mirage* bowl had an 11-inch diameter.

254. Covered cheese or butter plate in *Jersey* pattern. Cover was 5 inches in diameter.

256. *Milton* sugar and creamer.

257. *Minerva* bowl was available in only one size—6 inches in diameter.

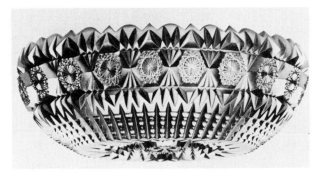

259. *Palmyra* pattern on a 10-inch bowl.

260. This *Panama* bowl came in four sizes.

262. Jug in *Ormond.*

261. Page from the Hawkes catalog showing six pieces of *Priscilla* stemware: goblet, saucer champagne, claret, wine, sherry, and cordial.

263. Three-light electric lamp, *Radiant.* Height was 16½ inches.

264. *Left: Raleigh* nappies came in four sizes—7, 8, 9, and 10 inches.

265. *Selkirk* 3½-pint jug and tumbler.

267. *St. Regis* jug.

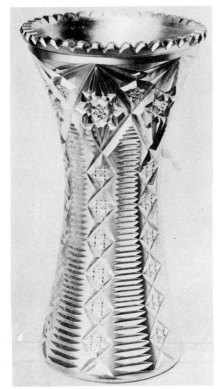

266. *Sherman* pattern on an 11-inch vase.

268. Quart *Tyrone* water bottle and tumbler.

269. *Weston* comport.

270. Tumbler and quart water bottle in *York*.

271. Salts were made in four shapes and various patterns.

272. Pattern *No. 3* decorated this sugar and creamer.

273. Puff box, 7 inches, in *Odd* pattern.

274. A 5-inch puff box.

275. Ten-inch vase in unidentified pattern.

276. Loving cup, 7 inches in height.

277. Another 7-inch loving cup.

278. Loving cup. Seven inches seems to have been the standard height.

279. Twelve-inch vase with delicate floral decoration was marked $17.

NOTE: Illustrations 280 to 330 are taken from pages of a Hawkes catalog dating in the 1910–15 period.

280. Hair receiver in *Empire* pattern.

281. Tea tumbler and teapot, *Alberta* pattern.

282. *Persian* colognes in three sizes. The two smaller ones have long stoppers.

283. *Chippendale* colognes. Again, note the variation in the stoppers.

284. Cream and sugar set in *Geneva*.

285. *Josephine* pattern cream and sugar set.

286. The pattern of this set was named *Cecil*.

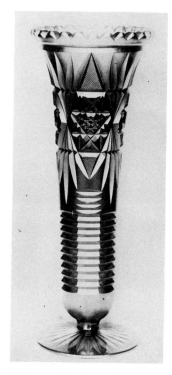

287. A 12-inch vase in *Bengal*.

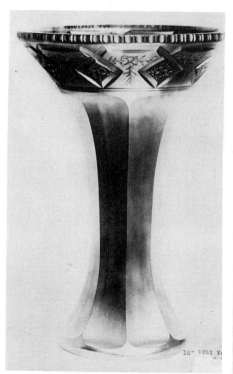

288. On the page picturing this flaring 12-inch vase, the identification is partly torn off: *Old Colony*. Price was $24.

289. Unidentified vase.

290. These two vases were identified as *Crete* (left) and *Dallas*.

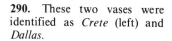

291. *Servia* pattern vases.

292. Tumbler and tall "jug" in *Empire*.

293. Pattern of these pieces is *Adam #2*.

294. *Hebe* tumbler and jug.

295. Pattern name on this page is illegible.

296. Tumbler and 3½-pint jug are identified as *Belmont*.

297. Pieces in *Doris* pattern.

298. *Manlius* pattern tumbler and jug.

299. *Oxford* pattern.

300. Pieces in *Conquest* pattern.

302. *Viking* pattern.

301. *Anson* pattern.

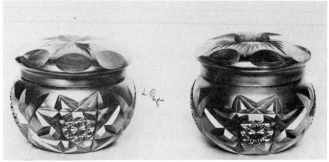

303. Dresser box and puff box in *Persian*.

304. Puff box and hair receiver in *Patricia*.

305. *Flora* pattern puff box and hair receiver.

306. Puff box and cologne in *Paul Revere*.

307. *Harmony* cologne and puff box.

308. *Argo* puff box.

309. Unidentified pieces.

311. *Satin Strawberry* sugar and cream set.

310. *Lawrence* pattern tall bonbon.

312. *Gravic Strawberry* comport with satin finish.

313. Six-inch nut bowl in *Gravic Meadow Rose*.

315. *Princess* bowl, 15 inches.

314. *Satin Iris* 6-inch fern dish with liner.

316. Finger bowl in *Alba* pattern.

317. *Naples* pattern celery tray, 11 inches.

318. Celery tray in *Pacific* pattern, 12 inches.

319. *Wild Rose* celery tray, 11 inches.

320. Domino sugar tray and container for cigarettes, both in *Strawberry Diamond*.

321. *Colonial* pattern finger bowl and plate. The bowls were $33 a dozen; the plates, $37 a dozen.

322. Bowl, 5 inches in diameter, and 7-inch plate in *Alpine* pattern.

323. *Argo* bowl came in several sizes.

324. Unidentified patterns.

326. *Virginia* pattern berry set.

325. Nappy and handled nappy in *Lamont*.

327. *Pilgrim* and *Queens* pattern nappies came in either 5- or 6-inch size.

328. Cold meat platter, 12½ inches; *Albany* pattern.

329. Altar cruets.

330. *Isabelle* photograph frame, 7 inches long.

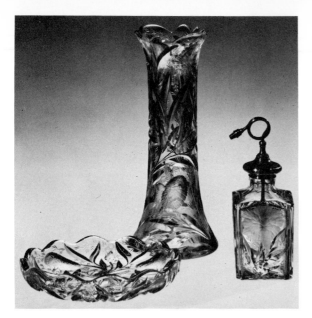

331. Vase and bowl in *Gravic Thistle,* cologne in a polished "Gravic" pattern. Cologne is mounted in Gorham silver with a date stamp for 1912. T. G. Hawkes & Co. *Coll. Mr. and Mrs. Marvin Ashburn*

NOTE: Illustrations 333 to 362 are pages from a Hawkes catalog of ca. 1925–35 showing chiefly various Waterford designs.

332. Bowl engraved in rock-crystal style in a rose pattern. T. G. Hawkes & Co., ca. 1920s. Diam., 20.3 cm. *Coll. Mrs. Estelle Sinclaire Farrar*

334. *Satin Iris* plate, 11 inches in diameter.

333. Comport, 7½ inches, in *Satin Strawberry,* was listed at $15. (*Comport* is the old form of *compote.*)

335. *Right: Old English* covered comport, 10 inches high, was listed at $37.

336. *Waterford* and *Georgian Flutes* pattern goblets were both listed at $54 a dozen. Also available in these patterns were saucer champagnes, clarets, sherry glasses, wines, cordials, cocktails, sherbets, highballs, and footed bowls with matching plates.

337. Covered comport in a somewhat different *Old English* pattern.

338. Another *Old English* pattern in a 11-inch covered comport.

339. Called a "covered vase" in the catalog, this piece was listed as available in colors.

340. *Waterford* 11-inch covered comport.

341. Another covered comport listed as coming in colors.

342. This *Waterford* pattern piece, 14½ inches high, was listed as a "vase." Price was given as $120.

343. *Waterford* covered comport, 14 inches. Price was given as $95.

344. Covered comport in *Old English Flutes* pattern. $100 was the price listed.

345. *Waterford* pattern comport.

347. This decanter was listed as coming in colors. Price was given as $29.

346. Comports, 9 and 6 inches, in a *Waterford* pattern, were priced at $55 and $30.

348. Another decanter listed merely by number, and as being made in colors. Again, price was $29.

349. The catalog identified this quart decanter as *Waterford*, $29.

350. A 12-inch *Waterford* vase available in blue, amber, and amethyst.

351. *Old English* pattern vase in 8-inch size was $30; in 11-inch, $60.

353. The catalog listed this oval vase in *Waterford* at $120.

352. A 10-inch vase available in "solid blue" was listed at $40 in the Hawkes catalog.

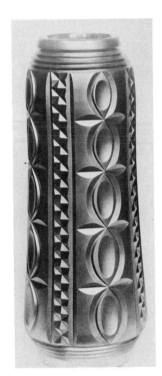

355. *Waterford* vase, 12 inches, listed at $36.

354. A *Waterford* pattern vase listed in the catalog as coming in two sizes and three colors: blue, amber, and amethyst.

356. Called a "center vase," this one measured 12½ inches and was decorated in *Old English* pattern.

357. Another *Old English* "center vase."

358. An *Old English* "center vase" for which matching "side vases" were apparently available.

359. Footed *Waterford* pattern bowl.

360. Smaller (6-inch) footed bowl in the same *Waterford* design.

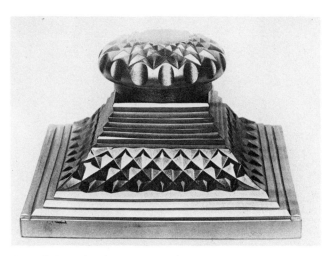

361. Inkstand, 7 inches square, in *Hajaby* pattern.

362A. Two different *Old English* pattern candlesticks. The one at left was more expensive. The one at right was 13½ inches high.

362B. Two more Hawkes candlesticks. The one at right was 10½ inches high.

NOTE: Illustrations 363 to 382 are from a Hawkes catalog ca. 1920–35.

363. Photograph frame in *Revere* pattern.

364. *Gracia* pattern photograph frame.

365. The pattern on this frame was called *Millicent*.

366. Frame in *Rococo* pattern.

367. This frame pattern was listed as *Eunice*.

368. Inkstand in an unidentified pattern.

369. Cologne and puff box with sterling fittings.

370. Cologne and puff box labeled "Celeste Blue" in the catalog.

371. This cologne came in three sizes.

372. A tray, lamp, and set of bowls.

373. Cigarette box.

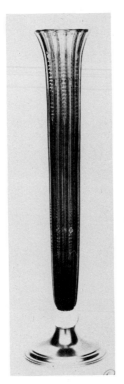

374. Tall vase.

375 & 376. Tall, slim vases with the notation "Stlg"—the customary catalog abbreviation for "sterling," when silver was used for decoration or mounting.

377. An unidentified vase.

378. Footed bowl with floral decoration.

380. Cocktail "mixer."

379. Glass basket in silver holder.

381. Covered candy jar.

382. Sherbet with the notation "Stlg" in the catalog.

NOTE: Illustrations 383 to 423 are taken from blueprint pages of a Hawkes catalog of ca. 1920–35.

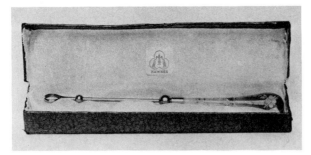

383. The notations on this catalog page picturing a cigarette holder read: "6 in. 5288 Stlg gold plated, blue handle/ Satin Eng'd/ Gregory Blank."

384. The cigarette holder shown here boxed with other items was also numbered 5288 in the catalog.

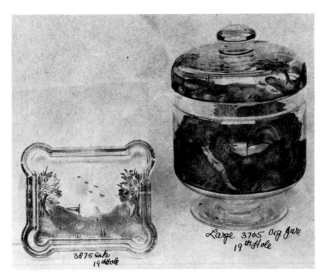

385. This ashtray and large "cig jar" with cover were both described as "19th Hole."

386. Two ashtrays, "satin engraved" and sterling mounted.

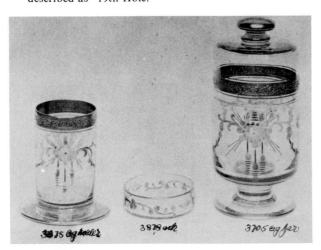

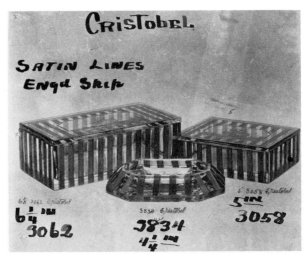

387. The catalog identified this cigarette holder, ashtray, and cigar jar as *Isis,* and at the top of the picture noted "Blue or Green."

388. *Cristobel* pattern set including two covered boxes and an ashtray was described in the catalog as decorated with "Satin Lines" and an "Eng'd Ship."

389. Three bottles identified, respectively, as *Sorento, Moselle,* and *Lexington.*

392. Pieces identified in the catalog as *Kashmir* pattern rock crystal.

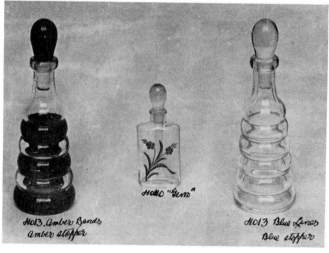

390. The three bottles on this page were described in the catalog as follows: "4013. Amber bands/amber stopper; 4010 'Gem'; 4013. Blue Lines/Blue Stopper."

393. Listed with the number 4011, this pattern was identified as *Milo,* stone-engraved satin.

391. Though differently shaped, these two perfume atomizers are both identified in the catalog as *Venus* pattern. Both came in green or blue.

394. Stemware set (4014) in *Old Waterford* pattern.

395. *Rosalie* rock crystal design.

396. Satin-engraved stemware in *Aragon* pattern; foot and stem were green.

397. *Eureka*, a satin stone-engraved design.

398. *Essex* pattern tumbler and "jug."

399. A similar set in *Premier*.

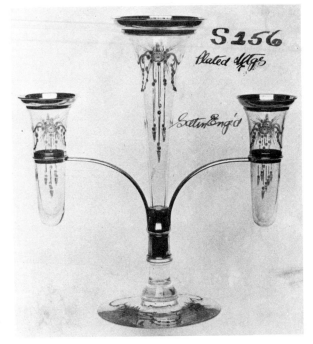

400. Satin-engraved triple vase with plated-silver mounting.

401. Polished and engraved *Avalon* pattern.

402. *Valencia* was another polished design.

403. *Deauville.* See Ills. 406, 415, 416, and 420.

404. *Grenada.*

405. Unnamed design; catalog noted a choice of blue or green.

406. These pieces in *Deauville*, a satin-engraved design, could also be ordered in blue or green. The fleur-de-lis was the major motif of the Deauville designs.

407. A satin-engraved 6-inch bowl.

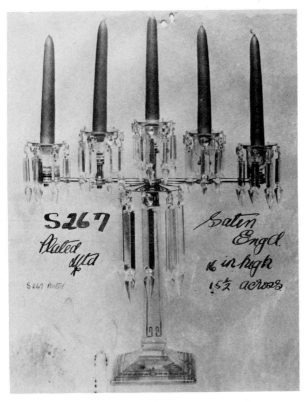

408. Satin-engraved five-light candelabrum with plated-silver mounting was 16 inches tall.

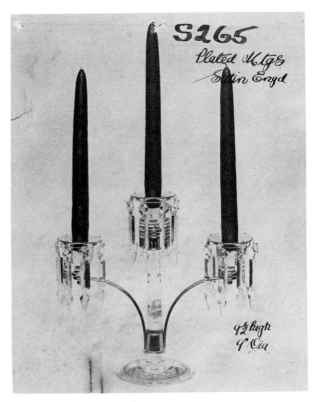

409. This three-light satin-engraved candelabrum also had a plated-silver mounting. Height was 9½ inches.

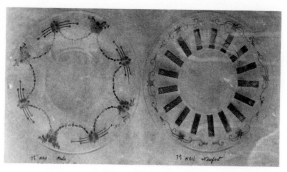

411. Two 7½-inch plates. *Milo*, at left, was identified as "stone engraved satin"; *Newport* was "satin cut and engraved." Heisey blanks.

410. Rock-crystal-engraved pattern called *Rosalie*.

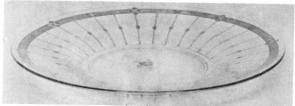

412. *Melba* was also a "stone engraved satin" design.

413. This 7½-inch salad plate bears the notation *Green Killarney*, indicating both the design and color.

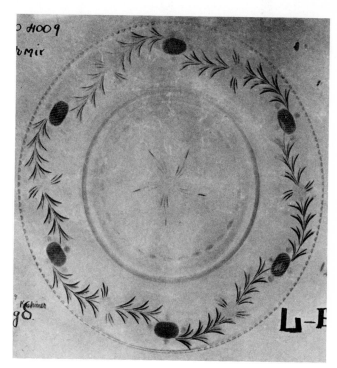

414. *Kashmir*, an engraved-rock-crystal design.

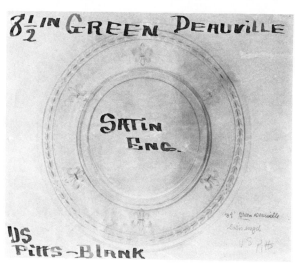

415. An 8½-inch plate in *Deauville*, apparently made on a United States Glass Co. (Pittsburgh factory) blank.

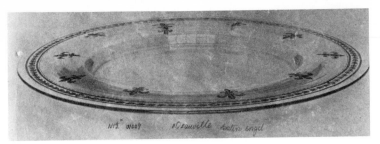

416. A 14-inch *Deauville* plate on a different blank.

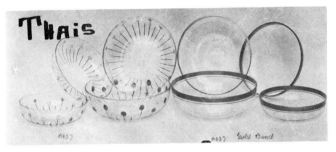

417. Flint glass bowls in *Thais* and in *Gold Band* evidently came in a "Nest of 4."

419. At left is a salt and pepper and vase combination; at right, a nest of ashtrays. Both items had sterling silver fittings.

418. Variously sized plates in amber, green, or blue were decorated with "Three Fishes" or "Birds & Bees," according to the catalog.

420. Three ½-pint footed jugs in *Vermont, Kashmir,* and *Deauville.* All have sterling mountings.

421. Sterling-mounted, satin-engraved bottle and matching glass. Note the lock that would secure the stopper (two keys are hanging on the side).

422. Flasks with sterling tops. Left one is marked "Frosted glass."

423. These two cocktail shakers—paled out almost to illegibility on the old blueprint pages—had either plated or sterling tops. The one at left was decorated with an enameled fighting cock. The same bird was engraved on the shaker at right. Matching glasses shown at bottom of the page have faded almost to invisibility.

424. Plate cut in *Kensington* pattern, ca. 1900–15. Diam., 33.3 cm. *The Corning Museum of Glass* (Gift of R. L. Waterman)

425. Goblet cut in the *Marquis of Waterford* pattern was designed by Herman Jacoby, produced ca. 1915–20. Height, 20 cm. *The Corning Museum of Glass* (Gift of T. G. Hawkes & Company)

426. Perfume set cut in *Gracia* pattern, T. G. Hawkes & Co., 1920s (both glass and silver are marked). *Coll. Mr. & Mrs. Marvin Ashburn*

427. Two bowls cut on the same blank. T. G. Hawkes & Co., ca. 1920–40. Diam., 20.2 cm. *Coll. Mr. & Mrs. Marvin Ashburn*

428. Two ice buckets, T. G. Hawkes & Co., ca. 1920–40. Height, without handle, 20.3 cm. *Coll. Mr. & Mrs. Marvin Ashburn*

429. *Left:* Group of engraved stemware, T. G. Hawkes & Co., ca. 1920–40. Height of tallest, 22.2 cm. *The Corning Museum of Glass*

430. Green-banded wineglass. T. G. Hawkes & Co., ca. 1920–33. Height, 13.2 cm. *Coll. Robert F. Rockwell III*

431. Goblet engraved in *Satin Iris* pattern on blank #7240. T. G. Hawkes & Co., ca. 1945–62. Height, 19.3 cm. *The Corning Museum of Glass* (Gift of R. L. Waterman)

432. Goblet engraved in *Satin Iris* pattern on blank #6015. T. G. Hawkes & Co., ca. 1945–62. Height, 19.7 cm. *The Corning Museum of Glass* (Gift of R. L. Waterman)

433. *Left:* Goblet engraved in *Satin Iris* pattern on blank #7227. T. G. Hawkes & Co., ca. 1945–62. *(Satin Iris is virtually identical to the Iris pattern on a wineglass marked "HAWKES GRAVIC" in the collection of the Corning Museum of Glass.)* Height, 19.4 cm. *The Corning Museum of Glass* (Gift of R. L. Waterman)

436. Goblet engraved in the *Carnation* pattern on blank #7227. T. G. Hawkes & Co., ca. 1945–62. Height, 19.4 cm. *The Corning Museum of Glass* (Gift of R. L. Waterman)

434. Goblet engraved in the *China Aster* pattern on blank #7240. T. G. Hawkes & Co., ca. 1945–62. Height, 19.3 cm. *The Corning Museum of Glass* (Gift of R. L. Waterman)

435. Goblet engraved in the *China Aster* pattern on blank #6015. T. G. Hawkes & Co., ca. 1945–62. Height, 19.7 cm. *The Corning Museum of Glass* (Gift of R. L. Waterman)

437. Goblet cut and engraved in the *Rock Crystal* pattern on blank #6015. T. G. Hawkes & Co., ca. 1945–62. Height, 19.8 cm. *The Corning Museum of Glass* (Gift of R. L. Waterman)

438. Goblet cut in an unknown pattern on blank #6015. T. G. Hawkes & Co., ca. 1945–62. Height, 19.7 cm. *The Corning Museum of Glass* (Gift of R. L. Waterman)

439. *Left:* Goblet cut in an unknown pattern on blank #6015. T. G. Hawkes & Co., ca. 1945–62. Height, 19.5 cm. *The Corning Museum of Glass* (Gift of R. L. Waterman)

440. Goblet cut in the *Kohinoor & Panel* pattern on blank #6015. T. G. Hawkes & Co., ca. 1945–62. Height, 19.6 cm. *The Corning Museum of Glass* (Gift of R. L. Waterman). This was Hawkes's most expensive pattern in later years and was rarely ordered.

441. Goblet cut in the *Queens* pattern on blank #7240. T. G. Hawkes & Co., ca. 1945–62. Height, 19.4 cm. *The Corning Museum of Glass* (Gift of R. L. Waterman)

442. *Above:* Goblet cut in the *Delft Diamond* pattern on blank #7240. T. G. Hawkes & Co., ca. 1945–62. Height, 19.2 cm. *The Corning Museum of Glass* (Gift of R. L. Waterman)

NOTE: Illustrations 443 to 452 are pages from a Hawkes catalog in use in the 1940s or 1950s. Several of the goblets pictured in Illustrations 431 to 442 are illustrated in this catalog also.

443. Three goblets (left to right): *St. George Waterford, Eardley Waterford, Delft Diamond Waterford.* All were $145 a dozen or more.

444. Three goblets: *Vernay, Delft Diamond,* and *Queens.*

445. Compote in a variation of the *Marquis of Waterford* pattern, ca. 1915–50. Diam., 30 cm. *The Corning Museum of Glass* (Gift of T. G. Hawkes & Co.)

446. *Strawberry Diamond and Fan* goblet and one in the rock crystal design called *Barclay.* The first was $126 a dozen; the latter, $75.

447. *Left: Francis I* pattern goblet. *Right: Strawberry Diamond & Fan.*

448. These three goblets are *C. Colfax, Revere,* and *Satin Iris.* Prices were, a dozen, respectively, $117, $117, and $159.

449. Goblets in *Satin Iris, China Aster,* and *Gravic Fruit;* prices were $261, $255, and $288 a dozen.

450. Goblet in *Worcester Rose,* $88 a dozen.

451. Page from a Hawkes catalog in use in the 1940s shows decanters cut in the Anglo-Irish style, probably part of Hawkes's Waterford line.

452. Water-damaged page from a Hawkes catalog in use in the 1940s shows a goblet in the pattern supplied to the President of Mexico early in the century. This was probably in the catalog merely for "show"; it was almost certainly not still in production.

SUMMARY

Dates: 1880-1962

Addresses: 1880-82—West Market Street, south side
 1882-1916—Hayt Building, 67-69 W. Market Street
 1916-62—Hawkes Building, 73-79 West Market Street
  (See text for branch locations.)

Blanks: Corning Glass Works, C. Dorflinger & Sons, Steuben Glass Works, H.P. Sinclaire & Co. Tiffin Glass Company, as well as a few from Baccarat, Val St. Lambert, Union Glass Company, Libbey Glass Company, Pairpoint Corporation, H.C. Fry Glass Company, Heisey Glass Company, and Duncan & Miller Glass Company

Trademarks: 1880-90—none
 1890-95—paper label
 1895-1962—acid-stamped "HAWKES" below a shamrock enclosing two hawks and a fleur-de-lis. The design of this mark changed somewhat around 1903 to 1905, but both marks were probably used concurrently for several years. Ca. 1903-20—a mark similar to the above but with "GRAVIC GLASS PAT'D" above it. Ca. 1900-1962—"HAWKES" acid-stamped on stemware

Products: Brilliant cut wares, copper-wheel and stone engraving. Cheaper lines added around 1905; enameled, gilded, and stained wares in 1920s and 1930s; simple cut and stone-engraved wares from 1940s until 1962

Employees: As Corning's largest cutting firm, Hawkes had many hundreds of employees during its long history; it is not possible to list them all. Some of those not already mentioned in the text are Nicholas Ambrosone (silversmith), Paul Ambrosone, Mildred Arnot, William Austin, Archie and Morris Bartholomay (cutters), Gerald A. Barton, Frank and Sam Bavisotto, Tom Bell, G. Bleichner, Charles M. Blodgett (cutter), Margaret Box, Cecil Bruce, James E. Burnes, Dennis Z. Calkins, Constantine Campanelli, O. Cartwright, J. Castellana, Thomas Castellana, W. Castor, Margaret Cavalier, Rosario Cavallaro, Ernie Cranage (cutter), W. Doyle, J. Drozda, Ralph Dukes, Thomas Edger, John W. Elliott, Mary Elwell, J. Faulisi (smoother and stone engraver), A. Fenderson, George M. Fish, John J. and William Gallagher (engravers), Emma Garty, G. Gerhart, Jessie Gorton, Joseph A. Hahne (engraver), Fred Haradon (engraver), William F. Hart (cutter), H. Hauptman (engraver), Carlton L. Hayes (gold dec.), Oscar Hepworth, Edith Herrick, G. Hess, H. Holman, L. Holton, Otto Horn (engraver), Adam C. Johnson (engraver), Emil Kaulfuss (engraver), N. Keck, Anthony Keller (engraver), G. Krebs, Charles Lee, N. Lincoln, George H. Lindstrom, C. McCarthy, Floyd Manwarren, A. Mayes, Mary Mellon, A. Miller, Alvah Miller, Arnold Miller, Warren Morse, Dennis O'Connor, George O'Dell, Edward Palme, Sr. & Jr. (engravers), Rudolph Palme (engraver), Alexander Perry, W. Phelps, Mary Pickrell, Simeon I. Powers, Wilmot Putnam (engraver), Minnie Reynolds, Lew Robbins, Joseph Salvini (cutter), Charles Sarter, K. Sarter (engraver), Joseph Shield (cutter), Adam Steltze (cutter), Benjamin R. Watson (cutter), Elmer Weaver, and F. Woods.

Customers: Leading jewelers all over the North American continent; department stores as well as jewelers after World War I

6
Hunt Glass Works, Inc.
(Hunt Glass Co.; Hunt & Sullivan)

Thomas Taylor Hunt, a second-generation glass cutter,[1] left his native Lancashire, England, for the United States about 1878. With him were his wife and their son Harry, then about eight years old. His first American employer was C. Dorflinger & Sons of White Mills, Pennsylvania.

In late 1880 or early 1881 Hunt moved on to Corning and the new little cutting company of Thomas Hawkes. The Hunts joined 12 or more other English cutting families, according to the 1880 census. These men were much in demand. Accustomed to finishing each piece of glass they began, they were acknowledged as more expert than cutters who had learned only to rough, smooth, or polish.

Harry Hunt learned to cut glass in Corning, probably at the Hawkes company under the eye of his father. His apprenticeship would have begun about 1884, and he stayed with Hawkes after earning his diploma.

In 1895 Thomas Hunt and Corning businessman Daniel Sullivan built a cutting factory behind Hunt's red frame cottage on the southeast corner of Sixth and Washington streets. This was in Corning's English section. The two buildings had a common wall; one could step from the cottage into the factory.

Sullivan took no part in the company's management. Thomas Hunt ran the business. Harry Hunt was its chief designer and salesman—Corning still remembers him as "a born salesman."

Hunt & Sullivan began the third generation of Corning cutting companies.[2] Thomas Hunt, a staunch Episcopalian and church organist, expected encouragement from Corning's other glass families, who were also Episcopalian. When he found that he could not buy blanks from Corning Glass and C.

Dorflinger & Sons, Hawkes's and Hoare's chief suppliers at this time, he left the church in protest.[3] The resulting coolness had ended, however, when the genial Sam Hawkes succeeded his father as president of T. G. Hawkes & Co.

Thomas Hunt turned to English blanks, which he selected on frequent trips to England. The *Corning Daily Journal* reported one such trip to "the land of his nativity" May 22, 1901.

Hunt & Sullivan began business with a few cutters and little capital. Hawkes and Hoare salesmen carried their samples in lined trunks; Harry Hunt took his to New York in a bushel basket. Davis Collamore & Co. was his first customer, and the sale was significant; this old and distinguished firm had had its own exhibit at the Universal Exposition in Paris in 1889, showing Hawkes glass and Rockwood pottery.[4]

By 1897 Hunt & Sullivan needed more room. The *Daily Journal* reported on January 14 that they had broken ground for an addition "to their glass cutting shop." Next day they had "secured the services of Ben O. Gore and Rees Lewis." On February 22, the addition was approaching completion—it would be "ready for business in about two weeks." A dozen or more frames, the *Daily Journal* added, would then be in operation.

In 1903 Cox & Lafferty, 32 Park Place, New York City, became Hunt & Sullivan's eastern representatives, and a trade journal reported:

The sample line they already show is very good and contains several things that are well worth attention. There is an evident desire to get away from the conventional and produce goods in really original and artistic cuttings. Shapes and color are all that they should be.

453. *Opposite:* Cut and engraved vase, probably on an English blank, made by Hunt & Sullivan ca. 1900. Height, 46.4 cm. *Coll. Mrs. Dorothy Hunt Sullivan*

The same magazine reported two weeks later "a tendency to get away from the conventional," adding that "this has been accomplished without the production of any 'freaks.' "[5]

The company's early unconventionality continued. In the 1920s it made a stone-engraved crystal radio case and horn, now in the collection of the Rockwell–Corning Museum.[6]

Hunt & Sullivan continued to grow slowly but steadily. James Sullivan inherited his uncle's interest in the company, probably early in 1905. The *Daily Journal* announced the next move February 25, 1905, in a story headlined CORNING CUT GLASS FIRM INCORPORATED WITH CAPITAL OF $20,000. The new partner, it added, "intends to look after the New York end of the business." Employees numbered about 25 to 30 at this time, including 4 roughers, 12 smoothers, and 3 to 4 polishers. Engraving was subcontracted to Corning's home shops until the 1920s.

Thomas and Harry Hunt bought out James Sullivan about two years later. The *Corning Leader* reported on January 10, 1907, that Sullivan had held a one-third interest. The announcement of a new name came in April. "In future the name will be the Hunt Glass Co., with Thomas T. Hunt, president, M. E. Hunt [Mrs. Thomas Hunt], vice president, and H. S. Hunt, secretary and treasurer."[7]

Thomas Hunt died in April 1909. His obituary in the *Corning Leader* of April 14 noted that Hunt had

> built up the business until he employed under ordinary conditions 50 to 60 men. The high grade glass and the fine quality of workmanship which was insisted upon spoke for itself and soon Mr. Hunt had a very lucrative business worked up, and at his death had one of the leading cut glass factories in the city.

Harry Hunt succeeded his father as president. He continued to concentrate on sales, making February and July trips to New York and covering also Chicago, Minneapolis—St. Paul, and other large cities. The February trip coincided with the arrival of western buyers on their way to Europe. Many companies sent their salesmen on the same route, and Hunt often traveled with one from the Steuben Glass Works.

Harry Hunt also continued to design cut glass. He patented *Royal,* his company's best-selling cutting until the late 1950s, in 1911.[8]

Hunt could count on outstanding and loyal employees to run his factory. Nella (Mrs. Fred) Fuller was the business manager and a vice-president. She left about 1916 to found a cut-glass company of her own, but this firm probably subcontracted for Hunt. Lee Carr, the company superintendent, was a vice-president by about 1920,

and kept the titles until his retirement some 30 years later. About 1915 Mary Krebs became the company's secretary-treasurer; she worked for the company until after Harry Hunt's death in 1935.

Harry Hunt was a jovial, popular company president, friendly with all Corning's glass families. He no longer used the English blanks his father had preferred. Suppliers included Libbey, Union Glass, and the H. C. Fry Co. Bottles with lapidary-cut stoppers came from France. The outbreak of World War I froze a shipment for Hunt Glass on the docks.

The company reached its peak during the 1920s. Its 80 employees included six engravers, all able to do copper-wheel work, and four or five salesmen. The company was a full partner in Corning's cut-glass industry, and on blank-borrowing terms with Steuben, Hawkes, and H. P. Sinclaire & Co. Its top line was a group of rock-crystal designs. Edward Palme, Jr., George Haselbauer, Hiram Rouse, and Nicolas Underiner engraved most of these in the factory; Emil Walter and Fred Haselbauer engraved the rest in their home shops. A Corning Chamber of Commerce pamphlet reported that "in 1920 the Hunt Glass Works, on commission of President Harding, furnished him with hundreds of pieces of stemware."[9]

Other designs of the 1920s included cuttings in the Anglo-Irish style, which the company called its "Waterford" designs. *Royal* and the Waterford cuttings were produced chiefly on bowls and vases; rock-crystal designs on decanters and stemware. The company also briefly cut floral designs on Pyrex brand glass for Corning Glass Works, but gave up the work because it did not pay enough.

454. The Hunt *Royal* design, patented in 1911, was the company's most popular cutting until the 1950s. Bowl diam., 24 cm. *Coll. Robert F. Rockwell III*

455. *Royal* pattern nappy cut by Nicolas Underiner. Diam., 19.2 cm. *Coll. Nicholas Williams*

456. *Royal* pattern tray cut by Underiner. *Coll. Miss Mary Krebs*

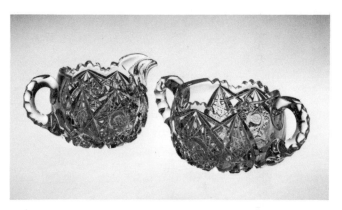

457. A Hunt Glass Works design of stars and rosettes on a sugar and creamer. Creamer height, 7.4 cm. *Coll. Robert F. Rockwell III*

458. Two of the Hunt "Waterford" designs, ca. 1910–30. Vase height, 17.2 cm. *Coll. Miss Mary Krebs*

459. A later, lighter Hunt cutting of the Waterford type, identified by an oval green sticker. Note the blank's similarity to that in Illustration 458. Ca. 1940–50. Height, 30.4 cm. *Private Collection; Frederic Farrar photograph*

460. Small pitcher cut at Hunt Glass Works by Nicolas Underiner, probably in the 1920s. Height, 8.7 cm. *Coll. Nicholas Williams*

462. Pair of engraved decanters in rock-crystal style, believed made between 1900 and 1915. Height, 32.9 and 33.1 cm. *Coll. Mrs. Dorothy Hunt Sullivan*

461. Demijohn cut by Lee Carr and engraved by Joseph Libisch for Hunt Glass Works, ca. 1915. Pairpoint Corporation blank. Height, 34.3 cm. *Coll. The Corning Museum of Glass* (Gift of D. J. and Russell Carr)

463. Flower-engraved plate in late rock-crystal style, ca. 1930s. Diam., 21.8 cm. *Coll. Miss Mary Krebs*

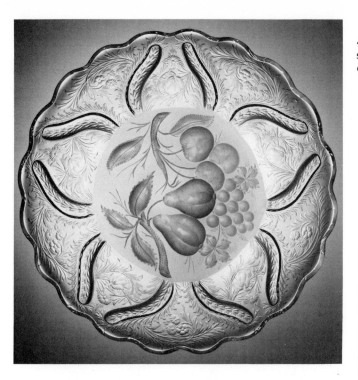

464. Heavy plate said to have been cut and engraved in seven of Corning's home shops. Diam., 30.4 cm. *Coll. The Corning Museum of Glass* (Gift of D. J. and Russell Carr)

465–468. Group of four pieces engraved for Hunt Glass Works by Nicolas Underiner. All date from the 1920s or early 1930s. Tumbler (465) is 9.7 cm. in height. The handled dish (466) is pink; diameter is 19.2 cm. Plate (467) is 18.5 cm. in diameter. The jar (468) is 12.2 cm. in height. *Coll. Nicholas Williams*

Though the 1930s were desperately difficult times for Corning's glass manufacturers, the Hunt company continued to produce high-quality wares until Harry Hunt's death in 1935. The company motto, "What sterling is to silver, Hunt's is to glass," appeared on its letterhead. The Hunt acid formula, which originated with Lee Carr, was a source of special pride. From 1920 on, however, quality blanks were increasingly hard to find.

Harry Hunt's son-in-law, Walter Sullivan, became president of Hunt Glass in 1935. He was unrelated to the Sullivans who were Thomas Hunt's early partners. Walter Sullivan had extensive experience in sales, but was new to the glass business. His sons, Walter, Jr., and John, joined the firm in 1945, young Walter as salesman, John as office manager.

Aside from home shops, only Steuben Glass, Hawkes, and Hunt were then decorating glass in Corning. Sullivan decided that the declining demand for fine-glass made advisable a shift in emphasis toward light pictorial cuttings. More women cutters joined the company's five; by 1948 there were 13.[10] In April 1948, Sullivan bought a larger building at East Third and Steuben streets, and announced plans for expansion in the *Leader* on the ninth of that month. Employees were to be increased from 50 to 100. These included a few veterans of World War II, who were learning to cut glass under the G.I. Bill of Rights. Walter Sullivan became chairman of the board; Walter, Jr., succeeded him as president. John Sullivan became secretary and office manager. Walter, Sr., planned to reopen the company's New York offices, and to add a second floor to the new factory. His sons were to manage the Corning business while he concentrated on "sales-expansion and liaison work here and abroad." Though Hunt customers still included jewelers, most were the department stores whose orders had become essential. The company still "owned or controlled" 150 designs, including their rock-crystal and Waterford lines. In 1951 a third son, Thomas J. Sullivan, entered the business as a shipping clerk. He became president in 1954.

In 1957, when Floyd Manwarren became Hunt's manager, the company was still cutting much of its patented *Royal*. Figured blanks were in use. Many pictorial cuttings imitated stone engravings. These were specialties of Hunt's women cutters. Hunt also employed some highly expert older men. The oldest was Thomas Dow, former superintendent of H. P. Sinclaire & Co. By 1961, when ill health forced Manwarren to leave the company, young men were no longer learning the trade.

A decline in business that had begun in the 1950s continued and deepened. During the 1960s Hunt's chief product gradually became its pictorial cuttings.

Shortly after 1970 control of the company passed from the Hunt-Sullivan family to a New York City group that manufactured and decorated glass for a door-to-door sales operation called Princess House. The closing of the factory, which occurred in about 1973, went virtually unnoticed in Corning. The building still stands, converted into an apartment house.

469. Cocktail shaker engraved in the rock-crystal design *Elegance,* ca. 1930–40. Height, 36 cm. *Coll. The Corning Museum of Glass* (Gift of Hunt Glass Works)

SUMMARY

Dates: 1895-ca. 1973. During its last years the company was no longer controlled by the Hunt-Sullivan family.

Address: 1895-1948: 196 West Sixth Street. 1948-ca. 1973: 300 East Third Street

Blanks: 1895-1905: chiefly English. 1905-37: Pairpoint, Libbey, Union, Fry. In the 1930s: Heisey; Indiana Glass; Fostoria; U.S. Glass Co. at Tiffin, Ohio; Bryce Brothers; Imperial. 1940-70: some of the above, plus Morgantown Glass Works; Federal Glass; West Virginia Glass; Viking Glass; Louie Glass. Figured blanks in use

Trademarks: 1895-1906: none. 1906-ca. 1915: script "Hunt" acid-stamped on glass. Later years: stickers of various colors, including pale blue and moss green

Product: a full line of wares; novelties include the Rockwell-Corning Museum's gramophone case. Early designs were chiefly rich cuttings; also some combinations of cutting and engraving. Rock-crystal engravings were the leading quality line of the 1920s. Waterford designs. *Royal* popular through the 1950s. 150 designs in 1948 included "Gray Cuttings," probably pictorial. *Spike:* simple pointed cuts raying upward. 1948-60: also *Trent, Cornwall, Beverly, Table Diamond.* Ca. 1960-ca. 1973: light pictorial cuttings most important

Employees: Cutters: Harold Andrus, Frank Bavisotto, Joseph Bevilaqua, Ernest Crannage, Robert Crozier, Fred Dann, Frank DeMario, Orvis Dillon, Thomas Dow, Martin Drew, Gust Eckstrom, Joseph Hill, Ed Hyland, Cornelius McGregor, Bert Owens, Lewis Rew, Dominick Reynolds, Walter Roberts, Wendell and Wesley Root, Harlo Rutledge; James, Percy, and Samuel Share; J. Richard Stubley, George Sundstrom, William Tahaney, George Van Gelder, Robert Webster, Ray Winfield. *Acid man:* Arthur Hurd, 1940-65. *Women Cutters:* Clara Acker, Ethel Travis Barnes, Alberta Carl, Eleanor Downing, Mrs. (?) Dunbar, Lorinda Freitas, Elsie Gerow, Minnie Holmes, Eva McNeil, Frances Negri, Lorraine Travis, Marjorie Wiles. *Engravers* (after 1920): Edward Palme, Jr., George Haselbauer, Hiram Rouse, Nicolas Underiner. Additional work subcontracted to home shops. *Managers:* Lyman Day, Lee Carr, Martin Drew, Floyd Manwarren, superintendents. Nella Fuller, Mary Krebs, Grace Hyde, John Sullivan, office managers

Customers: 1895, Davis Collamore & Co., New York; others unknown. 1906-37: Tiffany & Co.; Black, Starr & Frost; Ovington, and Plummer's, all in New York. Wright, Tyndale & Van Roden; J. E. Caldwell & Co. in Philadelphia; other jewelers, gift shops, and department stores throughout the country. After this time Hunt, like other fine-glass manufacturers, sold chiefly to department stores. Princess House ca. 1970-73

7
O. F. Egginton Co.

Oliver Egginton's cutting firm was the fourth in Corning, opening in October 1896.[1] Egginton, then in his seventies, for 15 years had been the manager of T. G. Hawkes & Co. He apparently felt that he would prefer to start his own business—and he did so with the backing of Q. W. Wellington, Dr. Henry Argue, a Mr. Hoyt, William Sinclaire, and possibly Marvin Olcott.

Born in 1822 in Birmingham, England, Egginton married an Irish girl, Ellen Brennan, when he was twenty-two. He worked as a cutter for Thomas Webb & Sons of Wordsley, where he probably knew John Hoare. Around 1865, Oliver brought his family to Portland, Maine, to join his brothers: Enoch, who was superintendent of the Portland Glass Company, and Joseph, who was head of the cutting department there. Enoch had previously worked at Hoare's cutting shop, in Dorflinger's Greenpoint factory.

In 1867, the Eggintons moved to Montreal, Canada, where Enoch, Oliver, and another brother, Thomas, helped found and run the St. Lawrence Glass Company. Here Oliver learned something about glass mixing, and at Enoch's death around 1870, he succeeded him as factory superintendent. Around 1873, Oliver and his sons—Joseph, twenty-six, and Walter, seventeen—came to Corning, probably at the invitation of John Hoare. Oliver worked as a foreman for Hoare until the 1880s, when he joined T. G. Hawkes in Hawkes's new glass-cutting shop. He is variously listed as a foreman, manager, and general superintendent for Hawkes, a position he held until 1896.

Egginton's sons probably worked for Hoare and Hawkes as well. Sometime in the 1880s Walter became one of Hawkes's designers—according to

family tradition, he designed some of the glass shown in Paris in 1889. Joseph was listed in the Corning directories as a glass cutter and as a glass decorator. As a sideline he designed and made stained glass windows. Two of these can be seen today in St. Mary's Church in Corning (a memorial to Oliver Egginton) and in the former Oliver Egginton house at 60 West Fourth Street in Corning. Joseph worked principally for Hawkes, but in 1900 he left to work for the International Silver Plate Company in Meriden, Connecticut. Although he returned later to Corning, he was never associated with his father's firm.

Oliver built his factory, which had two floors, each 30 feet by 76 feet, on a block of land at Fifth and State streets. As already mentioned, it opened in 1896, with Walter as the designer. By 1898, he employed 52 "skilled hands," and business was so good that Egginton expanded, putting on a 40-by-60-foot addition and nearly doubling his work force.[2]

On October 11, 1899, the business was incorporated as the O. F. Egginton Company, with Mrs. Walter Egginton, Dr. H. A. Argue, Joseph C. Moore, and William F. MacNamara as stockholders. In 1900, Oliver Egginton died and Walter took over the business. Oliver had repaid his backers some time before, and so the company was free of debt. Although Walter became president, family tradition has it that his father's capital had all been left to Walter's wife, who had more business sense.

The company remained prosperous for several years during the peak period of glass cutting, employing from 150 to 200 men during the fall busy season. By 1910, however, it had started to falter. The number of workmen dropped to 40 or 50, and

470. *Opposite:* Photograph of Oliver Egginton, ca. 1890.
Corning Daily Journal

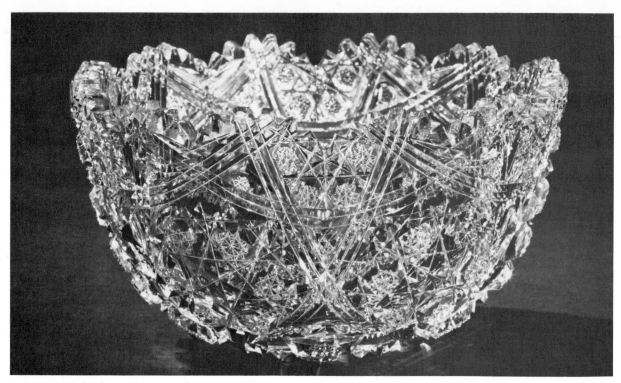

471. Bowl in *Cluster* pattern, O. F. Egginton & Company, ca. 1910. Diam., 15.3 cm. *Coll. Miss Lucille Egginton*

the lean years of the 1910 to 1918 period proved too much for the firm. By February 1918, the Egginton factory was bankrupt.

Walter Egginton was a good designer, and his patterns are among the best of the period. But he preferred heavy brilliant cutting to engraving, and his inability to compromise may have contributed to his downfall.

The Eggintons seldom bought blanks from Corning Glass Works, although they were on friendly terms with the Houghtons. Oliver considered Corning Glass Works's product inferior, and the Glass Works had an agreement to supply only John Hoare and Thomas Hawkes with blanks. For special orders, Egginton occasionally bought from Corning. His preferred suppliers, however, were Baccarat, Val St. Lambert, Libbey, the Jeannette Glass Company, and the Union Glass Company.

Egginton did not advertise much, but he did issue catalogs. Every piece of glass was acid-stamped with a crescent and star. Although Walter did not like engraving, a few of his designs used stone-engraving; no copper-wheel work was done. From the beginning, the Eggintons used an acid-dip to polish that was a special recipe of Walter's. He mixed the solution and did the dipping himself about once a month, but a wheel polisher was also employed in case polishing was needed before enough work had accumulated for the regular acid-bath. Egginton also employed one of the few lapidarists in Corning, who cut faceted or "lapidary-cut" stoppers. Most of Corning's smaller firms used imported stoppers that were already cut.

472. Vase and cologne bottle in *Calvé* pattern, O. F. Egginton & Company, ca. 1910. Height of vase, 17.6 cm. *Coll. Miss Lucille Egginton*

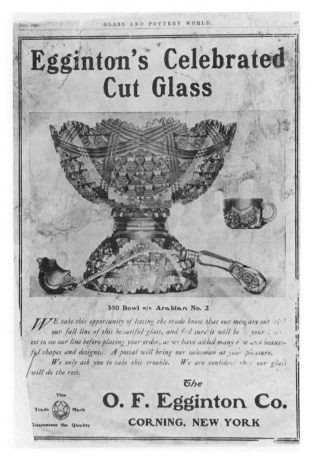

Egginton's Celebrated Cut Glass

350 Bowl w/s Arabian No. 2

WE take this opportunity of letting the trade know that our men are out with our fall line of this beautiful glass, and feel sure it will be to your interest to see our line before placing your order, as we have added many new and beautiful shapes and designs. A postal will bring our salesman at your pleasure.

We only ask you to take this trouble. We are confident that our glass will do the rest.

The

O. F. Egginton Co.

CORNING, NEW YORK

This Trade Mark Guarantees the Quality

473. Advertisement for punch-bowl set in *Arabian* pattern from the *Glass and Pottery World,* June 1906.

474. Powder box, O. F. Egginton & Company, ca. 1910. Diam., 13 cm. *Coll. Miss Lucille Egginton*

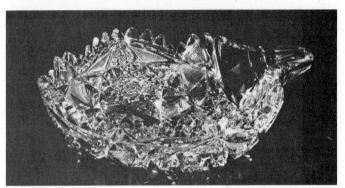

475. Nappy in *Creswick* pattern, O. F. Egginton & Company, ca. 1910. Length, 18.5 cm. *Coll. Miss Lucille Egginton*

476. Compote in a variation of *Lotus* pattern, O. F. Egginton & Company, ca. 1912–18. Height, 13 cm. *Coll. Mr. and Mrs. Keith Price*

477. Nappy in a variation of *Lotus* pattern, O. F. Egginton & Company, ca. 1912–18. Diam., 15.4 cm. *Coll. Mr. and Mrs. Joseph O'Bryan*

The patterns produced at the Egginton factory included *Arabian, Berkshire, Calvé, Cluster, Creswick, Diadem, Dogwood, Dryden, Genoa, Gounod, Iris, Iroquois, Lemons, Lyre, Lotus* (patented 1903), *Magnolia* (patented 1903), *Marquise, Orient, Orleans, Prism, Russian, Sherwood, Spartan, Steuben, Strathmore, Tokio, Trellis* (patented 1908), *Vendix, Vendome, Verdi, Virginia,* and *Warwick.* All were designed by Walter. Since he also designed at least one pattern for Thomas Hawkes (*Valencia,* 1893), it seems likely that he produced this at his own factory as well. The glass was sold to Marshall Field of Chicago, Shreve, Crump & Low in Boston, Nathan Dorman in New York, and other firms.

The number of employees varied from nearly 200 at peak in 1900 to only about 40 when the business closed. About half the employees in the later years were women, who cleaned, washed, and waxed the glass to prepare it for the acid-dip.

Although in operation for only 22 years, Egginton produced much fine-quality glass, some of it among the finest made in Corning.

SUMMARY

Dates: 1896-1918

Address: Fifth and State streets

Blanks: Baccarat, Val St. Lambert, Libbey Glass Company, Jeannette Glass Co., Union Glass Co.

Trademark: "EGGINTON" in a crescent with a star, acid-stamped on glass

Products: primarily brilliant cut glass; some stone-engraved wares

Employees: up to 200 men and women at peak season during the early years

Customers: Marshall Field & Co., Chicago; Shreve, Crump & Low, Boston; and other jewelers

8
Engraving in Corning, 1868-1968

Corning's early importance as a center of copper-wheel engraving has long been overlooked. Collectors have preferred cut glass to engraved, perhaps in part because the time-consuming copper-wheel technique made engraved glass far more expensive than cut glass. Today engraving is so misunderstood that it is often called intaglio cutting or even etching.

Those who do love and collect engraved glass tend to think that it originated in Corning with the 1933 reorganization of Steuben Glass. This is not so. Corning has had fine engravers since 1869; before 1890 she was a leader in the field. Perhaps nowhere else would the taxing assignments of modern Steuben's designers have been achievable.

The story of Corning's engraving begins slowly.[1] The articles "lettered and most beautifully ornamented with flowers" at Hoare & Dailey in 1869 were engraved. Their engraver had left Corning when the 1870 census was taken. We believe that he was Augustus Haselbauer, a Bohemian who appeared in Brooklyn directories of 1870 and 1871. Haselbauer lived in Brooklyn's eastern section during these years, where Hoare & Dailey's Greenpoint cutting shop was situated. In 1870, when the Corning Flint Glass Works was in receivership and its furnaces were cold, Hoare & Dailey cut and engraved an order for the White House. We believe that Augustus Haselbauer worked on it in Brooklyn, and that he was already training a younger relative, Joseph Haselbauer. But the Corning directory indicates that both were back in Corning by 1873, in time to engrave the *Philadelphia Public Ledger* order described in Chapter 4.

Most of Corning's fine-glass was geometrically cut in the 1870s and 1880s. The engraver's chief subjects were the monograms, coats of arms, and floral designs commissioned by jewelers. More elaborate

work was rare enough to warrant newspaper stories; it was invariably pictorial, two-dimensional, and unpolished. Institutions or public figures like the Astors and Vanderbilts ordered it. Augustus and Joseph Haselbauer engraved such orders for Hoare & Dailey (perhaps including Brooklyn orders of 1869 to 1873) until 1880. Then Thomas Hawkes opened his company, for which Joseph Haselbauer seems to have been the first engraver. Master engraver Max Roland Erlacher has recently studied the work of the two men at our request. He confirms that Joseph, though younger, was the better engraver. Indeed, his work is extraordinary.

As Joseph Haselbauer worked on William Vanderbilt's punch bowl in 1883, Thomas Webb's blowers in England were fashioning the blank for a piece of glass that changed Corning's glassmaking history. Completed in 1886 after two and a half years of intermittent engraving by the Bohemian William Fritsche, it became known as the Fritsche ewer. Its high-relief engraving would have been called *Hochschnitt* in Fritsche's native Meistersdorf. The Webb company polished it, and called the result "rock crystal." Webb had introduced rock crystal in the 1870s. The ewer became and remains the archetype of the genre.

New York City jeweler Theodore Starr, an important Corning customer, bought the ewer. He also printed and distributed a four-page article about it by Alfred S. Johnston, F.R.G.S. Johnston called Fritsche "as true an artist as ever breathed." Meistersdorf, he wrote, was "the Village of Masters ...where the best art-workers...lived." The ewer, he concluded, should not have left England. It belonged in the South Kensington Museum.[2]

The Irish-born John Hoare and Thomas Hawkes had worked together to prove that Corning could surpass England in the Anglo-Irish idiom. It is unlikely that either had pondered the distinction between skill and art. They were sensitive to English innovations because of 1) the competitive disadvantage caused by high American wages; 2) European copying of American designs;[3] and 3) eastern retailers' refusal to acknowledge that American cut glass could equal the English in quality.

Hoare and Hawkes reacted immediately with a permanent change of course. Fortunately, Thomas Hawkes's company secretary, H. P. Sinclaire, Jr., strongly preferred engraving to cutting, and he had been designing engravings for some time.

Hawkes may already have decided to exhibit at the Paris Universal Exposition of 1889. Now he acceded to Sinclaire's preference. The Hawkes exhibit would include elaborate engravings of Sinclaire's design, which Joseph Haselbauer would engrave.[4]

As Haselbauer devoted all his time to the Paris engravings (Ill. 14), Hieronimus William Fritchie of Meistersdorf came to Corning, with or immediately after Joseph Haselbauer's brother Ignatius.[5] Fritchie was probably related to the Webb Master. He (or his employer) emphasized the relationship by listing him as William in directories until 1895, when the Corning directory first called him Hieronimus W.[6] Fritchie took over Haselbauer's regular duties at the Hawkes company.

The Grand Prize Hawkes was awarded at the Paris exposition seemed to Corning a firm answer to the English challenge. But it was also a watershed in Corning's glassmaking history. H. P. Sinclaire's stubborn preference for engraving seemed less egregious. His designs became a Hawkes special-order line, and slowly began to make their way.

As J. Hoare & Co. began to prepare its exhibit for the 1893 Columbian Exposition, Augustus Haselbauer died and Fridoli (or Fridolin) Kretschmann arrived in Corning. Kretschmann, another Meistersdorfian, called himself a "glass carver." He came from the Webb company, and stayed only long enough to see the Hoare exhibit completed. Perhaps he executed all its award-winning engraved and rock-crystal designs. Certainly he wrote to his compatriots at Webb that Corning needed engravers.[7] Joseph Nitsche and Adolf Kretschmann, both from Meistersdorf, answered the appeal. Nitsche came directly to Corning, and replaced Fridoli Kretschmann at J. Hoare & Co. Adolf Kretschmann detoured via the Columbian Exposition, where he demonstrated his craft for the Libbey company.

By 1894 Corning had five copper-wheel engravers, all Bohemian. Ignatius Haselbauer may have worked with Joseph Nitsche at J. Hoare & Co. Hawkes employed foreman Joseph Haselbauer,

478. Decanters made for John Magee to commemorate the opening of the Corning, Geneva & Syracuse Railroad December 10, 1877. The engraving is believed to be the work of Augustus Haselbauer of Hoare & Dailey. Height, 33 cm. *Coll. Mr. and Mrs. George Wyckoff*

Hieronimus William Fritchie, and Adolf Kretschmann. The work of the last four is known and of the first rank. Clearly, the two companies were expecting increased sales of engraved glass.

The Bohemians brought with them their foot-powered lathes, expecting to set up the home shops traditional in Central Europe. These were important to Corning for several reasons. First, the Bohemians might train their sons at home. Second, they worked extra hours at home during their employers' busy seasons. Finally, they became engraving subcontractors for smaller cutting companies that opened after 1904. We have found no home engraving shop that worked only for its proprietor's in-factory employer.

These engravers, and those who followed them, found in Corning a German-speaking enclave eager to welcome them. They became enthusiastic members of the Saengerbund, the singing organization that had met weekly since the early 1860s. Its annual balls and outings were family affairs that continued well into the 1930s.

The newcomers brought with them more than their skills. Chosen for apprenticeship because of their sobriety and probity as well as aptitude, they became the solidest of new citizens. Several invested in Corning's future by acquiring income-producing real estate.

Corning's fine engraving made its way steadily but slowly until 1900, when T. G. Hawkes and Co. began to prepare for the introduction of its Gravic glass. Now Joseph Haselbauer began to train Corning's first American-born engravers. These were Hiram Rouse, Wilmot Putnam, and William Morse. All seem to have been somewhat older than the traditional age of fourteen. Haselbauer was paid again for instruction in 1902, according to the Hawkes Cash Book. These pupils may have been William Beebe, Francis Quinn, George Kennedy (or Kenneda), and R. Shepherd.

This year also brought Corning's first Alsatian engravers. A Corning tradition that the Hawkes company sent Nicholas Bach on a recruiting trip is supported by a Cash Book entry: "to be acctd [sic] for $1025" October 15, 1902. This was the form the company used for prepaid traveling expenses. The trip closely followed H. W. Fritchie's departure for work at the Libbey company, presumably to work on their exhibit for the 1904 Louisiana Purchase Exposition. The Alsatians who came to Corning shortly after this date were John Illig and Emile Walter. We shall see that their engraving style was more closely related to the bolder, deeper Germanic Jugendstil than to the painterly tradition of Bohemia. Nicolas Underiner (originally Undreiner) also immigrated from Lemberg in 1905. All three engravers went to work for T. G. Hawkes & Co., where the Gravic glass that required their talents was the special responsibility of H. P. Sinclaire, Jr.

The opening of H. P. Sinclaire & Co. in 1904 again overtaxed Corning's engravers. Sinclaire intended to specialize in fine engravings. Fired by his enthusiasm, most of the Hawkes engraving department followed him, including foreman Joseph Haselbauer, who brought with him his son Fred from the Haselbauer home shop. H. W. Fritchie returned to the Hawkes company from Toledo.

From 1905 to 1909 three more Bohemians arrived in Corning; and young American engravers' names appeared increasingly in company and city records. Although Corning's cutters decreased from 490 to 340 during these years, the number of engravers increased to 45. Why?

First, Corning had temporarily overtaken England in sales of engraved glass. Fred Carder spoke specifically of rock crystal in the 1903 interview quoted in Chapter 2. The article said:

Another branch of the trade which was being gradually taken from the English manufacturer, Mr. Carder averred, was the celebrated rock crystal glass.

479. The Fritsche ewer deeply influenced Corning cut-glass manufacturers by its rock-crystal style of engraving. Height, 38.5 cm. *Coll. The Corning Museum of Glass*

"This," he said, "has been kept as a specialty of the Stourbridge district for many years, and the best of our productions have found their way to the States. It looks as if this, too, will eventually be as well done by them as is the cut glass. There are one or two firms who are laying themselves out for this class of work, and I was impressed by the number of designs, emanating from the Wordsley district, which were being copied and produced in *fac-simile* there for houses who had originally bought from this district . . . It is only the little novelties for which Stourbridge is famous that the Americans will continue to buy."

Second, taste was changing. Technical virtuosity had outrun inspiration in cut glass. Those who could afford engraving now had an alternative to the overdecoration of the nineteenth century.

Third, Hawkes Gravic glass was an immediate success, and Sinclaire & Co. at once established a reputation for fine engravings.

Finally, the fine, hand-polished cuttings of Corning's quality manufacturers were increasingly imitated on cheaper blanks and with handwork skimped. The discerning buyer sought a glass more difficult to imitate, and found it in engraved glass. The Tiffany & Co. *Blue Book* for 1907, for example, listed glass in both rich cuttings and rock crystal. On comparable items the rock crystal was higher in price.

As cut-glass quality declined, the center of the industry shifted to New York City. Corning, however, consolidated her position as the center for engraving. More Bohemians were needed, and more arrived: Anthony and Henry Keller, Ernest and Emil Kaulfuss, Edward Palme. The first of three Hauptmanns, relatives of the Kellers, came in 1908. In 1910 a Libbey engraver who signed himself "Emil" wrote Corning's Emil Kaulfuss urging him to "come back to Toledo and bring Ernst [Kaulfuss] with you."[8]

A second generation of Bohemians was also at work: Clement Nitsche; Fred and George Haselbauer, trained by their father Joseph, who died about 1910; Francis Fritchie. It is not clear whether engraver John A. Haselbauer was the son of Augustus or of Ignatius, both of whom had sons named John.

Corning may also have attracted one of England's Woodall family. Hiram Rouse noted an "English fellow" named "Woodhull" in his work notebooks. The misspelling would be natural; Woodhull is a village only a few miles from Corning. Rouse also noted engraving designs by this "Englisher."

By the century's second decade Corning's Bohemian enclave was well known. Several engravers stopped in Corning before going on to other cities. Others came to stay. Among them were Joseph Oveszny, Frank Konigstein, and the May family. Joseph Hahne came from Alsace.

The year 1911 brought a young Master to replace Joseph Haselbauer. This was Joseph Libisch, who became the link between Corning's early engraving and the artistic leap forward of modern Steuben Glass. All these men opened their own engraving shops even as they worked in Corning's factories. They also worked for out-of-town companies. Two are known to have subcontracted for C. Dorflinger & Sons.

Even when the Hunt Glass Co. and Steuben Glass opened engraving departments in the 1920s and 1930s respectively, Corning's home engraving shops continued. They have never died out. All worked for individuals as well as for companies. Much of their glass, of course, was stone-engraved; the market for copper-wheel engraving has always been limited by its high cost.

In the factory and at home, engravers designed many pieces. Frederick Carder and H. P. Sinclaire, Jr., are the only "bosses" known to have designed much of their own engraved glass; Hawkes-

employed designers probably also designed engravings.

Engravers' designs were not necessarily original—the engravers often worked from books of designs. It seems clear that these illustrated flowers, putti, hunting scenes, and other motifs used again and again in Central European engraving. Indeed, their familiarity doubtless contributed to the immediate success of modern Steuben Glass's simpler artist-designed glass in 1933.

The Bohemians' training in drawing enabled most of them to portray buildings as well, and some were talented portraitists. Each had his specialty. Joseph Libisch's unequaled animal engravings rival the most delicate work on canvas.

Many superb Corning engravings have been lost in recent years. Some were given away by their engravers or sold to dealers. Other collections have been dispersed by the engravers' widows. Several can be described, and will be listed later in the appropriate sections. It is our hope that they will again come to light so that they can be photographed and recorded.

The engraving shops described below operated throughout the year, year after year. Those engravers who worked occasionally at home for their in-factory employers have been omitted. Shops that are presently in operation are included in Chapter 20.

Corning's Home Engraving Shops

Joseph F. Haselbauer

Joseph Haselbauer was born in Bohemia—probably in Meistersdorf[9]—doubtless in 1852 (as the 1880 census gave his age as twenty-eight). When he left, at the age of fourteen, to study engraving in the United States, the villagers gave him a cow. He sold it and used the money to buy shoes.

There were as yet no *Glasfachschulen*. Apprentices studied privately with a Master, a relative whenever possible. Haselbauer reached the United States in 1866, the *Daily Journal* said 40 years later (September 19, 1906). We believe that he began to work at once with engraver Augustus Haselbauer, eight years older and probably a brother.[10] Circumstantial evidence suggests that their employer was Hoare & Dailey, whose shop was in the Dorflinger factory in Greenpoint.

The Haselbauers may have been the engravers observed at Hoare & Dailey's Corning shop in 1869. In 1870, as already explained, Augustus was in Brooklyn, presumably to work on a Hoare & Dailey White House order. Joseph, still a minor, was unlisted in Brooklyn directories, but we believe that

480. Joseph and Mary Smith Haselbauer about 1875, the year of their wedding. *Coll. Mrs. Catherine Haselbauer Dencenburg*

he also worked on the order. Directory evidence indicates that both men were in Corning in 1873, when John Hoare moved his Brooklyn "operatives" upstate.

In 1875, when Joseph's training had ended, he married Mary Smith in Corning. He had found a competent and tough-minded business manager, who knew that her husband had far surpassed his teacher. (Compare Ills. 14 and 478.) Joseph began to behave with a Master's independence. Mary, daughter of a German who had Anglicized his name, understood the dignity that the degree conferred. In 1876 she insisted that they go to Philadelphia and set up a tent on the Centennial Exposition fairgrounds. There, Joseph engraved glass on his foot-powered lathe and Mary sold it. She was pregnant at the time—their son Frederick was born that year. He was later followed by Ellen, and in 1889 by George.

Haselbauer seems to have operated his own shop from this time on. Until 1910 it was in the woodshed of his house. We do not know that he ever again worked in the Hoare factory, though he is reported

to have engraved for the company. The same *Daily Journal* story of September 19, 1906, indicates that C. Dorflinger & Sons was another customer. "Since coming to this country about 40 years ago," it said, "he has worked on nearly every order for the White House." Several of these were supplied by Dorflinger, including the one for Theodore Roosevelt that prompted the article.[11]

Haselbauer's skill as a teacher also betokened the Master. His first pupil was his son Fred, who probably began engraving studies about 1890. H. P. Sinclaire's decision to entrust all his Paris exposition designs for Hawkes to Joseph provides another indication that Joseph had surpassed his teacher.

Haselbauer was clearly doing the work of a Master at the Hawkes company in 1900. Entries in the Cash Book show that he was in charge of preparations for the introduction of Gravic glass.

During 1901 the company paid Haselbauer for "decorative books" and "for instruction one boy H. Rouse." In addition to a regular semiannual bonus, he received another for "3 lathes to his model." In 1902 the company paid him $15 for a "German book of designs," $1.73 for "carborundum wheels billed to himself," and $100 for further instruction. In 1903 T. G. Hawkes & Co. paid him for "engraving books to date" and $27.30 "for work at home." The size of this payment supports other evidence that son Fred was then engraving in the Haselbauer home shop.

Haselbauer left the Hawkes company with H. P. Sinclaire in 1904. We do not know whether he engraved at home for the new company, or busied himself with designing glass and equipment and hiring engravers. When the factory opened, he took charge of the largest group of engravers ever assembled in a single Corning factory, and stayed as foreman "for quite a number of years," according to Clement Nitsche—probably until his death. His son Fred also engraved in the Sinclaire factory.

Meanwhile, the Haselbauer shop continued to operate. Though son George had learned to engrave at an unusually early age, the shop still had more orders than it could fill. Hiram Rouse's notebooks indicate that Fred left Sinclaire & Co. in March 1906. The Dorflinger White House order followed two orders for the Hawkes company that were completed at home in June of that year and recorded in the Hawkes Cash Book on June 6 and 16.

It was perhaps about this time that the three Haselbauers decided to turn their home shop into a small business, J. F. Haselbauer & Sons. Though this is usually considered to date from 1910, when they built a two-story building behind the Haselbauer house at 84 West Third Street, the Hawkes Cash Book records payments to the company before that year. (Its story is told in a later chapter.)

481. T. G. Hawkes & Co. included this photograph of the mature Joseph Haselbauer in a publicity folder printed ca. 1900–1903. *Coll. The Corning Museum of Glass*

The engraving on White House stemware of the 1880s can confidently be attributed to Joseph Haselbauer, as can the Paris exposition vase in Illustration 14. Perhaps Christian Dorflinger, who must have known Augustus and Joseph Haselbauer's work in Brooklyn, had them engrave his well-known Centennial decanter set. Its seals are clearly the work of *two* copper-wheel engravers, and none are known to have worked in White Mills.

Other known Joseph Haselbauer work has been lost. This included a wine jug depicting the adventures of Ulysses, and several pieces of gold-ruby glass. These can be accounted for until the 1950s; they are believed to have been sold by Fred Haselbauer's widow. A dime-sized crystal disk on which Haselbauer had engraved a legible Lord's Prayer was still in Fred's possession in the late 1930s or early 1940s.

Joseph Haselbauer was Corning's founding engraver and one of the great engraving Masters. Let us hope that additional examples of his work will come to light.

SUMMARY

Dates: Ca. 1876–ca. 1906; thereafter J. F. Haselbauer & Sons
Address: 84 West Third Street
Blanks: chiefly supplied by customers
Trademark: none known
Product: custom engravings of all kinds and of superlative quality
Employees: Fred Haselbauer worked in his father's shop after 1890; George may have done so in the last year or two before it became J. F. Haselbauer & Sons. Mary Smith Haselbauer managed business matters. Others, if any, unknown

Customers: T. G. Hawkes & Co., C. Dorflinger & Sons; reportedly J. Hoare & Co. Other customers, including the Hunt and Steuben companies, may have used the later company. Also, unknown private customers

Hieronimus William Fritchie
(originally Fritsche)

H. W. Fritsche left Meistersdorf in 1873, at the age of thirteen. On his passport he added two years to his age, perhaps because the apprentice was supposed to have finished school. The boy's destination was Scotland, where he learned engraving from an uncle, but he traveled by way of England.

By 1881 the young man was engraving glass in Dublin, where he met and married an Irish girl. He had already Anglicized the spelling of his name. In 1885 his engraving won a medal at the Dublin Artisans' Exhibit. His employer, we believe, was the firm of T. & R. Pugh.

Fritchie brought his family with him to Corning about 1888.[12] This was unusual—evidence that a thoroughly satisfactory job awaited him. As we have seen, it was with the Rich Cut Glass Works of Thomas Hawkes, whose only engraver was fully occupied with the engravings for the Hawkes exhibit at the Paris Universal Exposition of 1889. A family tradition of Samuel J. Share's descendants says that Share made several recruiting trips to Great Britain for the company, and brought back engravers. We may suspect that Fritchie was one of them.

The Hawkes company had, in Fritchie, a first-rank engraver whose specialty was hunting scenes. He engraved them as long as he lived. One of the

482. Hieronimus William Fritchie (*left front*) and his fellow engravers in Dublin ca. 1885. *Coll. Mrs. Helen Fritchie Arnoldy*

two that he made for himself was in the polished rock-crystal finish; the later one was unpolished. At the Hawkes company he earned a regular bonus in addition to his wages, though at first this was smaller than Joseph Haselbauer's.

Fritchie brought with him his own foot-powered lathe. It is probable that he used it to engrave in the family's first three homes: on Jennings Street, Sly Avenue, and at the top of hilly Walnut Street. Fritchie owned and rented a second house in downtown Corning, which he bought in case walking up his hill each day became too much for him.

Fritchie taught his son Francis to engrave in the home shop. His in-factory teaching may have begun in 1901, when Hawkes Gravic glass was soon to be introduced. The Hawkes Cash Book records a payment to Fritchie of $50 on February 27 for "instruction 2 boys W Putnam W Morse." Together with Hiram Rouse, mentioned earlier, these were Corning's first American engravers except for Haselbauer's sons.

In 1902 Fritchie left Corning to work for the Libbey company in Toledo, which was preparing its exhibits for the Louisiana Purchase Exposition of 1904. "The Manufacture of Incised, or Cut Glass," an article about the Libbey company, appeared in the *Scientific American* of April 30, 1904. Rufus Denman, cutting the Libbey World's Fair punch bowl, was pictured on the cover. In the article itself, H. W. Fritchie was shown at his lathe, to illustrate the engraving process. Inasmuch as glass companies have always photographed their premier workmen, publication of his photograph would indicate that Fritchie was Libbey's leading engraver. The fact that *Scientific American* published a description of rock crystal engraving (even a somewhat inaccurate one) implied that the technique had become so popular its inclusion in a major exhibit was *de rigueur,* and that Fritchie had been borrowed to work in that technique.

The Romans and the Orientals [the anonymous author wrote] were fond of both the cameo and the intaglio processes of engraving, and they had a peculiar combination of both which we now designate as "rock-crystal engraving." This is a long and expensive process, but the superb and highly artistic results fully warrant the expenditure of labor. The somewhat formal and mathematical lines give way to

483. Plate, *Apotheosis of Transportation,* exhibited at the Louisiana Purchase Exposition in 1904 by the Libbey Glass Co. Probably engraved by Hieronimus William Fritchie, borrowed from Corning 1902–4. Diam., 31.1 cm. *Coll. Smithsonian Institution; Smithsonian photograph*

floriated designs, or free rein is given to the plastic fancy by the possibility if not the ease of modeling. The sculptor in his studio adds clay while he is working...while his marble-worker cuts off the marble to attain the same effect, in one case addition and in the other subtraction—the glass engraver does both.

It is doubtless unnecessary to remark that we know of no time when an engraver added glass as his work progressed.

Following Haselbauer's departure from the Hawkes company, Fritchie returned just before Christmas of 1904. Next day Hiram Rouse wrote in his notebook that he had worked on *"Olive, Fritchie's first pattern after he came back."* The Hawkes Cash Book left no doubt that Fritchie had returned as the Hawkes company's leading engraver. His "special" pay was double what Haselbauer's had been, and paid weekly. Later it was raised again by 50 percent, to six dollars a week. No other engraver received special pay.

The Fritchie family was now complete. "Romie" Fritchie, as his friends called him, built a big frame house at the top of Walnut Street. An extension at the back housed his engraving shop. The house overlooked all of Corning, and had its own reservoir. The shop was in use in 1905, when the

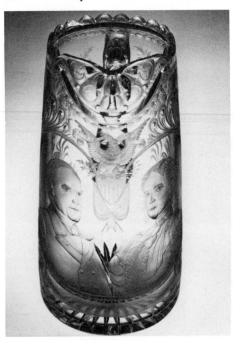

484. Pitcher designed and engraved by H. W. Fritchie. The portraits are the campaign photograph of President and Mrs. William McKinley. Probably begun in Corning ca. 1901 and completed in Toledo ca. 1902. Height, 25.6 cm. *Coll. The Corning Museum of Glass* (Gift of Mrs. Helen Fritchie Arnoldy); *Frederic Farrar photograph*

485. Goblet engraved with a view of Carpenters Hall, Philadelphia, by H. W. Fritchie ca. 1917–30. Height, 5.3 cm. *Coll. Mrs. Helen Fritchie Arnoldy; Frederic Farrar photograph*

Hawkes Cash Book recorded a payment to him "for work done at home." Francis Fritchie was now also engraving, more to please his father than from personal inclination. He engraved for T. G. Hawkes & Co., and in 1913 and 1914 for John Hoare, Inc., in Wellsboro, Pennsylvania. After serving in the army he gave up engraving, realizing that his work would never equal his father's.

H. W. Fritchie's Corning engraving shop was widely known as "a quality shop," but there is no record of its customers. We do not know that it ever employed other men, or where its blanks came from.

About 1916 Fritchie again left Corning. This time he opened an engraving shop in Philadelphia. He was employed steadily by J. E. Caldwell & Co., and Wright, Tyndale & Van Roden, two of the city's leading jewelers. He also engraved antique reproductions of all sorts for the city's largest antique dealer, then on Chestnut Street. His work for Caldwell included a hunt-scene trophy for the Devon Horse Show.

Fritchie later gave up his downtown shop, but carried on in his large suburban house and continued to work for the Caldwell company, which, his son-in-law says, "would take anything he engraved." He kept in touch with Corning friends by frequent visits. Special friends (according to information supplied by Erwin Wood) included Sam Hawkes, for whom he engraved a punch bowl for the Chicago World's Fair of 1933, Joseph Libisch, and Adolf Kretschmann. However, the Hawkes company did not exhibit at the 1933 fair, and we do not know for which customer they may have supplied the punch bowl.

As he entered his seventies, Fritchie, a widower, became restless in his big house. He took a job with the Strawbridge & Clothier department store, commuting each day, and engraved monograms in a little shop set up for him in the store's glassware department. He also "kept his hand in" by engraving more elaborate work at home. At seventy-seven, he still refused to retire. His children, increasingly worried about his safety, resorted to an elaborate ruse: they persuaded his reluctant employer to "lay him off" for his own good. "He was wild," his daughter says, "but he never knew."

486. Detail from the bottom of an umbrella stand engraved by H. W. Fritchie shortly before his death in 1940 shows the Bohemian style of his work. *Coll. Mrs. Helen Fritchie Arnoldy; Frederic Farrar photograph*

Fritchie's daughter persuaded him to move in with her and her husband by setting up an engraving shop in her basement. Fritchie engraved there until a stroke felled him at his lathe in 1940. He was eighty-one years old.

SUMMARY

Dates: ca. 1888-1916, with the exception of 1902-04, when Fritchie worked in Toledo; 1916-40, in Philadelphia

Addresses: he engraved at all the Fritchie Corning addresses, but the best known and most active Corning shop was in the house at the head of Walnut Street (1904-ca. 1916)

Blanks: chiefly supplied by customers

Trademark: usually none; an occasional piece made for

his own use is signed "H. W. Fritchie" in diamond-point script.

Product: elaborate polished and unpolished engraving on glass that ranged from stemware to punch bowls. Hunting scenes were a specialty.

Employees: Francis Fritchie sometimes worked in his father's shop in Corning. No others known

Customers: individuals and companies; during the years in Philadelphia, J. E. Caldwell & Co., Wright, Tyndale & Van Roden, T. G. Hawkes & Co., and a Philadelphia antique dealer

Joseph Nitsche
Clement Nitsche

Joseph Nitsche was born in Meistersdorf about 1855, and learned his trade there, according to his son Clement. He and his family joined the Thomas Webb company's colony of Bohemian engravers in England about 1882. Although Clement was only two years old, he remembers the stay in England as "very hard for my mother. She didn't speak any English. One of the neighbor women would go to the store with her and tell her the English words."

When word came from Fridoli Kretschmann that Corning needed engravers, Joseph Nitsche was one of the two Meistersdorfians who responded. He sent his wife and sons home to Bohemia, and sailed for the United States with Adolf Kretschmann.

487. Mr. and Mrs. Joseph Nitsche about 1900, with sons Clement (*left*) and Ernest. *Coll. Mrs. Grace Nitsche Barker*

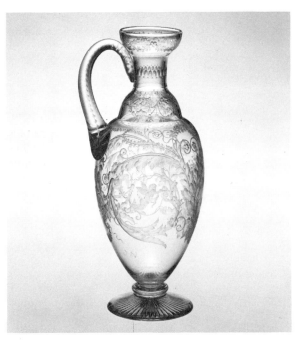

488. Ewer designed and engraved by Joseph Nitsche ca. 1893. The initials were added later by a childish hand. Height, 26.4 cm. *Coll. Mrs. Grace Nitsche Barker*

489. *Rich Carnations* tray, designed and engraved by Clement Nitsche for H. P. Sinclaire & Co. from a sketch by Sinclaire ca. 1915. Length, 29.3 cm. *Coll. Mrs. Estelle Sinclaire Farrar*

Nitsche's first employer was J. Hoare & Co.; he replaced Fridoli Kretschmann, who returned to England about the time that Nitsche arrived in America. Augustus Haselbauer, the Hoare company's first Corning engraver, had recently died.

By 1895 Nitsche's family had joined him; Corning directories indicate he then owned a house at 366 Walnut Street. His home engraving shop was already operating; Clement, now fifteen, learned engraving there. He remembers this training well; he worked "for weeks and weeks on any old bottles that were around the house." A later shop where he and his father worked still stands, facing the alley behind 138 West Fifth Street. Here a younger brother, Ernest, learned to engrave; Ernest, however, became a cutter.

Joseph Nitsche move to the Hawkes company some time before 1901, when the Hawkes Cash Book records the first "special" or "extra" payments to him.[13] But he continued to work with Clement in the Nitsche shop until his death in 1923. The Hunt and Steuben companies were among the Nitsches' customers. They also worked for individuals, doing both copper-wheel and stone engraving.

We suspect that the wine jug in Illustration 488 was the first piece that Joseph Nitsche engraved at home after reaching Corning. Made for his own use, it has an American eagle, unrelated to the rest of the design, below its handle.

The greater part of Clem Nitsche's in-factory engraving was for H. P. Sinclaire & Co. He moved from the Hawkes to the Sinclaire company in 1904 because, he said, "Sinclaire was going to make better [engraved] glass."[14] Except for a brief period at the Hoare Bridge Street plant, he stayed with the Sinclaire company until it closed in 1928.

Clem Nitsche created many simple designs "for the young fellows to copy," but he was also responsible for several more elaborate ones. He designed the celery tray in Illustration 489 from a sketch by H. P. Sinclaire. When Sinclaire saw the finished piece, he was so pleased that he had it wrapped and took the first train to New York to show it to Tiffany & Co.

After the Sinclaire closing, Clem Nitsche worked mainly in his Fifth Street shop for almost a decade. He worked briefly in Jeannette, Pennsylvania, for the Westmoreland Glass Company for a few months also. Most of his work after 1928, however, was for Steuben.

In 1937 the engravers' advancing age became a matter of concern to the reorganized Steuben Glass, which decided to set up an apprenticeship program. Clem Nitsche closed his engraving shop for good and went to work in the Steuben factory to "train the young fellows." Thomas Miller, a former

Steuben engraver, told us that Nitsche was their only teacher during the program's first years. He continued to engrave for Steuben until he retired at the age of about seventy.

490. Tumbler designed and engraved for his wife by Clement Nitsche ca. 1920s. Height, 10.3 cm. *Coll. Mrs. Grace Nitsche Barker*

On September 8, 1977, Clement Nitsche celebrated the birthday that made him 97 years young. He plays euchre with a group of cronies several times a week, and regrets that he was a bit too old to demonstrate engraving for the Corning–Painted Post Historical Society. They invited him to do so in the Storefront Museum that they operated from about 1973 to 1976. "A few years ago I would have done it," Clem Nitsche says.

SUMMARY

Dates: ca. 1894-1937
Address: for most of the 1894-1937 period, at the rear of 138 West Fifth Street
Blanks: most supplied by customers
Trademark: none
Product: copper-wheel and stone engravings of the Nitsches' own designs and those of the companies for which they worked

Employees: none
Customers: the Hunt and Steuben companies and individuals

John N. Illig[15]
(See also Chapter 17)

Johann-Nicolaux Illig was born in Alsace in 1879; Corning Glass Works records say that he learned his trade at the Cristalleries de St. Louis. His engravings for Désiré-Christian & Sohn won an honorable mention at the Paris exposition of 1900. A historian of this exposition wrote:

> In their exhibits of architecture, the fine arts, the decorative arts, and...in the...industries, the Germans were shockingly good. It was clear to everyone that the German Empire...had chosen the exposition as a favoured area for international competition.[16]

The certificate awarded to Illig named him specifically; the name of his employer followed. This fact strongly implies that Illig had his Master's certificate (as does the character of his later life), though he was only twenty-one. Illig's youth earned him the envy of his older colleagues. The strained atmosphere that resulted may have predisposed him to emigrate.

In 1902, when H. W. Fritchie left Hawkes & Co. for Toledo, Nicholas Bach made a recruiting trip to his native Alsace-Lorraine looking for engravers for the company. He brought back John Illig.

Illig engraved for T. G. Hawkes & Co. until H. P. Sinclaire & Co. opened, when he moved to the new company. Hiram Rouse first mentioned him at the

491. John Illig won this award for engraving at the Paris Universal Exposition of 1900 when he was only twenty-one years old. *Coll. Mr. E. J. Illig*

Sinclaire company in July 1906. He stayed until about 1915,[17] specializing in deeply stone-engraved fruit and vegetable designs that were usually unpolished.

Reports that Illig also engraved for the Egginton company are probably correct, for Illig also operated a thriving home shop. His brother Joseph, who followed him to Corning, worked with him until about 1917, when poor health prompted him to move to California. This is the only home shop that we can document as having a wholesale outlet while its proprietor was a full-time factory craftsman. Illig's agent in 1910 was W. F. Upham of 66 Murray Street, New York City.[18] Giometti Brothers was another customer.

About 1915 Illig gave up factory work to devote full time to the John N. Illig company. It is the subject of Chapter 17.

SUMMARY

Dates: ca. 1902-ca. 1915
Address: 235 Pearl Street
Blanks: sources unknown
Trademark: none known
Product: presumably the engraved and cut-and-engraved fruit and flower designs that his company later made. These were usually stone engraved and unpolished.
Employees: Joseph Illig; others unknown. Agent: W. F. Upham of New York
Customers: probably the Egginton company; Giometti Brothers; wholesaler Upham; individuals

493. Vase engraved by John N. Illig on a broken and salvaged Sinclaire & Co. blank, 1905. Height, 19.3 cm. *Coll. Mrs. Mary Illig*

Emile Walter[19]

Handsome, blue-eyed Emile Walter was born in Soucht, Alsace-Lorraine, in 1865, and learned his trade at the St. Louis glassworks, about five miles away. He moved to Corning about 1902, sending for his family the following year. The date suggests that he too immigrated as the result of Nicholas Bach's recruiting trip for Hawkes & Co.

Mrs. Walter dressed their eight children alike on their trip over, so that she could find them easily on the ship. Her husband was late in meeting them, and they were held on Ellis Island until he arrived.

The Walters' first Corning home was a tiny house on Chemung Street; they moved about 1904 to 161 West Fourth Street. Two more children were born in Corning.

Walter fitted up an engraving shop in his barn. This was operating by July 23, 1904, when the Hawkes company Cash Book records they paid him "for work at home." Here he worked for himself, for private customers, and for other Corning companies. T. G. Hawkes & Co. was his only in-factory employer during his life in Corning. For them, his daughter says, he engraved a number of pieces that became famous in Corning. One was a vase on

492. Basket engraved by John Illig, ca. 1903. Length, 13 cm. *Coll. Mr. and Mrs. Fred Gillard*

which he engraved the figure of a woman. The only piece of his work that we have seen (Ill. 494) shows him to have been an excellent craftsman in the Alsatian style.

Once Walter overcame his initial homesickness, he was instrumental in bringing other Alsace-Lorrainers to Corning, and he became an American citizen, as did most of Corning's European immigrants. About 1912 he bought, and two daughters ran, a confectionery store at 39 West Market Street. This operated until about 1916, according to local directories. It is not clear whether or not he continued to engrave for the Hawkes company, to which the local directory indicates he returned full time about 1918. According to his passport, he visited France in the summer of 1927.

Walter retired from the Hawkes company about 1936. After his wife's death in 1942, four of his daughters took care of him. He lived with each of them three months of the year. In 1949 he visited a son in Chicago between two of these stays, and there he died at the age of eighty-three.

SUMMARY

Dates: 1904–ca. 1942
Address: 161 West Fourth Street

494. Pitcher engraved by Emile Walter at an unknown date between 1904 and 1936. Height, 25.6 cm. *Coll. Thomas V. Welch*

Blanks: sources unknown; many supplied by customers
Trademark: none known
Product: stone and copper-wheel engravings
Employees: none known
Customers: individuals and Corning companies

Anthony F. Keller
Anthony J. (Tony) Keller

Anthony F. Keller was born in Meistersdorf about 1870.[20] He learned his trade there, probably in a fine-glass company that the family owned. This had a retail shop in Warsaw, Poland. Keller left Bohemia rather than serve in the army, but the year is uncertain. His first American employer was in Houston; his son Anthony J. (Tony) was born in Corning in 1902.

Keller may have come to Corning with a relative, Jordan May, who was engraving for T. G. Hawkes & Co. by the spring of 1903, as established by the Hawkes Cash Book, in which entries on May 6 and 14 for "exps of engravers $45" indicated unusual

495. Tumblers engraved by Anthony F. Keller between ca. 1920 and ca. 1940. Height of taller tumbler, 9.7 cm. *Private collection*

activity in the engraving department. A Hawkes company payment on December 16, 1905, "for work at home" indicates Keller's home shop was operating at that date. He left the Hawkes company to engrave for H. P. Sinclair & Co. in November 1906, and was reported by Clyde Hauff as still there in 1916. His brother Henry also worked for the company; in 1908 they were joined by an uncle named Hauptmann, who was also an engraver, according to Hiram Rouse's notebooks. The Hauptmann and May families gave seven engravers to Corning, but we have found none of their work. They too were natives of Meistersdorf.

Keller trained his son Tony at home; from about 1922 through 1926 the two worked together at

496. This Pyrex brand glass trivet may have been engraved by Anthony F. Keller. Diam., 28.2 cm. *Coll. Mr. and Mrs. Thomas Dimitroff*

Hawkes. Keller also operated an engraving shop at 228 East Market Street for a number of years. It may have opened as early as 1920; it closed about 1932. During part of this time it was a full-time operation, though it was unlisted in Corning directories.

By 1937 Keller had moved to Gibson, just east of Corning, and listed himself as retired. Several Corningites have reported that the two Kellers engraved together here for several years, and that their customers included the Steuben Division of Corning Glass Works.

The senior Keller enjoyed engraving representations of buildings, and a piece that depicts the White House is known. We believe that the portrait of Corning Glass Works and its railroad siding shown in Illustration 496 may be his work.

We have found one stone-engraved oval tray of good quality that its owner attributes to the earlier shop. She reports that Tony Keller engraved it for the Steuben Division, but that it was withdrawn from the line because it did not sell well.

The older Keller's excellence as a teacher is attested by the high skill of his son, who in 1938 became one of the first in-factory engravers of the reorganized Steuben Glass. Steuben engraver Kenneth Van Etten remembers him as a "fine, fine" craftsman. Tony Keller's career was cut short by ill health. He gave up engraving for other employment at Steuben Glass about 1960, and retired a few years later.

SUMMARY

Dates: home shop 1905-ca. 1920 and ca. 1936-1940. Larger shop ca. 1920-ca. 1932

497. Candlestick and salad-dressing bottle engraved by Anthony F. or Anthony J. Keller, probably in the 1920s. Height of bottle, 17.4 cm. *Private collection*

Address: 79 West Fifth Street, 25 West Fifth Street, 376 Commerce Street before 1920; 228 East Market Street ca. 1920-ca. 1932; ca. 1936-40, Main Street, Gibson
Blanks: sources unknown; some supplied by customers
Trademark: none
Product: stone and copper-wheel engraving. Representations of buildings were a specialty of the older Keller.
Employees: Tony Keller worked in the Market Street shop and reportedly also in Gibson. Others, if any, unknown
Customers: individuals, Steuben Glass Works, Steuben Division of Corning Glass Works; others unknown

Nicolas Underiner (originally Undreiner)

Underiner was born in Lemberg, Lothringen, in October 1862,[21] and emigrated to Corning in 1903. His wife was a Lemberg woman; she and the children followed Nicolas to Corning in 1905. Her "Departure Certificate" called Underiner a factory worker rather than an engraver, perhaps because he was equally adept as a cutter (Ills. 460, 465–468).

Though Underiner's first Corning employer was probably T. G. Hawkes & Co., the Rouse notebooks show that he was engraving for H. P. Sinclaire & Co. by April 30, 1906. Hauff reported he was still at that company in 1916. Other reports that he was engraving for J. Hoare & Co. suggest that he was operating his own shop also. On May 7, 1910, Underiner became an American citizen.

From about 1920 into the 1930s, according to

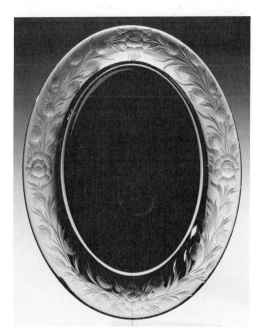

498. Picture frame engraved by Nicolas Underiner ca. 1930 in the polished rock-crystal style. Height, 18.6 cm. *Coll. Nicholas Williams*

directory listings, Underiner engraved in the factory of the Hunt company, whose engraved rock-crystal designs were its highest-quality line at this time. He also cut glass for the company from time to time, but he continued to work for other companies and for individuals in the barn behind his house at 317 Wall Street, as well.

Underiner engraved in his home shop and for the Hunt company virtually until his death, which came about 1932.

SUMMARY

Dates: ca. 1906-ca. 1932
Address: 317 Wall Street
Blanks: sources unknown; many supplied by customers
Trademark: none
Product: copper-wheel and stone-engraved glass
Employees: none
Customers: J. Hoare & Co. has been reported; others unknown

Edward Palme, Sr.

Edward Palme was born in 1867 in Kreibate, Bohemia.[22] Though "Palme" is part of the company names of glass firms in Zvečevo (Slavonia) and Stein-Schönau, Edward Palme learned his trade in Meistersdorf. Family memories are that he "finished" in Vienna; presumably this was the city in which he earned his Master's certificate.

Palme became an engraving teacher. He often said that he had "a record few men could equal," alluding to the five countries in which his children were born as his teaching took him as far east as Constantinople and perhaps to Egypt. Anton Libisch, who knew Palme in Europe, said that he

499. Pitcher, "Before the Storm," adapted from a painting and engraved by Edward Palme ca. 1900–1910. Height, 25.2 cm. *Coll. Mrs. Edward Palme, Jr.*

had held a supervisory position with the Lobmeyr company of Vienna at one time.

The Palme family sailed into New York harbor late in December of 1905.[23] Their first stop was Charleroi, Pennsylvania, where relatives were employed in a glass factory. There they stayed for two years before moving to Corning, where Palme's employer was T. G. Hawkes & Co.

By 1907 Palme was training Edward, Jr., in his home shop. This operated for many years at 264 West Second Street. Edward, Jr., worked in it until he opened his own engraving shop. The two men subcontracted for companies that had no engraving departments, and also engraved for private customers.

Palme, Sr., was the Hawkes company's leading engraver in the 1930s. He received the most difficult assignments, including the presidential seals on glass for the White House, according to Kenneth Van Etten of Steuben Glass, who worked at Hawkes's before World War II. Illustration 499 shows Palme's duplicate of *Before the Storm,* a pitcher that he engraved for Hawkes & Co. and copied for his wife.

In the late 1940s, when Palme was almost eighty, he moved to California in order to be near his daughter. He engraved there until his death in 1951.

500. Mr. and Mrs. Edward Palme, Sr., on the occasion of their 50th wedding anniversary dinner, ca. 1940. *Coll. Mrs. Edward Palme, Jr.*

SUMMARY

Dates: 1907-ca. 1947
Address: 264 West Second Street
Blanks: sources unknown; many supplied by customers
Trademark: none known
Product: chiefly copper-wheel engravings
Employees: Edward Palme, Jr., worked with his father until about 1925
Customers: individuals; Corning companies that lacked engraving departments

Ernest Kaulfuss[24]

Ernest Kaulfuss, born in Meistersdorf in 1878, learned to engrave glass there. We do not know who his early employers were. He came to Corning in 1903, and his wife and two children followed about two years later. Two more children were born in Corning.

Kaulfuss was working for H. P. Sinclaire & Co. by July 1905, according to Hiram Rouse. He stayed until the company closed, or shortly before (he was not listed in the 1927 directory but had returned in 1929). Then he engraved for T. G. Hawkes & Co. until 1948, the year of his death, judging from the Hawkes Cash Book entries.

During much of Kaulfuss's career in Corning he also worked in an engraving shop in his own house. His daughters remember particularly his work for the Hunt and Steuben companies, done at 48 Conhocton Street, his home from about 1908 to 1920. He also engraved there for individuals and reportedly for T. G. Hawkes & Co.

Ernest Kaulfuss is recalled by Clement Nitsche, who engraved with him at the Sinclaire company, as a "first-class engraver." Two younger brothers, Emil and Louis, were also engravers. Directory evidence indicates that Emil joined Ernest in Corning about 1908, after engraving for the Libbey company in Toledo. He engraved for them again later, probably in the 1920s, but returned permanently to Corning about 1929. Hawkes & Co. records show both brothers in the engraving department in the 1940s.

It is not certain that Louis Kaulfuss came to the United States, but he may be the "Louis" who wrote Emil Kaulfuss from Toledo in 1910, urging him to return and "bring Ernest with you."

Ernest Kaulfuss died in May, 1948. His work shows him to have been highly competent in both design and execution. The vase in Illustration 501 achieves an unusual, fairy-tale atmosphere. The considerable variation in Kaulfuss's engraving depth is largely responsible; heavier elements such as rocks and tree trunks are far deeper than the smaller figures on the vase. One of Kaulfuss's daughters remembers watching her father engrave service plates for the White House, but she is not sure

501. Vase designed and engraved by Ernest Kaulfuss. The blank, a broken and salvaged one from H. P. Sinclaire & Co., suggests a date not much later than 1928, when the company closed. Height, 27.2 cm. *Coll. Mrs. Dorothy Kaulfuss Coats*

whether the work was done at the Sinclaire or the Hawkes company.

SUMMARY

Dates: ca. 1908–ca. 1948

Address: 48 Conhocton Street until about 1920; it was at this address that Kaulfuss's home shop was most active. Some engraving also, after 1920, at 185 Chemung Street and 107 East Erie Avenue

Blanks: sources unknown; often supplied by customers

Trademark: none

Product: copper-wheel and stone engravings

Employees: none

503. Tumbler engraved on a Sinclaire & Co. *Plain* blank by Henry Keller in the early 1920s. Height, 10.4 cm. *Coll. Mrs. Edna Hanley Rotsell*

502. This goblet-shaped vase, designed and engraved in ornate Bohemian style by Ernest Kaulfuss, includes a series of storytelling vignettes in both the upper and lower register. Ca. 1908–20. *Coll. Mrs. Dorothy Kaulfuss Coats*

Henry Keller[25]

Henry Keller, born in Meistersdorf in 1878, was a younger brother of Anthony Keller. Directory information indicates Henry reached Corning about 1906. He worked first for T. G. Hawkes & Co., but Clyde Hauff says he had moved to the Sinclaire company by about 1909 or 1910. We assume that he worked in the family glass company until he emigrated.

Henry Keller and his wife had no children. They saw little of the Anthony Kellers.

Henry Keller engraved for the Sinclaire company through 1921, and perhaps until the company closed. He probably engraved at home from about 1909, when he bought his first house in Corning. About 1912 he built or bought a house at 376 Watauga Avenue. This had an extremely well-equipped shop in an extension at the back. Three of its lathes are still in use in the shops of Steuben Glass engravers.

Keller did a brisk business with Corningites, who bought sets of the Sinclaire company's plain table-wares and had him monogram or otherwise decorate them (Ill. 503). This private work continued throughout his life, though he worked increasingly for the Steuben Glass Works. A neighbor remembers Joseph Libisch's delivering blanks from Steuben. "Sometimes it would be a good deal more than Mr. Keller wanted," she says. Later, Steuben engraver Thomas Miller, another neighbor, brought engraving assignments to Keller.

Henry Keller was highly skilled.[26] Among the pieces he engraved for his wife were a cake plate with a hunting scene, a plate bearing a portrait of Abraham Lincoln, and a nude classical figure. These can be accounted for until the 1960s, when Keller's widow sold them or gave them away.

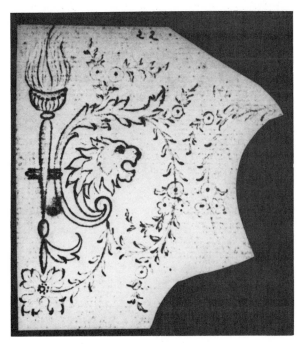

504. Henry Keller's pattern No. 22, one of many that he engraved in his home shop. *Coll. Max Roland Erlacher; Frederic Farrar photograph*

Engraving was not Keller's only means of livelihood. He was also a landlord whom former tenants remember with great affection. One treasures a piece that Keller engraved on a Steuben blank in honor of the birth of her first child.

Master engraver Max Erlacher bought about 40 of Keller's patterns during the 1960s. Many combine scrolls, stylized flowers, and foliage. Several include birds in flight; three have lion heads in profile as their principal motif.

Henry Keller worked until a few days before his death in 1950 at the age of seventy-two. Though his doctor had warned him to slow down, he preferred not to. Like many of his fellow Bohemians, he "really put in a day's work," to quote a Keller friend.

SUMMARY

Dates: ca. 1909-1950

Address: 337 East First Street before about 1912; thereafter, 376 Watauga Avenue

Blanks: many supplied by customers; a few from Steuben; other sources unknown

Trademark: none

Product: stone and copper-wheel engravings, including portraits

Employees: no regular employees. Several Bohemian engravers who lived with the Kellers when they first moved to Corning may have helped Keller while they lived with him.

Customers: individuals, Steuben Glass Works, Steuben Glass; others unknown

Hiram Rouse[27]

Hiram Rouse, born in 1883, was one of Corning's first native-born engravers. His teacher was Joseph Haselbauer, who taught him at T. G. Hawkes & Co. when the firm was preparing to introduce its Gravic glass. Rouse's training seems to have been completed in February 1901. His fellow apprentices were Wilmot Putnam and William Morse (Ill. 505), who studied with H. W. Fritchie at the same time, according to Hawkes Cash Book records. Though Haselbauer later taught other young Americans, Rouse is the only pupil whose name we know other than Haselbauer's own sons.

Rouse's engraving for the Hawkes and Sinclaire companies is singularly well documented. He recorded each of his engraving jobs from August 1902 through February 1910, illustrating many with sketches of their designs. He also entered the time each took, and the names of engravers with whom he worked.

Rouse's notebooks show that he was a highly competent craftsman. He did his share of drilling bobèches, engraving simple borders, and helping other engravers. Yet, by October 1902, he had engraved a cologne bottle that required 39 hours of work and a bowl that took 55. He noted a "raise" on October 14, the day he finished three engraved plates on which he had worked a total of 114½ hours.

By December 1903, Rouse had begun to engrave first examples of new designs. In 1904 he noted "Raise to $12 week ending Sat. Oct. 15." A single notation of "intaglio" suggests that Rouse may have been a cutter before he studied engraving: the Corning area used the word to describe pictorial cutting.

In July 1905, Rouse left the Hawkes company to work for H. P. Sinclaire & Co., as did several other

505. Bowl designed and engraved for T. G. Hawkes & Co. by William Morse in the 1920s. Diam., 20.3 cm. *Coll. Mrs. Sheldon Smith*

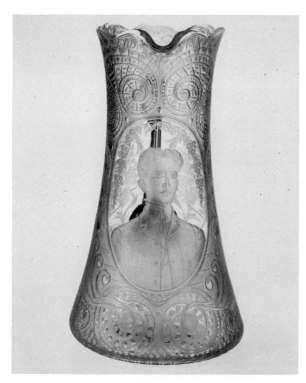

506. Pitcher designed and engraved by Hiram Rouse about 1905. Made for Rouse's wife, the pitcher features a self-portrait. Height, 24.5 cm. *Coll. Mrs. Jennifer Jacoby Dawson*

Hawkes engravers. Still others had preceded them. He stayed for about ten years.[28] As time went on he engraved many first examples of the simpler Sinclaire designs, and also originated several. Doing first examples required him to set the time that should be required for future production. Rouse was a conscientious workman. He regularly noted, apparently as records to emulate, any other engraver's ability to engrave a given design more quickly than he could.

A brief record of engraving for the Hunt company in 1910 shows that Rouse was working at home by this time. Hunt assignments seem to have required him to establish the engraving time required for a number of new designs.

Rouse gave up in-factory engraving about 1915. He became a salesman, and during the 1920s, the manager of a grocery store. He worked twice for Corning Glass Works: in 1919 in the finishing department, and in 1935 as smoother and hand-wheel grinder in the apparatus department, according to company records. During all this time, however, he also worked in an engraving shop to the side and rear of his house at 237 Chestnut Street. It is not clear when this was built. He engraved in the Hunt Glass Works and Fuller factories during the late 1920s and for Hunt in the 1930s, and reportedly also

subcontracted for the Hunt company in his home shop thereafter.

Rouse seems never to have worked full time in his shop; it operated chiefly during the evenings and over weekends. He did a great deal of stone and copper-wheel engraving for individuals. Blanks ranged from the cheapest pressed wares to the finest productions of modern Steuben Glass.[29] Most, of course, were supplied by his customers.

Rouse engraved in the Bohemian style. He is the only American-born Corning engraver presently known to have engraved a portrait.

Rouse continued to engrave in his home shop until a few years before his death, which occurred in 1970 when he was eighty-seven. His heirs gave his engraving shop and equipment to the Corning-Painted Post Historical Society, which hopes to set up the shop permanently, and offer demonstrations of engraving in it, within the next few years.

SUMMARY

Dates: 1910 or earlier–ca. 1967
Address: rear of 237 Chestnut Street
Blanks: usually supplied by customers
Trademark: none
Product: stone engraving and copper-wheel engraving. Rouse's own designs were in the Bohemian style.
Employees: none
Customers: Hunt Glass Works, the Fuller company; individuals

Joseph Libisch[30]

Master engraver Joseph Libisch's career spans the turning point between Corning's early engraver-designed work and the new conceptions of modern Steuben Glass's artist-designers. Joseph Libisch can be compared only with Joseph Haselbauer. His knowledge of the Corning engravers' specialties made him as fine a foreman as he was an engraver. It was a stroke of good fortune for Corning that Libisch arrived in town shortly after Haselbauer's death.

Joseph Libisch was born in Zvečevo, Slavonia (then in Austria-Hungary), in 1886. He was the eldest son of a glass cutter. Zvečevo was a hamlet in the wood; it had sprung up around the glass factory founded there by J. & L. Lobmeyr in 1842.[31] Here each glassblowing shop (team) had its religious statues, and the working day began with prayer. A miniature train ran into the forest to fetch wood for the furnaces.

Libisch began work at the age of twelve. His duties included starting the fires at 5:00 A.M. and preparing the shop for the glass craftsmen.

The Zvečevo cutting and engraving apprenticeships were known for their excellence—graduates could find work anywhere in Europe. One of Libisch's engraving teachers was Master engraver Edward Palme, who preceded him to Corning.

In 1904, when the Zvečevo factory went into bankruptcy,[32] Libisch engraved briefly in Essek. He returned to Zvečevo after the glassworks reopened under new management.[33] It was presumably at this time that Libisch completed his Master's studies at an unusually early age. About 1906 he moved to Vienna, where he engraved for the Wiener Werkstätte.

In April 1911, Libisch arrived in New York with his Masterpiece under his arm and the now-forgotten name of a glass expert in his pocket. The expert looked at Libisch's work and told him that he belonged in Corning, and Libisch took a train that very day, arriving in Corning with $17. He was at work at H. P. Sinclaire & Co. within three days of his arrival in the United States.

Libisch began to work at home very soon. H. P. Sinclaire would suggest or sketch a new design, which Libisch roughed out on his lathe. The two men then worked out refinements together, or altered the conception, until a first example was ready to be photographed and offered to retailers.

After his marriage to a Corning girl, Libisch and his wife lived with her parents, and his engraving shop was in their home at 109 West Market Street. In 1921 he left the Sinclaire company to devote full time to work in this shop.

In 1924 Libisch bought a house of his own on the southeast corner of Dodge and Pulteney streets. An extension at the back housed his engraving shop. Libisch designed a new lathe for it, but had to engrave with his old one during the 13 months that he waited for the new one to come from Europe.

Joseph Libisch was a lover of the outdoors. His engravings of birds and animals have probably never been surpassed. His drawing was impeccable, his designs outstanding, and his hand sure. Though Corning companies and the engravers themselves cleaned up the outlines of engravings as a matter of course, a cutter who did this work for the modern Steuben Glass, Louis Lentricchia, recalls that Libisch's work rarely required cleaning up.

Libisch's devotion to his craft was complete. "His whole life was glass engraving," his daughter says. But the tensions of fine engraving are great, for as an elaborate piece approaches completion, it is increasingly likely to crack. Libisch's favorite relaxations were hunting and fishing. Occasionally he would steal half a Sunday to visit his favorite fishing spot, where his luck was so good that other anglers called it "Joe's hole."

As the years passed, Steuben's engraving took up an ever increasing share of Libisch's time, though he worked for other companies and individuals. In

507.   Two plates in H. P. Sinclaire & Co. designs engraved by Joseph Libisch in the 1930s. Larger plate, diam., 21.5 cm. *Coll. Mrs. Helen Libisch Elmer*

addition to engraving for Steuben, he assigned its work to Henry Keller, Adolf Kretschmann, Clem Nitsche, and other Corning engravers, sometimes distributing the blanks in baskets. Thus, he was in effect foreman of a citywide engraving shop.

During the Great Depression, when there was little work, Libisch turned his skilled hands to renovations of his house and to engravings for his family. He had enjoyed selecting pieces of colored glass at the Sinclaire factory; now he engraved these and also uncolored Steuben pieces. Characteristically, he often elected to engrave birds and animals. Libisch made plaster casts of many of his smaller pieces. His daughter has kept them all.

When Steuben set up an in-factory engraving department and training program in 1937, Libisch closed his shop. As engraving foreman, he continued for some years to distribute glass to Corning's home shops. He also did some teaching of Steuben apprentices after the program's first years, according to Thomas Miller.

The first examples of most elaborate Steuben Glass engravings from 1933 to 1956, when Libisch retired, were his work, according to the late Robert Leavy, former president of Steuben Glass. These included the *Gazelle Bowl, Zodiac Bowl,* and the *Merry-Go-Round Bowl* (see Chapter 20). Libisch's last presentation piece was probably the *Papal Cup* (Ill. 738).

Libisch retired in 1956 at the customary age of seventy. He was a genial and familiar figure in Corning during his retirement years, but he engraved no more. His house and shop were razed as part of Corning's Urban Renewal Program after the flood of June 1972.

SUMMARY

Dates: ca. 1911-1937
Address: 109 West Market Street; after 1924, 102 West Pulteney Street
Blanks: chiefly supplied by customers; those for his own use, from Steuben Glass (or the Steuben Division of Corning Glass Works) and H. P. Sinclaire & Co.
Trademark: none
Product: virtually all copper-wheel engravings; those for his own use chiefly depict birds and animals.

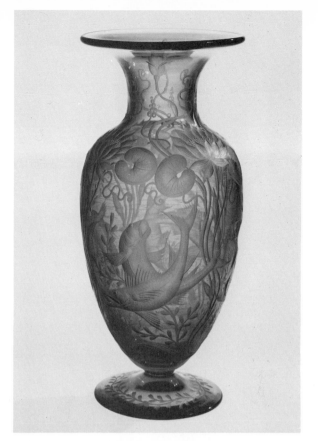

508. Vase, *Kingfishers,* adapted from a picture in a children's book and engraved by Joseph Libisch. in 1931. *Coll. Mrs. Helen Libisch Elmer*

509. Vase depicting game fish, designed and engraved by Joseph Libisch on a Colonia blue vase made by H. P. Sinclaire & Co. Engraved ca. 1930–37. Height, 27.9 cm. *Coll. Mrs. Estelle Sinclaire Farrar*

Employees: none
Customers: Hunt Glass Works, Steuben Division of Corning Glass Works, and the later Steuben Glass; individuals

Adolf Kretschmann[34]

Adolf Kretschmann was born in Meistersdorf in 1871, and learned to engrave in Bohemia. The neighboring towns of Haida and Stein Schönau had glass technical schools that offered engraving courses, and it may be that he studied at one of them.

Like many other Bohemians, Kretschmann emigrated to avoid military service. The year may have been 1889, when the annual number of recruits was increased. He was engraving for the Webb company in England in 1893 when word came from Fridoli Kretschmann in Corning that engravers were needed. He traveled to the United States with Joseph Nitsche.

Kretschmann's first destination was Chicago, where he demonstrated engraving for the Libbey company at the World's Columbian Exposition. We may assume that he saw J. Hoare & Co.'s exhibit, which included engraving and rock-crystal work by

Fridoli Kretschmann, probably a kinsman. Adolf may also have met the three young Corning cutters who, the Corning *Daily Journal* reported on June 12, 1893, were "at work upon the World's Fair grounds." Kretschmann enjoyed this work, and later often spoke of it to his children.

Kretschmann's first Corning employer seems to have been the Hawkes company. Later he worked for H. P. Sinclaire & Co., probably until it closed, and then returned to Hawkes. According to his daughter, he was laid off about 1936 because an old knee injury made climbing the stairs difficult for him. Though Kretschmann was about sixty-five, he was far from ready to retire. He engraved for a year or two after this date in Middletown, New York.

During many of his years of factory work Kretschmann also operated an engraving shop at 345 West First Street. At first his lathe was in his bedroom; later he fitted out a shop over his garage. This was his only source of income during the two years or more during the 1920s when his knee injury kept him at home. His daughter remembers a Mr. Dorflinger bringing baskets of work for him from White Mills.[35] He also engraved for the Hunt and Hoare companies and J. F. Haselbauer & Sons during various periods.

510 & 511. *Left:* Some of the sample goblets that Adolf Kretschmann designed and engraved for use in his home shop. Height of tallest in 510, 17.3 cm.; in 511, 15.8 cm. Ca. 1920–40. *Coll. Mrs. Esther Kretschmann Patch*

Kretschmann did a great deal of engraving for individuals, as well. For private customers he made a dozen or more samples of stemware in his own designs. Occasionally he found time to buy undecorated seconds from Steuben Glass Works or Corning Glass Works, Steuben Division, and eliminate their imperfections as he engraved them.

Adolf Kretschmann worked at his lathe until he had passed the eighty-year mark, but during his last years he spent more and more time in his garden. He also kept chickens, and enjoyed selling their eggs. He died in 1955 at the age of eighty-four.

SUMMARY

Dates: 1918 or earlier–ca. 1951
Address: 345 West First Street
Blanks: subcontracting on blanks supplied by customers; engraving for himself, often on Steuben seconds; other sources unknown
Product: stone and copper-wheel engravings; much stemware for individual customers
Employees: none
Customers: C. Dorflinger & Sons, the Hunt, Hoare, and Steuben companies; and individual customers

Peter Kaulfuss[36]

Engraver Peter Kaulfuss was born in Europe in 1841, and came to the United States as a trained young engraver. His preferred subjects strongly suggest that he was Bohemian. Peter was unrelated to Ernest and Emil Kaulfuss.

Peter settled in Saratoga, New York, where he operated an engraving shop for many years. He engraved forest scenes, deer, and buildings on crystal and flashed ruby wine jugs, pitchers, and vases, but also engraved most of the souvenir pieces that visitors to Saratoga took home with them.

Kaulfuss family tradition, supported by some documentary evidence, says that Peter set up his own booth at many major fairs and expositions. His grandson's belief that Peter's work won a prize at a

512. Windmill engraving by Adolf Kretschmann on a tumbler, ca. 1920–40. Height, 9.6 cm. *Coll. Mrs. Esther Kretschmann Patch*

Paris exposition suggests that his shop may have engraved for the Hawkes company in 1889.

Kaulfuss moved to Corning late in life. Directories show that the engraving shop Corning remembers on Steuben St. operated from about 1919 to 1926. Clyde Hauff recalls Peter Kaulfuss as an H. P. Sinclaire & Co. engraver from about 1913 to 1915. His last customers for wares engraved in his home shop were Corning Glass Works and Tiffany & Co. Kaulfuss died in 1927.

SUMMARY

Dates: ca. 1919-26
Address: 160 Steuben Street
Blanks: sources unknown; probably supplied by customers
Trademark: probably none
Product: We know only that Kaulfuss did custom engraving for individuals.
Employees: probably none
Customers: individuals, Corning Glass Works, Tiffany & Co., others unknown

Wilmot Putnam[37]

Wilmot Putnam was born in 1881 in the town of Dix, New York, not far from Corning. He was a first-generation glass craftsman. Putnam was a close friend of William Morse, later a well-known Hawkes & Co. engraver, and it was Morse who interested him in learning the craft. The two young men learned together from H. W. Fritchie in the Hawkes factory while Joseph Haselbauer taught Hiram Rouse. Cash Book records indicate that the three probably completed their training in February 1901. Except for Haselbauer's sons, they were the first of Corning's American-born engravers.

513. Wilmot Putnam, *center,* engraving at J. Hoare & Co.'s Bridge St. plant, 1915-20. The other engravers are George McQuade, *left,* and Joseph Sidot, *right.* The man on the stepladder is unidentified. *Coll. Wilmot Putnam, Jr., copy print by Frederic Farrar*

Putnam's later employers included J. Hoare & Co. when its factory was on Bridge Street (1915-20) and H. P. Sinclaire & Co. He worked for the Sinclaire firm until it closed in 1928. Returning to the Hawkes company, he stayed until its 1962 closing; his picture appeared in its final publicity folder.[38]

Putnam taught engraving at both the Hawkes and Sinclaire companies, beginning early in the century. After his retirement he put down a few notes about his career and about Corning's glass industry. "At one time," he wrote, "I had about fifteen young men trying to learn it [engraving] at Hawkes." Most of his pupils were unable to master the craft. Exceptions were Earl Sturtevant, who deserted Corning to engrave in Texas, and Aiden Johnson.[39]

Putnam's father, a carpenter, built his son's engraving shop for him in the early 1920s; the young man had long engraved at home (Ills. 514-515). The shop, in his house at 202 Baker Street, had one foot-powered lathe. In 1940 Putnam moved the shop to the second floor of his garage, where his son installed an electric line and a motor.

Putnam worked at home for his employers, for the Hunt company, and for individuals. During the Depression years, when Hawkes & Co. operated at half time or less, private customers were a welcome source of extra income. Like other home shops, Putnam's was especially busy as Christmas approached. He engraved a number of fine copper-wheel pieces for his own use, but sold these to a Rochester dealer after his retirement. The pitcher in Illustration 516, however, shows his designing skill. He occasionally did cutting also.

Putnam's home shop enabled him to continue engraving after Hawkes & Co. closed in 1962. He was then eighty-one. For about four years the Bacalles Glass Shop in Corning was his most important customer. His work was chiefly stone engraving on blanks that the shop provided. Blanks that Putnam used for individual customers came from remaining Hawkes stock or from an Elmira hardware store.

Putnam died in 1969. His shop still stands, and his son has all his father's equipment.

SUMMARY

Dates: ca. 1920-1969
Address: 202 Baker Street
Blanks: most supplied by customers; after 1962, from remaining Hawkes & Co. stock also, and from an Elmira hardware store
Trademark: none
Product: stone and copper-wheel engravings
Employees: none
Customers: additional work for his in-factory employers (the Sinclaire, Hawkes, and Hoare companies); the Hunt Glass Works; Bacalles Glass Shop; individuals; the Fuller Cut Glass Co.

514 & 515. *Above and right:* Three of many paper patterns that Wilmot Putnam used for the engraving he did at home. *Coll. Wilmot Putnam, Jr.; Frederic Farrar photograph*

516. Pitcher designed and engraved by Wilmot Putnam, ca. 1910–20. Height, 11.6 cm. *Coll. Wilmot Putnam, Jr.*

Nathaniel O. Phelps[40]
(See also Chapter 19.)

Phelps was born in Gouverneur, New York, in 1890. He learned his trade at T. G. Hawkes & Co., beginning in 1905. Presumably his teacher was H. W. Fritchie. Phelps engraved for H. P. Sinclaire & Co. between about 1910 and 1916, according to Clyde Hauff, then served in World War I. During Phelps's years with the Sinclaire company, Joseph Libisch was the leading engraver, and Phelps credited Libisch with teaching him a great deal more about the craft. Phelps met and married his wife at the Sinclaire company.

It is not clear whether Phelps returned to the Sinclaire company after World War I, though we know that Mrs. Phelps worked there in the early 1920s.[41]

Phelps engraved at home for the Hunt and Steuben companies from about 1921 to 1927. In 1928, he and his family moved to Rochester. The company that he founded there is discussed in Chapter 19.

SUMMARY:

Dates: ca. 1921-27
Address: 315 East Market Street
Blanks: supplied by the companies for which he worked
Trademark: none
Product: stone and copper-wheel engraving
Employees: none
Customers: the Hunt Glass Works and Steuben Division of Corning Glass Works

Charles May

Engraver Charles May is the last proprietor whom we can document in the cutting shop at 63 East Erie Avenue. He was listed there only in the 1925 Corning directory. At this time he was living with Gerald May. We assume, therefore, that Charles was a member of the May family of engravers from the Meistersdorf area,[42] and a relative of Gerald's. The Mays were in Corning by 1903, when engraver Jordan May's name appeared in the Hawkes & Co. Cash Book.

The Mays were all copper-wheel engravers. Their names are occasionally mentioned in Corning as those of men who "helped out" in Corning's home engraving shops.

We have found no May engraving. Charles's absence from Corning directories by 1927 suggests that he had left town.

SUMMARY

Dates: ca. 1924-ca. 1926
Address: 63 East Erie Avenue
We have found no information about *blanks, trademark, product, employees,* or *customers.*

Harry Goodman[43]

Harry Goodman was born in Latvia; he came to this country about 1900, at the age of seventeen. Goodman was an engraver of jewelry and silverware. Since seventeen was the usual age for finishing a journeyman's apprenticeship, we assume that he learned his trade in Europe.

Goodman first joined sisters, who lived in New York, then worked at his trade in Coudersport and Honesdale, both in Pennsylvania. Honesdale was in the glass-cutting area that surrounded the White Mills factory of C. Dorflinger & Sons, and so Goodman could hardly have escaped becoming aware of fine American cut glass.

Harry Goodman was a highly skilled engraver when he moved to Corning about 1919 and opened his own jewelry store at 26 West Market Street. In the 1925, 1927, and 1931 Corning directories, he listed himself as a manufacturer of cut glass in addition to his listings as a jeweler. However, the only glass production that his daughter recalls was of jewelry. Customers brought bits of fine crystal or art glass to him and Goodman fashioned engraved glass hearts from them, adding to each a gold enclosing wire and hanging loop.

Goodman's interest in cut and engraved glass seems to have ended in the early 1930s. Corning remembers him well, but as a jeweler only. He died about 1961, when he was in his late seventies.

SUMMARY

Dates: ca. 1925-ca. 1928 and also around 1931
Address: 26 West Market Street
Blanks: Goodman used no blanks as such.
Trademark: none
Product: Goodman fashioned engraved jewelry from bits of crystal and colored glass. His listing as a manufacturer of *cut* glass, however, suggests that he also marketed glass in his own designs cut in Corning's home shops.
Employees: none known
Customers: retail customers for his engraved jewelry

Joseph Hahne[44]

Joseph Hahne of Meistersdorf came to Corning just after World War I. He was a cousin of engraver Frank Konigstein, and hence was related also to the Keller and Hauptmann families, all of whom were engraving in Corning when he arrived, according to local directories. Hahne was a man of mature years when he began work for T. G. Hawkes & Co., his only Corning employer.

517. Decanter and matching glasses designed and stone engraved by Joseph Hahne, ca. 1930–40. Height of decanter, 21.9 cm. *Coll. Mrs. Matthew W. Cammen*

Hahne married a Corning woman in the 1930s, when both were middle-aged. He had boarded in her home since his arrival in town, and after marriage they continued to live at 60 West Third Street, where his engraving shop was located in the attic.

Though Hahne may also have been an engraving subcontractor, the few pieces of his glass that we have found were stone engraved for private customers, on inexpensive blanks in the shapes of the 1930s. We cannot identify their manufacturer.

Hahne's shop seems to have operated until his death, which came about 1944. He had left Hawkes & Co. only a short time earlier.

SUMMARY

Dates: ca. 1930-ca. 1944
Address: 60 West Third Street
Blanks: sources unknown
Trademark: none
Product: Only stone engravings have been identified.
Employees: none
Customers: individuals

518. T. G. Hawkes & Co. *Gravic Iris* wineglass. Originally copper-wheel engraved, the design was later stone engraved and finally cut, with engraved detail added as in this example. Aiden Johnson executed Hawkes engravings of all these types. Height, 13.3 cm. *Coll. The Corning Museum of Glass*

Aiden Johnson[45]

Johnson was born in Corning in 1889. He followed the example of his brother Fred (see Chapter 19; Fred eventually became secretary of Ideal Cut Glass Co.) by learning to cut glass at T. G. Hawkes & Co. However, he cut glass only briefly before learning to engrave from Wilmot Putnam, and switching permanently from the cutting frame to the engraver's lathe.

519. A postcard of the 1960s shows Aiden Johnson engraving for the Bacalles Glass Shop in Corning. *Coll. Wilmot Putnam, Jr.; Frederic Farrar copy photo*

Johnson worked for the Hawkes company for more than 50 years of his 60-year career—during World War I he worked for the Hunt Glass Works. He was one of the many Corning craftsmen who had a second trade. With Sam Hawkes's blessing, he took an examination that qualified him to be a substitute mail clerk, and he worked in the post office when the fine-glass business was in the doldrums.

An accomplished violinist, Johnson was a charter member of the Corning Philharmonic Society. He played also in Corning's Methodist and Grace Methodist Episcopal churches. As a hobby, he shared Corning's passion for fishing.

Johnson fitted out a shop over his garage at 24 West Sixth Street, and engraved there for a number of years; later he moved his shop equipment to the basement of his house. It remains there just as he left it. The Hunt company was one of his home shop customers.

Johnson was seventy-three when Hawkes & Co. closed in 1962, but he continued to engrave at home almost until his death, which came in 1969. During those last years the Bacalles Glass Shop of Corning was his most important customer, but he engraved occasionally for individuals. Though he did stone and copper-wheel engravings for Bacalles (Ill. 519), he infinitely preferred copper-wheel work, and deplored the recent habit of calling pictorial cutting "engraving."

Johnson's favorites among the pieces he made for his wife were a deeply engraved eight-inch bowl in his own wild-rose design, and a wineglass engraved with several fruits. He also executed his own designs for the Bacalles Glass Shop.

SUMMARY

Dates: ca. 1930–ca. 1968
Address: 24 West Sixth Street
Blanks: most supplied by customers
Trademark: none
Product: stone and copper-wheel engravings. Some of his designs incorporate birds, grapes, and wild roses.
Employees: none
Customers: the Hunt Glass Works; Bacalles Glass Shop; individuals

Edward Hauptmann
Frank Konigstein

Frank Konigstein and his great-uncle, Edward Hauptmann, were copper-wheel engravers from Meistersdorf.[46] Henry Keller, Hauptmann's nephew, brought him to Corning to work at H. P. Sinclaire & Co. in 1908, according to Rouse's notes. Konigstein reportedly reached the United States in 1911,[47] when he was seventeen years old. He and Hauptmann worked together in Brooklyn at this time.

Konigstein first appeared in Corning directories in 1915/16, when he lived with engraver Joseph Oveszny. He was probably already working for H. P. Sinclaire & Co., where, his daughter reports, he helped engrave a punch bowl for the White House. This may date from 1916. (See Chapter 14.) Konigstein married in Corning, and his daughter was born there in 1918. In 1921, the directory indicates, he was still engraving for the Sinclaire company, but a few years later he left the industry for higher pay as a machinist. He worked first for Corning's Hood Foundry and then for Ingersoll-Rand. From time to time, however, he helped out in Corning engraving shops.

About 1929 Konigstein and Hauptmann moved to a farm on Rose Hill, outside Corning. The farmhouse had a room at the back where the two men engraved for a number of years. We do not know when it closed. During this period both men reportedly also engraved during busy seasons in the shops of Henry Keller and Joseph Oveszny.

SUMMARY

Dates: ca. 1930–?
Address: Rose Hill, R.D. 2
Blanks: makers unknown, but it is believed blanks were bought from the Hawkes company.
Trademark: none
Product: copper-wheel and stone engraving
Employees: none
Customers: unknown

Edward Palme, Jr.

Edward Palme, Jr., was born in Serbia in 1893,[48] the son of a Master engraver who brought his family to Corning early in 1906 (see Edward Palme, Sr.). Young Edward began to study with his father in 1907 at the traditional age of fourteen.[49] His first employer was H. P. Sinclair & Co. There, he felt, his engraving benefited from the high quality of the company's work.

During World War I Palme saw service in England. When he returned, he worked with his father both in the senior Palme's home shop and at T. G. Hawkes & Co. About 1932 he opened his own shop at 91 West Third Street. Joseph Libisch's recommendation brought him work from the Steuben Division, Corning Glass Works, though he continued to work in the Hawkes factory.

Palme left T. G. Hawkes & Co. to work as a copper-wheel engraver for Steuben in 1936, and for four years continued to work at home for the company.[50] He later engraved in the factory, from which he retired in April 1960. He continued to engrave at home until 1966, when he suffered a stroke. Palme died in 1968.

SUMMARY

Dates: ca. 1932–1966
Address: 91 West Third Street
Blanks: chiefly supplied by customers
Trademark: none
Product: stone and copper-wheel engravings
Employees: none
Customers: individuals, Steuben Division, Corning Glass Works

Joseph Oveszny[51]
(also spelled Ovescny and Ovesney in Corning records)

Joseph Oveszny's engraving shop is one of the best-remembered in Corning, yet we know little about its proprietor's life there. Together with the Hauptmanns and the Mays, to whom his wife may have been related, Oveszny was among the nomadic minority of Corning's engravers.

Joseph was born in Hungary in 1884. He learned to engrave glass in Bohemia, where he met and married his wife, but worked chiefly in Hungary before emigrating to the United States.[52] He reached

520. Blue-stained bowl designed and engraved by Joseph Oveszny, ca. 1940. Diam., 21.3 cm. *Coll. Mr. and Mrs. Lawrence B. Hausheer*

Corning about 1914, according to local directories; we do not know whether he had earlier American employers.

The Sinclaire company was Oveszny's first documented employer. He began work there after 1916, and was still with the company in 1921, but he was absent from Corning directories in 1923 and 1927. In 1925 he was again working for Sinclaire & Co.; by 1929 he was working for Corning Glass Works. He left Corning again about 1933. This is the period, we believe, when he was employed by the Westmoreland Glass Company, which was introducing a line of colored engraved glass. Henry Hauptmann was with him in Jeannette, Pennsylvania.

After Oveszny returned to Corning about 1935, he operated an engraving shop in his house at 24 East Fourth Street; directories give the address as both his place of business and his residence. In 1939 he became an engraver for Steuben Glass. Except for a few months in 1943, when he worked in the bulb-finishing department of Corning Glass Works, Oveszny stayed until 1949, according to company records. Thereafter he seems to have engraved at home until his death in 1955.

A great many individuals bought stone-engraved glass from Joe Oveszny. Among extant pieces is some cameo work on the Sinclaire company's hard, opaque Nubian black glass. Oveszny's employment at the company was during the period when it was experimenting with this difficult glass, and it may be that cameo engraving, rare in Corning, was his special task at the company.

In his home shop Oveszny also stone-engraved stained pieces, possibly from the Westmoreland company, and crystal. Thomas Miller, retired Steuben Glass engraver, remembers delivering Steuben jobs to Oveszny. These were presumably copper-wheel designs. Oveszny also made some floral-cut pieces, the petals of which were executed with a gang-cut wheel. This evidence that the Oveszny shop had a cutting frame as well as a lathe or lathes gives weight to Corning reports that other craftsmen helped out at 25 East Fourth Street from time to time.

SUMMARY

Dates: ca. 1935-ca. 1955
Address: 24 East Fourth Street
Blanks: some bought from Hunt Glass Works, according to Lawrence Hausheer of the Corning Glass Works; stained pieces perhaps of Westmoreland manufacture; some Sinclaire & Co. colored wares
Trademark: none
Product: stone and copper-wheel engravings, including cameo work; floral cutting
Employees: Other Bohemian engravers helped out from time to time.
Customers: a great deal of work for individuals; Steuben Glass

9
Small Companies and Home Shops in Corning and Adjacent Villages

In 1894 Frank Wilson & Sons began to expand the goals of Corning's cutting industry beyond those of John Hoare and Thomas Hawkes. These were simple: to make the best cut glass in the world and, by extension, to establish Corning as the Crystal City. Corning's engravers long shared these aims. (See Chapter 8.) Corning's small cutting shops and companies diverged from them. The Wilson Company, for example, was a subcontractor for a New York importing firm.

During the prosperous years of the early twentieth century Corning's cut-glass business flourished as never before and never since. In response to avid buying of cut glass, many little companies sprang up. Though Corning's fine cut glass, retailed chiefly by jewelers, remained almost as expensive as the diamonds it resembled, smaller companies began to produce a cheaper grade of cut glass—meant for "the middle class of people," to quote Hawkes. They, he added, "have a great deal more money than they did 20 years ago, and they buy more cut glass."[2] They bought much of it from department stores.

Many of Corning's small firms aimed to tap this vast market. For a few euphoric years sales seemed to be on an endless upward course, and Corning's pool of skilled craftsmen seemed to promise quick cut-glass profits to the daring entrepreneur. The owners of the new cut-glass companies, however, might be businessmen who knew nothing about the business. They invested a few thousand dollars—or even a few hundred—and hired a competent cutter as manager. Several went out of business almost as quickly as they had begun. Companies like these produced a flood of glass that does not bear comparison with the finer work of Corning's premier manufacturers. Some of it, though, equals the middle-grade work that Hoare, Hawkes, and Sin-

claire, for example, were forced by competition to manufacture.

Corning also had more professional small cutting shops; earlier chapters have described the Hawkes and Hoare annexes. In addition, there were subcontractors and repair shops by 1905, most of them headed by expert cutters. Branch shops of out-of-town companies had begun to open about 1903. Home cutting shops were still few, but increased in later years. Occasionally these became small companies. A substantial percentage of these little enterprises operated almost sub rosa, unlisted in Corning directories. Because we have chanced upon them in trade journals, newspaper stories, and business records, we assume that others will come to light in the future.

The owners of at least five commercial buildings in Corning fitted up parts of them as cutting shops. The known ones were 134–136 West Tioga Avenue, the Corning Building Co. warehouse on the southeast corner of Tioga Avenue and Cedar Street, 227 East Market Street, an unnumbered frame building on the north side of West Market Street, and the Heermans & Lawrence building at 63 East Erie Avenue. The Heermans & Lawrence building is the best documented; its second-floor cutting shop housed six cutting companies between 1902 and 1913. In 1925 an engraving shop operated there; we have no information about possible cutting-shop tenants during the intervening twelve years.

Earlier chapters have shown that Corning Glass Works blanks were unavailable to these companies. The reasons that Corning was "peppered with little cutting shops," to use a local expression, were doubtless those of James Sebring, quoted in Chapter 3. Briefly recapitulated, these were Corning's reputation in the trade for fine-glass, the lack of unionization, and the availability of trained cutters. The second of these was crucial to out-of-town companies. The supply of craftsmen was more important to local cutting-firm proprietors. Both groups benefited from Corning's reputation. The Hoare and Hawkes companies, together with Corning Glass Works, were responsible for all three.

The work that home shops and small companies did could include subcontracting, repairs, retail cutting for private customers, matching broken pieces of sets made elsewhere, and the manufacture of their own lines of cut glass. Yet some were nudged by circumstances into specializing in one line of work. Cutter Michael Moore, for example, operated an acid-etching shop at his home at 233 Baker Street from perhaps 1910 to about 1920.[3]

Home cutting shops often had two or more cutting frames, and perhaps a polishing frame, so that the owner could move from one operation to the next with a minimum of wheel-changing. When business was brisk, he hired a helper or two. Most home shops were part-time operations; their wheels hummed in the evening or on Sundays because their owners had other jobs. During slow periods in the industry they might work full time at home. Cutting glass at home was typically a source of extra income; it also permitted the craftsman to continue working after his formal retirement.

Most of the cutting was of excellent quality. Hand polishing was the rule. On the other hand, the home cutter usually did not, and perhaps could not, buy wholesale quantities of fine blanks. Often the retail customer provided his own blanks, which ranged from the cheapest of pressed wares to pieces of free-blown crystal. Single blanks of fine quality might be bought from an employer. Undecorated glass was also available from Steuben from about 1904 to 1933, and from H. P. Sinclaire & Co. from 1920 to 1927.[4] Pyrex brand glassware, extremely popular in floral cuttings, was readily available, as was inexpensive glass from local hardware stores. These pieces the home cutter regularly used for his samples.

Branch shops used their Corning premises as insurance against labor trouble at the parent plant as well as for increased production. At least one worked for Corning's giants and also made its own line of cut glass. They seem to have employed no designers, and probably ordered no blanks. Trademarks, if any, would have been those of the parent firm.

Cutting subcontractors specialized in their customers' simpler and more popular designs. In the absence of evidence that they had acid rooms, we assume they delivered their work roughed and perhaps smoothed, but not polished. Deliveries were weekly; payment was immediate, according to the Hawkes Cash Book. The subcontractor might employ several men; he hired more during busy seasons.

It is possible that contract cutting for large department stores or wholesalers was a source of income for more small companies than we yet know about.

Repair work was accepted by every Corning cutting company, large and small. Former cutter Gerald Davis recalls being summoned back to the industry by Corning Glass Works's Steuben Division about 1930. Steuben needed him to help repair blue-cased candelabra made by H. P. Sinclaire & Co. Only Elmira Cut Glass can be documented as specializing in repairs, and only during its last years.

The list below excludes, so far as possible, cutters who worked extra hours at home for their employers only during busy seasons. This seems to have become common practice during the 1920s.

* * *

Frank Wilson & Sons

This little company has great historical interest. It was the first to open in Corning after the Hoare and Hawkes companies; it is the only one known to have been run by union men, and it was the earliest local cut-glass contractor.

English-born C. Frank Wilson came to the United States in 1872.[5] His large family included at least three sons who became cutters. Robert and Joseph, born in England in 1864 and 1867, were associated with their father in Frank Wilson & Sons, according to the Corning Directory.

C. Frank Wilson cut glass in Cambridge, Massachusetts; Monaca, Pennsylvania; and in Connecticut

521. Low bowl cut by Frank Wilson & Sons. Diam., 20.5 cm. *Coll. The Corning Museum of Glass*

522. Wilson & Sons cologne bottle. Height, 19.3 cm. *Coll. The Peddler's Horn, Corning*

before moving to Corning in 1880. He was one of the earliest cutters of the Hawkes Rich Cut Glass Works. A February 17, 1887, newspaper story reporting Robert Wilson's testimony for the prosecution in a hearing when Hawkes strikers were charged with riot suggests that Robert also was then working for Hawkes.

Joseph Wilson left Corning in 1888. The whole family was unlisted in the 1891 Corning Directory, but Frank had returned by 1893.

The AFGWU *Proceedings* of 1896 printed letters from, to, and about Joseph Wilson. Their subject was strike benefits that he claimed and eventually received. The exchange shows that he and Robert were members of Local Union 28, founded by cutters at the Libbey company in Toledo in September 1888.[6] Joseph was a working foreman or working superintendent for Libbey. He returned to Corning after a strike in 1894.

"If any member of LU No. 28 deserved benefits for that strike, I did," he wrote, "and I think you know so, too." He left Toledo "to start business for [himself]," he added.

Though Joseph Wilson used his father's name for the Corning company (as was customary), he himself was clearly its moving spirit. It employed "a couple of men" at first, but in 1896 the Wilsons were

alone. Joseph wrote: "Part of the time I...acted as salesman." It has been reported that the Wilsons had eight cutting frames, and that customers included a number of eastern retailers of quality glass.

When Frank Wilson & Sons opened, however, it seems to have had only one customer. Thomas Hawkes testified in 1904 that "Wilson wasn't in business really for himself, he was a representative of Bawo and Dotte[r]."[7] He added:

> I knew Wilson; he used to work for me....He was hired by a large importing house in New York who were doing an extensive business and they had Wilson start a little shop here. They bought foreign blanks for the express purpose of having them cut in Corning because Corning...had an enviable reputation in Cut Glass.[8]

The blanks, Hawkes said, were Baccarat's.

The fact that Bawo & Dotter were importers doubtless explains the English style of known Wilson cuttings. We assume that contract work for Bawo & Dotter had ended or decreased by 1896, when the Wilsons worked alone and Joseph became a part-time salesman. He wrote the union in April 1896: "Nor do I know when I may have to go to work for others."

Frank Wilson & Sons closed about 1897. Joseph moved to Brooklyn, where he became a principal of the Becker & Wilson cutting company.[9] Frank Wilson joined Joseph about 1901, according to information in the *Daily Journal* on March 14 of the following year. Directories indicate that he returned to Corning about 1903, and cut glass there until his retirement about 1912. He died around 1920.

SUMMARY

Dates: late 1894-ca. 1897
Address: 19 Sly Avenue, the address of C. Frank Wilson
Blanks: from Baccarat, supplied by Bawo & Dotter; others unknown
Trademark: none known
Product: a full line of glass, much or all of it in European style during the affiliation with Bawo & Dotter
Employees: two unknown cutters employed in 1894; thereafter, C. Frank, Robert, and Joseph Wilson only
Customers: Bawo & Dotter only, 1894-95. We do not know whether other customers, who reportedly included Tiffany & Co. and Marshall Field & Co.,[10] bought Wilson glass directly or through Bawo & Dotter.

Charles G. Tuthill's Glass Cutting Shop

Corning directories show that Charles Tuthill was operating a cutting shop at the rear of his father's home in 1895. It seems to have closed by 1899, when the directory no longer listed it. This shop is discussed in Chapter 19 as the forerunner of the Tuthill Cut Glass Co.

The Bronson Inkstand Co.

This company was the forerunner of George W. Drake & Co. Founded in Painted Post, New York, about 1896, it was bought by Clute & Drake in 1898. It is discussed in Chapter 10.

Corning Glass Works

The cutting operation of Corning Glass Works was very small. We know of its cut crystal from testimony given by Amory Houghton, Jr., and his son Alanson in 1904. In response to a lawyer's question, the elder Houghton said: "We make the glass but do not *to any extent* cut it. We have arrangements so *we do something in that way.*" Later he testified: "The Corning Glass Works has not *to any great extent* ever engaged in the business of manufacturing and selling cut glass for the market" (italics added).[11] Alanson Houghton testified that the Glass Works did somewhat more cutting than his father believed, and implied that cutting continued.

523.   Plaque experimentally engraved by Corning Glass Works (ca. 1940s) directly from a photograph of Mrs. Otto Hilbert. *Coll. Otto Hilbert*

Extensive questioning of elderly Corning Glass Works employees has yielded one memory of the reshaping of blanks on the cutting frame. This was done to provide customers—presumably the Hawkes, Hoare, and Sinclaire companies—with new shapes for their approval. The piece could then be used as a pattern for free-blown blanks, or a mold could be made. Even assuming that such pieces were then decorated by cutting, however, this process does not explain the small amount of cut glass manufactured "for the market."

Corning Glass Works also used cutting frames to remove the fins from pressed commercial products. By 1922 the company was cutting Pyrex-brand glassware. Though Corningites call such pieces "engraved Pyrex," the light floral designs were cut. They were so successful that Corning Glass Works subcontracted the work to other companies, including Giometti Brothers and, briefly, the Hunt Glass Works. This seems to have been the last cutting of consumer glassware that Corning Glass Works undertook. It ended by about 1930.

Experimental work continued, however. We show (Ill. 523) an experiment in engraving on glass directly from a photograph. This dates from a decade or more later; the experiment was abandoned as unsuccessful.

SUMMARY

Dates: ca. 1900-ca. 1929
Address: foot of Walnut Street
Blanks: the company's own Best Metal, and Pyrex brand glassware
Trademark[12]: none on Best Metal; the Pyrex trademark impressed in Pyrex brand glassware
Product: Best Metal blanks partially reshaped by the cutting wheel; a small production of cut glass cannot be accounted for. Pyrex brand wares of all sorts cut in light floral designs
Employees: probably no more than two or three; names unknown
Customers: presumably the Hoare, Hawkes, and Sinclaire companies for reshaped blanks. Cut-glass customers unknown. Light-cut Pyrex brand glass widely distributed through kitchen-ware retailers

Ernest Mulford

Ernest Mulford was a Hoare & Dailey cutter who began work there in late 1880.[13] We do not know whether he stayed with Hoare until 1901, when he opened Corning's first subcontracting shop. Corning directories list several other Corning addresses for him before he moved to 94 John Street about 1901. This was the site of his cutting shop. Payments "on acct." to Mulford entered in the T. G. Hawkes & Co. Cash Book early in 1901 show that the company was one of his backers.

Mulford's shop was about 25 by 60 feet in size, according to Percy Johnson, a former neighbor. He employed four or five cutters,[14] and perhaps more in peak seasons.[15]

The Hawkes Cash Book records Mulford's first delivery of glass to T. G. Hawkes & Co. as on August 30, 1901, and gives evidence that his deliveries were irregular but averaged two a month until 1902. Thereafter they became almost weekly. In 1903 some 50 payments to him from the Hawkes company ranged from $14.25 to $194.32, with a median payment of about $85. He was paid on delivery. The modest size of his payments suggests that he worked also for J. Hoare & Co.

Corningites remember no acid room in the Mulford shop. This lack indicates that Mulford's product was dipped, polished, and trademarked after it reached his customers. He reportedly cut Hawkes's simpler designs on fast-selling items such as tumblers. He may also have had retail customers.

The absence of Mulford's business from the 1913/14 Corning Directory suggests that it closed about 1912.

SUMMARY

Dates: 1901-ca. 1912
Address: 94 John Street
Blanks: many probably supplied by Hawkes and other companies for whom Mulford may have subcontracted. Pairpoint records show, however, that he also bought directly from that company.
Trademark: none
Product: simpler cuttings for Corning's larger companies; perhaps also a small line of his own glass
Employees: four to ten cutters, of whom only John Robbins is known
Customers: T. G. Hawkes & Co.; others unknown

Joseph Blackburn[16]

Blackburn was of English birth and training. The Corning Directory indicates he was a cutter in Corning by 1891, but we do not know which company was his employer.

Blackburn's subcontracting company began operations a few months after Mulford's, but seems to have been longer in the planning. The Hawkes Cash Book shows payments to T. G. Hawkes for "Expenses for Jos. Blackburn," and for loans to Blackburn that began in 1900. And the Cash Book also provides evidence that Hawkes regularly paid for insurance on Blackburn's life from this time until Blackburn died in March 1905. This fact strongly suggests that Hawkes had paid to equip the Blackburn shop.

Blackburn first delivered glass to the Hawkes company December 31, 1901. His deliveries were less regular than those of Ernest Mulford. His lowest payment in 1903 was $14.85. The largest was $97.32; the median was about $45.

Blackburn's cutting shop was in a barn behind his house at 300 Baker Street. It had four or five frames. Blackburn hired additional cutters at various times, but his company was smaller than Mulford's. He too may also have subcontracted for other companies.

SUMMARY

Dates: Dec. 1901-spring 1905. Hawkes's Cash Book records a few payments after Blackburn's death in March.
Address: 300 Baker Street, in a barn behind Blackburn's house
Blanks: probably supplied chiefly by customers
Trademark: none
Product: unknown cuttings for Hawkes & Co. and perhaps other customers
Employees: other unknown cutters from time to time
Customers: T. G. Hawkes & Co. and perhaps other Corning companies

T. G. Hawkes & Co. Cutting Shops Numbers 2 and 3

These wholly owned branch shops, which also opened during the cut-glass boom of the early twentieth century, are described in Chapter 5.

Crystal Manufacturing Co.

This company was incorporated August 1, 1902, by Philip A. McCrea, Joseph W. Borst, George A. Bronson, and Wilhelm H. Warns of Painted Post, and Hosea A. Clark of Corning, according to the firm's incorporation papers. The five men were equal owners and directors. Beginning capital was $15,000, unusually large for one of the area's small companies. It was situated in Painted Post, but appears in no Corning directories, although these included Painted Post listings.

The company's principals are also elusive. Philip McCrea is unlisted in directories, as is the business of Hosea Clark. Borst was proprietor of the Bronson House in Painted Post. Bronson was secretary-treasurer of the Bronson Heater & Supply Co.; Warns was its superintendent. Was there a practical glassmaker in the group? Perhaps; the name Bronson had been connected with the Bronson Inkstand Co., sold to Corning owners in 1898 or before, as noted in Chapter 10. That too was unlisted in directories before its sale.

The purposes that Crystal listed in its incorporation papers suggest that it was connected with the Bronson Heater & Supply Co. The company was "to make, manufacture, and deal in glass, cut glass, furnaces, engines, iron, stoves, heating apparatus, tools and machinery, and to acquire letters patent and inventions." Perhaps it occupied part of the older company's premises.

It is clear that Crystal was not called by that name in Corning: two Corning groups considered using similar names later in 1902 and again in 1903. Chapter 19 will show that this was common local practice. For these reasons we assume that the Bronson Cut Glass Co. that has been reported elsewhere was in fact the Crystal Manufacturing Co. Of its products, we know only that inkstands were probably not among them.

SUMMARY

Dates: Aug. 1, 1902-?
Address: Painted Post; street address unknown
Blanks, trademark, and *product* unknown
Employees: number and names unknown; but see Chapter 11, note 9.
Customers: unknown

Knickerbocker Cut-Glass Company

Knickerbocker is the first known tenant of the second-floor cutting shop in the Heermans & Lawrence building at 63 East Erie Avenue. It was incorporated September 10, 1902, with capital of $2,000. Maud Cochran, Tony Miller, and Gottlieb H. Tobias of Corning and attorney Julius D. Tobias of New York each owned 40 shares of the 50-dollar stock. Directors were the Tobiases and Dwight Cochran,[17] who was probably Maud's husband.

Cochran, Knickerbocker's manager and secretary, was a former bicycle manufacturer, according to local directories. G. H. Tobias's later career suggests that he had no experience in the glass business. In fact, from the absence of directory listing, he and Miller, who was a glassblower in 1907, would seem to have been newcomers to Corning in 1902.

Knickerbocker's incorporation papers gave the following aims:

> To manufacture, buy, sell and deal in all sorts... of glassware . . . whether . . . cut, pressed, edged [etched is probably meant] or engraved, to manufacture...machinery and...useful in connection with the preparation of glassware [etc.]

The *Corning Journal* reported on the incorporation date that the company "intends to begin business with about ten frames." The January 12, 1903, issue of the *Daily Journal* carried a report that Knickerbocker had hired Mary Farly, a bookkeeper

at the O. F. Egginton Co. Later that month, January 21, the newspaper said Thomas Kinsella of Painted Post had bought Tony Miller's stock. In February the new little cut-glass company of Almy & Thomas bought Knickerbocker.[18]

Knickerbocker's five-month span suggests that it produced little or no cut glass. Yet the Pairpoint Corporation sent the company its 1905 catalog of blanks as—one assumes—it had sent earlier ones.[19] By this time, according to the Corning Directory, Cochran was selling carriages. Tobias had gone on to a busy career as a merchant tailor, camera and typewriter dealer, and owner of three moving picture theaters.[20]

SUMMARY

Dates: 1902-3
Address: 63 East Erie Avenue
Blanks: The only known supplier is the Pairpoint Corporation.
Trademark: none known
Product: cut, engraved, and etched glass planned, but little or none was produced
Employees: up to ten cutters planned, but only known employee is bookkeeper Mary Farly
Customers: unknown

Ideal Cut Glass Co.

Founded in Corning in 1902, Ideal Cut Glass moved to Canastota, New York, about 1904. For this reason it is discussed in Chapter 19.

Almy & Thomas

A story in the *Daily Journal* titled "Cut Glass Change" told Corningites on February 25, 1903, that

> Messrs. Charles H. Almy and G. Edwin Thomas, former grocers...yesterday bought the stock and fixtures of the Knickerbocker Cut Glass Company ...and took possession today....The shop is located on the second floor of the Heermans & Lawrence machine shop building...with entrance on Erie Avenue, east of Cedar.
>
> Messrs. Almy and Thomas, who are enterprising and successful businessmen, intend to enlarge the business to the extent of forty frames, at least. In order to do this, it is expected to extend their shop to the alley, on the north, thus giving twice the present floor space.

The following month—actually only a few days later, March 2—the paper reported they had rented for use as a storeroom the former East Market

524. Cut Almy & Thomas bowl. Diam., 20.3 cm. *Coll. The Corning Museum of Glass*

525. Almy & Thomas bowl and nappy. Diam. of nappy, 15.6 cm. Bowl, *The Corning Museum of Glass;* nappy, *Coll. Frances Trachtenberg*

Street store of Dwight Cochran's Senate Wheel [bicycle] Company.

Despite *Journal* reports in 1903 and 1904 that Almy and Thomas had bought land on East Market Street, the cutting shop, at least, did not move. It made a general line of geometrically cut glass on blanks from Tiffin, Ohio, and from the Pairpoint Corporation.[21] Its quality was variable.

In January 1907, Almy and Thomas sold the company. A *Leader* story on January 7 gave its total employees as 35, and the purchaser as "a stock company formed at Troy, N.Y." Some of the employees, presumably the cutters, were expected to move to Troy. Almy and Thomas had "permanently retired" from the glass business.

Almy & Thomas used the acid-stamped trademark described below. No engraved Almy & Thomas

glass is known. We do not know who ran the cutting shop, which can have accommodated few more than 15 cutters.

SUMMARY

Dates: Feb. 25, 1903-Jan. 1907
Address: cutting shop at 63 East Erie Avenue
Blanks: The known sources are the U.S. Glass Co. at Tiffin, Ohio, and the Pairpoint Corporation.
Trademark: acid-stamped concentric circles. At the center of the inner one, a cipher of the letters **A** and **T**. Between the circles, above, "Almy & Thomas"; below, "Corning"
Product: a full line of geometrically cut glass of variable quality
Employees: 35 in 1907, probably including no more than 15 cutters, all unknown
Customers: probably eastern department and gift stores

Elmira Glass Cutting Co.
Elmira Cut Glass Co.
(See Chapter 15 for a discussion of the parent firm.)

Many characteristics of Corning's small cutting shops can be documented in connection with the Elmira Cut Glass Co. Its Corning shop was the branch of an out-of-town company. It operated sub rosa for a decade or more. It manufactured, repaired, and subcontracted cut glass. Its nicknames, Ferris Brothers and Ferris Cut Glass Co., have caused confusion. It was founded by Corning-trained men. Its enlargement in Corning followed labor trouble at the parent firm. Finally, it was relatively short-lived.

By 1902 the Elmira Glass Cutting Co. was working on glass for T. G. Hawkes & Co. The Hawkes Cash Book entries related to the Elmira firm extend from June 7, 1902, to October 13, 1904. The wide variation in its bills, which ranged from $214.60 down to $5.10, indicates that it was cutting glass, though it may also have been making repairs. When Hawkes & Co. last used the firm in October 1904, the Corning shop was already open at an unknown address.[22] The company name changed to Elmira Cut Glass Co. about 1906.[23]

By November 1910, the Corning branch employed 15 men, and the company was in the news because of a strike at the main plant. Some of the cutters had demanded that the American Flint Glass Workers' Union be recognized. *The Leader* reported on November 11: "Mr. Ferris [Elmira's president] is emphatic in his statement that he will not conduct a union shop."

ELMIRA CUT GLASS CO. COMING HERE was the headline of a November 29 story in the *Leader.* There were now 35 men working in the Corning shop, and only 15 in Elmira.

The parent company made a full if modest line of cut glass. Among its blank-suppliers was C. Dorflinger & Sons (two items) and the Pairpoint Corporation.[24] News stories leave no doubt that it expected to continue manufacture in Corning, and perhaps it did for a year or two. *Thomas' Register* gave its capital as over $5,000 in 1912. By 1913 its fortunes had declined, however, and it moved into the 63 East Erie Avenue cutting shop. Only a few weeks later fire destroyed the company's stock. A newspaper story reported "the wholesale value of the product was $3500, and this is a total loss."[25]

By this time the company had only three steady employees in addition to its owners. A 1975 newspaper piece by Corning's popular columnist Joe Hayes quoted John Ferris, Jr., to describe the company's last years.[26]

> "We were not cut glass manufacturers," Johnny explained, "but we did a lot of work for the dozen manufacturers operating here...."
>
> "For instance...we got 24 cocktails from a New York store. Some...were badly chipped and it was our job to remove those chips. In order to do a good job we had to grind down and polish all 24, to make them alike."
>
> A Chicago firm sent two punch bowls that were blanks....They weighed 40 pounds each but were chipped and scratched. "Too big for our wheels," said Johnny Ferris. "Dad took them to Joe Haselbauer....Together, Dad and Joe made those punch bowls like new." He thinks the bowls are still in Corning—the Chicago firm refused to pay the "exorbitant cost of repairing them."

The 1913 fire effectively ended the life of the Elmira Cut Glass Co. Though a newspaper story reported that J. Hoare & Co. and Giometti Brothers had bought its cutting frames, the Hoare company seems to have bought its name as well. Elmira Cut Glass's only listing in Corning directories, in 1913, gives its address as "foot of Walnut St."—that of J. Hoare & Co. and Corning Glass Works. Its president was H. W. Baldwin, Hoare & Co.'s treasurer.

SUMMARY

Dates: in Corning ca. 1903-ca.1914
Address: unknown 1903-13. 1913: 63 East Erie Avenue; later in the year, foot of Walnut Street
Blanks: from Pairpoint Corporation; two items from Dorflinger. Blanks for subcontracting supplied by customers. Other sources unknown
Trademark: None known or mentioned in catalog of the parent firm.
Product: subcontracting and repairs from 1902 or earlier. Cutting of the parent firm's line of cut glass also
Employees: 15 to 35, dwindling to three in 1913. Only

members of the Ferris family are known: John C., George, and John, Jr.
Customers: subcontracting for Corning's larger firms, including T. G. Hawkes & Co. Repairs for out-of-town dealers also. Customers for the company's own line of glass unknown

Ernest L. Bradley, Cut Glass Manufacturer

The Bradley company was one of Corning's more transitory ones. It opened in the cutting shop at 134 West Tioga Avenue in late 1904 or early 1905 and had closed by 1907.[27]

Cutter Ernest Bradley was himself one of Corning's more transient residents. Directories seem to show that he came to Corning about 1900, left again a year or two later, and returned to open his small cutting company. He lived a few doors down the street from it, at 124 West Tioga. Neither he nor his company is listed in the 1907 Corning directory.

The West Tioga Avenue cutting shop was small; we assume that Bradley hoped for subcontracting and repair work, but we have found no glass that can be attributed to him. None of the Corningites interviewed remembered the man himself.

SUMMARY

Dates: ca. 1904-ca. 1906
Address: 134 West Tioga Avenue
Blank suppliers, trademark, product, employees, and *customers:* unknown

Painter Glass Cutting Shop

The *Daily Journal* reported May 12, 1904: "Robert Painter, of this city, has opened a glass cutting shop in the barn of Dental Surgeon F. A. Fenderson, of East Third St." The story added that

526. Two nappies cut at the Painter Glass Cutting Shop. Diam. of handled piece, 12.8 cm. *Coll. Mrs. Louise Painter Hallahan*

the shop had two steam-powered cutting frames. According to family memories, the shop's address was incorrectly given. The shop was located in the alley between East First Street and East Erie Avenue (now Denison Parkway), in the block bounded by Chemung and Pearl streets.

Painter's brother Ernest also cut glass for the shop. It presumably had closed by May 19, 1906, when the Hawkes Cash Book indicates Robert Painter was cutting glass for that firm. Ernest Painter also later worked for Hawkes & Co., where both brothers may have learned their trade, and also for the O. F. Egginton Co. Dr. Fenderson seems to have been their shop's financial backer.

Robert Painter left the glass industry to become a plumber; Ernest H. Painter became a self-employed carpenter[28]—unfortunately, perhaps, as the Painter cut glass that we have seen is of excellent quality.

SUMMARY

Dates: May, 1904-ca. May, 1906
Address: in the alley between East First Street and East Erie Avenue, and between Chemung and Pearl streets. The snack bar of Corning Hospital now occupies the site.
Blanks: suppliers unknown
Trademark: none known
Product: Geometric cuttings on nappies and bowls are known.
Customers: unknown

J. J. Byrne

J. J. Byrne had been a blacksmith at 123 West Market Street for many years when he began, in 1906, to receive the Pairpoint Corporation's catalogs of blanks. He received one in 1907 also, but not in 1908.

Corning had just reached its peak as a cutting-industry center. We assume that Byrne briefly tried his hand at the cutting trade. Alternatively, one of many other Byrnes, some of whom were glass blowers, may have used his premises to cut glass for him.[29] Or Byrne may have backed other small shops.

The Byrne family left Corning during World War I. We have found no descendants to interview, no memories of Byrne's cutting operation, and no glass known to have been cut by him.

SUMMARY

Dates: ca. 1905-ca. 1907 or later
Address: the Byrne blacksmith shop, which also sold agricultural implements, at 123 West Market Street
Blanks: from the Pairpoint Corporation; other suppliers, if any, unknown
Trademark, product and *employees* unknown

527. Bowl cut by Samuel T. Share at Standard Cut Glass Co. Diam., 21.5 cm. *Coll. Miss A. E. McCloskey*

Standard Cut Glass Co.[30]

The Standard Cut Glass Co. opened early in 1905 in a frame building at the end of West Market Street, on the north side. Its proprietor was Samuel T. Share, an English-born cutter who had formerly worked for T. G. Hawkes & Co. Gerald Davis, who cut glass there one winter, calls Standard "a little shop with two or three cutters" in addition to Share. One of them was James Share, his brother.[31]

Sam and Jim Share were sons of Samuel Jabez Share, one of the Hawkes company's early English cutters. Samuel J. Share "crossed the ocean eight times for T. G. Hawkes," to quote his granddaughter. He brought back engravers, who lived with the senior Shares when they first arrived.

Standard was a Hawkes & Co. subcontractor from March through June of 1906, receiving $64.20 to $154.10 for near-weekly deliveries of glass, according to the Hawkes Cash Book.

On January 11, 1906 (Hawkes Cash Book), James Harry Guest left T. G. Hawkes & Co.'s employ and became co-proprietor of Standard Cut Glass. The company had prospered sufficiently to take over the larger shop at 63 East Erie Avenue that Almy and Thomas vacated in 1907. It remained only briefly, however, before moving to 136 West Tioga Avenue, its address in 1908. In this, the last year Standard was listed in Corning directories, Sam Share was president; Guest was secretary.

We assume that the depression of 1907/08 caused the company to close. Samuel Share later cut glass for the Hunt Glass Works; Guest seems to have left Corning, judging from the directories.

Share and Guest are reputed to have been expert cutters, and glass attributed to them bears out this judgment. Pairpoint Corporation's "Blank Negatives" records list Standard as a customer.

SUMMARY

Dates: 1905-ca. 1908
Address: end of West Market Street on north side, 1905-7; 63 East Erie Avenue, 1907; 136 West Tioga Avenue in 1908
Blanks: probably supplied by T. G. Hawkes & Co. and other customers, if any, during the period when Standard Cut Glass was a subcontractor; also the Pairpoint Corporation. Other suppliers unknown
Trademark: none known
Product: cut glass of good quality in rich cuttings
Employees: Two or three cutters in addition to the working owners included Gerald Davis (1905-6) and James Share.
Customers: Only T. G. Hawkes & Co. (1906) is known.

American Cut Glass Co.

On February 24 and March 3 of 1906, T. G. Hawkes & Co. recorded in its cash book payments to American "for work on glass." Despite American's absence from Corning records, it may have been a local cutting shop. The Hawkes company's unique payment to American "for bbls." also, however, suggests that it was an out-of-town firm that freighted the glass to Corning. We have found no further information about the company.

SUMMARY

Dates: in business 1906
Address: unknown; American may have been an out-of-town firm.
Blanks and *trademark,* if any, unknown
Product: included subcontracting
Employees: unknown
Customers: Only T. G. Hawkes is known.

Delos V. Olin

Eight payments to Olin "for work on glass" appear in the Hawkes Cash Book between March 3 and May 5, 1906. A mention of his name in August 1905 shows that he was a Hawkes employee at that time. The Corning directories list him as a cutter in 1905 and 1907. Presumably he started a small business of his own with the encouragement of his former employers.

Olin delivered glass to the Hawkes company more irregularly than did Ernest Mulford. The relatively small size of the Hawkes company's payments suggests that he probably employed no more than one other cutter. Olin's largest bill was $47.65; the smallest, $8.41.

Olin was in business with his father as a grocer by 1909, the local directory indicates. Though this fact by no means proves that he gave up glass cutting, we have found no other information about him.

SUMMARY

Dates: 1906-ca. 1908
Address: 136 Myrtle Avenue
Blanks: probably supplied by customers
Trademark: none
Employees: probably no more than one additional cutter
Product: Only subcontracted cutting for Hawkes & Co. is known.
Customers: Only T. G. Hawkes & Co. is known.

Augustus Rose

Augustus Rose of Gibson finished his cutting training in the middle or late 1890s.[32] The T. G. Hawkes & Co. Cash Book provides evidence that he was working for that firm by November 13, 1905. The entry was a single payment to "Gus Rose for work on glass," for $31.75.

By late 1906 or early 1907, he had left the Hawkes company's employ, and was in business for himself as a grocer and cut-glass manufacturer on Gibson's Main Street, according to the Corning Directory. In 1909, Rose listed himself in the directory as a carpenter, but he seems to have continued to operate his cutting shop for some years.

Though Rose may have subcontracted for other Corning firms, he is remembered in Corning for his work for individuals. The Rose family gave Corning a number of highly competent cutters. Another of them, Frank Rose, is reported to have worked with Augustus.

SUMMARY

Dates: 1907-?
Address: Main Street, Gibson
Blanks: sources unknown; many supplied by customers
Trademark: none
Product: unknown
Employees: Frank Rose reportedly worked with Augustus.

Patrick Callahan[33]

Callahan was born in Corning about 1856. He learned the cutting trade at Hoare & Dailey, where he worked for 12 years. His older brother, Andrew, also cut glass for the Hoare company. They finished

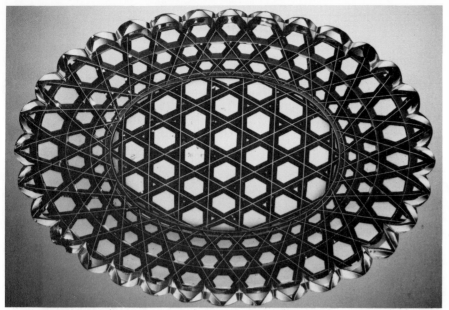

their training at about the same time, and were first listed as cutters in the 1874/75 Elmira and Corning directories.

Patrick's next employer was T. G. Hawkes & Co., where he worked for 20 years. However, glass cutting was not his only means of livelihood. During the depression of the 1890s local directories listed him as a grocer as well. These dates make the simple career sketched above extremely interesting. Callahan (originally Callaghan) must have apprenticed in 1868, the year that Hoare & Dailey began operations in Corning, and must have switched to the Hawkes company when it opened in 1880.[34] He was thus one of the Corning industry's pioneer cutters.

Callahan left the glass industry in 1902; he ran a shoestore in Corning until about 1907. He died in 1916.

Patrick Callahan ran a cutting shop behind his house at 73 West Fourth Street, across the alley from J. F. Haselbauer & Sons; he may have been one of the cutters who "helped out" when that company was busy. The Callahan shop operated almost until his death, and may have opened before his 1907 retirement as a merchant.

SUMMARY

Dates: 1907 or earlier-1916
Address: behind 73 West Fourth Street
Blanks: suppliers unknown; many doubtless supplied by customers. The only known piece of Callahan glass is of fine color.
Trademark: none
Product: Only rich-cut glass is known.
Employees: probably none
Customers: individuals and perhaps other home shops

Majestic Cut Glass Co.
(See also Chapter 19.)

This company was founded in Elmira, New York.

Its Corning operations are known from only a single news story, which appeared in the *Leader* November 29, 1910. This concerned the labor trouble of Elmira Cut Glass Co. The story said, in part, that the

trouble seems to be a sequel of the difficulties of the Majestic Cut Glass Company a few years ago which resulted in the firm removing to Corning, where it is now enjoying a flourishing business. [Saul] Spiegel of this city, is now at the head of the Corning concern.

The company never appeared in Corning directories. Mrs. Beatrice Perling, the founder's daughter, was unaware that it had a Corning branch when we interviewed her.

We assume that Majestic of Corning cut the same geometric cuttings as the parent firm, and used the same blanks. Some of these came from Belgium, Mrs. Perling says. The Pairpoint Corporation was another supplier. This company's records noted that Majestic was "out of business" in 1908, however, which is clearly untrue of the Corning branch.

We have found no information about employees; we assume that the company closed shortly after the *Leader* article was published.

SUMMARY

Dates: ca. 1907-ca. 1911
Blanks: some from Belgium; others possibly from Pairpoint Corporation in the company's first year or so in Corning
Trademark: none known
Product: presumably the same full line of rich-cut glass that the parent firm made
Employees: unknown
Customers and *address* in Corning unknown

Eygabroat-Ryon

The parent firm of this Lawrenceville, Pennsylvania, company is discussed in Chapter 19. The Corning branch followed Standard Cut Glass in the cutting shop at 63 East Erie Avenue, according to the Corning Directory. We have seen that this could accommodate 15 or more cutters. Eygabroat-Ryon clearly opened with fewer: on November 13, 1908, the *Leader* said the company had hired more and begun to work overtime.

This new branch and its seeming prosperity were unusual in 1907/8, a period that brought bankruptcy to many cut-glass companies.

The Corning shop's manager was listed in the 1909 directory as William Jones. (No other officers were listed.) The name Jones is so common that we cannot be sure whether this was the same William Jones who was listed in the 1905 directory as foreman at T. G. Hawkes & Co.; and in *China, Glass & Lamps* on May 19, 1906, as an incorporator of the Avis, Pennsylvania, Cut Glass Works. After World War I, a William Jones cut glass for H. P. Sinclaire & Co.[35] Yet a consolidation of the Avis and Lawrenceville companies is a tempting explanation of Eygabroat-Ryon's need to expand during a sharp business downturn.

We have found no glass that can be attributed to the Corning shop. The parent firm was at this time producing both geometric and floral cuttings. We assume that the two shops used the same sources of blanks.

Eygabroat-Ryon's Corning operation seems to have closed by early 1911, since it was absent from the directory. The *Leader* reported on August 18, 1911, that the parent firm had closed.

SUMMARY

Dates: 1908-ca. 1911
Address: 63 East Erie Avenue
Blanks: Pairpoint Corporation and C. Dorflinger & Sons records list the parent company as a customer for blanks. We assume that the Corning branch was also.
Trademark: none on known Eygabroat-Ryon glass
Product: probably a full line of geometric and floral cuttings
Employees: William Jones, manager, and perhaps 15 cutters, all unknown
Customers: unknown

Climax Cut Glass Co.

The *Leader* informed Corning on August 4, 1911, that the cutting shop in the Heermans & Lawrence building, formerly occupied by the Knickerbocker,

529. Rich-cut plate made by Peter Eick in his home shop ca. 1912–20. Diam., 30.5 cm. *Coll. Misses Florence and Evelyn Eick*

Almy & Thomas, and Eygabroat-Ryon companies, would be reopened by Climax Cut Glass Co. The story gave no company officers; nor did Climax's listing in the 1911/12 Corning directory.

Climax has been forgotten in Corning, and is undocumented after 1912. We have found no glass that can be attributed to it. It had left 63 East Erie Avenue by the spring of 1913, when the Elmira Cut Glass Co. moved into the premises.

SUMMARY

Dates: August, 1911-ca. late 1912
Address: 63 East Erie Avenue
Blank-suppliers; trademark, if any; *product, employees,* and *customers* unknown

Peter A. Eick[36]

Peter Eick was born in Brooklyn in 1875. His German-born father, Joseph Eich, was a glass cutter for Corning's Hoare & Dailey by 1880, according to a story in the *Journal* on October 14 of that year. The family name was Anglicized about 1892, as directories show.

Young Eick went to work for the Hawkes Rich Cut Glass Works at the age of ten. He learned to cut glass there, and also met his future wife, who worked in the packing department. Around 1912, while still employed by the Hawkes company, he built a five-frame cutting shop behind his West Fifth Street house. When work was slack at the Hawkes factory, he carried on his own business.

In normal times Eick's five frames enabled him to move from one operation to the next without changing cutting wheels. When sales were brisk, cutter William McMahon helped out. Mrs. Eick did the clerical work; she and the Eick daughters washed and wrapped the glass and assisted in packing and shipping it. Eick's shop became one of Corning's most successful. During these years Eick also worked from time to time for John Illig's company.[37]

By 1919 Eick had left the Hawkes company, where his salary was $17 a week. His Corning Glass Works employment record shows that he was hired to "engrave" in the Pyrex finishing department August 4; it listed John Illig as his former employer.

Eick now set up a second cutting shop with one frame in the basement of his house. Here he did additional work on Pyrex brand glass, and put in extra hours monogramming glass for a local store. He was expert at cutting Old English letters. At the same time he was working full time for Corning Glass Works.

Eick's billhead of the 1920s read: "PETER A. EICK/MANUFACTURER OF/RICH CUT GLASS/SPECIALIST IN REPAIR WORK AND ENGRAVING PYREX TEAPOTS." He also decorated and monogrammed other Pyrex brand glassware; his "engraving" was, in fact, pictorial cutting.

Corning newspaper columnist Joe Hayes remembers that Eick also ran a dancing school, one of three in Corning. It was well patronized.

When his own glass business was not too pressing, Eick still cut glass for the John Illig company. Illig's financial backer remembers Eick as the company's last employee in the 1920s.[38]

Death came to Peter Eick in 1935, when he was at the peak of his career (his obituary in the *Leader* was dated April 22). A few years later his larger shop was razed, and the equipment in both shops sold.

Eick's high-quality blanks were from the Union Glass Company. His rich cuttings of his own designs were shipped all over the United States. Most items were priced between five and ten dollars, but a lamp sold for $300 in 1920.

SUMMARY

Dates: ca. 1912-35
Address: 131 West Fifth Street
Blanks: crystal from Union Glass Co.; Pyrex brand glass from Corning Glass Works
Trademark: none
Product: rich cuttings on vases, bowls, lamps, and tableware in particular; floral cutting and monograms on Pyrex brand glass, especially teapots

Employees: cutter William McMahon occasionally; the Eick family
Customers: perhaps Corning Glass Works for floral-cut Pyrex brand glassware 1919-21; a local store; individuals throughout the United States.

Signet Glass, Co., Inc.

The Signet company's incorporation—the papers, dated November 6, 1913, were prepared by attorney Francis B. Williams, its chief stockholder—was reported in the *Corning Leader* of November 7. The other stockholders were Louise Haradon, his stenographer; and Holland B. Williams, his cousin, both of whom seem to have been inactive partners.[39] The company began business with a capital of only $500; 45 of its 50 shares of stock were unsubscribed. Its three stockholders were also Signet's directors. The company's purposes were "manufacturing, buying, selling and dealing in glass ware and metal mounted goods of any and all kinds and descriptions."

Francis Williams was the lawyer for T. G. Hawkes & Co., according to Mrs. Walter Schaefer, the Hawkes company secretary during the 1920s. At that time, she says, there was no sign of the Signet company, yet there is reason to think that the Hawkes company controlled Signet during its brief life. A Signet sales-transfer ledger covering the period from February 18, 1914, through December 31, 1915, began on sheets headed "T. G. Hawkes & Co. Sales Journal."[40] A number of Signet sales marked "with Hawkes" are evidence that glass from the two companies was shipped together from the Hawkes factory. A 1915 handwritten list of blank prices for the Hawkes company included one item marked "Signet." Finally, the Signet sales book was recovered recently from the former Hawkes building with other Hawkes & Co. records. Secrecy about matters like this also characterized Thomas Hawkes's Steuben and Hawkes & Co. incorporation papers.

Signet's glass was of moderate price. The several floral designs that the sales book named (*Rose of Sharon, Wild Rose, Calliopsis, Lily, Iris,* and *Violet* among them) suggest stone engraving. Sales of sterling silver "Tid Bit Stands," cocktail mixers, baskets, bowls, and vases, and of silver- and gilt-mounted objects, remind us that Hawkes & Co. had opened a metal department in 1912.

Signet's principal agent was Henry Creange, Inc., of 200 Fifth Avenue, New York. Merchandise for Marshall Field & Co. of Chicago, the Heintz Art Metal Shop of Buffalo, and other retailers was shipped through Creange. Perhaps the most thought-provoking is a shipment of "Edenhall Crystal

Goblets 8080" at $8.75 a dozen. These were modestly priced even by 1913 standards. The name recalls the Hawkes & Co. Edenhall goblet, a good-quality engraving signed by William Morse that has usually been dated from about 1920.

Signet also sold such novelty items as "Domino Sugars, Nabiscos, and Uneedas." It ground stoppers, made mountings, and matched broken and unbroken glass. Higgins & Seiter and Tiffany & Co., both of New York, were among the customers for this special-order work.

Signet's monthly sales in 1914 ranged from a low of $11.25 to a high of $2,207.34. Sales improved in 1915; monthly totals varied from $82.66 to $3,930.84.

We have found no later information about Signet. Holland Williams, an incorporator, has no memory of it; Hawkes employees of the 1920s are unfamiliar with the name. We believe that it closed at the beginning of 1916, or shortly thereafter. Perhaps it was a marketing and production experiment designed to protect the Hawkes & Co. name from association with its own modestly priced glass. Signet's dates suggest further that it implemented a final business decision of Thomas Hawkes, who died only a few months before the Signet incorporation papers were filed. Certainly the kind of work Signet did was done by Hawkes & Co. shortly thereafter.

We have found no glass that can be attributed to Signet.

SUMMARY

Dates: November, 1913-ca. early 1916
Address: Signet glass was shipped from the Hawkes & Co. factory on West Market Street; we believe that it was also made there.
Blanks: Signet's name appears on a 1915 Steuben Glass Works list of T. G. Hawkes & Co. blank prices. Other sources are unknown; presumably they include other Hawkes suppliers.
Trademark: possibly an acid-stamped script "Signet"
Product: inexpensive stone-engraved or pictorially cut glass of small size; matchings; sterling silver pieces; silver and gilt mountings
Employees: presumably those of T. G. Hawkes & Co.
Customers: chiefly department stores, including Marshall Field & Co. (Chicago), John Wanamaker (Philadelphia), Gimbel Brothers (New York), and the Frederick Loeser Company (Brooklyn). Also jeweler Richard Briggs of Boston. Customers for matchings and/or repairs included Higgins & Seiter and Tiffany & Co. (New York). Signet's agent was Henry Creange, 200 Fifth Avenue, New York.

Harry Jones [41]

Harry Jones, born in 1881, came from an old Corning family and was its first member to cut glass.

He was unrelated to William Jones, manager of Eygabroat-Ryon's Corning shop. There is no family memory of whether Harry Jones learned his trade at the Hoare or the Hawkes company. Payments to "H. Jones" entered in the T. G. Hawkes & Co. Cash Book during 1901 and 1902, however, suggest that Harry Jones was a Hawkes cutter during these years.

Jones was foreman at G. W. Drake & Co. by the spring of 1903, when he was twenty-two; in late 1907 or early 1908 he became the company's superintendent, according to Corning directories. The company closed in the latter year. Thereafter, directories listed him as a cutter until 1918, when he was "foreman 77 Market St.," the Hawkes & Co. address.

Jones operated a cutting shop and small retail store for many years behind his house at 210 East Second Street.[42] The building faced the alley, and is still standing. We do not know what year it opened, but a Christmas advertisement in the *Leader* on December 15, 1917, offered "a complete line of glass" and "factory prices." Some of it was on fine,

530. Harry Jones and his family about 1930. The small building, center, is probably his home shop. *Coll. Mrs. Thomas Hanley*

531. Prism-cut candlesticks, on Heisey blanks, cut by Jones in his home shop. Height, 18.8 cm. (Other Jones-cut pieces are shown in Illustration 537.) *Coll. Mrs. Thomas Hanley*

free-blown blanks; other pieces were pressed wares from the Heisey company.

Jones's wife was the sister-in-law of a Corning Glass Works vice-president. These were years when relatives tended to work for the same company; about 1925 Jones went to work for Corning Glass Works, beginning as a shop boy.[43] By about 1928 he was in charge of drawing automatic tubing. When the Glass Works's Fall Brook, Pennsylvania, plant opened in 1930, Jones became production foreman of automatic tubing, and closed his home shop.

Jones retired because of ill health less than two years later. He died of tuberculosis in 1934.

Harry Jones was generous in his gifts of cut glass to relatives. These show that his work was excellent. Most, perhaps all, are hand-polished. The high quality of the blanks, however, suggests that the great majority were made at G. W. Drake & Co. (See Chapter 10 for examples.)

SUMMARY

Dates: ca. 1915 or earlier-1930
Address: facing the alley behind 210 East Second Street
Blanks: Many are of superior quality but unknown maker. Others are pressed Heisey glass.
Trademark: none
Product: geometric cuttings of excellent quality, hand polished. Jones advertised "a complete line of glass."

Employees: none known
Customers: individuals in Corning; others unknown

Wellsboro Glass Co.

The glass industry has long called glass companies by the names of the area in which they were situated. For this and other reasons, we assumed until recently that the single mention of the Wellsboro Glass Co. in Corning's newspaper referred, in fact, to John Hoare, Inc., of Wellsboro.[44] Further research has shown that the assumption may be incorrect.

The *Leader* reported on June 20, 1916, that the Wellsboro Glass Co. of Corning had "secured an order from a single firm for 300,000 dozen cut glass tumblers," adding that it was one of the largest "single piece orders" ever received. Its size may indicate why the company had recently moved to Corning.

China, Glass & Lamps gave additional information about the company in its issue of June 26, 1916. It said:

> According to northern Pennsylvania reports the Wellsboro Glass Co., Wellsboro, Pa., has purchased the Corning Cut Glass Co.'s former plant at Centerville from James O. Sebring and Warren J. Cheny [*sic*], and after the building has been remodeled will move there from Wellsboro. The company is to use at its new plant a glass cutting machine developed and patented by E. O. Ryon of Wellsboro, president of the company.

The plant that Wellsboro Glass had bought accommodated up to 50 men.[45] It was on Hart Avenue, a few hundred yards west of Corning, in a village once called Centerville (now Riverside).

We have found no further information about this company, which was unlisted in Corning directories. We assume that it was short-lived, and that its products were relatively small items, inexpensively cut by machine. The company's Wellsboro factory may have been the one situated on Main Street in the first decades of the twentieth century.[46]

SUMMARY

Dates: in the Corning area 1916-ca. 1917 or slightly later
Address: Hart Avenue, Centerville (now Riverside)
Blanks: inexpensive; sources unknown
Trademark: none known
Product: cut by a machine of the owner's invention, at least in part; hence, simple geometric cuttings. Only tumblers can be documented.
Employees: unknown; the company's Corning plant could accommodate 25 or more cutters.
Customers: unknown

533. Engraved tumbler and cut pyramid from the Fuller company. Tumbler height, 10.4 cm. *Coll. Mrs. W. H. Kresge*

532. Cased amber plate from Fred Fuller, Cut Glass Manufacturer. Diam., 28.1 cm. *Coll. Mrs. Emil Schrickel*

Fred H. Fuller, Cut Glass Manufacturer

World War I was under way in Europe when Nell Fuller left the Hunt Glass Works to found the company that bore her husband's name. The only Corning cutting company known to have been founded and run by a woman, it was first listed in the 1917 Corning Directory.

The Fuller company was situated in a frame building behind the house of Mrs. Fuller's "adopted mother" on Washington Avenue, just outside the Corning city limits.[47] The building still stands. The two-story half had a stockroom on the ground floor and the cutting shop above. A one-story section to the right was the office. The house was the first in Corning to have heavy-duty electricity; this also powered the cutting wheels and lathes, according to Mrs. Swen Johnson, wife of the present owner.

The company operated until Nell Fuller's death in the late 1920s.[48] It employed three or four men, all of whom also worked for the Hunt company. Though no formal record of a subcontracting arrangement is remembered, it is clear that Nell Fuller's company did cut and stone-engrave glass for Hunt's.

Employees included cutters Ernest Crannage and Art Schaffer, and engraver Hiram Rouse, all of whom also worked for Hunt. Rouse was related to Fred Fuller. Other relatives helped with the washing and packing when the company was busy. Fred Fuller worked there when he could, but also held other jobs.

Nell Fuller was an extraordinarily efficient businesswoman. A dozen or more years as the Hunt

company's business manager had given her a thorough knowledge of the glass business. Her product included cut and stone-engraved wares; crystal and colored blanks were used. The colored pieces that we have seen were stained. The company did no copper-wheel engraving, and we know of no Fuller stemware.

SUMMARY

Dates: ca. 1916-ca. 1927
Address: Washington Avenue beyond city limits, on east side of road
Blanks: uncolored and stained, usually pressed; suppliers unknown
Trademark: none
Product: tumblers, plates, vases, bowls, candlesticks, etc., and decorative items of modest price
Employees: cutters Ernest Crannage and Art Schaffer; engraver Hiram Rouse; Fred Fuller and relatives from time to time
Customers: the Hunt Glass Works; others unknown

Louis Kling

The Corning Directory of 1919/20 listed Kling as a glassworker at 2-4 West Erie Avenue. This was the Howell Building. We know of no cutting shop in the building, though it had housed the offices of the Corning Cut Glass Co. early in the century.

We have found no further information about Kling, who may have operated a small repair shop.

Ambrose Van Etten[49]

Ambrose Van Etten was born in 1884 in Gibson, adjacent to Corning's eastern border. Gibson had been a busy canal port, and the Van Ettens canallers. Ambrose's father, however, was a farmer. The several branches of the family gave the industry a number of expert cutters.

Van Etten and his twin, Eugene, learned their trade at T. G. Hawkes & Co. Their apprenticeship began in 1898, at the customary age of fourteen. An older brother, Archie, was already a Hawkes cutter.

Sometime before 1912 Ambrose Van Etten became cutting foreman of the Ideal Cut Glass Co. in Canastota, New York. (Ideal is discussed in Chapter 19.) Here there was no formal apprenticeship, but Van Etten trained willing and able boys. Among them was young Floyd Manwarren.[50] Van Etten returned to Corning about 1915.

Van Etten's adventurous life took him away from Corning at least twice more. From about 1917 to 1920 he worked for an uncle in New York as pilot of an excursion boat. Thereafter he cut for the Hunt company, and from 1933 to 1936 for a now-forgotten employer in New York City.

During his Corning years Ambrose Van Etten operated a cutting shop "just about all of his life," his son says. In the 1920s it was in Gibson, possibly at two locations. Alec Perry, one of the Hawkes company's highest-paid cutters in the 1940s (he was also a preacher), worked there with him. Later the Van Etten shop was in Horseheads, New York, a few miles east of Corning. Its site is now occupied by Iszard's department store, in the Horseheads shopping mall.

When World War II began, Van Etten switched from cutting to war work for Corning Glass Works, and stayed until his department was discontinued. He continued to operate a shop after his retirement, and died in 1953.

SUMMARY

Dates: ca. 1920-ca. 1950, with interruptions during the 1917-20 and 1933-36 periods
Addresses: "behind Robinson's grocery store" in Gibson; in the present shopping mall at Horseheads, New York
Blanks: Those we have seen are inexpensive pressed glass or Pyrex brand glass. Much of Van Etten's work was on glass supplied by his customers.
Trademark: none
Product: We know of straight-line floral cuttings, initials, and names, but presumably Van Etten did geometric cuttings also.
Employees: cutter Alec Perry in the Gibson shop; none in Horseheads
Customers: chiefly individuals

Benjamin R. Watson[51]

Joseph Watson, Benjamin's father, was one of a group of English glass cutters who came to Corning in 1884 to work for Thomas Hawkes. Thomas Shotton and George Nokes were also in the group (see Chapter 16). They were most apprehensive about living conditions in western New York, where they expected to find Indians; one of them brought along his own tin bathtub, to be prepared for primitive living.

Young Ben had been born in 1880 in Birmingham, England. He learned his trade at the Hawkes company, for which he cut glass for the rest of his life. He also operated a cutting shop in the basement of his house at 164 Columbia Street, beginning in the early 1920s. When Watson's future son-in-law, Ranald McMullin, gave up the study of forestry in 1925, Watson undertook to train him as a cutter.

A few years later Watson was operating a small cutting factory in a building behind his house, and employing four or five men. They included McMullin until 1932, and cutters Ernest Crannage and Arthur Hyland. Blanks came from Glassboro, New Jersey, and from Watson's customers. Among these was the Steuben Glass Works.

When the Fred Fuller company closed, Watson bought a truckload of its equipment: two cutting frames, deep-cutting equipment, a line shaft, and other machinery. His shop also had four lathes, one of them for stoppering.

Watson's company made chiefly floral and geometric cuttings, but Watson himself, who was also a painter, occasionally did copper-wheel engraving. One such piece was a picture frame on

534. Two whiskey bottles and a sandwich tray from Benjamin Watson's small backyard company. The tray, 30 cm. in diameter, has Watson's initials worked into the design. Left to right: *Colls. Mr. & Mrs. Fred Gillard, the Rev. Roger Alling, Mr. & Mrs. Campbell Rutledge, Jr.*

535. Cased amethyst Steuben bowl engraved by Benjamin Watson, perhaps as a Steuben Division subcontractor. Diam., 35.2 cm. *Coll. The Corning Museum of Glass* (Gift of Mrs. R. M. McMullin)

which he engraved little boys and dogs. Little of the company's work was signed, but Watson occasionally worked his initials into the designs of his best pieces or initialed them on the bottom.

During the Great Depression, when most Hawkes cutters worked half time or less according to the firm's Cash Book, Watson's company provided extra income that was especially welcome. During these years Watson paid local boys a quarter each for all the empty uncolored whiskey bottles they could find.[52] He cut or engraved them, added stoppers, and sold them locally for a dollar or so. Those we have seen are little darker than inexpensive or World War I blanks. The work on the geometrically cut ones, especially, is very good.

Watson's company operated until shortly before his death in 1942. His frames continued to work in the shop of the Wellsboro, Pennsylvania, cutter who bought them.

SUMMARY

Dates: ca. 1921-1942

Address: 164 Columbia Street, first in the basement, later in a building behind the house

Blanks: from Glassboro, New Jersey; commercial whiskey bottles during the depression years; others supplied by customers

Trademark: none, but occasionally the initials "B.W." or "B.R.W." were worked into Watson's best engraved designs or incised on the bottom of a cut piece.

Product: chiefly cutting designed by Watson on a wide range of wares. Cuttings were both floral and geometric. Watson also did occasional copper-wheel engravings. Work for Steuben executed from samples they supplied

Employees: Ranald McMullin, 1925-32. Also cutters Ernest Crannage and Arthur Hyland

Customers: chiefly individuals; also the Steuben Division, Corning Glass Works

John Denson[53]
Denson & Cosgrove

John Denson was born in 1886 in Cooper's Plains, near Corning. He learned his trade as a J. Hoare & Co. apprentice, beginning at the customary age of fourteen.

By 1913 Denson was a cutter for Hunt Glass; he also worked briefly for the O. F. Egginton Co. He was a Steuben Division and Steuben Glass cutter from 1922 to 1935, retiring in the latter year because of poor health, according to Corning Glass Works records.

Beginning about 1920, Denson and a fellow cutter named Cosgrove operated a small cutting shop in Gibson. This seems to have preceded that of Ambrose Van Etten in the barn behind Robinson's grocery store. By the mid-twenties, Denson worked alone in a three-frame shop on the enclosed porch of his home at 270 East Third Street. His chief customer was Steuben; he did stoppering for the company and shipped the finished product. He also cut glass for individual customers.

Denson's shop was in operation until about 1930 or a bit later.

SUMMARY

Dates: ca. 1920-ca. 1930

Addresses: barn behind Robinson's grocery store, Gibson, in early 1920s; ca. 1925-ca. 1930, 270 East Third Street

Blanks: chiefly supplied by customers

Trademark: none

Product: chiefly stoppering for Steuben after about 1925; also cutting, both pictorial and geometric

Customers: individuals; the Steuben company

10
Bronson Inkstand Co.; George W. Drake & Co.

George Drake crammed as much living into his forty-year life as some men manage in twice the span. He was the very type of the gentleman-glassmaker, attracted by the beauty and excitement that the business offered, but active also in other fields. Corning's elders remember him as "a splendid fellow" and "a man with a wonderful sense of humor." Because Drake's story illuminates its period, we tell it at length although we can show little of his glass. (Three of his designs are shown in *American Cut and Engraved Glass* by A. C. Revi, pages 199–200.)

Drake was the scion of a successful and public-spirited family.[1] His grandfather, Franklin Drake, originator of the family wealth, moved to Corning with a lumber fortune in 1867 and set about making a larger one in the coal fields a few miles south. When George was born in 1870, Franklin Drake was extending his coal-carrying Tioga Railroad to Elmira. Later he founded Corning's Stove Works and First National Bank.

George Drake's widowed mother married Dr. A. M. Gamman in 1878. George clerked in the family bank after graduating from military academy. In 1890 he became the junior partner in Marvin Olcott's real estate and insurance firm. Doubtless Olcott was the manager and larger investor, but he may have owed his later interest in cut glass to young Drake (Olcott became a partner in H. P. Sinclaire & Co.).

In 1891 Drake married. The union produced the beautiful and charming Gladys and Doris Drake, who would later have "all the boys in Corning crazy about them," to quote an admirer.

In 1892 Drake succeeded his grandfather as president of the Corning Stove Works, a position he held until the company closed in 1904. The Cleveland–Harrison election found Democrat Drake working hard for Cleveland. "He was one of the organizers . . . of the Anti-Snap Convention. . . in Syracuse," his obituary recalled. This political affiliation was unusual in glassmaking Corning, which needed the Republicans' high tariffs to protect them from European low-wage glass.

Cleveland rewarded Drake by appointing him postmaster in 1894. He was also a partner in Clute & Drake, a book, paper, and notion business. Yet Drake's immense vitality prompted him to embark on another venture before his term as postmaster expired. The *Journal* announced it on July 20, 1898:

> Clute & Drake have purchased the business of the Bronson Inkstand Company of Painted Post, and will push the sale of the inkstand, which is one of the best of the kind on the market.

On September 14 the *Journal* added that the inkstand had been "invented by the Rev. Mr. Smith, now of Painted Post, and should have been called the Smith Inkstand."

The company seems to have been founded by George Bronson, later a principal of the Crystal Manufacturing Co. of Painted Post. A Clute family tradition says that Corning Glass Works manufactured the blanks, and owned the company when Clute and Drake bought it. The Glass Works reportedly had had trouble patenting the inkstand, and so did the company's new owners.

The inkstand company is listed in the Corning Directory of 1899 only, when it was situated at 16 East Market Street, Clute and Drake's address. Cutting, however, was done in George Drake's barn on the southeast corner of Cedar and Fifth streets.[2] This company led George Drake into the cut-glass business when he took over the inkstands and Frank Clute retained their book and stationery business.

Drake's new business soon was cutting more than inkstands. The *Journal* reported his next move on August 21, 1901, under the headline NEW GLASS CUTTING SHOP:

> The G. W. Drake Cut Glass Company has leased the Hungerford Building on Bridge Street...for... six years....(It) will begin to fix the building up for a glass cutting shop and...by Sept. 1, upward of 70 frames will be in operation. The company was organized a few months ago with a capital of $10,000. G. W. Drake is president. (He), A. M. Gamman and Mrs. G. W. Drake comprise the Board of Directors.

The announcement exaggerated. Former employee Gerald Davis, as well as Clyde Hauff, estimates that cutters numbered between 20 and 35. The lower figures are substantiated by the *New York Industrial Recorder* of 1901, in which an article stated that the company was an

> extensive manufacturer of high grade cut glass. (It) was established two years ago and under able and progressive management the business is fast assuming very gratifying proportions and today the steadily increasing patronage extends throughout... the United States. The plant...consists of a large three story building 45 x 60 feet...and employment is given to 40 skilled and practical hands, together with several experienced and clever traveling salesmen. The reputation of the house is unexcelled.... No concern in the world can produce...cut glass superior to this one....

The article showed the company's trademark, which we reproduce. Because it has never been reported on a piece of glass, we assume that it was used as a sticker.

In March of 1902, the company closed for a week because of flood damage, but by May it was enlarging its capacity.[3] According to local directories, its manager by 1903 was Harry M. Jones, who later operated his own cutting shop (see Chapter 9). Drake & Co. cut geometric and brilliant designs of good quality, but employed no engravers in the factory. Cutters in 1904–5 included John Rowe, later a Corning policeman; Charles Hotalen, Carl Hotalen, and John Robbins. There was no apprenticeship program, but at least one ambitious fourteen-year-old, Gerald Davis, learned to cut glass from the older men.

Drake & Co.'s blank suppliers included C. Dorflinger & Sons and the Pairpoint Corp.[4] Dorflinger supplied five stemware sets, ten vases, four bonbons, a celery, a nappy in five sizes, a cheese plate and cover, ice tub and plate, a bowl, and open-foot oyster cocktails. Some of these blanks have been pictured with Dorflinger cuttings.[5]

Drake & Co. prospered. The *Journal* reported July 1, 1904, that it was "not suffering from the summer dullness of the trade, but is even working overtime." This was unusual, and especially so in 1904, when Hawkes & Co.'s business was apparently off about 20 percent from that of 1903, judging from the payroll recorded in the Hawkes Cash Book.

Drake's immense good humor was remarked in a trade-journal tribute to the man and his product, published in 1906—*China, Glass & Lamps* wrote of the company in its September 29 issue:

> Of the twelve or fourteen concerns in Corning, this company has been a leading exponent of push and energy. Beginning not so many years ago, Mr. Drake by strict attention to business has built up an enviable trade. Personally of a genial nature he makes a favorable impression in all quarters and no little success can be attributed to this fact. The factory...is...distinguished by the beauty and artistic finish of its wares, which adds so materially to their selling qualities in the hands of the retail jeweler.

Drake's stepfather-partner, Dr. Gamman, was now more interested in oil than in cut glass. The 1905 and 1907 Corning directories listed him as an "oil producer." It was perhaps he who interested Drake in prospecting for oil.

In 1906 the company again expanded. The *Journal* wrote on February 5 that it had "increased its working force by a dozen men and...(would) install eighteen more frames." Employees would total "upwards of eighty men." Not all, of course, would have been craftsmen. Business remained good into the fall. Overtime work began in September, the *Daily Journal* reported on the twentieth of that month.

The depression that began in 1907 brought so many glass-company bankruptcies by 1908 that *China, Glass & Lamps* sometimes reported several in a single paragraph. It reported Drake & Co.'s on February 29:

> A petition that the...Drake...Co....be subject to an involuntary bankruptcy was filed...by Charles Kuhn of Corning, and N. C. Cropp, and W. J. Warner, of Buffalo...to prevent the sale of the property to satisfy a judgment obtained by Lucy Denton Burt of Corning.

But the account may not have been entirely accurate—Corning directories list no Charles Kuhn in or around 1908.

The company's debts were variously reported at $80,000 and $9,400. Harry Hunt and Michael Grady, foreman at the Corning Cut Glass Co., were appointed to appraise the stock, which was advertised for sale. W. J. McKee, said to be a Corning hardware dealer, bought it for $2,225. According to *China, Glass & Lamps* of July 4, 1908, McKee was rumored to have made the purchase "for interested parties"; but this story too may have been inaccurate, as we have found no record of a Corningite by the name of W. J. McKee.

Drake was in Corning very little after this time. When he died suddenly December 18, 1910, his obituary noted that he had spent much of his time in Oklahoma, exploring for oil. The barn in which his glass was first cut has been razed, but his Bridge Street factory still stands.

G. W. DRAKE, Corning, N. Y.

...ufacturing must ever remain the keynote of suc... ...every great community. The Crystal City, aptly... ...has become renowned as a great glass industria... ...and in this connection we desire to mention th... ...of G. W. Drake, extensive manufacturer of high... ...cut glass. This enterprise was established two...

...and under able and progressive management

536. Trademark of G. W. Drake & Co.

SUMMARY

Dates: 1898 (as Bronson Inkstand Co.)-1908
Address: 1898-ca. 1901, 16 East Market Street (the address of Clute & Drake) and rear of 52 East Fifth Street; 1901-8, 56-58 Bridge Street
Blanks: from C. Dorflinger & Sons and the Pairpoint Corp.; other sources unknown
Trademark: See Illustration 536. Probably used as a sticker
Product: geometrically cut crystal of good quality
Employees: 20 to 35 cutters, who included John Rowe, Charles and Carl Hotalen, John Robbins, and Gerald Davis. Manager, cutter Harry M. Jones
Customers: chiefly jewelry stores

537. Vase and decanter cut and perhaps designed by Harry Jones, probably at G. W. Drake & Co. Height of vase, 30.6 cm. *Coll. Mr. and Mrs. Fred Gillard*

11
Corning Cut Glass Co.

Lawyer James O. Sebring moved to Corning in 1895 at the age of thirty-four.[1] His legal acuity became legendary in Corning; when he died in the 1940s he was said never to have lost a case. Sebring was a dynamic and driving entrepreneur. During the years when his cut-glass company operated, directories indicate that he was also president of a manufactory of artificial stone and of a grape and wine company. His real estate holdings included Corning's "Pinewood Park and pleasure grounds" and Pinewood Sanitarium property, presumably nearby.[2]

Sebring's Corning Cut Glass Co., however, was the enterprise that most interested Corning. It opened in 1901. Corning Glass Works sued in 1902 to prevent Sebring from using the name. The suit dragged on until 1911, when Sebring won it and closed the company.

Sebring's sister-in-law and her husband, Mr. and Mrs. Frank Hendryx, were co-incorporators of the company. A few months later W. J. Cheney, Sebring's law partner, became vice-president. None of them knew anything about manufacturing cut glass. Sebring testified:

> The Corning Cut Glass Company was formed in 1901....I never had any practical experience in the manufacturing or cutting glass....Hendryx had no practical experience....He had been an employee of a company manufacturing commercial glass...for some time prior. I think the suggestion of the formation of this company came from me....I think [Hendryx] was visiting at my house; his wife is my wife's sister; and I may have talked it over with my partner Mr. Cheney prior to that time. Mrs. Hendryx had no experience whatever in the manufacture or cutting of glass. Her name was used

largely to comply with the statute to make the necessary number of directors or incorporators.[3]

Cheney was a director as well as vice-president of the company. According to testimony in the Glass Works suit, he owned "not quite" one-third of the stock. The local directory listed Hendryx as secretary and treasurer.

The company's cutting factory was built for its purpose on Hart Avenue, just west of Corning in a village now known as Riverside.[4] In Corning directories, the company address was given as that of Sebring & Cheney's Corning law offices—2 West Erie Avenue until about 1908, when they moved to 2 West Market Street.

Michael Grady, who had learned his trade at J. Hoare & Co. and worked there for a decade, held the title of foreman, but in reality he was the factory manager. He testified in 1906:

> My duties have been the overseeing of the cutting and finishing, and in fact my duties have been everything....I have worked at the frames most every day and now I have charge of the business. I have sold glass several times and I made several trips on the road....
>
> I went out the first trip to Rochester the first year we started and I have been out about twice a year ever since....[5]

Grady's son Justin, formerly of Corning Glass Works, says his father left the company in 1908 when the owners refused to give him a stock interest; he became a grocer. We do not know who succeeded him at Corning Cut Glass.

The company's employees varied from 15 to 50 between late 1901 and 1906. Twenty to 25 were at

538. *Opposite:* Manager Michael Grady of Corning Cut Glass Co. with the young ladies who worked there. The photograph dates from before 1908. *Coll. Justin Grady*

187

539. Representative R. B. Reineck had this display of Seneca Glass and Corning Cut Glass wares at Monongahela House in Pittsburgh. The cut glass is that of the Corning company. *China, Glass & Lamps,* Feb. 6, 1904; *Coll. The Corning Museum of Glass*

work in August 1906,[6] perhaps including the young ladies we show pictured with Mike Grady. The late Francis Conroy, an employee during school vacations, remembers Ernest Ferris and Thomas Durkin of Painted Post and Ray Troll of Corning as among the cutters, and the company's product as geometric cutting of good quality. The shop was "small but progressive," he said, "and had quite a success for a number of years." This is borne out by an extant bill for cut glass from the J. D. Bergen Co., "Popular-Priced Cut Glass," introduced as evidence in the Glass Works suit. Clearly, Corning Cut Glass had more orders than it could fill.

The company may also have employed rather briefly two early women cutters, Sylvia Davis and Mary Morse, who moved to nearby Painted Post about 1911, though these women may have worked for the Crystal Manufacturing Co. there.

Corning Glass Works's suit against Sebring and his company fascinated Corning. Newspapers commented on its progress frequently, as did trade journals. Corning Glass Works was granted a restraining order May 31, 1902, which prevented the new company from using the name "Corning." This order was reversed and later amended. Corning Cut Glass could use its name *if* each sale or advertisement was "accompanied by a statement...that the glass...[was] not manufactured by the plaintiff or from blanks manufactured by it."[7]

Corning Glass Works argued that 1) it had used similar names since 1868; 2) it was frequently addressed as the Corning Glass Company; 3) its glass was of "the very best quality and design"; and

4) the sale of Sebring's cheaper glass would impair the reputation of Corning Glass Works. They also argued that Sebring's company was situated outside Corning.

Sebring, with the help of his partner, acted as his own lawyer and finally won the suit in 1911. As it progressed, however, it forced the company to give up its original acid-stamped trademark, which included the full name. A second trademark used an acid-stamped "C.C.G." in an oval, Justin Grady says. The rarity of both suggests that Sebring later used a sticker.

Corning Cut Glass had started out briskly. The *Journal* reported on October 29, 1902, that it had begun to work evenings "on account of the holiday trade," and that "numerous new frames [had] recently been added."

Meanwhile, Sebring seems to have been considering the manufacture of blanks as a competitor of Corning Glass Works. This story is told in Chapter 18.

An article in *China, Glass & Lamps* described the company's products as of January 16, 1904.

The Coronation, the Amazon, the Snowflake and the Glendovere are four full new lines in elaborate patterns....The Coronation has the buzz-saw effect, the Amazon is a combination of sunbursts and similar designs. The Glendovere is one of those elaborate indescribable things and the Snowflake is as airy and delicate as its name. The Byron line, though much less expensive, comes in a complete line. The company's maiden line, the Alpha is still making good.

China, Glass & Lamps reported on February 6, 1904, that Corning Cut Glass's Pittsburgh representative was R. B. Reineck, whose display we show. On February 23, three years later, in the same publication, the company advertised for a salesman for the Indiana, Ohio, and Illinois territory. In February of the following year (1908), China, Glass & Lamps mentioned that Adam Duval was one of the travelers for Corning Cut Glass.

The company's glass did not rival the finest products of Corning's great manufacturers. An advertising letter from one of its agents said: "Almost anyone can now enjoy what was once a great luxury. Cut glass can be purchased at moderate prices."

James Sebring's reasons for opening a cut-glass company in Corning clearly were sound. We have quoted these at length in Chapter 2. Briefly recapitulated, they were: Corning's reputation for fine glass, the ready supply of trained workmen, and "the fact that [Corning] is not a union city." It was immaterial, he testified, that Corning Glass Works sold its blanks only to the Hawkes and Hoare companies.

His timing, however, was also important. His company rode the crest of Corning's greatest cut-glass boom, when, as Thomas Hawkes said, "the middle class of people" had a great deal more money and began to buy cut glass. Corning Glass Works, helped by Hawkes and James Hoare, was fighting to maintain Corning's reputation for high quality in its suit against Sebring; it was doomed to lose.

Some of Corning Cut Glass's blanks came from the Pairpoint Corporation, others from the Phoenix and Fairmont companies. Purchases from Union Glass Co. may have stopped after 1906, when a letter from the company urgently requested payment of past-due accounts.[8] The two signed Corning Cut Glass vases that we have seen were tall, heavy, brilliant-cut pieces of good workmanship. We have found no design patents assigned to the company, and believe that it employed no designer as such. Manager Michael Grady would typically have been hired because of his ability to design cuttings.

Despite the company's listing in *Thomas' Register* for 1912 (capital, over $5,000), directories indicate that it seems to have closed in 1911. On October 1, 1912, the *Corning Leader* reported that the American Flint Glass Workers' Union was considering buying the factory.

Sebring was apparently bitter over the Corning Glass Works suit. When he was Acting City Attorney in 1912, the Corning Board of Assessors raised Corning Glass Works's property valuation from $305,000 to $925,000; and the *Daily Journal* said on July 20 that the Glass Works had indicated it might move one plant. The following year the City Council overruled the assessors. The *Daily Journal* rejoiced. Its story of January 11 identified Sebring as the "moving spirit in the levying of an excessive assessment."

In 1921 Sebring was one of the owners who sold the factory of the former O. F. Egginton Co. to John Illig. He continued an active career as a lawyer until his death in the 1940s.

SUMMARY

Dates: 1901-ca. 1911

Address: factory on the corner of Hart and Erie Avenues, now in Riverside. Office at 2 West Erie Avenue, Corning, moved to 2 West Market Street about 1908

Blanks: from Pairpoint Corporation, Phoenix Glass Co., Fairmont Glass Works, and Union Glass Co. (perhaps until 1906 only). Purchases of glass from Niles, Ohio, and Vineland, New Jersey, have also been reported.

Trademark: for a brief period, an acid-stamped mark similar to that of J. Hoare & Co., giving the company's full name. Thereafter, the initials C.C.G. in an oval, also acid-stamped. The rarity of both trademarks suggests that a sticker was later used.

Product: a full line of geometrically cut and Brilliant cut glass. No chandeliers or lamps have been reported. Good work on goods of moderate price

Employees: Thomas Durkin, Ernest Ferris, George Lindstrom, Ray Troll, Clifford Stock, and Gerald Davis, all cutters.[9] Michael Grady was working foreman and manager until 1908. A total of 20 to 25 cutters was usual.

Customers: chiefly gift shops and department stores as far west as Wisconsin

12
Giometti Brothers

The Giometti family, including a young son, Cherubino, reached Utica, New York, from Tuscany in the early 1870s.[1] A second son, Lazare Clarence, was born in Utica in 1874. The Giomettis moved to Corning a few years later. By 1899 the brothers had Anglicized their names to Carbine and Lazarus Clarence (called Clarence).

Clarence Giometti learned to cut glass at T. G. Hawkes & Co., completing his training in the 1890s. The brothers opened a small glass-cutting factory in 1902. The *Journal*'s announcement, September 10, said:

> The firm of Giometti Brothers is composed of L. C. and C. J. Giometti. The former is an experienced glass cutter. The latter has for a series of years been salesman in the clothing store of Morris Ansorge, and will continue there. The shop of Giometti Brothers will be on their premises at No. 201 West Water Street. They expect to begin work this week with half a dozen frames.

Investors in the company included Thomas Chittick and Corning lawyer Claude B. Stowell.[2] Stowell was the company's treasurer; he wrote out the paychecks in his law office. Clarence Giometti was designer and working foreman; his brother, the bookkeeper and salesman, was on the road most of the time.

Corning directories were biennial, and Giometti Brothers appeared in every edition from 1903 through 1933. In fact, however, the company moved to Watkins Glen, New York, in 1907. On July 19 of that year, the *Leader* reported an agreement with

that town's Board of Trade. The company would move into the board's building on Twelfth Street. If it employed 25 hands, five-sixths of them men, ten months a year for ten years, and repaired and paid taxes on the building, it would receive a deed to the property. But the company returned to their former factory in Corning in 1909. The *Leader* wrote on April 2 that they would employ about 40 men, though the total was actually lower.

Giometti Brothers' billhead read "Manufacturers of RICH CUT GLASS." The company employed no in-factory engravers; John Illig engraved their special orders. Employees peaked at about 24. Designs included cane cutting, stars of up to 48 points, and floral cuts combined with geometric motifs.

During World War I, L. C. Giometti worked for T. G. Hawkes & Co. His work had to do with acid-dipping. After World War I, Giometti Brothers did flat glass work for automobiles, and also repaired old glass. The company's products changed with the times. During the 1920s its men made floral-cut Pyrex brand glassware for Corning Glass Works. The brothers held two design patents, assigned to Corning Glass Works, which only their company cut. (Actually, the two patents were for the same design applied to different shapes.) The circles in the one we show enclosed various flowers.

When autumn came, Giometti Brothers put aside other work. For two to three months they cut only for Marshall Field & Co. of Chicago, filling a boxcar with geometric- and floral-cut glass.

Giometti Brothers' last listing in Corning directories was in 1933. They closed later that year, one of many glass-industry victims of the Great Depression.

540. *Opposite:* Clarence Giometti and his wife in the Giometti Brothers factory early in the century. *Coll. Mrs. Louise Giometti Smith*

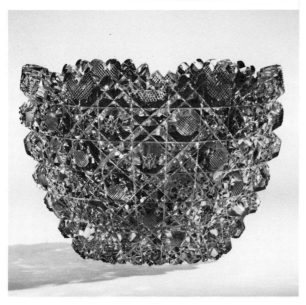

541. Green-cased bowl cut by Clarence Giometti between 1903 and 1920. Diam., 16.1 cm. *Coll. Mrs. Louise Giometti Smith*

542. Lamp cut at Giometti Brothers, probably before 1920. Height, 45.3 cm. *Coll. Mrs. Matthew Cammen*

543. Giometti Brothers sugar and creamer. Height of sugar with cover, 11.5 cm. *Coll. Mrs. Louise Giometti Smith*

SUMMARY

Dates: 1902-33

Addresses: 201 (later 205) West Water Street, 1902-7 and 1909-33. 1907-9, Twelfth Street, Watkins Glen, New York

Blanks: from McKee Glass Co., Jeannette Glass Co., a company in Washington, Pennsylvania, and a Belgian manufacturer. Many blanks were figured in later years.

Trademark: none

Product: a full line of rich-cut glass in early years; later, floral cuttings also. Floral-cut Pyrex brand glassware and commercial products after World War I

Employees: cutters included Jerry Quill (also spelled Quil), George Steers, George Krebs, Jack and Sid McGuire, Floyd Peters, Bob (or Bert) Ferguson, Ed Hyland, a Mr. Spear, and Raymond Powell. Hannah Fritchie, bookkeeper; Hannah Shay, wrapper

Customers: unknown before World War I; presumably department stores. After World War I, Corning Glass Works, Marshall Field & Co.

544. Clarence Giometti posed with some of his company's glass, ca. 1915. *Coll. Mrs. Louise Giometti Smith*

546. *Left to right:* Clarence Giometti and cutters Bert Ferguson, Ed Hyland, and Raymond Powell, about 1915. *Coll. Mrs. Louise Giometti Smith*

545. Vase cut on a figured blank by Giometti Brothers, ca. 1915. Height, 30.5 cm. *Coll. Mrs. Helen Fritchie Arnoldy; Frederic Farrar photograph*

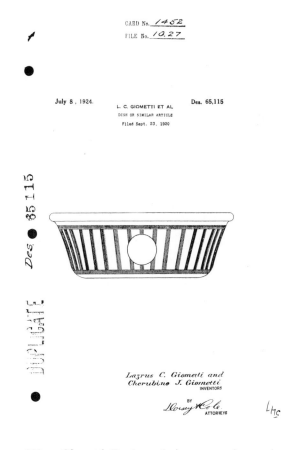

547. Giometti Brothers design patent for cutting on Pyrex brand glassware.

193

548. The crown shape of this cologne bottle, cut from solid glass, shows Frederick Carder's use of cutting-as-shaping in the 1920s. Height, 15.9 cm. *Coll. The Corning Museum of Glass*

549. Cut paperweight cologne with enclosed Cintra decoration. 1920s. Height, 22.5 cm. *Coll. The Corning Museum of Glass*

550. Cut console set in cobalt blue cased over pink, a combination that Carder called "Alexandrite." 1920s. Height of candlesticks, 30.5 and 30.8 cm. *Coll. The Rockwell-Corning Museum*

13
Steuben Glass Works (1903-18) Steuben Glass, Corning Glass Works (1918-33)

The artistic history of the Steuben Glass Works under Thomas Hawkes's ownership and that of Corning Glass Works form a unified whole until 1933. Its artistic direction was in the hands of Frederick Carder, who was responsible for its designs and glass formulas. From 1918 to 1933 Corning Glass Works employees called the company "the Steuben Division." Its letterheads in 1930 read "CORNING GLASS WORKS/Steuben Division." We shall use the nickname in order to avoid confusion with today's Steuben Glass, which embarked on a new course in 1933. Its story is told in Chapter 20.

Under Hawkes ownership Steuben was chiefly a glassmaking factory rather than a cutting company. The products it listed in the 1912 *American Glass Factory Directory* included jelly jars, "electrical goods," opal ware, and tubing, in addition to cutting blanks and cut glass. It also made quantities of undecorated art glass. Similarly, Corning Glass Works records show that cut and engraved glass totaled only 10 to 12 percent of Steuben's sales from 1918 to 1933. Inasmuch as all Steuben engraving and some cutting were subcontracted to Corning's home shops, its in-factory cutting operation was small.

Steuben's early history was shrouded in secrecy. Chapter 5 has shown that Thomas Hawkes bought the former Payne Foundry on West Erie Avenue in March 1901. Though he told the *Journal* that he "would use the property for manufacturing," he declined to be more specific. Two auxiliary Hawkes cutting shops opened in the building in that year and the following one. They operated through 1910, when relevant records end; the Hawkes Cash Book

provides no evidence that they closed before Hawkes's death in 1913.

In the spring of 1902 Samuel Hawkes interrupted a trip to England to invite Frederick Carder to manage a new glassworks in Corning.[1] Carder agreed, but the arrangement was kept secret. Only when he reached Corning in March 1903, ostensibly on a fact-finding trip for his County Council, was the new company announced.

Who was Frederick Carder? The following brief answer draws on Paul Gardner's definitive *Glass of Frederick Carder.*[2]

Carder was born in 1863 in Staffordshire, England, long noted for its china and glass factories. He left school at the age of fourteen to work in a local pottery, meanwhile studying art and technical subjects at night. His strong interest in John Northwood's cameo glass copy of the Portland Vase led to an introduction to Northwood, who taught him how to make cameo glass and recommended him to the Stevens & Williams glass company as a designer.

Carder designed under Northwood, who became the company's art director and works manager, until Northwood died in 1902. Carder designs included cuttings in the Anglo-Irish style and rock-crystal engravings. As Carder's reputation grew, Northwood's friendship cooled to the point of hostility. When Northwood's son succeeded to his father's position, which Carder had hoped to gain, Carder was willing to emigrate. His delay until 1903 is perhaps attributable to a tour of German and Austrian glass factories that he had agreed to make for the County Council in 1902.

Carder was thoroughly qualified to be artistic

director of a glassworks. The *Brierley Hill...Advertiser* wrote of his accomplishments as follows:

[Mr. Carder] has been associated with the [Wordsley Art] School and the art class which preceded it for the last fifteen or sixteen years, and has been art master since 1892....In his work at the school Mr. Carder happily combined the theoretical with the practical. It is twenty-three years since he commenced work at Messrs. Stevens and Williams's Moor Lane Glass Works, and his industry and ability raised him to the position of chief designer... and he is...the only holder in this district of a gold medal in the national competition, this having been awarded in 1890 for a design on glass. Under his superintendence the Wordsley Art Class was one of the foremost in the kingdom, and the school...has maintained that high reputation....

Last year Mr. Carder was appointed lecturer to the County Council, and on behalf of that body visited the glass works in Germany and Austria[3]...He had in 1897 visited France for a similar purpose, and when in March last he set out for the United States...he had ample material for making the most suggestive and informing comparisons.[4]

If Carder had reasons to keep his real mission to the United States a secret, so did Thomas Hawkes. Several suggest themselves. One is Hawkes's long collaboration with Corning Glass Works. His company was one of two Glass Works customers for blanks. His close friend was H. P. Sinclaire, Sr., the company's secretary;[5] Sinclaire, Jr., was Hawkes & Co.'s vice-president. Their loyalty to the Glass Works, and perhaps his apprehension about the AFGWU's reaction to his plans, may explain why Hawkes kept his own counsel until Carder arrived ten months later, before announcing Steuben Glass Works as an art glass factory. This was not Carder's understanding. The interview with him reported in the *Brierley Hill...Advertiser* said: "The firm under which Mr. Carder is engaged intend making the best quality of flint glass, similar to that used in the Stourbridge district."

The Hawkes Cash Book shows many Steuben-related payments before Carder reached Corning: for trademark registrations, a banker's draft on London, a survey of Erie Avenue. All repaid Thomas Hawkes for earlier disbursements, as did a payment March 7 for "drawing papers, S G W." Carder was now in Corning; Hawkes contracted with him that day "for delivery of one hundred shares of the capital stock of the Steuben Glass Works @ $100 per share."[6]

The same secrecy colored Steuben's incorporation certificate, filed March 9. It listed the owners of only three of Steuben's 500 shares of stock: Carder; Willard Reed, Thomas Hawkes's lawyer; and Estella Reed, presumably Reed's wife, who were also directors. Thomas Hawkes, who owned 355 shares of the stock when he died,[7] and testified in 1904 that he was the company's president, is nowhere mentioned.

Conversion of the Erie Avenue foundry had begun by April. Carder returned to England in late May and announced his move; his expenses were entered in the Hawkes Cash Book under June 1, 1903. Gardner writes that the news "startled and shocked the district." During his stay Carder must have arranged for English glassblowers to follow him. He was back in Corning by July 27.[8]

Now the Hawkes-Carder secrecy precipitated the first of two pregnant events. Distressing when they happened, they can be seen in retrospect as a foundation for Corning's continuing greatness as a fine-glass center. The first was a bitter struggle with the AFGWU, which the union won. The second was H. P. Sinclaire, Jr.'s, severing of relations with Hawkes & Co. Considered against the background of an already existing quarrel between Thomas Hawkes and C. Dorflinger & Sons, the two are seen to be related. For Sinclaire supported Dorflinger in the dispute.[9]

The union had warned the Englishmen not to work for Thomas Hawkes. When they crossed the Atlantic anyway, the AFGWU succeeded in having them intercepted at Malone, New York, on a New York Central train from Montreal, and taken to Ellis Island. After a three-month legal struggle they were deported.[10] In the hearings in Washington, Dorflinger did not support Hawkes's contention that he needed the workers to make "the same glass as the...Tiffany favrile glass." As a result (according to Hawkes's testimony in the Glass Works suit), his company stopped buying blanks from Dorflinger.

Thomas Hawkes and Carder found the blowers they needed in White Mills. Henning Overstrom, born in Sweden and brought to the United States by Christian Dorflinger, became the first man to blow the liquid aurene solution on Steuben's hot glass, according to his son Ralph Overstrom. Other Dorflinger men followed him to Corning. A former Steuben gaffer says that "you might say that C. Dorflinger & Sons was responsible for Aurene."[11] These men were doubtless also responsible for the notable similarity in the shapes of Steuben and Dorflinger finger bowls, tumblers, and a few other small pieces. Their competence ensured that no shape Carder designed was too difficult to produce. So many Dorflinger craftsmen followed Overstrom to Corning over the years that, one descendant says, "we used to say that half of Corning came from White Mills."

Steuben began to deliver cutting blanks by March

1904. H. P. Sinclaire returned from a sales trip to find that payments to Steuben had replaced payments to Dorflinger in the Hawkes Cash Book. He promptly quit. As Chapter 14 will show, the company he founded became Corning's specialist in fine engraving, employing and attracting to Corning many of the engravers on whom the reorganized Steuben Glass would depend after 1933.

Steuben Glass Works began to cut and engrave glass almost at once. Revi reports that cutting began in order to salvage blanks returned by the Hawkes company because of flaws.[12] These were chiefly stemware, according to testimony given in the Glass Works suit (p. 146). We may suspect that Carder either used the Hawkes & Co. cutters already working in his building, or sent a cutter or two of his own to work with them.

Beginning in September 1904, Carder earned a small additional salary as "consulting designer" for T. G. Hawkes & Co. This may have been payment for his services as a designer of special Hawkes blanks; we see no evidence of his style in Hawkes cutting, for which Thomas Hawkes continued to file patents. The Cash Book shows that the company was also training John Pearson as a designer in 1905 and 1906.

Carder·had a free hand artistically at Steuben, but the parent firm closely controlled business matters. T. G. Hawkes was president until his death, when Sam Hawkes succeeded him. Payments to Steuben "on acct" entered in the Hawkes Cash Book are too large and too frequent—sometimes twice a week—to be payments for blanks only.

T. G. Hawkes & Co.'s "travelers" at first sold Steuben glass; at least one continued to do so for a number of years. The Hawkes company continued to pay Steuben sales commissions through 1910, when relevant Cash Book records end. As late as 1915 Hawkes & Co. was setting Steuben prices for blanks.[13] We do not know whether this curious dependence on the parent company—and the Steuben custom of subcontracting its engraving—aimed at freeing Carder to develop his art glasses, or whether T. G. Hawkes insisted on tightly controlling an expensive investment.

Carder's status as one-fifth owner of Steuben was somewhat anomalous. Though he doubtless voted his stock, he paid only interest on its purchase price until after T. G. Hawkes died.[14]

Needless to say, Steuben Glass Works was a non-union company. Though Carder was perhaps not as relentlessly opposed to the AFGWU as was Hawkes, he had expressed reservations about it in his *Brierley Hill* interview. He said:

the [American] Glassmakers' Union is stronger than here; and it is conducted on lines less satisfac-

tory...Many of the best American firms...are employing only non-union men, solely because the rules and regulations of the Society are so arbitrary.

Steuben clearly prospered in its first decade; it expanded in 1908. We do not know, however, how much Steuben cutting and engraving was reaching the market. A fire that Corning papers reported in the Steuben cutting shops in December 1910 probably referred to the Hawkes-owned shops No. 2 and No. 3.[15] When Steuben expanded again in 1912, into an adjacent building to the east, the new quarters provided the third-floor salesroom and second-floor office that Corning still remembers; Gardner pictures the Steuben Glass Works building on page 38.

The beginning of World War I in Europe did not immediately affect Steuben operations. A trade journal (*China, Glass & Lamps,* June 26) reported during the slow summer season of 1916: "The various cutting shops at Corning, N.Y., are operating full tilt, as is the Steuben Glass Co.'s plant at that place."

The war affected all American fine-glass manufacturers by 1917. Steuben was classified as a non-essential industry. Cut off from the purchase of war-related materials, and restricted in the use of transportation, Steuben curtailed production. Corning Glass Works records show that they bought the company January 5, 1918. The Glass Works used the factory for commercial products, including light bulbs, but the making of fine glass never stopped entirely.[16] Presumably cutting also continued.

If Steuben had been known for Carder's colored glass before World War I, it retained its reputation during the craze for color of the 1920s. By 1930, however, crystal had regained popularity, especially in the heavy shapes of the international style. As the decade ended, so did Steuben's profits. Its reorganization in 1933, and the new life that resulted, is one of the subjects of Chapter 20.

Frederick Carder became art director of Corning Glass Works in 1933. As Gardner has related in detail in his book, Carder continued to work brilliantly with architectural glass, castings, and sculpture until his retirement in 1959 at the age of ninety-six, but he designed and manufactured no more cut or engraved wares.

* * *

Gardner's book on Carder contains catalog pages of Steuben cut and engraved crystal of the 1904–12 period, and additional pages of wheel-decorated colored blanks. We can add little to his detailed coverage.

Steuben Glass Works and Steuben Division cut crystal is rare and virtually always unsigned. Joseph

Sporer, former assistant to the Steuben blowing-room foreman, reports that cut glass was trade-marked only by sticker. We have, however, seen engraved colored pieces signed with an acid-stamped STEUBEN.

Unsigned cut or engraved pieces on Steuben blanks but in designs unreported in Gardner are plentiful. These should be suspected of being the product of one of the customers that bought Steuben company blanks. They show, however, that Steuben Glass Works cut many of the same blanks it also sold to others, and that the quality of its crystal was unremarkable.

T. G. Hawkes testified in 1904 in the Corning Glass Works suit (page 148):

> The Steuben Glass Works takes a cheaper...quality of glass, what they call half crystal, a great deal less lead in that than the glass manufactured by the Corning Glass Works....We don't know whether by the addition of more lead it could be made of the same richness.

Later Steuben Glass Works blanks, even when of full-lead weight, do not bear comparison with the brilliance of Dorflinger Best Metal. The half crystal was also continued; it may be this formula that the company sold as "gray English finish." Frederick Carder's interest and genius were expended chiefly on his colored glasses. Often their cutting was simple and dramatic.

Frederick Carder told Gardner that a squat vase (bowl) machine-threaded in green and stone-engraved in a simple floral design was Steuben Glass Works's first engraved piece.[17] H. P. Sinclaire & Co. made the design in quantity on Steuben machine-threaded blanks, usually in the green that Gardner shows. Given Carder's custom of subcontracting much of Steuben's wheel decoration, we may wonder whether his subcontractors included Corning cutting firms as well as home shops. Engravings before 1918 included polished work on blanks such as the one in Illustration 21. The three-dimensional effect imitated at lower cost the cut "pillars" of more expensive rock-crystal engraving.

Many of the designs and innovations that make Carder-Steuben cutting instantly recognizable date from between 1918 and 1933, when the company was Corning Glass Works's Steuben Division. During these years Carder often used cutting in ways new to Corning. His emphasis on cutting-as-shaping lifted the cutting wheel above its use as a decorating tool.

Carder carried further the Corning practice of cutting legs from the open bases of bowls, a relatively simple job. Carder had his cutters cut four-sided apertures above a glass rim (Ill. 548). This

was a feat that the reorganized Steuben Glass would repeat in its 1939 World's Fair Cup.

Such art objects as the Carder-Steuben birds illustrate another characteristic Carder use of cutting: as texture or background. In the Steuben eagle, cutting reminiscent of the hollow or St. Louis diamonds suggests the texture of feathers. But texture cuts were used on non-representational objects also. The cutting of a covered Moonlight glass bowl illustrated in Paul Gardner's book (page 94) is more reminiscent of the acid-etched background of French cameo pieces than it is of Corning's earlier decorative cutting.

Cutting-as-shaping distinguishes a group of paper-weight cologne bottles and vases made in the 1920s. Though enclosed color gives them much of their charm, deep channel cuts add a new drama to their shapes. Modern Steuben Glass's *Whirlpool Vase,* which we show in Chapter 20, is related to these pieces.

Frederick Carder's liking for such simple cut motifs as panels and punties was not new. H. P. Sinclaire, Jr., shared the predilection, as had C. Dorflinger & Sons. Made in sometimes startling combinations of Steuben colored glasses, however, Carder's bold cuttings had a style of their own. The twenties' word was "zip." The cut console set (Ill. 550) that we show is cobalt blue cased over pink, a combination that Carder called "Alexandrite."

Steuben combinations of air twist stems or controlled bubbles with cutting were unique in Corning.

The Steuben Division's engraving ranged from the simplest stone-engraved floral designs on crystal or color to sets of cased tablewares in the most elaborate of copper-wheel engraving. The strong similarity between a few of the former with Sinclaire & Co. designs suggests that both were engraver-designed. Finer work, such as the stemware we show, was of Carder's design.

By 1932, when the last Steuben Division catalog was issued, the company was making tablewares so modern in design that the reorganized Steuben Glass continued them for several years. The 1932 *Strawberry Mansion* urn, shown in Illustration 552, was another survivor of the Carder era.

Under both Hawkes and Corning Glass Works ownership the Steuben company produced acid-etched fine-glasses in myriad color combinations. Cut and acid-etched lighting globes were another important product.

* * *

We have seen that Frederick Carder may have used the Hawkes & Co. cutting shops in the Steuben

551. *Left:* Cased amethyst stemware, probably engraved by Henry Keller. Height of goblet, 25 cm. *Coll. The Corning Museum of Glass*

552. *Below: Strawberry Mansion* urn, inspired by an engraved goblet of the American Federalist period. The design was shown in the 1932 Steuben Division catalog, and continued after the company's reorganization in 1933. Height, 32.6 cm. *Coll. The Rockwell-Corning Museum*

building for his first tentative production of cut glass. Former employees remember that he had his own cutters when World War I began or just after it. This fine-glass cutting shop was very small: two roughers and a smoother or two. The late Robert Leavy, long Steuben's production manager, recalled three great roughers. Of these, however, only Leonard Dow was working for the company before its 1933 reorganization. Some cutting was subcontracted after about 1920; the number of cutters who listed themselves as employed by Corning Glass Works but who are absent from Glass Works employment records suggests that subcontracting was common. Benjamin Watson cut for Steuben in his home shop; John Denson did Steuben stoppering and shipped the finished product. In-factory smoothers were Marx Bernt and Nelson Doane. Polishers, stopperers, and erasers of engraver's slips included Denson (who also cut glass), John and Louis Lentricchia, and Henry Geisler. Ray Inscho was cutting foreman.

Engraving was entirely subcontracted. Virtually every home engraving shop in Corning seems to have worked for Steuben regularly or occasionally. Since they continued to do so after the 1933 reorganization, they are named in Chapter 20. An exception is Joseph Nitsche, who engraved for the Steuben Division until his death in 1923. Engraver Joseph Libisch became increasingly responsible for assigning Steuben's engraving jobs during the 1920s.

SUMMARY

Dates: 1903-the Steuben reorganization of 1933

Blanks: Virtually all were of Steuben's manufacture. Visual evidence (slight variations in color; the existence of large pontil marks on a few Steuben pieces) suggests that H. P. Sinclaire & Co. made an occasional lot for Steuben after 1920.

Trademark: stickers on cut glass; acid-stamped STEU-BEN on some engravings

Product: a full line of cut, cut-and-engraved, and engraved glass in color, cased crystal, and crystal

Employees: cutters: Leonard Dow, Marx Bernt, Nelson Doane; polishers and stopperers: John and Louis Lentricchia,[18] Henry Geisler; cutting foreman: Ray Inscho; factory saleswoman: Mrs. Betty Lynn McElroy; subcontractors included cutter Benjamin Watson, engraver Joseph Nitsche, and other engravers listed in Chapter 20.

Customers: for cut and engraved glass: department, jewelry, and gift stores across the country; for cutting blanks: the Hawkes, Hoare, Sinclaire, and J. F. Haselbauer companies in Corning. Also the Allen Cut Glass Co., the Pittston Cut Glass Co.; others unknown

553.   Cut plate, unsigned, made at Steuben Glass Works before 1918. Diam., 44.6 cm. *Coll. The Corning Museum of Glass* (Gift of Otto Hilbert)

554. Cut covered bowl in Moonlight glass, Steuben Division, Corning Glass Works, 1920s. Height, 22.5 cm. *Coll. The Rockwell-Corning Museum*

555. Rich-cut plate, signed "Steuben" in diamond-point script. Steuben signatures on cut glass are rare before 1933. Diam., 21.8 cm. *Coll. Miss Alice Keeler*

14
H. P. Sinclaire & Co.

H. P. Sinclaire, Jr., may have been the only person in Corning who thought, as he grew up, that he might not go into the glass business.[1] His mother was the sister of Mrs. Amory Houghton, wife of the founder of Corning Glass Works. Their brother had owned stock in Houghton's Union Glass Works in Somerville, Massachusetts, and—Glass Works records show—was the largest stockholder when the Houghtons bought the Brooklyn Flint Glass Works. Sinclaire's father was secretary of Corning Glass Works and one of its incorporators.

Harry Sinclaire, later called "H. P.," was born in New York City in 1864. The family moved to Brooklyn in 1866, and to Corning in 1868. Harry worked one summer for "Jimmy" Hoare at J. Hoare & Co. A natural artist, the boy was unimpressed by cut glass, which at this time was of the Anglo-Irish type.

Sinclaire's father believed that the big family library made college studies redundant. What his boys needed was business training. Accordingly, Harry went to Rochester Business University in 1882; his brother William followed two years later. From Rochester Harry wrote his father that he would like to go into business in New York. His father answered:

Mr. Hawkes came to me the other day & offered to give you a situation in his office. . . . The position would be a very good one for one so young as you are, and there is not one chance in a hundred that you would get as good a one in New York. Here you would be at once next to your employer, who is a rising business man, young, and making money. In New York you would probably have to take a boy's place.[2]

Harry agreed, and his father wrote again:

[Mr. Hawkes] is going to pay you Six Hundred Dollars the first year, which is an exceedingly liberal remuneration, & I told him so, stating that I would be perfectly satisfied with a smaller amount. His answer was that if you were worth anything you should be worth that. Now my dear Harry you are going to be placed in a responsible position at the very outset of your career, & you will have to work and think so as to fill it in a satisfactory manner. Always strive to do more than is required. . . . The next point for you is to determine to save at least half your salary. . . . I will not charge you for board, unless I find you should be inclined to waste your money.

Another position was also offered:

Mr. Wellington. . . offered to give you a position in his bank, saying that he had been watching you for the last two years. It was very gratifying to me to receive such an offer, & I thanked him for it, at the same time informed him that I had already made satisfactory arrangement for you.[3]

Harry went to work for the Hawkes Rich Cut Glass Works in March 1883, the *Journal* reported on the twenty-second. Perhaps his lifelong interest in copper-wheel engraving was awakened by the punch bowl for William Vanderbilt that Joseph Haselbauer was then engraving.

Though Harry's title was bookkeeper, he learned every facet of the cut-glass business under the tutelage of Thomas Hawkes, his father's close friend. As the reintroduction of curved miter cuts

556. *Opposite: H. P. Sinclaire, Jr., in June 1918. Coll. Mrs. Estelle Sinclaire Farrar*

203

557. Marvin Olcott, Sinclaire's partner from 1904 to 1921, during the 1920s. *Coll. Robert Olcott*

about 1886 led to the exuberant decoration of the Brilliant Period, Sinclaire's toleration for cutting cooled to antipathy. Hawkes encouraged his interest in engraving, and Harry designed simple stone engravings almost at once. Haselbauer engraved some of them, but none found their way into Hawkes salesmen's catalogs.

By 1888 Sinclaire was indeed "next to" Mr. Hawkes in the company. He was its spokesman in the *New York Tribune* article quoted in Chapter 2. In the years when the Hawkes family summered in Ireland, Sinclaire vacationed in the winter. The code used for the Hawkes Cash Book "Office payroll" entries designated Hawkes as "1" and Sinclaire as "2."

Sinclaire was responsible for the company's money management. Though accountant Walter Allen worked under him from 1887 to 1899,[4] Sinclaire kept in touch with production. He himself recorded all items supplied to the company through 1903.[5] Hawkes also encouraged Sinclaire's talent for sales. And the young man continued to design engravings.

As already explained, Corning's chief competitors for the lucrative East Coast markets were English,

and it was the challenge to Corning posed by the importation of the Fritsche ewer in 1886 that prompted T. G. Hawkes to include engravings in the exhibit he sent to the Paris Universal Exposition of 1889 (see Chapter 8). Sinclaire designed all the six or seven pieces. Joseph Haselbauer engraved them.[6]

In May, Charles Voorhees left J. Hoare & Co. to become bookkeeper at the Hawkes company, freeing Sinclaire to sail for Paris "in the interest of his employer," as the *Journal* put it on July 18, 1889. The engraving he saw at the exposition included exquisite work from Baccarat.[7] This company so impressed him that he later bought blanks from it. Henri Froment, the Hawkes company's only competitor as a cut-glass manufacturer in Group III, Class 19, showed engraved as well as cut glass and also demonstrated "the process of cutting and engraving glass," according to the exposition catalog. Sinclaire returned to Corning in mid-July.

We have described Corning's joy at the Hawkes company's Paris grand prize. When Hawkes reorganized his company in 1890, Sinclaire became the only other owner of more than one share of stock. In addition to the share that Sinclaire received "by subscription," he bought an additional 12½ percent interest.[8] He was to hold this until about 1925.[9]

Sinclaire signed an agreement to give Hawkes first refusal on his stock. If they disagreed about price, they were to appoint arbitrators. Sinclaire was formally named secretary and a director. His salary and Hawkes's were set at $1,800 a year.

Sinclaire began to travel for the company. In 1892 he married. His wife died in January 1900, following the birth of twin boys, their third and fourth sons. Sinclaire retired from an active social life, and threw himself into sales trips for Hawkes & Co. By the end of 1900, the Hawkes Cash Book shows he was regularly visiting New York, Boston, Philadelphia, Chicago, and other cities. His customers were jewelers, to whom he sold the company's best line of glass, including his own engraving designs. Whenever he was in Corning, he made the Hawkes engraving department his special interest.

Late in 1902 the death of Sinclaire's father loosened the bond that had tied him to T. G. Hawkes. Will Sinclaire took over as secretary of Corning Glass Works, of which the brothers became stockholders. Harry Sinclaire's sales trips were now so frequent that he was unable to serve as an executor of his father's estate.

By this time Sinclaire also headed a small china-decorating company, which used European blanks. Its trademark was a raven perched on a branch, and the name RAVENWOOD. H. P. Sinclaire & Co. would still stock its products in 1920.[10]

558. *Right:* Cologne bottle, *Pillars & Roses* engraving in rock-crystal finish, made at the Sinclaire company ca. 1905–27. Height, 18.2 cm. *Coll. Mrs. Estelle Sinclaire Farrar*

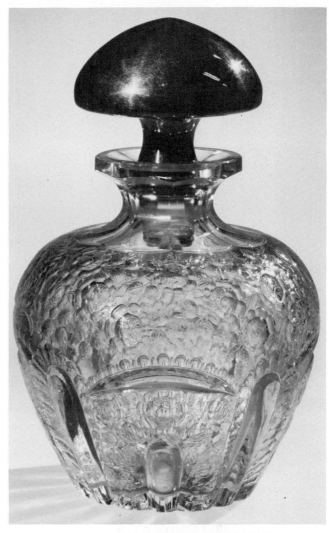

559. *Below:* Blue-banded tablewares made at the Sinclaire company, on Sinclaire blanks, in the 1920s. Diameter of plate, 16.4 cm. Plate and finger bowl, *Coll. Mr. and Mrs. John Marx;* sherbet and tumbler, *Coll. Mrs. Estelle Sinclaire Farrar*

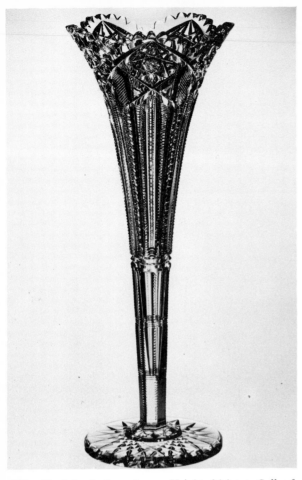

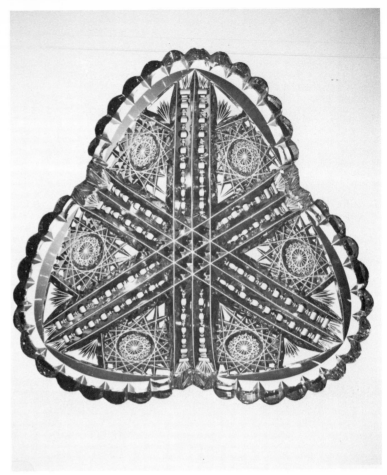

560. Sinclaire & Co. cut vase. Height, 36.1 cm. *Coll. of the Misses Mildred and Evelyn Durkin*

561. Sinclaire & Co. cut trilobe nappy in *Cumberland*. Length, 7.1 cm. *Coll. Mrs. Edna Hanley Rotsell*

Hawkes and Sinclaire agreed about little. Hawkes preferred rich-cut glass, for example; Sinclaire loved engraving. Hawkes believed strongly in advertising; Sinclaire was convinced that a quality product would find its own public. The differences had helped the company before 1902; Hawkes gave Sinclaire a free hand with the company's engravings.

The two men had one trait in common, however: an extreme reticence about their personal affairs. This was to drive them apart. Hawkes may never have known that Sinclaire had thought seriously of backing a competitor in 1895. When Oliver Egginton left the Hawkes company to found his own firm, Sinclaire proposed a partnership that Egginton declined.[11]

As Sinclaire's sons became lively and mischievous youngsters, and his engraving designs found increasing acceptance, he spent more time on design, and he began to design blanks also. When Corning Glass Works discontinued the manufacture of stemware blanks, Hawkes & Co. turned to C. Dorflinger & Sons. Sinclaire's later fondness for the Dorflinger crystal suggests that he was responsible for its use at Hawkes & Co.

By 1900 rock-crystal and unpolished engravings were selling well. Joseph Haselbauer was T. G. Hawkes & Co.'s engraving foreman. Thomas Dow, Oliver Egginton's nephew, was a cutting foreman; the Cash Book recorded his "special pay." This year saw the first preparations for the introduction of Hawkes Gravic glass; they continued through 1902. Sinclaire designed for the line; signed Gravic pieces with more copper-wheel detail than is usual date from these years.

Hawkes's secrecy about his plan to make cutting blanks at the Steuben Glass Works seems to have extended to Sinclaire too. H. P. clearly suspected that the company would compete with Dorflinger and Corning Glass Works, and his suspicions were shared. His own next steps were as clandestine as Hawkes's: Marvin Olcott became a salaried principal of a new company in November 1903; William Sinclaire bought $10,000 worth of stock in it on January 25, 1904.[12] Hawkes Cash Book entries indicate Sinclaire returned from a sales trip in late March. Hawkes & Co.'s bookkeeping entries for the first quarter of 1904 were complete early in April. In checking these, Sinclaire could not have failed to

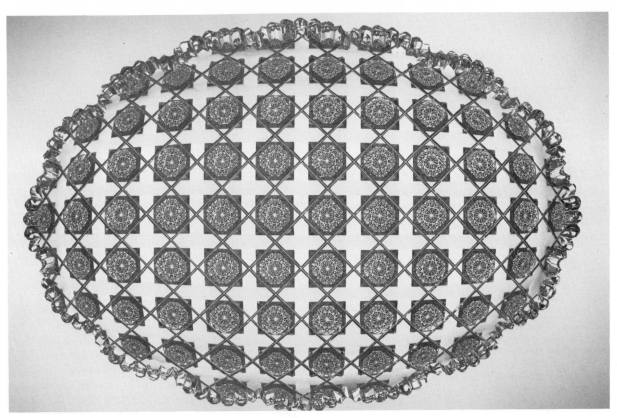

562. Tray cut in Sinclaire's patented *Assyrian,* ca. 1909–18. Length, 30.5 cm. *Coll. Mrs. Estelle Sinclaire Farrar*

563. Stone-engraved and "sterling silver inlay" pitcher, ca. 1920s. Height, 24.7 cm. *Coll. Mrs. Estelle Sinclaire Farrar*

564. Sinclaire & Co. cut and engraved stemware believed to be on Webb & Co. blanks. Ca. 1927. Height of goblet, 17.8 cm. *Coll. Mrs. Estelle Sinclaire Farrar.* Champagne glass, *Coll. Mr. and Mrs. Thomas Dimitroff*

notice the final payment, for packages only, to C. Dorflinger & Sons. In any event, on April 11, he threw his keys to the company on Hawkes's desk and announced that he was leaving.

Sinclaire's position with T. G. Hawkes & Co. was anomalous. His stock ownership was second only to that of Thomas Hawkes. His salary of $2,800 was the company's largest. On the other hand, Sam Hawkes was now first vice-president and Sinclaire was second vice-president, and Sinclaire had four sons to provide occupations for.

The very next day Tom Dow and a small group of Hawkes cutters began to work for Sinclaire in the White Mills factory of C. Dorflinger & Sons. Rumors reached the *Journal* on April 22. It reported:

> For a number of weeks there have been reports that a new glass cutting establishment was to be established in Corning, and the reports connected the name of a well known Corning young man having long experience in the glass business, and C. Dorflinger & Sons, wealthy glass manufacturers...as projectors of the enterprise....
>
> The rumors which have been prevalent for some time that C. Dorflinger & Sons...would shortly establish an important branch...at Corning...are taking more definite shape.... It is probable that the manufacture of glass cutters' blanks...will be largely carried on...and a branch cutting shop of great capacity will be installed.

The story correctly located the site of the future H. P. Sinclaire & Co. The Sinclaire brothers and Christian Dorflinger did nothing to stop the rumors. By May they were accepted as fact; T. G. Hawkes had reason to think that his Steuben Glass Works would have a formidable competitor in town.

CORNING WILL GET A NEW PLANT was the headline in *China, Glass & Lamps* on May 7. The story reported: "The new Dorflinger glass plant will be begun about the 20th of this month." It would start operations with two furnaces with 16 pots. Thomas Dow, "for the past month employed by the Dorflingers," would be foreman.

Construction of H. P. Sinclaire & Co.'s factory was now about to begin. The *Journal* reported on May 11 that H. P. Sinclaire had bought of J. A. Drake 36 vacant lots, and would "erect thereon a factory for glass cutting exclusively."

The two-story brick factory faced Cohocton Street, on the northwest corner of East Erie Avenue. Across Cohocton was Denison Park. Sinclaire landscaped his grounds as a continuation of the park, and designed the building so that each craftsman could look out at the trees and shrubs that he ordered from all over the eastern seaboard. Corningites were encouraged to stroll through the grounds; eventually they called them "Sinclaire Park." (See Ill. 5.)

Corning was proud of the factory. A later trade journal wrote:

> The factory is a triumph of architecture, well lighted, and the numerous departmental rooms are substantially and neatly furnished and equipped. The grounds, planned by a distinguished landscape artist, is [sic] indeed a beauty spot. The place is a fine example of...the creation of healthful and ideal surroundings.... Proprietors and agents come from far and wide to inspect the treasures made at the Sinclaire shops and make purchases. This is a reversal of the usual custom.... Articles are also manufactured on order from special designs supplied by art concerns in this country and from over seas.[13]

Cutting began in the fall, but interior painting continued. Spontaneous combustion of the painters' rags caused a fire on December 20 that did $20,000 worth of damage. Next day the company leased the former J. Hoare & Co. auxiliary shop on Cedar Street and Tioga Avenue,[14] and used it while repairs continued.

Sinclaire's partner, Marvin Olcott, was the genial scion of a founding Corning family. George Drake had been a partner in Olcott's real estate and insurance business. Olcott and Sinclaire were long-time friends, as their fathers had been. Olcott invested $20,000 in the company, but owned no stock until a second issue in 1909. William Sinclaire also made additional temporary advances to the company. He was so silent a partner that his sons never knew that he owned an interest. H. P. owned the remaining $40,000 worth of stock. He and Olcott did not draw their $150-a-month salaries until January 1909, when Olcott bought 166 of 500 new $100 shares, and Sinclaire 333.

Olcott's original investment may have been a loan, secured by the 13 shares of Sinclaire's Hawkes stock that Olcott owned by 1906.[15] T. G. Hawkes had refused to buy any of Sinclaire's stock at the $600 a share price set by arbitrators.[16]

The Hawkes & Co. stock transfer to Olcott exacerbated the ill feeling between Hawkes and Sinclaire. As the Hawkes company's second largest stockholder, Sinclaire attended its stockholders meetings of 1905 and 1906. He did not, however, attend a special directors meeting in May 1904, at which the directors sharply raised the salaries of T. G., Samuel, and Townsend Hawkes.

In 1906 Hawkes & Co. dividends dropped. Sinclaire's plummeted from $7,482.10 in 1905 to $2,000 in 1906.[17] Sinclaire sued, alleging that the salary increases, and the purchase of blanks from Steuben at a "much higher price than the same quality" cost elsewhere, were designed to lower dividends. The Hawkes lawyers answered that their clients were now doing Sinclaire's work in addition to their own, that competition from his company made them work harder, and the Steuben prices were not "much higher" in view of their "superior" quality. (See Chapter 13 for Hawkes's testimony that Steuben blanks were inferior to Corning's.) Sinclaire lost the suit. He continued to hold his Hawkes stock, and eventually reacquired Olcott's shares.

H. P. Sinclaire & Co. was known at once as Corning's engraving specialist. Sales reached a higher plateau after each glass-industry slump. Tiffany & Co. placed an order for the King of Bavaria, who required elaborate engraving on blanks so thin they would bend in his hand. The Sinclaire engravers obliged, though breakage was high and each goblet took three weeks of work.[18] Warren Harding bought two table services. The more elaborate was in the cut and engraved *Adam* design.[19] A five-foot punch bowl (doubtless including its cut-glass stand) for the White House that three Corningites have reported may be one that a White House curator writes was bought from Dulin & Martin of Washington in 1916. (See Chapter 6.)

World War I caused severe disruption. As fine blanks became unobtainable, H. P. Sinclaire cut back his company's line sharply. The Photographic Inventory of which we show a part was made for a 1917 stock-reduction sale. In November 1918, according to a private ledger, the company sent a large shipment of cut glass to C. Dorflinger & Sons.

Five or six personable salesmen sold Sinclaire & Co. glass coast to coast. In addition, there were New York and Philadelphia sales agents. K. P. Lockitt, New York agent during the 1920s, had previously represented C. Dorflinger & Sons.[20] The traveling salesmen reported directly to Sinclaire, who continued to personally sell his finest glass to jewelers. Many came to Corning to select it, as Sinclaire & Co. did not advertise and issued no catalogs to the trade.

In 1913 Corning heard a rumor that Sinclaire & Co. would begin making blanks. Marvin Olcott denied it; he was quoted in the *Leader* on September 18:

> The matter has never been considered even for a moment....I am at a loss to know how so silly a rumor...started unless it was from the fact that a man came to us and wanted...a special kind of glass for a mirror. We...took him to the Corning Glass Works.

In 1920 the imminent closing of C. Dorflinger & Sons prompted Sinclaire to open a tiny blowing factory in Bath, New York. It used Dorflinger formulas for crystal and colors in a two-pot furnace that Sinclaire bought from Corning Glass Works. The little factory was an immediate success. In the depression year of 1920 Sinclaire & Co. sales increased by more than 50 percent, and profits rose to an unprecedented percentage of sales. During the 1921 summer closing it added two more pots.[21] Its Dorflinger craftsmen and manager continued many Dorflinger shapes for both the Sinclaire company and its customers for blanks.

NOTE: Illustrations 565 to 602 are pages from an H. P. Sinclaire & Co. salesman's catalog of ca. 1914.

565. Two square bowls by Sinclaire. At left is *Corn Flowers & Lace Hobnail* (the 10½-inch size, $50). The engraved design at right includes canvas back, partridge, pheasant, and woodcock, combined with oak leaves and acorns. In 11-inch size, this bowl was $108.

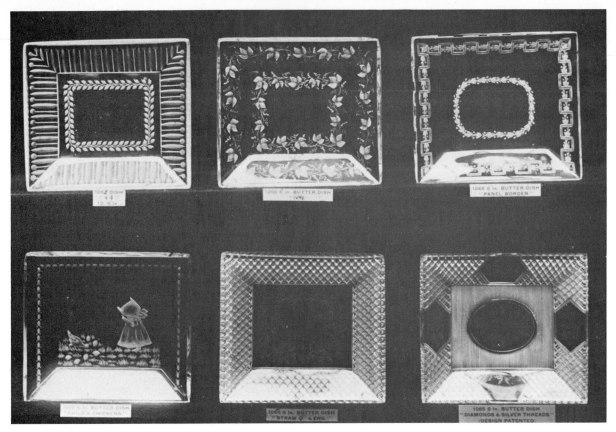

566. Sinclaire's 1914 catalog offered these six butter dishes, ranging in price from $5.30 to $11. Designs in the top row are *44, Ivy,* and *Panel Border;* those in the bottom row are *Child & Chickens, Strawberry Diamond & Engraved,* and *Diamonds & Silver Threads* (patented).

In early 1921 Marvin Olcott left the company to become vice-president of a Corning bank. Sinclaire bought his interest, and continued to seek his friendly advice. The coolness between the Hawkes and Sinclaire companies had ended after T. G.'s death, but began again about 1925.

Corning's fine-glass business was increasingly the prey of cheaper products from Europe. Sinclaire decided to emulate Corning Glass Works: he would subsidize his fine-glass by making commercial products. He had long made free-blown church wares. Now he planned to join the Fry, McKee, and Corning companies in producing oven glass. Its trademark was RADNT. After rebuilding an abandoned glass factory in Dunkirk, New York, at a cost of $250,000, he moved his Bath operation there in the spring of 1925. He had other products in mind too, but we know only that one was doorknobs.

Sinclaire hired a sales manager who had formerly worked for Corning Glass Works. Despite this precaution, Corning Glass Works records indicate he found that some RADNT designs infringed Glass Works patents on baking shapes per se. He had his decorators hand-paint these, so that they could not be used in an oven. Pending their redesign, a line of

RADNT pantry ware began to reach distributors in 1927.

Sinclaire had needed all his capital for the Dunkirk expansion. Hawkes & Co. passed several dividends without cutting officers' salaries. When Sinclaire pushed Sam Hawkes to buy his stock, the old disagreement surfaced again. Sinclaire resolved it by threatening to send his shares to a broker for sale to an outsider. Hawkes bought the stock. (See Reference Note 9, this chapter.)

Sinclaire had also planned to build a china factory in Dunkirk, and his second son went to work in a ceramic tile factory to learn the business. This plan, and the expansion of RADNT ware, were aborted by Sinclaire's sudden death of a heart attack June 22, 1927.

The Dunkirk factory closed at once. Cutting and engraving in Corning continued for about a year on undecorated stock. The plant was later sold to the Cortland Baking Company. About 1961 the building was razed to make room for a group of small stores, and Sinclaire Park became an asphalted parking lot.

* * *

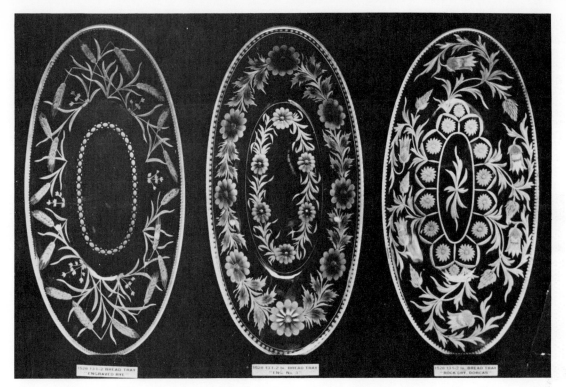

567. Sinclaire's ca. 1914 salesman's catalog showed these three bread trays, all 13½ inches: *Engraved Rye, Engraved No. 3, Dorcas* (Rock Crystal).

568. Four fruit salad bowls (each with liner). The designs at top and bottom left were designated, respectively, as *Engraved No. 4* and *No. 3 & Engraving.* The design at lower right is labeled *Rock Crystal* (the label at top right is illegible).

211

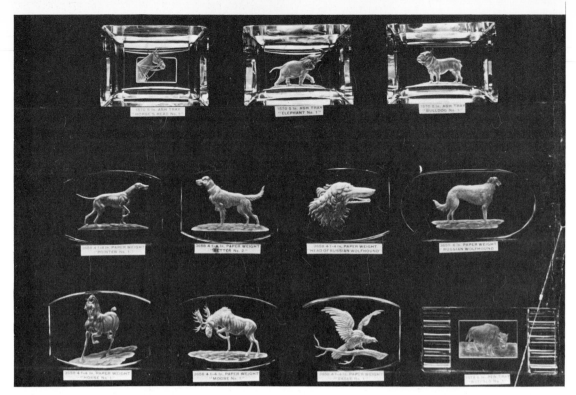

569. At top of this page from the ca. 1914 Sinclaire catalog are three 5-inch ashtrays with engraved decoration: a horse's head, an elephant, and a bulldog. The middle row displays four paperweights engraved with dogs; the weight at far right was 6 inches long. In the bottom row are three more animal weights and a pen tray with a buffalo.

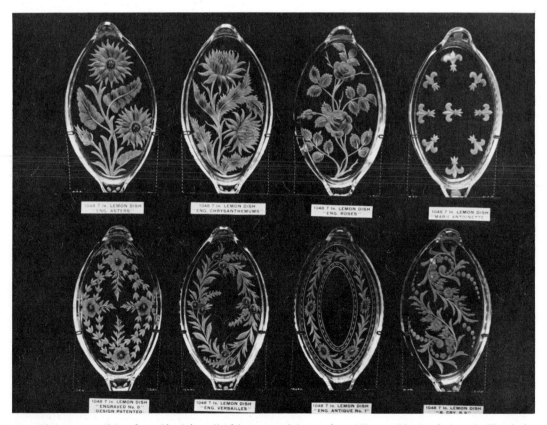

570. Eight lemon dishes from Sinclaire, all with engraved decoration. All were 7 inches in length. The designs in the top row were identified as *Engraved Asters, Engraved Chrysanthemums, Engraved Roses,* and *Marie Antoinette.* Those in the bottom row were labeled *Engraved No. 8* "Design Patented," *Eng. Versailles, Eng. Antique No. 1,* and *Rock Crystal S9.*

571. The Sinclaire catalog also offered 7-inch bonbon or jelly dishes. This page illustrates six of them. TOP ROW: *Corn Flowers, Peony,* and *Rose.* Those in the bottom row are labeled *Strawberry Diamond & Engraved, Assyrian & Border,* and *Snowflakes & Holly* "Design Patented."

572. Two engraved cold-meat platters from the ca. 1914 Sinclaire catalog. The one at top, 12¾ inches long, featured mallard ducks; the lower one, 14¾ inches, pictured "Adirondack deer."

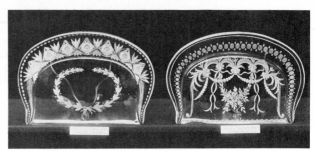

574. Two crumb trays from Sinclaire: *Cut No. 1 & Engraved* and *Engraved No. 3.*

573. Variously decorated small dishes and ashtrays from Sinclaire's ca. 1914 catalog. The designs of those in the bottom row are *Swallows, Fighting Cocks,* and *Setter No. 1.*

576. These Sinclaire "jugs" each held three pints. The design of the one at top left was identified as *Hollows & Border;* at lower left, as *Double Diamond & Border;* at lower right, as *Cut 22½ & Engraved.*

575. Four bowls from the Sinclaire ca. 1914 catalog. At bottom left, the design is *No. 4;* at right, *99.*

577. Here, four Sinclaire quart "jugs" are accompanied by their matching tumblers. Designs were identified as *Mitres & Festoons, Engraved Water Lilies, Engraved Rococo,* and *Flutes & Engraved Roses.*

578. The designs of these Sinclaire 3½-pint jugs were *Engraved Grapes* and *Engraved Strawberries.*

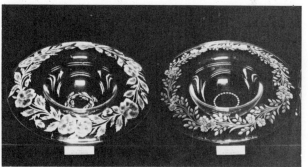

579. Sinclaire pansy bowls. The one at left is in *Engraved Pansy* design; at right, in *Engraved No. 1.*

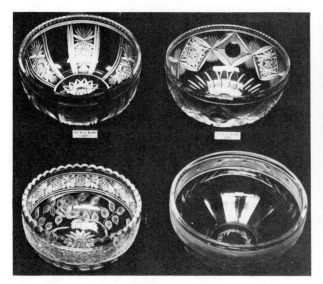

580. The four Sinclaire bowls shown here, from the ca. 1914 catalog, were identified as (top) *1027* and *1028;* (bottom) *Roses & Border* and *Flutes & Stars.*

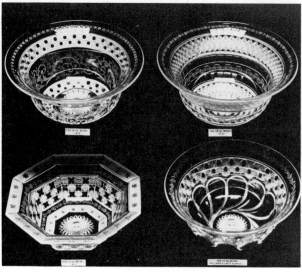

581. Four 10-inch Sinclaire bowls identified as *A5, A8, A1,* and *Pillars & Lace Hobnail.*

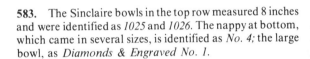

582. The design identifications on the Sinclaire bowls shown here are almost illegible. The two at bottom appear to be *47* and *1020*.

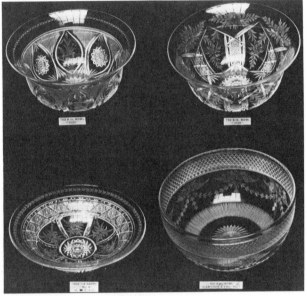

583. The Sinclaire bowls in the top row measured 8 inches and were identified as *1025* and *1026*. The nappy at bottom, which came in several sizes, is identified as *No. 4;* the large bowl, as *Diamonds & Engraved No. 1.*

584. Sinclaire bowls (8½ inches), "crystal glass." Prices listed ranged from $8.00 to $13.30. Designs were (top) *Engraved No. 1, Engraved No. 2, Engraved 183;* (bottom) *Engraved No. 3, Engraved No. 4,* and *Engraved No. 5.*

585. Compartmented trays in various designs by Sinclaire, ca. 1914. Designs in the top row are *Engraved 1000* and *No. 1*; at lower right, the design is *Engraved Ivy.* Label at lower left is illegible.

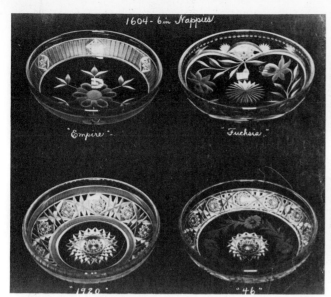

586. Sinclaire nappies in *Empire, Fuchsia, 1920*, and *46*.

588. Nine matching pieces of Sinclaire tableware in design *No. 20*.

587. Sinclaire "jugs" and matching tumblers: *Antique No. 1 & Engraved* and *Versailles & Engraved*.

589. Four Sinclaire "jugs" with matching tumblers. Designs are *1030, No. 4, Diamonds & Silver Threads* (patented), and *1028*.

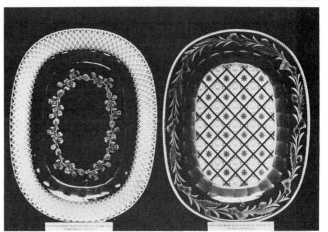

591. These Sinclaire trays (or platters) could be used for serving either cold meats or ice cream. Design at left was identified as *Diamond & Clover;* at right, as *Plaid & Thistles.*

590. Bowls and a compote. Designs are identified as *No. 4* and *70* at top and *Snow Flakes & Holly* (patented) at bottom.

592. Sinclaire "jugs," 3½-pint capacity, engraved in fruit and blossom designs; at left is *Engraved Apples* design; at right, *Engraved Oranges.*

593. "Doric" clock case engraved in *Thistles* design at Sinclaire. The dial is engraved with thistles to match the case.

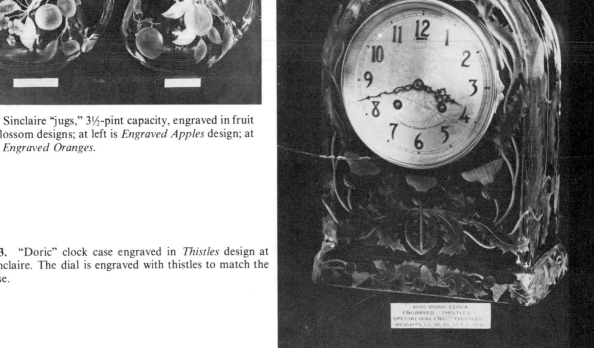

218

594. Sinclaire's 1914 catalog showed this set of stem- and tableware in crystal glass. The design was identified as *"Eng. No. 2."*

595. Identifications of these five pieces in the 1914 catalog are no longer legible.

596. Bowl at left is in *Strawberry Diamond & Fan and Engraving.* Bowl at right is *Versailles & Engraved.*

597. The Sinclaire bowls on this catalog page are in (top) *Hollows & Border* and *Double Diamond & Border;* (bottom) *Engraved No. 5* and *Strawberries.*

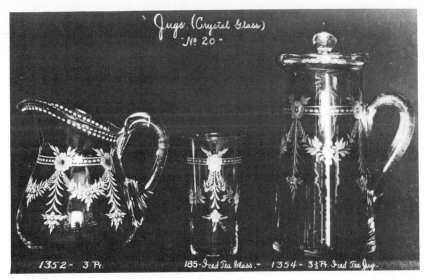

598. Sinclaire pieces in crystal glass, design *No. 20:* 3-pint jug, iced tea glass, and covered 3½-pint iced tea jug.

599. Three Sinclaire bowls, ca. 1914: *Lines, 1720,* and *Grapes.*

By the time H. P. Sinclaire & Co. opened, all of Corning was buying blanks from various sources. Blanks manufacturers did not copy one another's wares. If sales of a handled sandwich tray, for example, would not support the expense of an exclusive blank, the cutting company bought the blank that its competitors used. The Sinclaire company was unusual in that it bought most of its blanks from two sources as long as they could supply them. C. Dorflinger & Sons supplied 400 items, chiefly free-blown, including 19 sets of stemware.[22] Many were exclusive designs, blown to Sinclaire's own full-size drawings.[23] Sinclaire es-

pecially liked the marked transition from thick bottoms to thin edges that characterized Dorflinger tablewares. Thick vases, bowls, jugs, and soup plates came from Corning Glass Works. Most were blown in molds made to Sinclaire's designs by his pattern-maker, Gus Hammerstrom.

Sinclaire & Co. also bought blanks from the Pairpoint Corporation.[24] Baccarat supplied others, including ruby casings. After Dorflinger began to decline, H. P. kept track of the company's employees. Orders for blanks followed them to Toledo's short-lived Modern Glass Company, and to a little Brooklyn factory run by John Larson.[25] After

600. Four pieces in Sinclaire's *Belmont*.

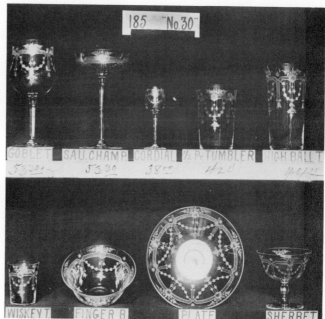

601. Page of Sinclaire's stem- and tableware is marked "No. 30."

Corning Glass Works bought Steuben, it too supplied blanks to Sinclaire & Co. After 1920, however, the Sinclaire & Co. blowing factory supplied most of the parent firm's blanks.

The Sinclaire & Co. Photographic Inventory shows little colored glass except for hock glasses. During the 1920s the company made and used a great deal of color, singly and in combinations. It also made iridized glasses in crystal and several colors, which were called "Pearl." Pearl Crystal is readily distinguishable from the Steuben Verre de Soie—its iridescence is on the inside; the exterior retains the original high luster.

* * *

As was customary in Corning when there was a parting of the ways, H. P. Sinclaire took with him to his new company all his designs for his former employer, who discontinued them. These included his Paris Exposition engravings of 1889 and later floral designs for Gravic glass.

Sinclaire designed most of his company's elaborate early engravings, and many of the later ones. Hiram Rouse's work notebooks show, as we have seen, that a number of Sinclaire & Co. engravers designed borders and motifs, and that some provided complete designs. These were usually stone engraved. Craftsmen who designed for the copper wheel will be discussed below.

H. P. Sinclaire's abiding love of nature ensured that his company would engrave many fruits and flowers. By 1917 it also offered series of birds, fish,

602. *Grapes & Lines* design by Sinclaire, ca. 1914.

and game animals, as well as scenes in England and/or Scotland. Corning's engravers especially admired the birds and animals; several copied the designs for their own use.

The company made many three-dimensional rock-crystal designs that incorporated pillars, but by 1917 the term "rock crystal" was describing any engraving in the polished finish.

Engravings were first offered in detailed versions, but, according to Rouse, a customer's order might specify "cheapen by" an hour, or any desired amount of time. Thus, various qualities of a given engraved (or cut-and-engraved) design sometimes come on the market.

Though Sinclaire still disliked heavily cut glass, which he privately called "God-awful," his company made it as long as customers bought it. His preference was for simpler cuts: flutes, panels, silver diamonds, and the delicate motifs of such designs as his patented *Assyrian*. His company made seven or more designs in the Anglo-Irish style and called them *English Antique*; at least eight in the style of early American glass were called *Antique*.

Sinclaire patented a few of his designs between 1909 and 1916. *Assyrian* (1909) was combined with engraved borders or other motifs more often than not. Other patents were *Engraving No. 8* (1909), *Flutes & Panel Border* (1910),[26] *Snow Flakes & Holly* (1911), *Diamonds & Silver Threads* (1913), *Adam* and *Adam No. 2* (1915), *Georgian* (1915), a salad dressing bottle (1916), and *Stratford* (1916). Despite the patents, the Sinclaire company allowed a few other companies to use his designs, perhaps under a licensing arrangement like the one between the Hawkes and Fostoria companies. The Steuben Division and Allen Cut Glass Co. cut Sinclaire designs.[27] The Sinclaire & Co. cutting of Allen's *Pond Lily* shows that reciprocal arrangements were not uncommon. (See Chapter 19.) It has already been mentioned that the Sinclaire, Hawkes, and Hoare firms often shared large orders for a given design.

H. P. Sinclaire's philosophy of design broke new ground. At an exhibit of Sinclaire & Co. glass at The Corning Museum of Glass (1972/3), Kenneth Wilson explained Sinclaire's aims as follows, the *Leader* reported on October 6, 1972:

> Sinclaire's designs are marked by more restraint than most cut...glass of the Brilliant Period. His delicate engraved designs were often based on natural forms, sometimes contrasted with cut elements. Typically, natural motifs appeared as medallions, bands, or panels set off by areas of undecorated glass. Sinclaire, with his architectural approach to design, succeeded in divorcing beauty from price; many inexpensive Sinclaire [pieces] were as attractive as the most costly ones.

In practical application, this philosophy meant that any of dozens of engraved motifs could be combined with any of dozens of cut ones, giving an unparalleled flexibility. By 1917 Sinclaire & Co. designs were so numerous that each of dozens of blanks had its own *No. 1* design.

Silver and gold mountings were common before World War I and for a few years thereafter. Enamel medallions or tops trimmed dressing-table and desk pieces during the 1920s.

Decoration in the twenties included a sophisticated use of high-luster semitransparent stains over copper-wheel outlining and shading of flower designs. The engraving was replaced by acid-etching about 1926. Acid-etched designs were used on color and on cased bands. Other techniques included the addition of embossed metals bands, "sterling silver inlay" (similar to silver-deposit), and hand painting. During these years Sinclaire & Co. introduced a number of simple cuttings, engravings, and combinations of the two on colored blanks, and also sold undecorated colored glass.

* * *

Sinclaire & Co. payroll figures for 1904 and 1905 suggest that factory employees numbered about 50. By early 1905 most of the engraving department that Sinclaire had built up at T. G. Hawkes & Co. was working for him. Joseph Haselbauer was engraving foreman; Nitsche says Haselbauer held the position for "a number of years"; he probably held it until his death in 1910.

When the company opened, it was probably Corning's fourteenth or fifteenth cutting firm.[28] In 1905 Corning had 33 engravers. Fifteen or more worked in the Sinclaire company's downstairs engraving shop, and at least a few more upstairs.[29] Allowing for clerical help, packers, washers, dippers, and a patternmaker, it would seem that Sinclaire & Co. employed as many engravers as cutters. This unprecedented proportion illustrates H. P. Sinclaire's devotion to engraved glass.

English-born Tom Dow served as plant superintendent from the first, though he and his brother Oliver both held the title of foreman for some years. A third brother, Leonard, one of Corning's great roughers, moved to the Steuben Division in the mid–twenties. Tom and Oliver Dow designed cut glass, as did cutter James Clark.[30]

The three Dow brothers, Bert Abbey, John Barenthaler, and smoother Nelson Doane were among the cutters who worked for Sinclaire & Co. in the Dorflinger factory from the spring to the late fall of 1904.[31]

Clement Nitsche was an engraver-designer for the company during much of its life. Master engraver Joseph Libisch began work in 1911 and stayed until 1921. It is not clear when he succeeded Joseph Haselbauer as engraving foreman. Libisch, too, often designed engravings. Other engravers who designed motifs, borders, and complete engravings included John Illig, Hiram Rouse, Ernest Kaulfuss, and an unidentified Englishman whose name Rouse's notebook gives as "Woodhull."

The name "H. Purdon" is prominently engraved on some sets of Sinclaire & Co. game birds. It also appears in diamond-point script on heavy fish-design soup plates. His is the only craftsman's signature that we have found on Sinclaire & Co. glass. No Woodhull (or Woodall) or Purdon appears in Corning directories. The fact that H. P. Sinclaire's given names were Henry Purdon has made some collectors suspect that he engraved the Purdon-signed pieces, but he did not.

Hand painting and gilding were the work of four or five women. A man variously reported as German and French headed the decorating department. We do not know who did the company's acid designs.

* * *

One of the Sinclaire trademarks was acid-stamped on each piece of glass after final inspection had shown it to be perfect. "And did we get it if we missed a piece!" a former employee recalls. Imperfect pieces were sold as seconds without a trademark and from a special salesroom. Corningites bought and subsequently repaired hundreds, perhaps thousands, of these pieces. Their present owners are likely to think, incorrectly, that Sinclaire & Co. glass was never signed. Unlike Hawkes & Co. and Hoare & Co., Sinclaire & Co. used a trademark from the first. Unsigned glass in Sinclaire & Co. designs should be considered either imperfect or a "matching" from another company. An exception to this rule is Sinclaire & Co. glass signed by a jewelry company. Some leading jewelers insisted on using their own trademarks on the glass that they sold.

SUMMARY

Dates: 1904-28

Address: northwest corner of Cohocton Street and Erie Avenue

Blanks: C. Dorflinger & Sons, chief supplier of free-blown blanks 1904-20. Corning Glass Works: thick blanks, mostly mold-blown, 1904-10. Pairpoint Corporation, 1905-9 and perhaps longer. Baccarat, Webb, Steuben, Libbey, Westmoreland, and Duncan & Miller companies were minor suppliers at unknown dates. After 1920 most crystal and colored blanks were of the company's own manufacture.

Trademarks: acid-stamped S in a laurel wreath interrupted by two shields. The left one encloses a fleur-de-lis, the right one a thistle. On tablewares: SINCLAIRE. Both acid-stamped but omitted from imperfect pieces

Product: Corning's largest line of copper-wheel engravings. A full line of stone-engraved, cut, and cut-and-engraved glass included lamps, candelabra, and chandeliers. Much colored and cased glass after 1920

Employees: Thomas Dow, superintendent; Oliver Dow, cutting foreman; Joseph Haselbauer, Joseph Libisch, engraving foremen. Cutters included (at various periods) Bert Abbey, John Barenthaler, Marx Bernt, Edward Canton, James Clark, William Custer (later an acid-dipper), Gerald Davis, Charles Dimick, Fred Denson, Nelson Doane, Leonard Dow, "Bouncer" Golden, Jean Georges Haar, James Hanley, Lew Hart, Mark Howard, Arthur Hyland, William Jones, George Lindstrom, Ernest Nitsche, John Schneider, Aloys Schneider, Watson Scouten, Arthur Stevens, Louis Strutz, Fred Terrell, Alfred Wilcox,———Warren.

Dippers, polishers, and stopperers included: George Bievalacqua, Charles Chilson, John Edger, Charles Jacobs, Louis Lentricchia,———Maurer, Henry Morgan, Jacob Wheat. Patternmakers: Gus Hammerstrom, succeeded by Charles Dean ca. 1920.

Engravers: William Beebe, Orange T. Benson, Richard Dorn, Davis Everson, Fred Haselbauer (ca. 1904-6), Edward and Herman Hauptmann, John Illig, "Bob" Johnson, Ernest and Peter Kaulfuss, Anthony (Sr.) and Henry Keller, George Kennedy, Frank Konigstein (ca. 1916-21), Adolf Kretschmann, John Lesh,———Manning, Jordan May, William Morse (ca. 1905-6), Fred Myers, Joseph Oveszny, Edward Palme, Jr., Nathaniel Phelps, H. Purdon, Wilmot Putnam, Francis Quinn, Joseph Rasinger (ca. 1918), Hiram Rouse, Randolph Sensabaugh, Joseph Sidot, Nicolas Underiner, Fred Winson,———Woodhull (Woodall?).

Women employees included Margaret Dow, Elizabeth Dwyer, Mary Elwell, Fanny Eygabroat, Julia Foster, Thelma Foster, Edna Hadley, Wilfreda Hanrahan, Kitty Hart, Hazel Hilk, Dagny Johnson, Esther King, Bessie Leavenworth, Florence McQuaid, Ruth Nichols, Lena Flaspheler, Maggie Relihan (forelady), Laura Stevens, Dolores Tietje, Minnie Tobias, Ruth Walling.

Packers: John Flynn, John McGannon. Work unknown: Joseph Bevilacqua, Joseph Bevy, Frederick Curry, James Jordan, Valentine Passetti, James Phenes.[32]

Salesmen and agents: travelers included W. J. Hopkins, J. W. Swann, A. N. Hull, and B. F. Robinson. Later, also J. Victor Jugo, Harrie Pritchard, and (briefly) Harrie Millspaugh, office manager, 1921-27; and Karl Gaiss. K. P. Lockitt, New York agent in the 1920s, R. E. McCormick in Philadelphia.[33]

Customers: jewelers included Tiffany; Black, Starr & Frost; Gorham; Bailey, Banks & Biddle; J. E. Caldwell; C. D. Peacock; Richard Briggs; and Cowell & Hubbard companies. Department and gift stores: the Ovington, John Wanamaker, and Marshall Field companies. Other customers coast to coast and in Canada unknown.

NOTE: Illustrations 603 to 636 on the following 34 pages are the concluding plates (67 to 100) of the 100-plate photographic inventory made at H. P. Sinclaire & Co. ca. 1917, when war restrictions made it necessary for most Corning glass companies to discontinue—at least temporarily—a considerable number of their designs. The preceding plates of this photographic inventory are reproduced in *H. P. Sinclaire, Jr., Glassmaker,* Vol. II, "The Years Before 1920," by Estelle Sinclaire Farrar.

603. Plate 67 of the Sinclaire 1917 Inventory: TOP ROW: plate in *99;* pudding dishes in *Stars, Pillars & Engraving* and in *Lace Hobnail & Grapes.* SECOND ROW: pudding dishes in *Panel Border* and *Lattice Border;* soup plates in *Rock Crystal 100* and *Rock Crystal 101.* THIRD ROW: soup plates in *Rock Crystal 102* and *Rock Crystal 103;* cake plate in *Snow Flakes & Holly;* plates in *Blackberries* and in *Panel Border.* BOTTOM ROW: plates in *98, Adam, 1021,* and *Diamonds & Silver Threads.*

604. Inventory Plate 68. The designs in the top row are *Snow Flakes & Holly, Lace Hobnail & Fruits, Boston,* and *1028.* SECOND ROW: *1009, Grapes, Dots,* and *Georgian.* THIRD ROW: salad plates in *Key Border, Panel Border, Roses & Lines,* and *1012.* BOTTOM ROW: service plates in *Albany, No. 3, No. 9,* and *53.*

605. In the top row of this inventory photograph, items 1 and 3 are in *Daisies & Lines* design; the remaining two (salad plates) are in *Bristol* and *No. 2.* SECOND ROW: These small and large oil bottles are *Albany, 777, Mitres & Border, 1000* (two bottles), *Adelphia, Regent, Queen Louise,* and *1000.* THIRD ROW (oil and salad dressing bottles): *Flutes & Panel Border, Ivy, No. 1, No. 2, No. 3, No. 4, Roses & Lines, Daisies, Flutes, Flutes & Panel Border,* and *1008.* BOTTOM ROW: The first three compotes are in *Adam No. 2,* the last in *1028.*

606. The 19 compotes in this Inventory Plate range from the very small to large size. TOP ROW: *Empire, Stratford, Cut & Engraved 112,* and *Regent.* SECOND ROW: *Adam, Adam No. 2, Adam Scalloped Edge,* and *Ivy.* THIRD ROW: *Ivy, Panel Border, No. 4, No. 6, 1000, Albany.* BOTTOM ROW: *Regent, Albany, Regent, Daisies & Lines,* and *Adam No. 2.*

607. TOP ROW: mayonnaise bowl and plate in *112*, cake stand in *No. 1*, mayonnaise bowl and plate in *Flutes & Panel Border*. SECOND ROW: compotes in *Adam No. 2, Cut & Engraved 112*, and *York*. THIRD ROW: *Engraved No. 1, Flutes & Panel Border*, and *Stratford*.

608. Inventory Plate 72 pictured 16 sugar and cream sets, along with a few other small items. TOP ROW: Compote in *Cornell*, mayonnaise bowl-and-plate sets in *1000* and *Albany;* Worcestershire sauce bottle in *Flutes & Panel Border,* mustard jars in *1000* and *Snow Flakes & Holly,* horseradish jar in *1000,* and another mustard in *Daisies & Lines.* SECOND ROW: sugar bowls and cream pitchers in *72, Cut No. 1 & Engraved, Engraved No. 3,* and *Boston.* THIRD ROW: *Daisies & Lines, Adam, Flutes & Panel Border, Flutes & Engraving.* FOURTH ROW: sugar bowls and cream pitchers in *Regent, Adelphia, Diamonds & Silver Threads,* and *Empire.* BOTTOM ROW: sugar bowls and cream pitchers in *Fuchsia, Georgian, No. 4,* and *1000.*

609. The top row of Inventory Plate 73 pictures three sugar bowl and cream pitcher sets— *1009, 1021,* and *1028;* another sugar in *Flutes & Panel Border,* and a sugar and cream set in *York.* SECOND ROW: sugar and cream set in *Engraved 183,* two sets in *777,* and a spoon tray in *Adam.* THIRD ROW: spoon trays in *Adelphia, Flutes & Panel Border, No. 4, Assyrian,* and *Strawberry Diamond & Engraved.* FOURTH ROW: bells in *Rock Crystal No. 2, Snow Flakes & Holly,* and *1003;* rum jugs in *Chrysanthemums, Diamonds & Silver Threads, Snow Flakes & Holly, Stars & Roses, No. 4, 1000, 1003.* BOTTOM ROW: two two-piece caviar sets—in *Fishes & Seaweed* and *40;* jam pot with silver cover in *89,* jam pots with glass covers in *S11, Currants,* and *Oranges.*

PLATE 74

1441 1442 1443
1444 1445 1446
1447 1448 1449 1450 1451 1452 1453 1454

610. The designs of the three "lacquered jars" at top are *Prunus Blossoms, Chinese No. 1,* and *Chinese No. 9.* SECOND ROW: three covered jars in *Adam, Pillars & Flowers,* and *Flutes & Prunus Blossoms.* BOTTOM ROW: glass-covered jam pot in *No. 1,* silver-covered jam pots in *Snow Flakes & Holly, Mitres & Border, Double Diamond & Borders, Flutes & Panel Border, Hollows & Border;* glass-covered jam pots in *No. 40* and *1023.*

611.   Fifteen covered jars are shown in Inventory Plate 75. TOP ROW: *Adam, Queen Louise, Antique No. 1, 111,* and *Regent.* SECOND ROW: *Engraved No. 1, Stratford, Chippendale, Queen Louise, Adam No. 2.* THIRD ROW: *Flutes & Borders, Empire, Old English No. 1, Adam,* and *Flutes.*

612. The top row of Inventory Plate 76 shows jars in these designs: *Adam No. 2, Flutes & Panel Border, Stratford, Empire, Adam No. 2.* SECOND ROW: Jars are in *Regent, Adam No. 2, Empire, Daisies & Lines,* and *Boston.* THIRD ROW: cologne bottles in *San Remo, Diamonds & Silver Threads, Flutes & Panel Border, Albany, York, Daisies & Lines, Albany, York, York,* and *1000.* BOTTOM ROW: First eight cologne bottles are in *Daisies & Lines, Adam, No. 4, Flutes & Panel Border, Empire, 1000* (shown in two sizes), and *Albany;* remaining six colognes have silver tops and are atomizers—*No. 4, Lilies of the Valley, Mitres & Border, No. 4,* (amethyst) *Violets,* and (spun amethyst) *Carnations.*

613. The top row of Plate 77 begins with three tall colognes in *No. 40, Ivy,* and *Flutes;* the remaining items are toilet-water bottles in *Sweet Peas, Marie Antoinette, Mitres & Border, Panel Border, Pansies, Violets, Roses, Carnations, Ivy, Adam,* and *Diamond & Engraving.* SECOND ROW: Candlestick with long pendants is in *Flutes* design; remainder are *Flutes, B, Flutes, Rock Crystal Daisies, C, Rock Crystal No. 3,* and *Flutes.* THIRD ROW: Designs are *Adam, Cut Odd, Odd & Engraved, Rock Crystal No. 1, Odd, Flutes & Panel Border, No. 40, Gooseberries,* and *Engraved No. 4.*

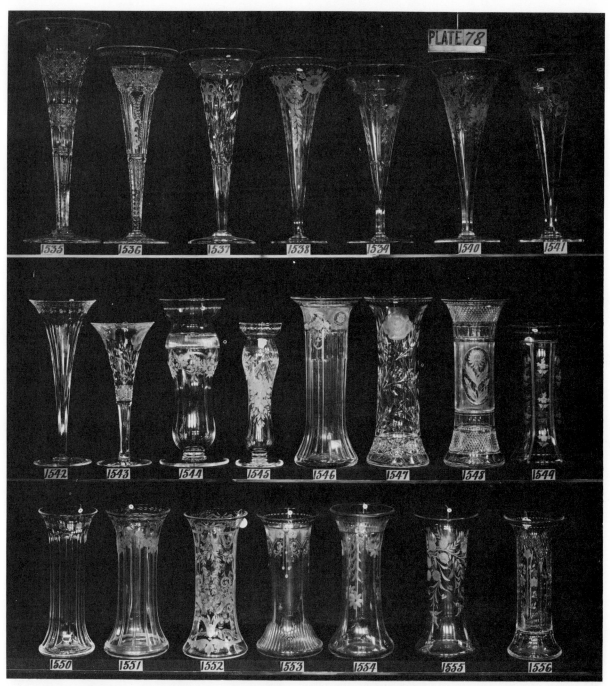

614. Inventory Plate 78. TOP ROW: *Antique No. 1 & Engraved, No. 4, Empire, 183, Regent, York,* and *1000.* SECOND ROW: *Flutes & Panel Border, Adelphia, Queen Louise, York, Adam, Adelphia, Diamonds & Silver Threads,* and *Daisies & Lines.* THIRD ROW: *Flutes & Panel Border, Georgian, 35, 112, Regent, 1000,* and *1021.*

PLATE 79

615. In the top row are vases in these designs: *No. 3 & Engraved, Snow Flakes & Holly, No. 4, 183, Adelphia, Flutes & Panel Border,* and *Empire.* SECOND ROW: *Adam, Diamonds & Silver Threads, Empire, 1000, Medallions,* and *1000.* THIRD ROW: *31, 1010, Albany, Adam,* and *No. 4.*

616.   Vases in the top row are in these designs: *Engraved Fuchsia, Queen Louise, Lilies, 35, Hops, Poppies & Rye, 183,* and *1000.* SECOND ROW: vases in *No. 8, 1000, Stratford, Queen Louise;* baskets in *Fuchsia, Odd,* and *Daisies;* small vase in *Albany.* BOTTOM ROW: vases in *Diamonds & Silver Threads* and *1021;* rose bowl in *Empire;* vases in *Albany, York, Adam No. 2,* and *34.*

PLATE 81

1598   1599   1600   1601   1602

1603   1604   1605   1606   1607   1608

617. Eleven vases of various sizes and shapes, but all in *Adam* design.

618. All the vases on Inventory Plate 82 are in *Adam No. 2* design.

619. All the vases in the top row of Inventory Plate 83 are in *Adam No. 2* design with the exception of the first and fourth ones, which are in *Adam*. Vases in the second row are *No. 4, Queen Louise, Regent, 183, Queen Louise,* and *112.* In the bottom row are vases in *1000, Regent, York, Flutes & Panel Border,* and *Snow Flakes & Holly.*

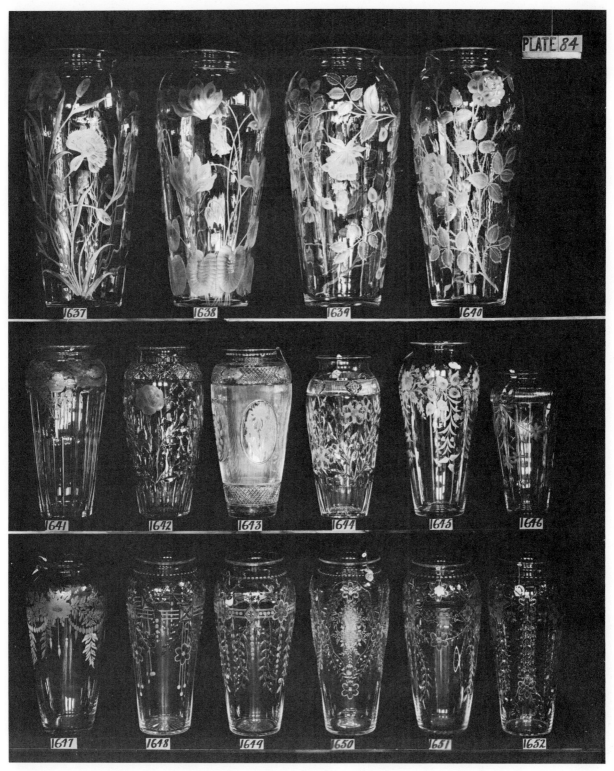

620. Here, the vases in the top row are all in floral designs: *Carnations, Cyclamen, Fuchsia,* and *Roses.* SECOND ROW: *Adam, Adelphia, Diamonds & Silver Threads, Empire, 1000,* and *Regent.* THIRD ROW: Vases in this row are all in numbered designs: *183, 1005, 1006, 1007, 1008,* and *1009.*

621. The top row illustrates baskets in *Regent, 1000, Boston, 1028,* and *No. 8.* SECOND ROW: vases in *Odd, 1021, No. 4, No. 8, 1000, 183, 1000* (the last two). In the bottom row, all the vases are in *1000.*

PLATE 86

1675   1676   1677   1678   1679

1680   1681   1682   1683   1684

622. The vases pictured on Inventory Plate 86 are all in *Stratford* design except the very last one, which is *Special Roses*.

623. The top row of vases illustrates *Queen Louise* design, as do all those in the second row with the exception of the last one, which is in *No. 1*. The designs in the bottom row are *112, No. 8, Ivy, No. 8, No. 4, Engraved, No. 8, No. 9, No. 1, Ivy,* and *Albany*.

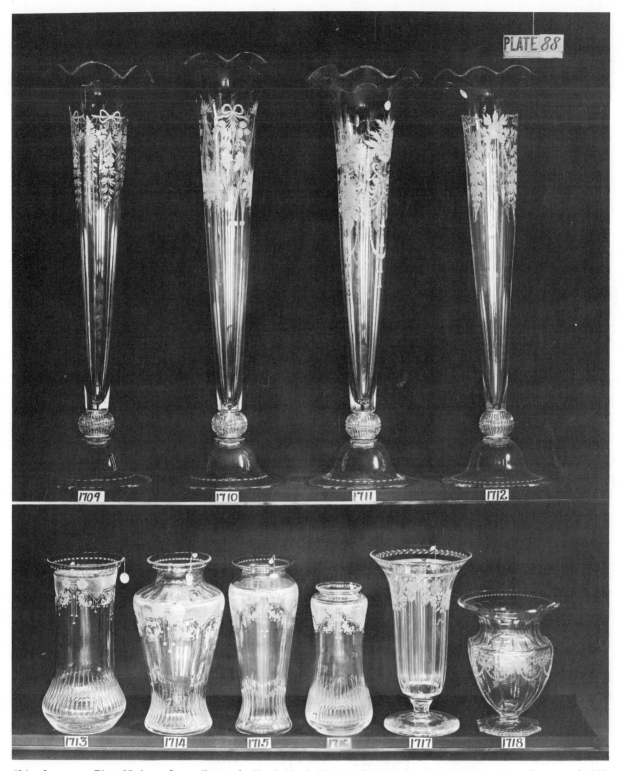

624. Inventory Plate 88 shows four tall vases in *No. 2, No. 3, No. 4,* and *183* designs. In the lower row are four vases in *112,* followed by one each in *Georgian* and *183.*

625. The designs pictured in the top row here are *Poppies, Roses, Chrysanthemums, Tulips & Jonquils,* and *Carnations.* In the bottom row are five vases in *York,* two in *Albany,* and a final one in *York.*

626. The top row of Inventory Plate 90 pictures vases in *Cut & Engraved No. 1, York, 1000, 1008,* and *Albany.* In the second row, the vases at either end are in *183;* the two in the center are *Queen Louise.* BOTTOM ROW: First two are *Daisies & Lines,* followed by *Flutes & Roses, No. 4, Engraved 34,* and *Special.*

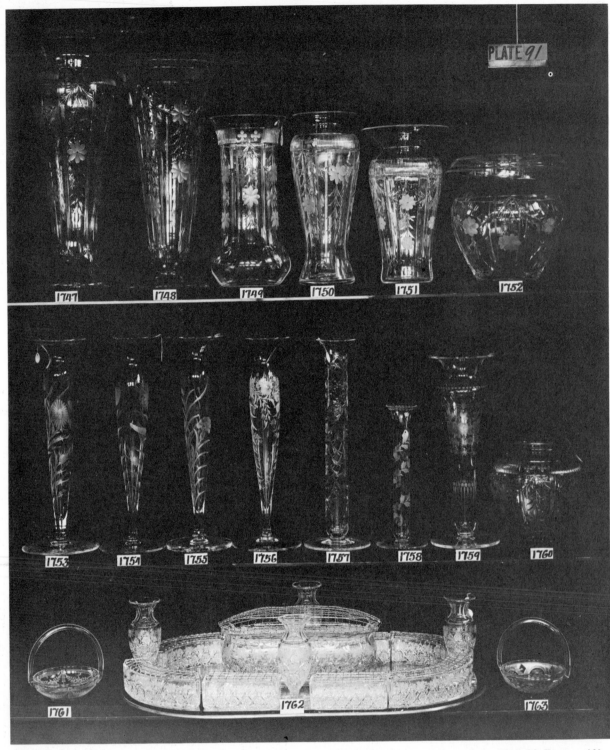

627. The six vases in the top row are all in *Regent* design. SECOND ROW: *Daisies, Asters, Carnations, 1000, S9, Engraved No. 1, Ivy,* and *Regent.* BOTTOM ROW: a basket in *Engraved No. 1*, a centerpiece in *Snow Flakes & Holly*, a basket in *Adam No. 2*.

628. In the top row of Inventory Plate 92 are two vases in *No. 4*, one in *1010*, then three more in *No. 4*. The second row begins with three vases in *No. 4*, followed by one in *Snow Flakes & Holly*, then four in *1021*. In the bottom row are a vase in *183*, followed by three in *Empire*, then *Adelphia*, *Roses & Lines*, *Flutes & Panel Border*, and *Adelphia*.

629. At top, the two baskets and first vase are in *Daisies & Lines* design, followed by two vases in *Boston,* and one each in *No. 1* and *No. 2.* SECOND ROW: The designs are *183, Carnations, Poppies, 1000, Ivy, 183,* and *112.* THIRD ROW: First three vases are in *Cut & Engraved No. 1, 1012,* and *Boston;* next three (bracket vases for automobiles) are in *Flutes & Carnations, Flutes & Panel Border,* and *Vera.* The two low rectangular vases are in *Diamonds & Silver Threads* and *No. 1 & Engraving.*

630. Inventory Plate 94 featured centerpieces. The two in the top row are in *Flutes & Panel Border* and *Adam* designs. SECOND ROW: flower pan & holder in *No. 1*, centerpiece in *Ivy*, flower pan & holder in *Roses & Lines*. BOTTOM ROW: *Prunus Blossoms* vase, *Wild Roses* centerpiece, and *Asters* design vase.

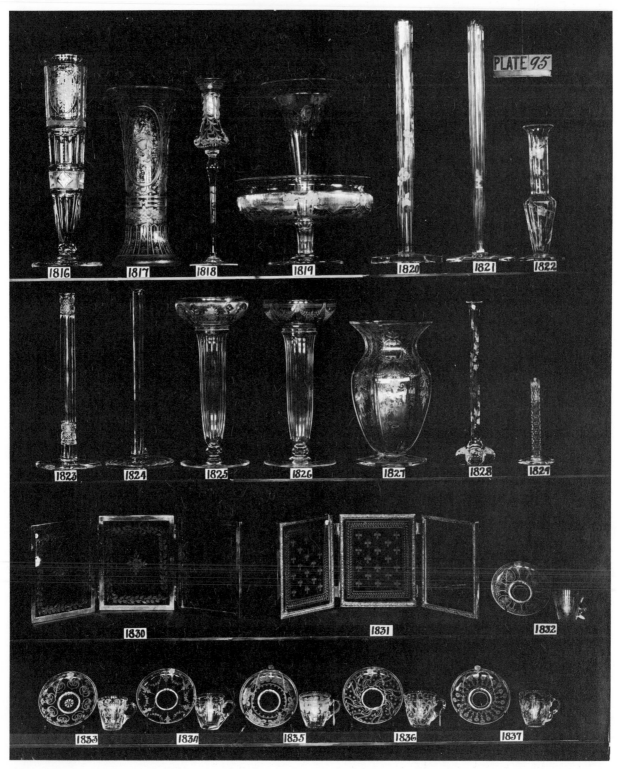

631. TOP ROW: vases in *Cut & Engraved No. 1, 3121,* and *No. 5;* centerpiece in *112,* then vases in *Flutes & Prunus Blossoms, Flutes,* and *Flutes & Prunus Blossoms.* SECOND ROW: vases in *Stars, Pillars & Engraving, No. 1, Adam No. 2,* three more in *No. 1,* and a small vase in *Hollow Diamonds.* THIRD ROW: wind screens in *Roses* and *Marie Antoinette,* a cup and saucer in *Trees & Roses.* BOTTOM ROW: cups and saucers in designs *No. 3, No. 5, No. 8, No. 9,* and *No. 10.*

632. In the top row of Inventory Plate 96 are a plate and decanter in *Birds & Bees* design and a three-piece bread and milk set in *Alphabet*. SECOND ROW: boxes in *Daisies & Lines, No. 3, No. 2, Prunus Blossoms, Adam,* and *No. 2.* THIRD ROW: a box in *Asters* design, puff boxes in *1000, No. 4, 777,* and two in *Ivy*; then a hair receiver in *Diamonds & Silver Threads.* FOURTH ROW: a puff box in *York,* three boxes in *No. 1,* one in *No. 3,* and still another in *No. 1.* BOTTOM ROW: a box in *No. 1,* glove boxes in *Adam* and in *Adelphia,* a puff box in *Adelphia,* and a card case in *No. 1.*

633. Inventory Plate 97, clock cases. In the top row designs are *Engraved Grapes, Thistle, No. 1;* followed by two in *No. 3.* SECOND ROW: *Thistle, Diamonds & Silver Threads, No. 1,* and two in *No. 3.* The case at bottom is *No. 1 & Engraved.* All the cases in the top row except the middle one, along with the second and third cases in the center row and the one at bottom, were fitted with Chelsea movements and had special dials with raised figures. The middle clock in the top row had a cheap eight-day movement, and the two at the end of the second row had cheap one-day movements.

634. The two large picture frames in Inventory Plate 98 are in *Louis XVI* and *Chinese Chippendale* designs. The six paperweights in the second row are *Horse No. 1, Eagle No. 1, Moose No. 1, Head of Russian Wolfhound, Russian Wolfhound,* and *Silver Threads & Roses.* BOTTOM ROW: Thermometers are in *Ivy, No. 1,* and *Thistle;* stamp boxes are *Engraved* and *Silver Diamonds & Roses;* mirror is *Engraving No. 1;* plates are designs *64* and *65.*

635. Here, in the top row, are five teapots: *Grapes, Versailles & Engraved, Mitres & Border 1, Antique 1 & Engraved,* and *Cut No. 1 & Engraved.* SECOND ROW: three teapots, in *No. 40, Marie Antoinette,* and *1009;* two plaques, in *Roses* and *Ivy.* THIRD ROW: four teapot stands, in *No. 4, Roses, Mitres & Border,* and *Snow Flakes & Holly;* card holders in *Dots* and in *Roses & Lines.* BOTTOM ROW: vase in *1012* design, plate and jar in *Pears & Oranges,* sponge bowl in *Panel Border,* basket in *Mitres & Border,* and a vase in *Adelphia.*

636. Two "spun green" electroliers—*Roses* and *Engraved No. 1* designs—pictured on Plate 100 of the Sinclaire 1917 Photographic Inventory. The blanks are almost certainly from Steuben.

637. Fred Haselbauer, top right; George Haselbauer, bottom right; Mrs. Joseph Haselbauer, center left, with a group of relatives and friends about 1920. *Coll. Mrs. Catherine Haselbauer Dencenburg* (then the little girl in the front row).

15
J. F. Haselbauer & Sons[1]; Frederick Haselbauer, Engraver

Mrs. Joseph Haselbauer decided in 1910 that the Haselbauers' volume of business required construction of a two-story building behind their West Third Street house. Joseph Haselbauer was fifty-eight, and at the peak of his powers. Fred was thirty-four, a steady, serious-minded bachelor. George, at twenty-one, was more brilliant and more volatile. He had been engraving since childhood because, as his father said, "If you won't go to school, you'll learn to engrave." Their mother said of her sons' talents that "George was a born engraver; Fred had to line everything out."

The J. F. Haselbauer & Sons shop had cutting frames as well as lathes, and an acid room. Its equipment was of the highest quality. In one room, high shelves held books of patterns along with broken glassware that the Haselbauers had matched. Among the latter were many pieces with the engraved shield of White House orders.

Like Augustus and Ignatius Haselbauer, Joseph died young. He never worked in the new shop, but his sons continued to use his name. The company letterhead and advertisements read "Rich Rock Crystal, Copper Wheel and Stone Engraving/Monograms, Letters, Etc." Ellen Haselbauer, their sister, worked in the business when and where needed. Mrs. Joseph Haselbauer ran it with a firm hand. Besides keeping the company's books, she prepared the glass for George to acid-dip.

Corning reports that the shop had 12 cutting frames and 6 lathes may be exaggerated. Yet there is little doubt that the company throve during its first years, hiring additional craftsmen as needed, and subcontracting some of its engraving to Corning's one-man shops. The company was "a quality shop" by any standards.

J. F. Haselbauer & Sons made every kind of engraved and cut-and-engraved glass. It was perhaps Corning's busiest subcontracting company, working for firms that probably included Christian Dorflinger's.[2] The Haselbauers also made repairs. We have quoted John Ferris of Elmira Cut Glass Co. about one such job. They also did matchings, and made a small line of their own glass as well. Some blanks for this came from Steuben.

The Haselbauer brothers were temperamentally mismatched. Despite their mother's peacemaking efforts, relations became strained when bad times began for the glassmaking industry. Fred was dependable, conservative, and active in Masonry. Young George was impatient, ambitious, and eager for the company to become known as a manufacturer. He set up displays of Haselbauer glass at a John Wanamaker department store, at Garrett's winery in Hammondsport, and in Buffalo shops. "You have to spend money to make money," he said. When the 1920 depression began, he returned to his second trade as a machinist, though he again engraved, for the Hunt Glass Works, in the 1930s.[3]

Fred Haselbauer continued alone, hiring Henry Hauptmann as an additional engraver from time to time, and eventually dropping the company name. The Great Depression was as hard on him as on the rest of Corning. He was glad to have monogramming and polishing work from the Steuben Division. In 1938, when his mother decided to have the Haselbauer shop torn down, Fred went to work in the Steuben factory. He was sixty-two. With characteristic kindness, he insisted that young Floyd Manwarren take the shop's cutting equipment, and pay the low asking price whenever he became able to do so.

Fred Haselbauer moved to the Hawkes company as a cutter in October 1947, and again became an engraver the following spring, when one of the department left, according to the company payroll records. It is characteristic of the industry, but nonetheless touching, that Haselbauer's rate of pay, now that he was in his seventies, was lower than that of the younger men. He adjusted the discrepancy by working longer hours than they did, remaining in the trade he loved until his final illness in 1949.

SUMMARY

Dates: J. F. Haselbauer & Sons, ca. 1910-21. Fred Haselbauer, glass engraver, ca. 1921-38

Address: rear of 84 West Third Street

Blanks: chiefly from the companies for whom the Haselbauers worked. Some from Steuben. Other suppliers unknown

Trademark: none

Product: 1910-20, subcontracted and independently made engraved and cut-and-engraved glass of all kinds, including chandeliers. Repairs and monogramming. 1920-38: subcontracting, gradually diminishing to monograms and polishing

Employees: several unknown cutters and/or engravers during the early years. After 1920, engraver Henry Hauptmann from time to time

Customers: private customers unknown. Widespread subcontracting; C. Dorflinger & Sons probably a customer

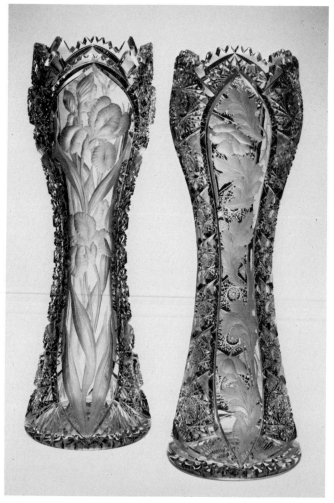

638. Cut and engraved plate (unfinished) and cut and engraved vase. Both are from J. F. Haselbauer & Sons; the vase is by George Haselbauer. Plate diam., 27.6 cm. *Coll. Mrs. Catherine Haselbauer Dencenburg; vase, Coll. The Corning Museum of Glass* (Gift of Mrs. Catherine Haselbauer Dencenburg)

639. Pair of vases cut and engraved for their mother by Fred and George Haselbauer, ca. 1911–20. Heights, 40 cm. and 39.8 cm. *Coll. The Corning Museum of Glass* (Gift of Mrs. Catherine Haselbauer Dencenburg)

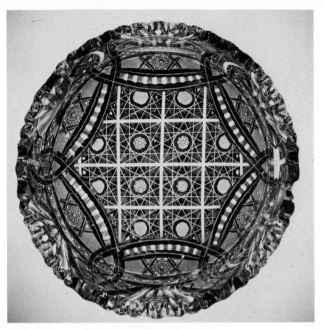

640. Haselbauer & Sons rock-crystal-finish bowl. Diam., 21 cm. *Coll. Mrs. Catherine Haselbauer Dencenburg*

641. This cut bowl shows that Haselbauer & Sons' cutting was as expert as their engraving. Diam., 21.1 cm. *Coll. Mrs. Catherine Haselbauer Dencenburg*

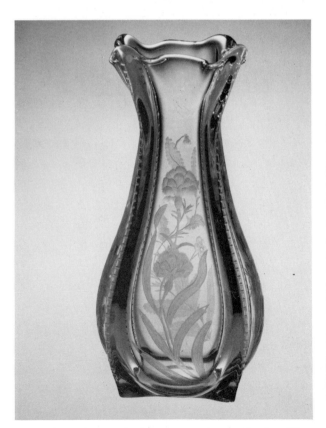

642. Carnations and wheat engraved on a Steuben Division blank by George Haselbauer. Height, 29.4 cm. *Coll. Mrs. Catherine Haselbauer Dencenburg*

643. Small stone-engraved plate from Haselbauer & Sons or from Fred Haselbauer's shop. Diam., 11.5 cm. *Coll. Miss Mary Krebs*

16
Thomas Shotton Cut Glass Works

The Shotton company is the largest one that fled to Corning as a haven from union agitation.[1] Its move came in 1912.

Thomas Shotton was an English cutter who came to Corning in 1884 as part of a group hired by T. G. Hawkes.[2] George R. Nokes, or Noakes (incorrectly spelled Noxe in one Corning directory), was another group member. Nokes boarded with Shotton in Corning.

Shotton had left Corning by 1893, according to the directory. He went to Brooklyn and founded a glass-cutting company. Nokes joined him in 1894. By 1912 the Thomas Shotton Cut Glass Works was Brooklyn's largest, with capital of over $50,000. (*Thomas' Register* claimed its largest Brooklyn competitor was capitalized at over $10,000.) Shotton, Nokes, and William Waldman of New York were the company's principals.

Shotton respected the craftsmanship he found in Corning; a period of work for his company is part of the biography of several Corning cutters.

In 1912 Shotton's company had two plants in Brooklyn, and reported $600,000 worth of business for the previous year. It also reported 600 men in its main plant and 166 in its annex, "with a demand for more." Though these totals were probably exaggerated,[3] the company was clearly a large one. Thomas Hazelbauer, son of engraver Ignatius Haselbauer, managed one of the plants;[4] later developments indicate that it was the annex.

In May of 1912, Shotton closed one or both of his Brooklyn factories. The reason was "the attempt of the glass cutters' union to prevent the establishment of [t]he open shop." By July the company was ready to move part of its operation to Corning. Each development of this important business story brought headlines in the *Leader*. The first came July 19:

SHOTTEN [sic] ANNEX OF BROOKLYN CUT GLASS COMPANY TO OPEN PLANT HERE. Firm Headed by Former Corningites Will Start 100 Frames . . . in Old Drake . . . Plant August 1— Company . . . Promises to Double Size of Local Plant Soon.

Shotton had leased the 56-58 Bridge Street plant for three years, with an option for two more. Twenty-five frames would be added to the building's 75; electric power would be installed. Thomas Hazelbauer was manager, but the *Leader* continued to spell the name with the original "s." The paper ended its story with the following editorial comment:

> The opening . . . will be welcomed by the glass cutters of Corning as its establishment is expected . . . to better local conditions by creating a better demand for experienced glass cutters, a fact which will tend to improve certain conditions which have made it difficult for cutters to change their places of employment without leaving the city.

The phrase "certain conditions" alluded to agreements among the larger firms not to hire one another's workmen.[5] These anti-piracy measures required a craftsman to work outside Corning for a period before applying for work with a second Corning employer.

The Shotton company's move did not end these gentlemen's agreements, but it did bring higher wages. Though the *Leader* refrained from attributing a cause in a story printed on July 26, the implications was clear. "EMPLOYEES OF J. HOARE & CO. GET 10 PER CENT WAGE INCREASE" was the headline. The story added that there was "a greater demand for first class cutters than there [had] been for a considerable period."

644. *Opposite:* Cut powder box and hock glasses designed by Thomas Hazelbauer and cut at the Shotton company's Brooklyn factory. The glasses reportedly were made for a Pope, ca. 1910–20. Height, 19.6 cm. *Coll. Mrs. Thomas Hazelbauer, Jr.*

More news followed on August 2: "SHOTTON COMPANY LEASES ANOTHER PLANT TO EMPLOY 75 MEN HERE." This was the "old cut glass plant in the [Corning] Building Compan[y]'s building on Tioga Avenue." It had served as J. Hoare & Co.'s annex and H. P. Sinclaire & Co.'s temporary quarters. This story reported that men would be "set at work next week [at 56–58 Bridge St.] to operate 75 frames, with the promise that this number [would] be doubled within a few weeks." The Shotton company planned an apprentice program as well; Thomas Hazelbauer had hired his brother John as foreman.[6]

Actually, the Shotton company cut glass in Corning for a few weeks at most. The *Leader* reported August 7 that union men had arrived "to break up the operations of the new Corning plant." Seven more, "delegates" of Shotton's Brooklyn strikers, "arrived today," the paper said. An organizer from Toledo was also in town. The company closed, though it is not clear when. Thirty employees went to work for O. F. Egginton Co. in October. Few went to Brooklyn, where the Shotton company continued to operate until about 1923, according to the *Glass Trade Directory.*

The American Flint Glass Workers' Union did not take the defeat lightly. "UNION CUTTING SHOP IS SOUGHT. National Officers of Union Here to Look Over Plant. Ohio Firm Coming?" was the headline of a *Leader* story of October 1. An unnamed Ohio firm would come to Corning if assured of 100 employees and three months' use of the plant without cost. Neither materialized.

The balance of the story indicated that the Shotton company had used union employees rather than hiring Corning cutters. The union organizer, it said,

feels very bitterly toward the Shotton company which closed its shop just after he had brought men ...from cities throughout the country to work for it....He also has the same feeling toward the men he believes were responsible for the Shotton plant leaving town.

The story's last sentence, above, calls to mind a long-standing rumor in Corning that the city's cut-glass manufacturers paid Thomas Shotton to leave town. Other than Thomas and John Hazelbauer, no Corning men seem to have returned to Brooklyn with the company. Thomas stayed with the company as foreman and designer until his premature death. John returned to Corning a year or so later.

The Corning operation presumably made the same kind of glass that the Brooklyn plants cut. In 1912 and later, this included good-quality but relatively simple geometric cuttings and combinations of floral and geometric designs. The pieces we have seen are on blanks of excellent color; some, however, are pressed and figured.

SUMMARY

Dates: 1912, from July to about October

Addresses: 56-58 Bridge Street and the southwest corner of Cedar Street and Tioga Avenue

Blanks: suppliers unknown; of good color, but some pressed and figured

Trademark: none known

Product: a full line of geometric cuttings and combinations of floral and geometric motifs

Employees: more than 30 and perhaps as many as 150 cutters. Only manager Thomas Hazelbauer and apprentice-foreman John Hazelbauer are known.

Customers: probably chiefly department stores. An order for a pope that Hazelbauer family tradition reports indicates that some glass may also have been made for jewelers.

17
John N. Illig, Manufacturer of Artistically Engraved Glassware

Chapter 8 discussed John Illig's early years in Corning, and the unorthodox arrangement by which he had a New York representative even while he worked in the factory of H. P. Sinclaire & Co.[1] About 1915 Illig gave up factory work to devote full time to his business. His brother worked with him, though he disapproved of the move. Joseph Illig was correct; John could have chosen no worse period to found a fine-glass company.

Illig's first factory was at 136 West Tioga Avenue, from which address he presumably issued his first catalog. A fire had forced him to move to 227 East Market Street by the time he issued a slightly revised one in 1917. By this time he had a West Coast agent, H. G. Gute & Co. of San Francisco. It is the Gute copy of the Illig company's catalog that we reproduce.

The catalog is especially strong in engraved flowers and fruits. Some are reminiscent of H. P. Sinclaire & Co. work, since Illig had designed for that company and took his designs with him when he left. As was customary, his former employer discontinued them.[2]

Illig's talent for design is apparent even in his inexpensive *Stars and Stripes,* which effectively used the gang-cut wheel.[3] His specialty, however, was fruits, in which his work was unexcelled.

Though Illig's company was never large, it throve briefly. Joseph Illig moved to California about 1917, but cutters included Gerald Davis, Dominick Reynolds, and Peter Eick, all of whom worked part time for the company, according to Davis, and Ada Rew, who was a full-time cutter, Manwarren says.

Illig remained optimistic as the war in Europe cut off shipments of foreign blanks and lowered the quality of domestic ones. His optimism continued as the depression of 1920/1921 began. Chapter 2 has shown that this lowered glass-industry wages in New York State by almost 42 percent in a single year. Yet on February 7, 1921, Corning read in the *Leader*: "ILLIG CUT GLASS COMPANY BUYS SITE FOR NEW FACTORY TO GO UP . . ." Illig changed his plans in May, however, and moved his company into the vacant O. F. Egginton factory. The *Leader* reported on May 2 that as the factory could "accommodate 150 men Mr. Illig's business [would] have opportunity for expansion." The purchase seemed a rare bargain; Illig's later partner says that the owners[4] lowered the price steadily from $25,000 until finally they "mostly gave him the building, for $5,000."[5]

Illig's conviction that business would improve was perhaps based on the renewed availability of fine blanks. Yet the depression made it impossible to collect from the jewelers all over New York State who bought his glass. In 1923 Corning Glass Works gaffer Joseph Fox agreed to invest in the company. Fox says of the next blow to the American fine-glass industry:

> Lots of glass was coming in from Europe. Nobody [here] wanted to work for two dollars a day. But if the men had been paid enough to live, their glass would have been too expensive for anyone to buy.

Illig stopped regular work at the factory about 1924, though Corning directories continued to list it for a few years. Fox later converted it into apartments.

Illig continued to engrave his handsome glass at home until 1929, when he worked briefly at Corning Glass Works, as he did again in 1934, according to company records. But like the Master that he presumably was, "he didn't want anyone telling him how to engrave," his daughter says. He sold his tools, and turned to any jobs he could find. His last employer was again Corning Glass Works, where he worked as a night watchman. He died in 1948.

SUMMARY

Dates: ca. 1915-ca. 1924-29
Address: ca. 1915-17, 136 West Tioga Avenue; ca. 1917-21, 227 East Market Street; 1921-ca. 1924, 152-174 West Fifth Street; ca. 1924-ca. 1929, 230 Pearl Street, Illig's home
Blanks: The Illig catalog seems to show that the Steuben Division supplied some. Suppliers of lower-quality blanks unknown

Trademark: none known
Product: a full line of engraved and cut-and-engraved glass. Deeply engraved fruits and flowers, often unpolished, were a specialty. Also matchings and subcontracting. See catalog.
Employees: Cutters included Joseph Illig, Gerald Davis, Dominick Reynolds, Peter Eick, and Ada Rew. Most worked part time for the company. John Illig was designer-engraver.
Customers: West Coast sales through H. G. Gute & Co., San Francisco. Eastern sales chiefly to New York State jewelers, presumably through W. F. Upham of New York, Illig's representative in 1910. Subcontracting customers included Giometti Brothers.

NOTE: Illustrations 645 to 679 represent the major part of the Illig company's second salesman's catalog, ca. 1917. *Coll. Corning–Painted Post Historical Society*

645.   Matching sugar, creamer, and spoon tray made by the Illig company about 1917. *Athens* is penned in lightly as the name of the design or pattern.

646.   Another page of matching pieces from the Illig catalog.

647. Large pitcher and matching cup with a design of lemons and leaf sprays, Illig, ca. 1917.

648. Pitchers and matching tumblers. Both pitchers held four pints. The design at left is of jonquils. That at right, called *Spray 1*, consists of flowers and fernlike leaf sprays.

649. Tall, 3-pint pitchers and matching tumblers, patterns not identified in the catalog.

650. At far right in the top row is a tall cordial bottle decorated with grapes. The other five containers on this page are all pinch bottles. Those at the bottom are decorated with rye, a thistle, and a shamrock (respectively).

267

651. At bottom of this page from the Illig catalog is a highball set consisting of a decanter and six glasses. At top are three "tumble-up" sets.

652. The rock-crystal glass pictured on this page all bears identical or closely similar engraved flower motifs.

653. A page of goblets from the Illig catalog of ca. 1917.

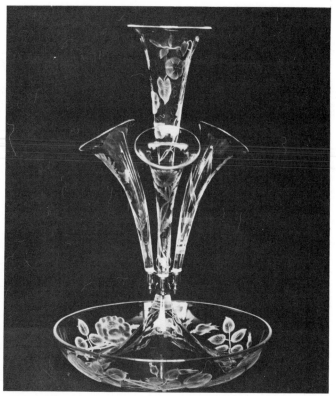

654. Epergne with four removable trumpet-shaped vases. Each part is decorated with a different kind of flower.

655. Two 12-inch vases from the Illig catalog. Each is decorated with cut motifs and engraved flowers.

656. Tall vase with engraved Easter lilies, Illig catalog, ca. 1917.

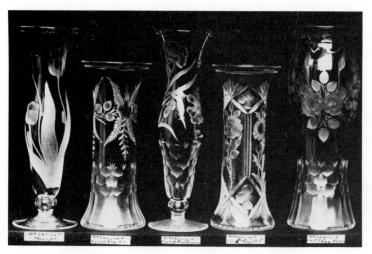

657. Group of Illig vases decorated with engraving or a combination of cutting and engraving.

658. Another page of Illig vases. All are decorated with flower motifs.

659. Three Illig vases. The one at far right is decorated with a "sculptured" chrysanthemum.

660. Four Illig flowerpots. Three of them have a butterfly motif in addition to the floral sprays.

661. Three puff boxes and a hair receiver, Illig, ca. 1917. Items one and three are both in *Athens* pattern. The box second from left is identified as *Louis XV,* and the one at far right as *Spray 2.*

662. Two Illig flower bowls. One at left has a pansy motif.

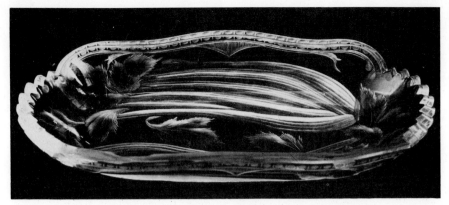

663. A 12-inch celery tray by the Illig firm. Main decorative motif is a bunch of celery.

664. Two Illig plates, identified on the catalog page as *Spray 1* and *Spray 2*.

665. These plates from the ca. 1917 Illig catalog are *Morning Glory* and *Rye* designs.

666. The design on this 9-inch bowl by Illig is identified as *Raspberries*.

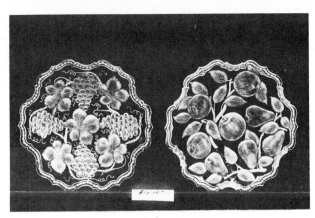

667. Two more handsome fruit designs by Illig. At left is *Grapes;* at right, *Apples & Pears*.

668. A group of Illig pieces in fruit and floral designs.

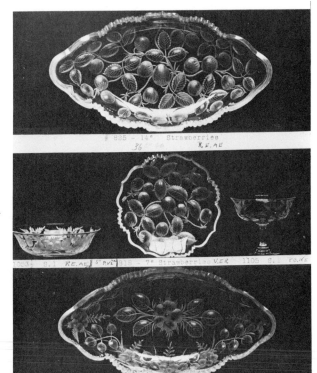

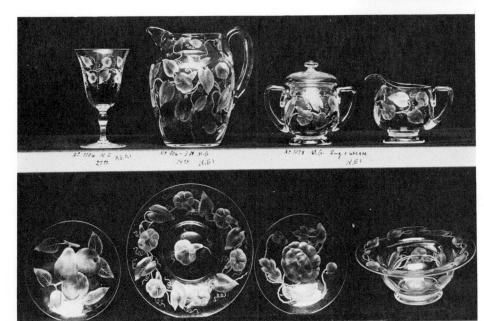

669. More Illig pieces with fruit or floral designs. First and third items in lower row are 6-inch plates in *Apples & Pears* and *Poppy* designs. The melon bowl and its matching 8-inch plate are *Morning Glory* pattern.

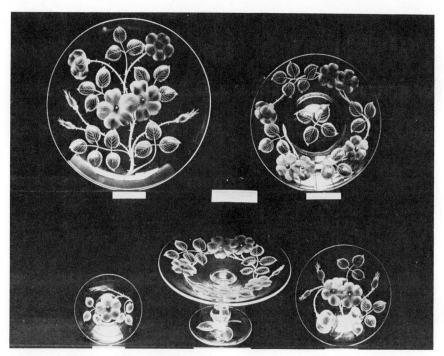

670. Group of Illig pieces in *Wild Rose* pattern.

671. Page from the ca. 1917 Illig catalog depicting pieces in a wide variety of shapes, including an oil and vinegar set, celery dish, basket, bedside water set (tumble-up), and candlestick.

672. Another varied group of pieces, most of them decorated with simpler, plainer designs.

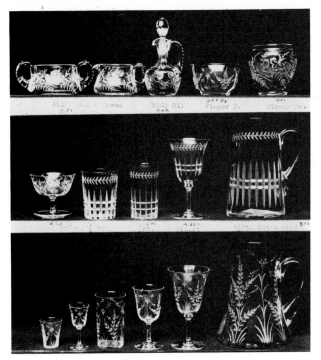

673. Engraved Illig designs, ranging from flowers to delicate sprays to the geometric.

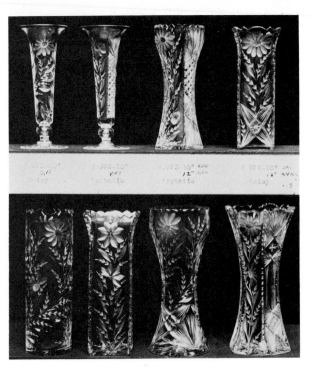

674. All eight vases on this page of the Illig catalog are decorated with floral motifs and sometimes further embellished with cutting. The two at center in the top row are identified as *Arctotis* pattern; the second vase at bottom is *Clematis*. The remaining five are all in some variation of the *Daisy* pattern.

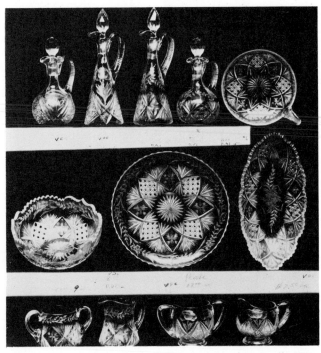

675. Several cruets and other serving pieces; all are decorated with a combination of engraving and cutting.

676. Again, the pictured pieces are decorated with a combination of cutting and engraving.

677. Punch bowl and matching punch cup, Illig catalog, ca. 1917.

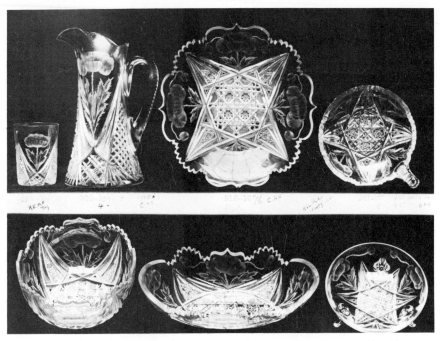

678. Seven matching pieces with engraved poppies and elaborate cut motifs, Illig, ca. 1917.

679. Another punch bowl from the ca. 1917 Illig catalog.

18
Corning's Ghost Companies

Research has brought to light the names of several Corning cut-glass companies that seem never to have existed or to have existed under other names. We call them "ghost companies."

Corning's ghosts were misidentified for any of several reasons. One was the industry custom of calling factories by the names of their owners or managers. Bath, New York, for example, called H. P. Sinclaire & Co.'s blowing plant, which Ivan Larson managed, the Larson Glass Works. Another cause of confusion is a proprietor's association with more than one company. Sometimes the announcement of a new company was rushed into print, only to be followed by a change of name or a decision not to open. In one case a simple lapse of memory seems to be to blame for an inaccurate company name. Again, printed rumors might prove to be unfounded.

The following list of Corning's ghost companies is based on research through the autumn of 1977. We offer it as a summary of likelihoods, inasmuch as proving non-existence is virtually impossible.

The Allen Glass Co.

This company was reported by a knowledgeable informant as operating on the southeast corner of Cedar Street and Tioga Avenue. J. Hoare & Co. had used this shop, owned by the Corning Building Co., early in the century. William Allen was a Hoare & Co. foreman who later founded the Allen Cut Glass Co. in Johnstown, Pennsylvania. We assume that Corning's "Allen Glass Co." was in fact the Hoare & Co. annex, and that Allen ran it. His grandson, who has thoroughly researched the Johnstown company, knows of no branch shop in Corning.

Arcadian Cut Glass Co.

Two trade publications placed this company in Corning in 1902.[1] We have found no mention of it in Corning newspapers or directories. One of the Ferris brothers, proprietors of Elmira Cut Glass Co., however, was also associated with an Arcadian Cut Glass Co.,[2] We judge that the Arcadian name was considered for the Elmira Cut Glass Co. branch shop that opened in Corning about this time.

Joseph Black

The Corning–Painted Post Historical Society has reported Joseph Black as a subsidiary of T. G. Hawkes & Co.[3] We believe the name was in fact Joseph Blackburn, a Hawkes & Co. subcontractor.

The Bronson Cut Glass Co.

This seems to have been a local nickname for the Crystal Manufacturing Co. of Painted Post; its incorporators included George Bronson. Only the widespread use of a nickname can account for the fact that two other Corning cutting company proprietors considered using company names that included the word "Crystal." The use of this nickname has also caused confusion with the Bronson Inkstand Co. of Painted Post. This was sold in 1898 to Clute & Drake of Corning; the sale led to the founding of George W. Drake & Co.

Crystal City Cut Glass Co.; Crystal Glass Co.

These names have been connected in print with the principals of three Corning cutting companies. Yet neither seems to have been used.

George W. Drake considered calling his company the Crystal City Cut Glass Co.; so did James Sebring, president of the Corning Cut Glass Co.[4] So far the record is clear.

On May 10, 1902, however, *China, Glass & Lamps* printed two confusing stories. The first said that Sebring and his partners had incorporated Crystal Glass Co. for the purpose of making cutting blanks. The second said that the Addison, New York, glass factory would begin making blanks (and lighting goods) as the Crystal Glass Co. It had briefly manufactured blanks and cut them as Egginton & Brewster about 1895. To compound the confusion, the second story said that Crystal was reputed to be "controlled by the Imperial Cut Glass Co. of Corning, New York" (see below). The Addison factory neither resumed making blanks nor used the Crystal name.

The name appeared again in a *Daily Journal* story of June 22, 1903. This reported:

A new company has been organized by Northside residents, who will start a new cutting factory . . . in the near future. The concern will be known as the Crystal City Cut Glass Co. Incorporation papers were sent to Albany.

No such papers were filed, though Northside residents incorporated the Ideal Cut Glass Co. that week. Next month the Crystal Manufacturing Co. of Painted Post filed incorporation papers.

Ferris Brothers; the Ferris Glass Co.

Corning usually called its branch of the Elmira Cut Glass Co. by one or the other of these names.

The Holton Glass Co.; Holton Glass Cutting Co.

These names have been mentioned by descendants of several glass cutters. A January 7, 1902, letter to the Holton Glass Cutting Co., applying for a job, was introduced as evidence in the Corning Glass Works–Corning Cut Glass Co. suit.[5] Corning Glass Works was attempting to show that its frequent receipt of mail intended for Corning Cut Glass showed the similarity of the two companies' names had caused confusion. The letter's existence suggests that Corning Cut Glass had a foreman named Holton when it opened.

No Holton Glass Co. appears in Corning directories, nor have we seen it mentioned in Corning newspapers.

Imperial Cut Glass Co.

China, Glass & Lamps reported June 27, 1903, that Imperial had been incorporated recently. The principals it listed were those of Corning's Ideal Cut Glass Co., which was incorporating at this time.

Sebring Brothers; Sebring Cut Glass Co.

These were Corning's nicknames for James Sebring's Corning Cut Glass Co. James Sebring's brother was a principal of another of James's businesses; a brother-in-law was secretary and treasurer of the cut-glass company.

19
Neighboring and Corning-Founded Companies

Earlier chapters have shown that Corning's cut-glass industry peaked about 1905, then began to decline as America's cut-glass companies continued to increase. Cut glass had begun to reach the vast department-store trade. Little companies sprang up, said Thomas Hawkes in 1904, "like mushrooms in a night," as we quoted in Chapter 1.

By this time no company made top-grade glass exclusively. Most new companies produced glass of moderate price; some so indicated in their advertisements or on their billheads. Yet several companies founded by Corning cutters produced quality glass. Among them were the Tuthill and Allen companies. Earlier companies founded by Corning men also produced quality glass, as one would expect. The John S. Earl company was one of these.

The story of Corning's contributions to the fine-glass industry is still developing. Much of it lies beyond the scope of this book. We know, for example, that a group of Thomas Hawkes's cutters moved to Pairpoint before 1890. AFGWU *Proceedings* show that Philip McDonald, designer in 1882 of Hawkes's famous *Russian* design, was working for L. Straus & Co. in New York during the depression of the 1890s.

Future research will doubtless yield more examples of Corning-founded and Corning-area cut-glass companies. Corning was the great cutting school of the eastern United States in the late nineteenth century. We offer the list below as a suggestion of the influence that the Crystal City had on the industry.

Companies in New York State

McCue & Earl
John S. Earl (Brooklyn)

Corning read in the *Journal* of January 27, 1887, that John S. Earl, cutting foreman of J. Hoare & Co. "for about a dozen years," had resigned to become a partner in an established cutting shop in New York City.[1] Corning directories confirm that he had come to Corning about 1875. Though he was born in England, we do not know who his first American employer was.

Earl's first New York association was with McCue & Earl of Brooklyn. Before 1904 he was in business for himself in Brooklyn. His sons also worked in the company; William was salesman, and John J. was cutting foreman. C. Dorflinger & Sons records include a five-page listing of blanks supplied to the company; Pairpoint Corporation records of 1905 through 1908 also show that catalogs of blanks were sent to the Earl company.

A 1951 lecture to the Somerville, Massachusetts, Historical Society illustrated Earl's high reputation.[2] It described a 150-pound, $3,000 punch bowl that the Union Glass Co. blew for Tiffany & Co. of New York in 1904. The pedestal was 16½ inches tall. The bowl was 14 inches high and had a capacity of 30 gallons. The lecturer said:

> The bowl was richly cut by John S. Earl of Brooklyn, an especially rich cutting that he designated as the Tiffany pattern. Mr. Earl employed a system of blocks and pulleys to balance the great mass of glass . . . and thirty different workmen had a part in executing the design. The work occupied two hundred and ten days. The depth of the cut was five eights *[sic]* of an inch. In the cutting twenty-five pounds of glass was taken off. While the cutter was at work a man stood at each side of him steadying the bowl. . . . The December 9, 1904, Somerville Journal shows a picture of it.[3]

Earl family tradition provides a sequel to this story. When Tiffany & Co. displayed the bowl, Diamond Jim Brady saw and admired it. He wanted a larger one, however. Again the Earl company received the commission. When the Brady bowl was finished, John J. Earl and two assistants personally installed it for Diamond Jim. Its price was $5,000.

Six or seven years later, Earl sold his company. He and John J. retired. The older man died in April 1912.

The company made a full line of rich-cut glass, including ruby-cased stemware. Designs included many hobstars and strawberry diamond cuttings.

SUMMARY

Dates: McCue & Earl, 1887-ca. 1903; John S. Earl, ca. 1903-ca. 1911
Address: 22 Morton Street, Brooklyn; moved to First Street ca. 1905
Blanks: Suppliers included C. Dorflinger & Sons, Union Glass Co., and the Pairpoint Corporation.
Trademark: none known
Product: a full line of rich-cut glass, including ruby-cased stemware. Huge punch bowls a specialty
Employees: 30 or more cutters; John J. Earl, cutting foreman; William Earl, sales manager
Customers: Only Tiffany & Co. is known.

Elmira Glass Cutting Co.
Elmira Cut Glass Co. (Elmira)

This company's Corning branch is discussed in Chapter 9.

The Elmira Glass Cutting Co. may have been founded as early as 1893, when directory evidence indicates Corning cutter John Ferris seems to have left town. Its name changed to Elmira Cut Glass Co. about 1906.[4]

The catalog that we show can be dated between 1906 and 1910. It lists the company's officers as John C. Ferris, president; Joel E. Ferris, treasurer;

680. Tray cut on a brilliant blank by the John S. Earl company, ca. 1903–11. Length, 18.4 cm. *Coll. Mrs. Arthur Corwin; Frederic Farrar photograph*

and Benjamin F. Levy, secretary. Levy was listed as an Elmira attorney in the telephone book. These men were directors, as were George R. Ferris and Isaac Levy.

The company made a full though modest line of cut glass. Its 38-page catalog, which showed 27 designs, stated:

> The Elmira Cut Glass Company manufactures only a high grade of cut glass. Each article sent out by the factory is guaranteed.
> This catalog contains a few leading sizes and designs. Other sizes, shapes and designs furnished on application.

The catalog pictured the plant as a brick building three and a half stories tall in front and two and a half in back.

Elmira Cut Glass was having labor trouble by 1903. Corning's *Daily Journal* reported on it February 10. The company had refused to discharge an employee whom his fellow workers disliked. Fifty employees struck. The story gave the company officers as the three Ferrises named above, and located the firm at Fox and Market streets.

Next day the (weekly) *Journal* reported that the men's grievance was with the union. Though a cutter was behind in his dues, the union refused to fine him.

More trouble followed. The *Daily Journal* reported on August 3 that 31 journeymen and 7 apprentices had stopped work. The dispute was still unsettled September 17, when the paper reported that most of the company's work was being done in Corning. We assume that its own Corning branch was doing the work.

A more serious strike came in 1910. A *Leader* story on November 11 was headlined MEN AT WORK IN CORNING SHOP. Elmira Cut Glass's factory was now on East Water Street. Union members had demanded recognition of the union. President John Ferris refused, and "the men were given a chance to return to work last Monday as non-union men." A statement that the factory had closed was contradicted later:

> Fifteen non-union men, some old employees, have been at work in the Elmira plant, and as many more in the Corning branch. More will be employed as required.

The *Leader* reported further developments in a November 29 story, ELMIRA CUT GLASS CO. COMING HERE. This too contained a seeming contradiction, for the writer added that the business had been moved to the Elmira factory's first floor. There were still 15 men working in Elmira, and 35 in Corning. George Ferris was quoted as saying that

> only two cut glass companies paid a higher wage scale than the Elmira Glass Cutting Co. in the United States. [They] paid about five per cent more but their plants [operate only] part of the year.

The Elmira operation seems to have closed later that year or early in 1911.

Pairpoint Corporation records from 1905 through 1908 show that their catalogs of blanks were sent to the company. Elmira bought a small, handled nappy and a horseradish jar from Dorflinger & Sons.[5] The company trained a number of its own cutters. Corning cutters who worked in the Elmira factory included Patrick and John Sheedy, according to their sister Delia.

NOTE: Illustrations 681 to 692, pages from an Elmira Cut Glass Co. catalog of ca. 1906–10, show most of the company's designs. A few others were listed but not pictured. *Coll. The Corning Museum of Glass*

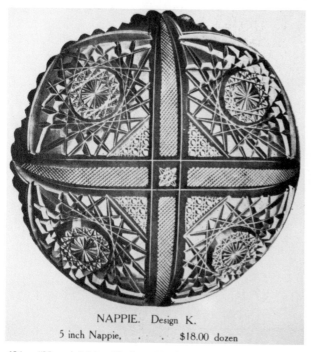

NAPPIE. Design K.
5 inch Nappie, . . . $18.00 dozen

681. "Nappie" identified as "Design K."

NAPPIE. Design No. 80.
5 inch Nappie, . . . $22.00 dozen

682. Another nappy, "Design No. 80."

NAPPIE. Design No. 6.

5 inch Nappie	.	.	$18.00 dozen
5 " "	hld.	.	18.00 "
6 " "	.	.	24.00 "

683. Nappy, "Design No. 6."

BON BON No. 1306
Design No. 33
7 inch, . . $36.00 dozen

685. Bonbon dish by Elmira Cut Glass Co. The 7-inch size is listed at $36 a dozen.

OBLONG BOWL. Design 38.
10½ inches Long, 8 inches Wide. $10.00

BOWL. Design No. 6.
10 inch Bowl. $9.00

BOWL. Design K.
8 inch Bowl. $4

BOWL. Design No. 28.
8 inch Bowl. $5.00

BOWL. Design No. 39.
8 inch Bowl. $5.50

684. Group of Elmira bowls. The one at top right is also identified as "Design No. 6." Bowl in the center, like the nappy in Ill. 681, is designated as "Design K." Bowl at top left is "Design No. 38"; at bottom left, "Design No. 28"; at bottom right, "Design No. 39."

686. Elmira cut "wine jug." It came in 2-, 3-, 4-, and 6-pint capacity. Heights ranged from 10 to 14 inches. "Design No. 51."

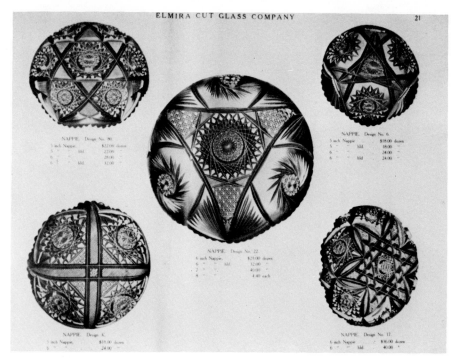

687. Several of these nappies have the same design as already pictured in the immediately preceding Elmira illustrations.

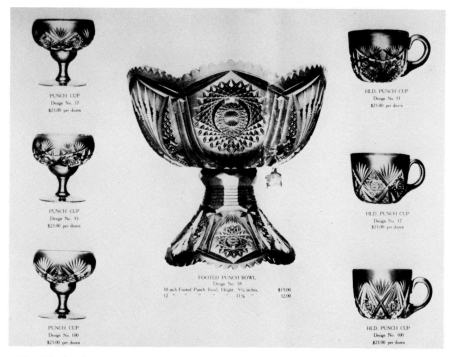

688. Elmira footed punch bowl was identified as "Design No. 18." Punch cups, either footed or handled, were available in three designs. None of those pictured have the same design number as the bowl, but the main motifs were similar and compatible.

SQUAT CARAFE. Design No. 23. $4.50.

GLOBE CARAFE. Design No. 23. $4.50.

WHISKEY JUG
Design No. 17. 2 pints
$9.00.

GLOBE CARAFE. Design No. 22. $4.50.

GLOBE CARAFE. Design No. 1. $4.50.

689. Four carafes and a stoppered whiskey jug (center) from Elmira Cut Glass Co. Note the use of the most popular and familiar motifs.

DEEP BON BON
Design No. 20.
Length, 7½ inches. Width, 4½ inches. $$28.00 dozen.

SPOON TRAY
Design No. 20.
Length, 7½ inches. Width, 3½ inches. $28.00 dozen.

SPOON TRAY
Design No. 39.
Length, 7½ inches. Width, 3½ inches.
$2.00 each.

CRIMP BON BON
Design No. 20.
Length, 7½ inches. Width, 5 inches. $28.00 dozen.

BROAD BON BON
Design No. 20.
Length, 7 inches. Width, 4½ inches. $28.00 dozen.

690. Four Elmira pieces cut in "Design No. 20." The spoon tray (center) is identified as "Design No. 39."

691. Two more Elmira cut "wine jugs." These too were available in four sizes, the heights ranging from 10 to 14 inches.

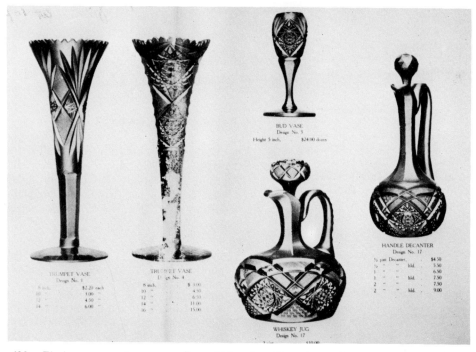

692. Elmira vases, a decanter, and a whiskey jug. Note the cutting on the stopper of this jug (bottom center).

SUMMARY

Dates: ca. 1893-1911
Address: in 1903, Fox and Market streets. By 1910, East Water Street
Blanks: Suppliers included the Pairpoint Corporation; two small items came from Dorflinger & Sons; other suppliers unknown
Trademark: none mentioned in catalog
Product: a modest line of geometrically cut glass in 27 known designs; other shapes and designs, however, "furnished on application"
Employees: may have totaled 65, including apprentices. Corning cutters included Patrick and John Sheedy.
Customers: unknown

Thomas Shotton Cut Glass Works (Brooklyn)

The Thomas Shotton company and its abortive move to Corning have been discussed at some length in Chapter 16. The summary below adds facts relevant to the Brooklyn operation.

SUMMARY

Dates: ca. 1894-1920s
Address: main plant at 482 Driggs Avenue in 1912. Annex address unknown. Offices and/or salesrooms at 48 West Broadway, New York City
Blanks: Shotton may have used Sèvres blanks, for which S. Herbert, cosponsor of at least one Shotton advertisement, was agent. Other suppliers unknown. Shotton glass that we know is of excellent color, but much of it is on figured blanks.
Trademark: we have seen none; none mentioned in advertisements
Product: a full line of rich-cut and floral-cut glass, much of it designed by Thomas Hazelbauer of Corning after about 1910
Employees: numerous, but presumably far fewer than the 766 reported in Corning news stories. Thomas Dow and Joseph Wilson reportedly cut glass for the company.
Customers: unknown. One order for hock glasses reportedly went to a pope.[6]

The Linford Cut Glass Co. (Jamestown)

William H. Linford was employed at Hoare & Dailey in 1880, according to the *Journal* of October 11. The census of that year gave his age as thirty-eight, his birthplace as England, and his occupation as glass cutter. The directory of 1891 listed both William Linford, Sr. and Jr., as cutters. The younger man had left town by 1895. This is perhaps the year that he opened the Linford Cut Glass Co. in Jamestown, New York.

By August 1900, the company was having labor trouble. The *Corning Daily Journal* of September 1 reported it as follows:

W. H. Linford, formerly of Corning, who conducts a glass cutting establishment at Jamestown, N.Y., has a strike on his hands. About thirty men are involved, mostly from Corning. A special to the *Buffalo Evening News* says:

JAMESTOWN, Aug. 31.–Recently the Linford Cut Glass Company reduced the wages of two or three men to what they considered a fair figure. Yesterday noon the thirty glass cutters in the factory went out on strike, and have not yet returned to work. The company alleges that the men whose wages were cut were not earning the money paid them. It is expected the matter will be amicably settled.

Apparently it was.

The company was listed in the *Glass Trade Directory* of 1902. When the *Directory* resumed its cut-glass listings in 1914, however, the Linford company was gone; we assume that it closed between 1903 and 1913. We have found no Linford glass, and no indication that the company used a trademark.

SUMMARY

Dates: ca. 1895-1913 or earlier
Blanks: suppliers unknown
Trademark: probably none
Product: unknown
Employees: about 30 cutters in 1900, most of them from Corning
Customers and *address* in Jamestown, unknown

Egginton & Brewster (Addison)

A glass manufacturing plant called the Addison Mosaic Glass Co. operated a few miles west of Corning from about 1890 to about 1894.[7] In 1895 the factory reopened. Its new owners planned to add a cutting shop. The *Daily Journal* reported the story on October 15.

Walter Egginton, of this city, has resigned his position with T. G. Hawkes & Co., and has gone to Addison, where with G. H. Brewster... he will revive the defunct Mosaic Glass Company....The firm will be known as Egginton & Brewster. Mr. Egginton has been connected with Mr. Hawkes' shop here since it was established, being for a large portion of that time the foreman. The new firm expects to start business within a week, with a force of twenty men. William Harrup, of New Bedford, Mass., will be foreman of the factory.

The paper wrote on October 25 that Harrup had hired ten men for "cutting and fancy ware." Clearly, the new owners planned to cut their own blanks.

Walter Egginton was the son of Oliver Egginton, who had recently retired from the Hawkes company as manager or superintendent. The following year he would open his O. F. Egginton Co., a high-quality cut-glass concern. Walter later became president of it, following his father's death. We do not know what connection, if any, there was between the two firms.

Egginton & Brewster had closed by May 10, 1902, when *China, Glass & Lamps* printed two contradictory reports about a possible reopening under new ownership. At this time Brewster was still an owner of the factory, but Egginton was president of O. F. Egginton Co. in Corning.

SUMMARY

Dates: 1895-ca. 1901
Address: "over the creek"
Blanks: of the company's own manufacture
Trademark: none known
Product: cut glass and "fancy ware"
Employees: 10 men making "cutting and fancy ware" in 1895. William Harrup, factory foreman. Walter Egginton presumably cutting foreman and designer
Customers: unknown

Erhardt & Schaeffer
(or Schaeffer & Erhardt)
Schaeffer & Co. (Syracuse)

Joseph Erhardt, born in Alsace-Lorraine in 1872, immigrated in the late 1880s as a trained glass cutter.[8] His close friendship with Jean Georges Haar of Corning, with whom he may have come to the United States, suggests that Erhardt, like Haar, "got his trade" at the St. Louis glass company.

Erhardt's first American home was in Syracuse, where he married about 1894 and established a small cutting company about 1895 with his brother-in-law, Jacob Schaeffer. Erhardt was its designer. The men seem to have worked in Erhardt's home at 316 Wyoming Street, where Schaeffer boarded, according to the Syracuse directory.

The company was short-lived; the two men were incompatible. The 1897/98 Syracuse City Directory showed Schaeffer operating as Schaeffer & Co. at 106 South State Street.

Erhardt worked briefly in Tiffin, Ohio, before settling in Corning. Corning directories say he cut glass for T. G. Hawkes & Co. from about 1899 to 1903. Dissatisfaction with the work prompted him to give it up and join the Corning police force. He died in 1929.

Erhardt's cutting was of excellent quality, as were his blanks. Family pieces are not trademarked, and are cut in rich geometric designs.

SUMMARY

Dates: ca. 1895-ca. 1897; thereafter, Schaeffer & Co. for an undetermined period
Address: 316 Wyoming Street; Schaeffer & Co.: 106 South State Street
Blanks: suppliers unknown
Trademark: probably none
Product: geometric cuttings
Employees: Erhardt and Schaeffer only
Customers: unknown

Becker & Wilson (Brooklyn)

A. C. Revi has discussed this company and its successors in his book, *American Cut & Engraved Glass.* It opened immediately after the closing of Frank Wilson & Sons in Corning about 1897. The Wilson of Becker & Wilson was Joseph, Frank's son. The *Corning Daily Journal* of March 14, 1902, however, reported the father as also "engaged in the glass business" in Brooklyn. Though he returned to Corning, he was presumably working in Becker & Wilson at the time of the report.

SUMMARY

Blanks and *trademark:* unknown
Product: rich geometric cuttings
Employees: included Frank Wilson in 1902
Customers and *address:* unknown

The Tuthill Cut Glass Co. (Middletown)

This company was one of Corning's most distinguished offspring. Its predecessor was the cutting shop that Charles G. Tuthill operated about 1895 in Corning. Directories list it at the home of his father, a prominent architect, and show that it was short-lived. In 1900 the Tuthill company opened in Middletown.[9]

Tuthill was a cutter, and the company's early work was rich-cut glass of excellent quality. By 1911, however, the company was doing well with the deeply engraved flower and fruit designs that became a specialty. The company manager was Susan Tuthill, Charles's sister-in-law; Tom Mortenson was foreman. Leon Swope, who stone engraved for the company for two years, reminisced about it as follows, in a letter of October 27, 1976:

> When Tom Mortenson was foreman for Tuthill he called and said to come down to Middletown and learn stone engraving. I was there January 7, 1911, to May 21, 1913....
> The way I remember Tuthill's, Mrs. Tuthill owned and ran the shop and Tom was foreman over the whole cutting and engraving. Mrs. Tuthill's husband was school superintendent.

The engravers were on the third floor, copper-wheel men by themselves and stone engravers also. Coming up the stairs, the first lathe was Bruno Hugo Palme, an Austrian; second lathe, Steve Case, a native former cutter; third lathe, myself; fourth lathe, Nicholas Rieber. He was *good,* a Dane. He had worked for Pairpoint and went back there when Tuthill shut down. Charles Tuthill worked all over the shop, had no regular job. I never saw him ...engrave....

Tuthill's was a quality shop.... Mortenson was a good workman, and preached it to me. I had to learn to work under my stone because that was the right way. My stone came towards me, and I could see what I was doing better....

Our so-called stones were carborundum. We could take a 3″ diameter stone off and put on an extension and use a stone down to ¾″. I used a diamond and made a gang stone to put feathers on birds.

Tuthill's was a small shop: about twelve to fifteen men.

Tuthill's copper-wheel engravers, Mr. Swope says, were named Sheperd and Benson. These were probably the R. Sheperd who, from Hawkes Cash Book evidence, left that firm in August 1906, and Orange T. Benson, who engraved for H. P. Sinclaire & Co. in the 1920s, according to the Corning Directory.

The Tuthill company reportedly closed in 1923, though there were short-lived attempts to revive it.

SUMMARY

Dates: 1900-23

Address: Wisner Avenue until 1903; thereafter, 36 Little Avenue

Blanks: six items from C. Dorflinger & Sons;[10] others from Pairpoint Corporation.[11] Other suppliers unknown

Trademark: acid-stamped script "Tuthill" for the latter part of the company's life

Product: a full line of rich-cut glass; by 1911 stone-engraved flowers, fruits, and the like, often combined with cut motifs; also copper-wheel engravings. High quality

Employees: 12 to 15 men, including stone engravers Leon Swope, Nicholas Rieber, Steve Case, and Bruno Hugo Palme; copper-wheel engravers Sheperd and Benson; cutters Louis Brandhurst, Harry Holmbraker, Ralph Salvati[12]

Customers: Glass of this caliber would have sold chiefly through jewelers; we can give no names, however.

693. Lamp cut in the Tuthill *Rex* design. The prisms are not original. 1900–1910. Height, 56.9 cm. *Coll. Mrs. Freda Lipkowitz*

694. Bowl stone-engraved by Leon Swope for the Tuthill company about 1912. Diam., 22.9 cm. *Coll. The Corning Museum of Glass*

695. Cut and stone-engraved punch-bowl set in the Tuthill *Vintage* design. Height, 41.2 cm. *Coll. The Corning Museum of Glass*

696. Cut decanter, finger-bowl set, and tumbler from Majestic Cut Glass Co. Height of decanter, 30.2 cm. *Coll. Mrs. Beatrice Spiegel Perling*

The Majestic Cut Glass Co. (Elmira)

The Majestic company's Corning branch, which outlived the parent firm, is discussed in Chapter 9.

The Majestic Cut Glass Co. was founded by Wolf M. Spiegel around the turn of the century.[13] It used the second floor of the headquarters of Speigel's junk business at the corner of South Clinton and Madison, judging from the listings in the 1915 telephone directory. Its product was a full line of rich-cut glass, including lamps and punch bowls.

Majestic cutting was expert, but some pieces show the faint wavy lines of the acid dip. Many blanks came from Belgium; others from the Pairpoint Corporation.[14] In 1908 Pairpoint records marked the company "out of business," but a Corning newspaper story of November 29, 1910, quoted in Chapter 9, shows that it had moved to Corning as the result of labor trouble.

The glass in family hands is not trademarked. The Majestic company's customers were leading stores in the eastern United States.

SUMMARY

Dates: ca. 1900-1908 in Elmira; thereafter in Corning
Address: corner of South Clinton and Madison
Blanks: from Belgium and Pairpoint Corporation; other suppliers unknown
Trademark: none on glass that we have seen
Product: a full line of rich-cut glass, including lamps
Employees: number and names unknown
Customers: leading stores in the eastern United States

The Ideal Cut Glass Co. (Canastota)

The Ideal Cut Glass Co. has a double connection with Corning. Founded there in 1902,[15] it gave Corning some outstanding cutters when it closed in 1933.

Charles Rose opened the Ideal company at the rear of his house at 75 West Pulteney Street, Corning, according to the directory. It was incorporated in 1903. Officers were Luman S. Conover, president; J. H. Scutt, vice-president; Fred Johnson, secretary; Charles Rose, manager; and George Velie, treasurer. Capital stock was $10,000. The incorporation papers indicate the directors were Conover, Rose, Johnson, Velie, and Scutt, each of whom owned five shares of stock. Rose and Johnson were the company's cutters; Rose ran the company. Conover was his father-in-law, and after 1903 his partner in a Corning hardware and sporting goods store.[16]

Johnson and Rose had learned to cut glass at the Hawkes company, where Rose became a foreman. The Hawkes Cash Book records his "special pay" of $50 twice a year.

By 1904 Rose was looking for larger quarters. Canastota offered him a former machine shop, with the understanding that it would become his if he

697. Pair of vases in *Diamond Poinsettia,* Ideal Cut Glass Co.'s most successful design. Cut by John Spear, ca. 1922. Height, 30.5 cm. *Coll. Mrs. Joseph O'Bryan*

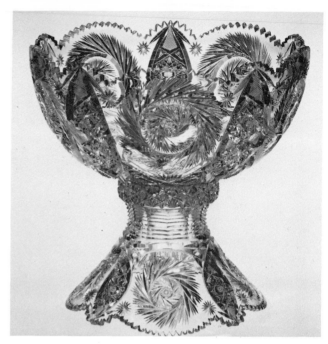

698. Punch bowl cut by Tom and/or Joe Burns in Canastota, N.Y., ca. 1915. Height, 32 cm. *Coll. Mr. and Mrs. John Jeppson*

stayed ten years.[17] The group that moved to Canastota probably numbered 10 to 12. Among them were Ambrose Van Etten, the foreman, and Rose's brothers, Fred and Benjamin. All were cutters.

In 1908 wholesale jeweler W. B. Hitchcock of Syracuse bought the company. Rose returned to Corning, where he became a popular alderman and active member of the Chamber of Commerce. At his death in December 1924, a *Leader* editorial called him "one of [Corning's] finest citizens."

Under Rose, Ideal used some Pairpoint blanks.[18] Most of its glass was geometrically cut, but there were also floral designs.

Under Hitchcock ownership and distribution, Ideal grew; at its peak it employed 125 persons. The ties with Corning continued. Orville Golden of Corning was superintendent in the early Hitchcock years; other Corning cutters are listed in the summary below. Most cutters, however, were local citizens trained at the company. By the 1920s they included about 30 women.

By 1912 Tom Burns was foreman of Ideal's best-cutters' shop. He was also the designer of *Diamond Poinsettia,* Ideal's best-selling design. Burns's bachelor brother Joe, also an expert cutter, headed cutting-wheel sales for the Norton Co. of Worcester, Massachusetts; he settled in Canastota when Tom moved there. His employers financed the operation of a small cutting in shop in Canastota, designed to experiment with the Norton wheels. When Norton introduced the gang-cut wheel in 1913, it proved a practical tool for making serrated knife blades, and Joe Burns founded the Burns Cutlery Co. in Syracuse.

Meanwhile, however, the Burns brothers and young Floyd Manwarren cut a great deal of high-quality glass in the Norton shop, which in effect was something of an Ideal Cut Glass Co. annex. The glass went to principals of the Norton Co.; some has recently been rediscovered, and has proved to be high-quality, hand-polished glass.

F. L. Morecroft, an officer of the Hitchcock company, became Ideal Cut Glass Co.'s president after Hitchcock's death. Floyd Manwarren managed the company from about 1921 until 1933, when the company closed after the bank holiday. Designs were chiefly floral in these years, but included some geometric cuts and copper-wheel engraving. Matchings were a specialty. Blank-suppliers then included the Fry, Libbey, and Union companies. Ideal used no trademark.

SUMMARY

Dates: 1902-33; in Corning until ca. 1904

Addresses: factory at 410 East North Street; main office in Elks Temple Building, Syracuse

Blanks: 1905-8, Pairpoint Corporation; other suppliers unknown. 1920-33, the Libbey, Union, and Fry companies

699. Tuthill cut nappy. Diam., 15.2 cm. *Coll. Mrs. Joseph O'Bryan*

Trademark: none
Product: originally geometric cuttings and a few floral designs; by the 1920s chiefly floral designs and a few geometric cuts and copper-wheel engravings. *Diamond Poinsettia* was the best selling of late designs. Matchings a specialty
Employees: Corning cutters included foreman Ambrose Van Etten, founder Charles Rose, superintendent Orville Golden, secretary Fred Johnson, Eugene Van Etten, Frank "Bouncer" Golden, Lee Stanton, Tom McIntyre, Ray Winfield, John Spear, Ed Rice, Archie Cass, and copper-wheel engraver Nathaniel Phelps. Cutters who worked in Corning after Ideal Cut Glass closed included Floyd Manwarren, Jemaine Kimball, Hazel Zimmerman, and——Maloney.
Customers: eastern jewelers and department stores; the Larkin Co. of Buffalo

Vallely Cut Glass Co.
International Cut Glass Co. (Buffalo)

Though Corning cutters took the industry to Buffalo, we know little about their companies. The following *Daily Journal* story of May 23, 1904, "Former Corning Young Men Have a Factory at Buffalo," was reprinted from the Buffalo *Evening News* of May 21:

Although the fact has been but little known, cut glass has been made...successfully in Buffalo for a year or more. The first local plant...was the Vallely Cut Glass Company at the Terrace and Franklin street, which was yesterday merged with the International Cut Glass Company, under which name the business will be continued. At a meeting of the directors...yesterday the following directors were elected: John C. Conway, President and Treasurer; John H. Vallely, Vice-President; J. Carroll, Secretary.

The new company will continue the manufacture of the finest grades and most artistic designs of cut glass at the present works, 59-61 Terrace, corner of Franklin Street...offices at 318 and 320 Ellicott Square.

Vallely and Charles (not J.) Carroll were brothers-in-law and Corning-area natives. Both had learned to cut glass at the Hawkes company, where Mary Ann Vallely Carroll was an inspector.[19]

We do not know when the company closed. Carroll returned to Corning, where he went into another business. Vallely went west to Ohio, and died in Toledo in 1955. He never left the glass business, but worked on lighting products and opened a glass and mirror shop.

SUMMARY

Dates: ca. 1903-?
Addresses: 59-61 Terrace, corner of Franklin; offices at 318-320 Ellicott Square
Blanks: Pairpoint Corporation is the only supplier known.
Trademark: unknown
Product: We know nothing more than the "finest grades" that the newspaper story reported.
Employees: unknown

Hazelbauer & Lundgren (Brooklyn)

We know this company from records of the Pairpoint Corporation, which sent catalogs of blanks to it between 1905 and 1908. Its factory was at 19 Hope Street. We believe that Thomas Hazelbauer of Corning, son of engraver Ignatius Haselbauer, was one of the principals. Thomas cut glass in Corning until 1894,[20] but may have left town soon after finishing his apprenticeship.

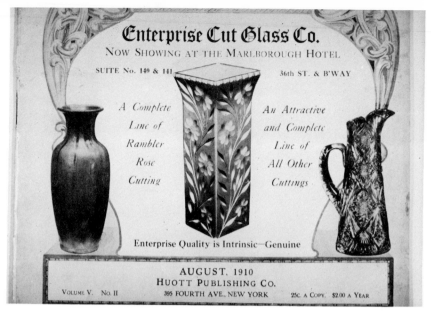

700. A 1910 advertisement for Enterprise Cut Glass Co.'s *Rambler Rose* floral cuttings. *Coll. The Corning Museum of Glass*

Presumably Hazelbauer & Lundgren was out of business before 1912, when Hazelbauer was general foreman of Brooklyn's huge Thomas Shotton Cut Glass Works. His role in this company's attempt to move to Corning is discussed in Chapter 16.

SUMMARY

Dates: 1905 or earlier-ca. 1910
Address: 19 Hope Street
Blanks: from Pairpoint Corporation; other suppliers unknown
Trademark, product, employees: unknown
Customers: unknown

Enterprise Cut Glass Co. (Elmira Heights)

The Enterprise company moved to Elmira Heights from Honesdale, Pennsylvania, July 1, 1906,, as the result of "a flattering offer from Elmira." Its principals, George Gaylord, James Bennett, and William Loring, had originally opened in Philadelphia "with a few hands." Employees in 1906 totaled 20.[21] Advertisements in 1910 described its floral-cut glass as "intaglio cut," and claimed: "No figured blanks used in our entire product."

Though Honesdale was near C. Dorflinger & Sons, that company supplied blanks for only 11 items to the Enterprise company; the Pairpoint Corporation was another supplier.[22]

Enterprise's 1912 listing in *Thomas' Register* gave its capital as over $10,000. Its last *Glass Trade Directory* listing was in 1915, when it was still listed in the Elmira telephone book. (See also Revi's *American Cut & Engraved Glass,* pages 158–66.)

SUMMARY

Dates: in Elmira 1906-ca. 1916
Address: College Avenue
Blanks: Pairpoint Corporation; 11 items from C. Dorflinger & Sons
Trademark: none known
Product: rich geometric cuttings and floral designs on a full line of glass
Employees: 20 in 1906
Customers: unknown

VanDeMark, Brace & Hall (Elmira Heights)

This company is remembered in Corning as having followed Enterprise Cut Glass Co. in Elmira Heights, and as having operated only briefly. It does not appear in glass trade directories, nor was it mentioned in Corning newspapers.

SUMMARY

Dates: Ca. 1916-ca. 1918
Address: perhaps in the College Avenue building of the Enterprise company
Blanks, trademark, product, employees: unknown
Customers: unknown

N. O. Phelps & Son
D. J. Phelps, Inc. (Rochester)

Nathaniel ("Nate") Phelps's home engraving shop in Corning is discussed in Chapter 8.

Phelps moved to Rochester in 1928.[23] He began engraving in his garage but worked full time at other jobs. His business grew slowly but steadily. In 1942 be began to teach his son Donald to engrave. When World War II ended, N. O. Phelps was subcontracting its cutting to Floyd Manwarren's and other home shops, and shipping glass all over the United States and to Alaska. Until 1961 N. O. Phelps & Son was situated on Thurston Road.

In 1958 Donald Phelps bought the business from his father. During the 1960s the firm worked chiefly as a contractor for R. J. Brodgaard & Co. of New York, an importer and wholesaler, The company name had then become D. J. Phelps, Inc.

The company's chief retail outlet is now Phelps Glass Studios, 4077 West Henrietta Road, though it has two other shops. It specializes in table fashions and decorates much of its own glass, but it has largely discontinued custom engraving. A third generation, Donald Phelps's son David, has begun to engrave for the company.

SUMMARY

Dates: 1928-to date
Addresses: ca. 1942-61, 681 Thurston Road; main shop now at 4077 West Henrietta Road
Blanks: suppliers unknown
Trademark: none
Product: originally engraving only. Cut wares also after World War II. Now exclusive designs, some stone engraved, for the company's retail shops only
Employees: Floyd Manwarren after World War II; aside from family members, others unknown
Customers: throughout the country, including Alaska, ca. 1942-60. R. J. Brodgaard of New York in 1960s. Now table and gift items for Phelps Glass Studio shops only

Companies in Ohio

The Sterling Glass Co. (Cincinnati)

The *Corning Journal* reported on August 6, 1902, that a new foreman had succeeded Edward J. Mayer at J. Hoare & Co. Mayer, the story said, was "to go to Cincinnati, O., and become manager of a glass cutting shop to be established in that city by Joseph Phillips, formerly head salesman for J. Hoare & Co."

The company was Sterling Glass. It bought a large proportion of its blanks, including one-quart and one-pint "mirrored" jugs, stemware, and ice cream trays, from C. Dorflinger & Sons, but also bought blanks from Pairpoint Corporation.[24]

We assume from the company's founding date and the background of its principals that Sterling specialized at first in the rich geometric cuttings that have been pictured elsewhere.[25]

SUMMARY

Dates: 1902-ca. 1950
Blanks: many from Dorflinger & Sons; some from Pairpoint Corporation; other suppliers unknown
Trademark: A script "Sterling" has been reported; we have not seen it.
Product: rich geometric cuttings in early years
Employees: unknown
Customers and *address:* unknown

Vallely Glass & Mirror Shop (Toledo)

John Vallely of Corning, a principal of Buffalo's International Cut Glass Co., opened his mirror shop in Toledo about 1924. It was at the rear of his house at 1765 Summit Street.

Vallely's obituary says that he

claimed to have been one of the pioneer makers of fancy wall mirrors, and to have created the first electric light shade with a chemical finish of brilliancy....

When General Electric entered the lighting glassware field, Mr. Vallely helped start the operation. He later was superintendent of GE's Fostoria plant.

A Toledo resident 35 years, Mr. Vallely operated his glass and mirror shop for 30 years....There he produced intricately decorated mirrors. He was a prize-winner in numerous hobby shows.[26]

Vallely died in 1954 at the age of seventy-six.

SUMMARY

Dates: 1924-54
Address: 1765 Summit Street
Blanks: suppliers unknown
Trademark: none known
Product: cut and engraved mirrors
Employees: unknown; perhaps none
Customers: individuals in Toledo

Companies in Pennsylvania

F. J. Eygabroat & Co.
Eygabroat-Ryon (Lawrenceville)

Corning-trained Fred J. Eygabroat founded the cut-glass industry in Lawrenceville, a few miles southwest of Corning.[27] Cutting companies operated there for almost half a century.

Eygabroat was born in Coopers Plains, New York, in 1874. About 1890 he began his training at T. G. Hawkes & Co. with his friend Everett Stage.[28] He had finished by 1895, and became a cutter for J. Hoare & Co.

Eygabroat was a natural athlete; he loved to play football and tennis, wrestle, and dance.

After 1895 Eygabroat moved to Wayne Junction, near Philadelphia, to manage a cutting shop. His sister says that "he was sent" there; perhaps this was one of the cutting shops in which J. Hoare & Co. owned an interest. Here Eygabroat taught dancing, and so met and married another dancing teacher.

China, Glass & Lamps printed the following item on January 18, 1902:

A NEW CUTTING SHOP

Fred Eygabroat, of Philadelphia, and formerly of Corning, N.Y., is going to open a small glass cutting shop in Lawrenceville, Pa. Work is expected to start about March 1.

F. J. Eygabroat & Co. employed only three or four men at first, but in 1903 Everett Stage became foreman of cutters. Before 1905 Burt Ryon became a partner, and the company name changed to Eyagbroat-Ryon. The growth was steady until Eygabroat died of typhoid fever in 1905, at the age of thirty-one. His obituary (name of newspaper unknown) said that he was

president and practical business head of the Eygabroat-Ryon Co., and a young man possessed of business ability to a marked degree being mainly responsible for the steady growth and success of the company. He...was very popular....While here he was much interested in athletics and for several seasons was a member of the local football team.

Glass we have seen that dates from Eygabroat's presidency is geometrically cut and of good quality, though designs lack the intricacy of the most expensive Hawkes and Hoare wares. None is signed. Blank suppliers included the Pairpoint Corporation and C. Dorflinger & Sons.[29] This combination, plus Eygabroat's background, suggests that his company may have subcontracted for J. Hoare & Co.

Everett Stage continued as foreman of cutters until 1909. In that year, according to the Tioga County (Pa.) directory, Wallace H. Ryon was president and general manager; Wallace P. Ryon was vice-president and treasurer. An unidentified and undated newspaper clipping says that Louis Levien was another part owner. The company's capital in 1909/10 was over $10,000.[30] A Corning. branch, which was operating at this time, is discussed in Chapter 9. A company advertisement in the August 1910 issue of *Pottery & Glass* gave E. W. Hammond, 65 West Broadway, as the company's New York representative.

Eygabroat-Ryon's Lawrenceville factory was a two-story frame building with outbuildings. The

701. Cut-handled nappy made by the Eygabroat-Ryon Co. Diam. with handle, 19.2 cm. *Coll. Mr. and Mrs. Harry Baker*

Corning Leader reported August 18, 1911, that Eygabroat-Ryon had closed, but gave no reason.

SUMMARY

Dates: 1902-11
Address: Main Street
Blanks: nine items from C. Dorflinger & Sons; others from Pairpoint Corporation; other suppliers unknown
Trademark: none known
Product: a full line of glass, at first in geometric cuttings of moderate complexity; also floral cuttings after the first years
Employees: cutters included Orvis Dillon and William Holton.[31] Fred Eygabroat and Everett Stage also cut glass.
Customers: unknown

Stage Brothers Cut Glass Co.
Stage-Kashins Cut Glass Co. (Lawrenceville)

Everett Stage was born in Lawrenceville in 1876. During his Hawkes & Co. apprenticeship he bicycled to Corning each morning. His wages at first were $3 per week, but they increased to $7 as his training progressed. By 1894 he had moved to Corning.[32] His younger brother, Leigh, completed his training at T. G. Hawkes & Co. by 1903.

About 1896, Everett Stage left Corning for a cutting job near Wayne Junction, Pennsylvania; he married there in 1903. Later that year he returned to Lawrenceville as cutting foreman of the F. J. Eygabroat Co. (later Eygabroat-Ryon). In 1909 he moved to Jeannette, Pennsylvania, as superintendent of the Louis Levien Cut Glass Co., loosely affiliated with Eygabroat-Ryon through Levien's financial interest in both. In 1911 he returned to Lawrenceville and went into business with his brother.

The Stage brothers incorporated two Lawrenceville companies on the same day in 1914. Incorporation papers say that Stage Brothers' principals and equal owners were Leigh Stage, James Miller, and William Barnes, and its purpose was "manufacturing cut glass and other glass ware." It began business on December 22 with $750 of its intended capital paid in. This corporation was never dissolved.

Everett Stage, his wife Lillian, and Herman Kashins incorporated Stage-Kashins Cut Glass Co. for the "manufacture and sale of cut glass and other glass and earthenware." Everett owned 15 shares of stock; his wife and Kashins held five shares each. This company began life with $2,000 of paid-in capital. Stage was president and treasurer. Kashins was the company's salesman.

The two incorporations have caused some confusion, but they probably provide the date when Leigh Stage withdrew from the original company after a fire in the factory. We know little about his company. Everett Stage and Kashins built a new factory on the corner of James and Cherry streets. When Kashins left the company, W. S. Wilcox became Stage's partner. This association lasted about two years, and brought the purchase of the Eygabroat-Ryon building. After Wilcox withdrew,

Stage moved his company back to Cherry Street. The name Stage-Kashins continued.

Stage was the company's designer, and he also cut glass. At the company's peak it employed 35 persons. At first it made geometric cuttings of high quality. Blank suppliers of this period are unknown.

The company also made floral-cut glass. In later years the cuts were light and on semi-pressed blanks, and finally on Depression glass.[33] Customers included G. W. Borgfeldt & Co., E. W. Hammond & Co., and jewelry and department stores throughout the United States, Canada, and Cuba. After World War II Stage-Kashins worked as a jobber for Borgfeldt, Hammond, and other large stores. Borgfeldt and Hammond sent their own blanks, but the cutting designs were Stage-Kashins'.

William Holton was the company's foreman for many years. During the 1940s a number of local girls were trained as light cutters by the company. However, Everett Stage continued to do all the company's stemming.

Stage-Kashins was legally dissolved in 1949 because of Everett Stage's poor health. At this time Lillian Stage was vice-president; Adeliene, the Stages' daughter, was secretary and treasurer.[34]

702. Cut and engraved tumble-up made at the Stage-Kashins company in its later years. Height, 17.8 cm. *Coll. Mrs. Willadene Liddick*

703. Cylinder vase cut by Stage-Kashins. Height, 16.6 cm. *Coll. Mrs. Willadene Liddick*

704. Vase cut by Everett Stage. Height, 35.1 cm. *Coll. Mrs. Adeliene Stage Butla*

705. Two-piece punch bowl cut by Stage. Height, 35.4 cm. *Coll. Mrs. Adeliene Stage Butla*

706. Wineglass by Stage. Height, 16.5 cm. *Coll. Mrs. Adeliene Stage Butla*

707. Cut and engraved Stage-Kashins nappy. Diam., 15.8 cm. *Coll. Mrs. Adeliene Stage Butla*

708. Footed bowl cut by Everett Stage, ca. 1910. Height, 25.2 cm. *Coll. Mrs. Adeliene Stage Butla*

SUMMARY

Dates: 1914-49

Address: For most of the company's life it was on the corner of James and Cherry streets.

Blanks: suppliers in early years unknown. By the 1930s, the Fostoria, Heisey, McKee, and Louie Weber companies; some blanks supplied by customers

Trademark: none

Product: a full line of geometric and floral-cut glass in early years; later, light floral cuttings. Jobbing work after World War II

Employees: 35 at the company's peak. Cutters included the Stage brothers, George Titus, Archie Brant,———Walker,———Grover, Sam Hubert, Henry Redfield, Henry Fischer, and (after World War II) Willard Robb. Local girls trained as light cutters were Marylou Totten, Norma Bostwick, Grace Brockway, Eileen Hackett, Genevieve Schenck, June Schenck, Ruth Huels, Dorothy Robinson, and Joanne Cole. Cutters when the company closed were Ruth Huels, Arland Cole, Lawrence Holton, William Holton, and Everett Stage.

Customers: unknown in early years. Later, G. W. Borgfeldt, E. W. Hammond, R. H. Macy, and other stores and jewelers across the United States and Canada and in Cuba

R. H. Pittman Cut Glass Co. (Lawrenceville)

This company has no known connection with Corning other than that its proprietor was presumably drawn to Lawrenceville because of a connection with Eygabroat-Ryon or one of the Stage companies. The Pittman company was operating in 1914; its trade directory listings ended in 1916.

W. S. Wilcox Cut Glass Co. (Lawrenceville)

Wilcox was Everett Stage's partner for about two years. When he withdrew from the Stage-Kashins company, he opened a cutting firm in the former Eygabroat-Ryon factory, which Pittman may also have used. This too was short-lived; our only tangible evidence of the firm is a crate-side stamped with the company name in The Corning Museum of Glass.[35] After the company closed, Wilcox converted the factory into a sawmill. This company also had no known connection with Corning.

William Allen Cut Glass Co.
Allen Cut Glass Co.
T. J. Callet Cut Glass Co. (Johnstown)

William Allen's family moved to Corning from Fall Brook, Pennsylvania, in 1883, when he was nine.[36] From 1887 to 1899 his father, Walter Allen, was an accountant under H. P. Sinclair, Jr., at T. G. Hawkes & Co. Earlier Allens had been glass marverers at the Holyrood Glass Works in Edinburgh.

Will Allen trained at J. Hoare & Co. under Bill Langendorfer from 1890 to 1893, and stayed on as cutter and designer. He headed J. Hoare & Co.'s 1901–4 20-frame apprentice shop at Cedar Street and Tioga Avenue; Corningites seem to have called it the Allen Glass Co. A younger brother, Walter Allen, was a T. G. Hawkes & Co. engraver.

In 1905 financial help from his father and brother enabled Will Allen to open the William Allen Cut Glass Co. at 11 Lewis (now Johns) Street in Johnstown. The *Daily Journal*'s story of August 30 was headlined WILLIAM ALLEN . . . BRANCHES OUT IN BUSINESS AT JOHNSTOWN. The story reported Allen's position with Hoare and also his future employees incorrectly, but added that his company would make a full line of glass from punch bowls to champagne glasses. Allen was to be chief designer, as he had been "for the Hoare people." The *Johnstown Tribune* correctly reported on October 11 that three cutters were at work and ten more were expected from Corning that day.

The William Allen company's product was of high quality. Most glass was fully hand-polished and fully cut until 1910; Allen family tradition says that the company subcontracted some of J. Hoare & Co.'s more difficult designs at first. Allen prices were higher than those of most new little firms. During this period the glass was signed with a diamond-point A. Allen inspected his glass himself, and sold no seconds.

Sales grew steadily; expansion became necessary in 1912. Allen continued as president-manager, but took in two local businessmen as equal owners. The company moved to 510–520 Wood Street, and its name became Allen Cut Glass Co. In 1913 the number of cutters reached a peak of 52.

The European war had begun to affect the company by 1915: sales and employees decreased, and the company moved to 86 Messenger Street. More investors bought stock in 1916. Then Samuel Fetterman became president, although Allen continued as manager and largest stockholder. Business improved briefly after the war, but the postwar recession closed the company on January 6, 1920.

Allen considered his company a part of Corning's industry rather than one of the western Pennsylvania group. By agreement, H. P. Sinclair & Co. cut the patented Allen *Pond Lily* design,[37] and the Allen company cut some Sinclaire designs. Allen employed a number of Corning cutters, and was occasionally exempted from Corning Glass Works's ban on selling blanks to companies other than H. P. Sinclaire, T. G. Hawkes, and J. Hoare. About 1906 William Allen went to Corning to buy discontinued blanks from the Hoare company. A few years later he bought end-of-production runs and terminal items of good quality directly from the Glass Works.[38]

The Allen Cut Glass Co. made hundreds of designs. After 1910 these included many of the period's floral cuttings, and fully cut glass became a smaller percentage of production. At this time the acid dip was used to polish the glass. Customers were department and jewelry stores from New York to Minneapolis, but chiefly in western Pennsylvania. Harry Dietz was the Washington, D. C., distributor. After 1909 or so the glass was marked by sticker only.

Allen blanks came chiefly from Steuben Glass Works and the Libbey Co. Minor suppliers included the Fry, Baccarat, and Union companies. Old employees believe that Dorflinger also supplied a few blanks, but the Allen name is missing from Dorflinger records. In the Allen company's last years it used a few pressed blanks from Heisey.

In 1921 William Allen and Tobias Callet set up the T. J. Callet Cut Glass Co. at 916–918 Fronheiser Street. This closed about a year later, and Allen became a food broker. He died in 1930.

SUMMARY

Dates: 1905-20

Addresses: 1905-12: 11 Lewis (now Johns) Street.; 1912-15: 510-520 Wood Street; 1915-20: 86 Messenger Street. T. J. Callet Cut Glass Co., ca. 1921-22: 916-918 Fronheiser Street

Blanks: chiefly from Steuben Glass Works and the Libbey Co.; the Fry, Baccarat, and Union companies were minor suppliers. Blanks from J. Hoare & Co. about 1906; terminal items from Corning Glass Works probably in 1910. A few pressed blanks from the Heisey company after World War I

Trademark: diamond-point A, 1905-ca. 1909; thereafter, an oval white sticker with red border

Product: a full line of rich-cut, hand-polished glass in early years; hundreds of designs, including some of H. P. Sinclaire & Co. Later designs with names that may help identify the glass include *Lilly, Blue Bell, Pond Lily* (patented 1913), *Daisy, Climatis,* and *Locust.*

Employees: Corning craftsmen included roughers Tom McAllister, Harry Clark, and Floyd Berleue, who also designed; smoother DeWitt Schenck, and a polisher named Baggs.

Customers: jewelry and department stores, chiefly in western Pennsylvania but also from New York to Minneapolis

NOTE: Illustrations 709 to 719 are Allen Cut Glass Co. shop photos. *Coll. Walter M. Allen*

709. Tall comport by Allen.

710. Hexagonal bowl by Allen was made in two sizes.

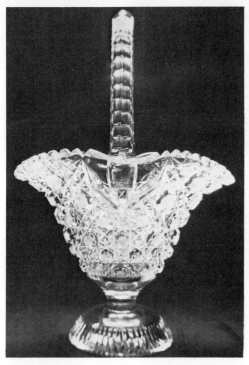

712. Bowl identified in the Allen shop photos as *Haverling*.

711. Basket by Allen Cut Glass Co.

714. Punch bowl and footed cups by Allen Cut Glass Co. The sticker identifies the pattern as *Cluster*.

713. Allen shop photos identify this pattern as *Magdaline*. It was used on bowls and nappies.

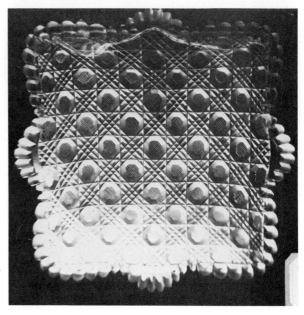

715. Another Allen shop photo.

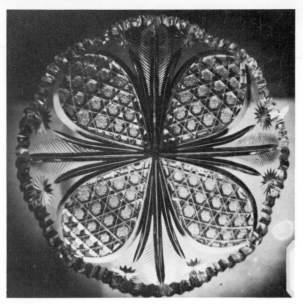

717. Two Allen sugar and cream sets.

716. This Allen shop photo shows a bowl identified as *Crystal* and priced at $15.

719. Footed sugar bowl and creamer by Allen.

718. An Allen plate available—according to the shop photo—in four sizes (6 to 10 inches) and priced at $3.50 to $13.00.

NOTE: Illustrations 720 to 724 are also Allen Cut Glass Co. products. The pieces shown in Ills. 720–722 are from the collection of Mrs. Helen Rorabaugh. *Photographs, Walter M. Allen*

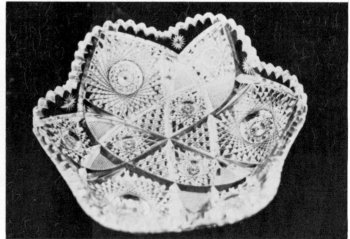

720. Pitcher in *Westmount* pattern. Height, 25.3 cm.

721. Bowl cut by Allen in *Carolyn* pattern. Diam., 25.4 cm.

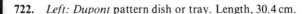

722. *Left: Dupont* pattern dish or tray. Length, 30.4 cm.

723 & 724. Two Allen cut bowls. The one at left measures 20.3 cm. in diameter. The second (above)—somewhat larger (25.4 cm.)—is identified as *Cluster Cut Special* pattern. Both are from the collection of Mrs. Arbutus Goenner. *Photographs, Walter M. Allen*

Berleue Cut Glass

Floyd Berleue learned his trade at T. G. Hawkes & Co., beginning in 1905 at the age of twelve. He cut and designed glass for the Allen and Callet companies, then opened his own shop at 1168 Solomon Street, Walnut Grove (near Johnstown).[39]

Berleue spent the years 1930 to 1934 in Maryland, then returned and operated his shop until 1940. His glass was of high quality for the period. Harry Dietz, former agent for Allen Cut Glass, distributed it in Washington.

SUMMARY

Dates: ca 1922-30 and 1934-40
Address: 1168 Solomon Street, Walnut Grove
Blanks: sources unknown
Trademark: none known
Product: cut glass of high quality for the period
Employees: none
Customers: unknown except for distributor Harry Dietz in Washington.

Pittston Cut Glass Co. (Pittston)

Hosea A. Clark, formerly of Corning, managed this company from February 1904 to an undetermined date after 1906.[40] Clark had worked in Corning since 1893, but said that before going to Pittston he had "practically no experience or knowledge in the matter of blanks for cutting and cut glass." Yet so great was Corning's reputation, presumably, that he had "general charge of the whole business": manufacturing, buying supplies, employing salesmen. He also sold glass himself to the general trade in New York, Boston, Philadelphia, and other large cities. In 1906 he was a member of the executive committee of the National Association of Cut Glass Manufacturers.

Pittston bought blanks from the Union, Dorflinger, Fry, Steuben, and Libbey companies, but "practically nothing" from Pairpoint Corporation.

Clark said: "The market demands a cheap article, of medium price, and high price. We sell all grades to the same concerns...[though] we do not go into

725. Cream pitcher and sugar bowl cut at J. Hoare & Co. (Wellsboro) or John Hoare, Inc., by Horace Taynton, ca. 1916. Height of bowl, 10.9 cm. *Coll. The Corning Museum of Glass* (Gift of Mrs. Forrest W. Marble)

726. Tumbler stone-engraved by Leon Swope for John Hoare, Inc. (Hoare & Millspaugh). Height, 9.2 cm. *Coll. Leon Swope*

the cheap goods...." His statement that there had been "some prejudice by some malicious persons who are hostile to...figure[d] blanks" implied that his company used them.

The Pittston company sold glass to jewelers, department stores, and "trading stamp people," with department stores taking "the greater quantity."

In discussing the Pittston company's cheaper glass, Clark also said:

The pattern and cutting is but very little and no fine work and it is given principally to apprentice boys. It depends upon the pattern whether it is given to a boy of one or two years experience, and it is smoothed by apprentice boys.... A good bowl is put in the hands of a skilled mechanic.

In 1906 the Pittston Cut Glass Co. was "running fifty frames."

SUMMARY

Dates: 1902 or earlier[41]-?
Address: street address unknown
Blanks: from the Union, Dorflinger, Fry, Steuben, and Libbey companies; probably included figured blanks
Trademark: none known
Product: a full line of low-, medium-, and high-priced cut glass
Employees: 50 cutters from all over, including Corning; local apprentices
Customers: jewelers, department stores, and "trading stamp people" in the East

John Hoare, Inc.
Hoare & Millspaugh (Wellsboro)

The J. Hoare & Co. branch shop in Wellsboro is discussed in Chapter 4. The later company discussed here was listed as John Hoare, Inc., in trade directories, though no incorporation papers were filed in New York or Pennsylvania. In Wellsboro it was known as Hoare & Millspaugh.

The *Corning Leader* reported the founding of the company on January 13, 1914, by John Hoare and Harrie Millspaugh. Hoare was a grandson of the founder of J. Hoare & Co. and the son of James Hoare. The company's capital stock was worth $10,000, the story said; the factory had 58 cutting frames.

China, Glass & Lamps ran a story about the firm on February 2, 1914, but the story was not entirely accurate, as J. Hoare had not opened in Wellsboro until 1906. It said that John Hoare had

for the past ten years...had charge of the Wellsboro plant of J. Hoare & Co. Mr. Millspaugh for sixteen years has been an employee of T. G. Hawkes & Co., and is thoroughly familiar with the sales department. The new concern has no connection with J. Hoare & Co., from whom they have leased the Wellsboro building.

Actually, the opening of Hoare & Millspaugh closely followed the Hoare family's loss of control of J. Hoare & Co.; perhaps the two events were connected.

Hoare & Millspaugh had six roughers, six smoothers, and a few polishers.[42] Horace Taynton was foreman of smoothers. Francis Fritchie of Corning was the company's copper-wheel engraver; he was later replaced by Fred Myers of Corning. Leon Swope designed and executed a number of stone engravings.

Swope was puzzled because the company stockpiled glass but never attempted to sell it. "I never knew Millspaugh to be on the road," he says. "I never knew what became of that glass, and I don't now." Perhaps it returned to Corning with John

727. Group of tumblers that Leon Swope stone-engraved for John Hoare, Inc. (Hoare & Millspaugh). Tallest is 11.1 cm. in height. *Coll. Leon Swope*

Hoare in 1917, when he and his father reassumed control of J. Hoare & Co.

The *Leader* announced the closing of the company on January 5, 1917, giving John and James Hoare's repurchase of J. Hoare & Co. as the reason.

The Hoare & Millspaugh pieces illustrated here were designed and stone-engraved by Leon Swope. Production, however, was small to the point of non-existence. Mr. Swope writes:

I still have about a dozen ten-cent tumblers that I put engraving on. They gave me one piece and said, "Put something on this." I never had a real job of anything to take out and sell.

It may be that these were later produced at J. Hoare & Co.

SUMMARY

Dates: Jan., 1914-Jan., 1917
Address: Industrial Grounds
Blanks: sources unknown
Trademark: none
Product: cut glass, some copper-wheel engraving, and stone-engraved samples
Employees: about 20 cutters; Horace Taynton, foreman of smoothers; copper-wheel engraver Francis Fritchie succeeded by Fred Myers, both of Corning; stone engraver Leon Swope
Customers: virtually none

Wellsboro Glass Co. (Wellsboro)

This company, which had moved to Corning by June 1916, is discussed briefly in Chapter 9. We know nothing of its life in Wellsboro; it may be the cut-glass company that older residents remember as having been on Main Street.

20 Corning Today

Corning today is a bustling center of fine-glass production, as she was a century ago. Since Corning Glass Works opened the Corning Glass Center in 1951, millions of visitors have watched the blowing, cutting, polishing, and engraving of Steuben glass. However, the Glass Center by no means exhausts Corning's interest for glass lovers.

Corning today still has home cutting and repair shops. Erlacher Glass accepts commissions for copper-wheel engraving, and retails cut and engraved glass in its own designs. The Bacalles Engraving Shop produces and wholesales pictorially cut glass. Other Corning craftsmen cut or engrave for Vesta Glass, which commissions glass of many sorts from "cottage craftsmen" across the country. Corning Community College offers a four-semester course in engraving.

The reorganization of Steuben Glass in 1933 is largely responsible for the creativity that characterizes the Crystal City. Yet the long life of the Hunt Glass Works, which did not close until the 1970s, and of T. G. Hawkes & Co. (which closed in 1962) have also contributed.

Corning's reaction to a disastrous flood in June of 1972, probably the worst in the city's history, is a paradigm of the relationship of challenge and response. Even as Corningites reconditioned their flooded homes, and restored their business section to its 1890s charm, glass craftsmanship in Corning also moved forward.

Corning today is as vital as she was a century ago. The future promises new directions in glass, and new enterprises, based on Corning's century-old devotion to handmade glass of the highest quality.

Steuben Glass

James Plaut's *Steuben Glass: a Monograph* and Paul Perrot's more recent *Steuben: Seventy Years of American Glassmaking* have exhaustively discussed the company's history and philosophy of design. We shall recapitulate them only briefly, then look at Steuben's glass as it relates to Corning's earlier glassmaking.[1]

The reorganization of the Corning Glass Works's Steuben Division in 1933 was an act of courage. The Division was unprofitable. Corning Glass Works was suffering from the Great Depression and preparing to lower its dividends briefly. European glass had won the price war that Corning's cut-glass manufacturers had been fighting. The most compelling reason for a new beginning was a dogged devotion to excellence, the conviction that the finest glass in the world would find a market regardless of its price. This ideal had inspired Amory Houghton, John Hoare, Thomas Hawkes, and H. P. Sinclaire. It was still alive in Corning's craftsmen, and in one other man: Arthur A. Houghton, Jr., great-grandson of Amory Houghton, Sr.

In the summer of 1933 the directors of Corning Glass Works considered closing the Steuben Division. Houghton asked for a delay. He had in mind a concept of glass new to Corning. It included design by artists to whom glass would be a new medium. Illustrations 730 through 748 show the result.

Houghton's dream looked toward the future. The conditions that made it achievable were firmly rooted in the past. Some twenty years after discontinuing production of its Best Metal, Corning Glass

728. *Opposite: The Venus Vase* shown here, like the engraved pieces pictured in Illustrations 729–732, shows the forceful style that Sidney Waugh established for Steuben Glass in the 1930s. Vase is 11¾ inches in height (Steuben Glass measures its pieces in inches). *Steuben Glass photograph*

Works had developed a crystal formula so pure that it required no decolorizer.[2] And Corning, New York, still harbored a group of craftsmen unmatched in the United States.

Houghton explored the implementation of his idea with a friend, architect John Gates, and the two consulted sculptor Sidney Waugh. The three young men decided that Houghton's ideals were achievable.

Houghton reported to the Glass Works board of directors:

> We have a small group of skillful and experienced workmen and an extraordinarily pure crystal glass. Let us take these, let us have a small amount of capital and a reasonable amount of time, give us a completely free rein, and we will attempt to make the finest glass the world has ever seen.[3]

The shades of John Hoare, Thomas Hawkes, and H. P. Sinclaire may have smiled when the directors agreed. Steuben Glass, Inc., was formed with Corning Glass Works as the only stockholder. Arthur Houghton, Jr., was president; John Gates director of design; Robert Leavy, a Steuben Division veteran, was production manager. Sidney Waugh became Steuben Glass's chief designer. The sale of blanks and the manufacture of most colored glasses ended. Some Frederick Carder designs, however, continued to be made in the first years.[4]

Steuben Glass's first major exhibitions came in 1935, at London's Fine Arts Society Gallery and at the Knoedler Gallery in New York. The glass was immediately successful. London, especially, was astonished at the brilliant, innovative glass made by the "three young men." This included designs by Fred Carder in his millefiori, intarsia, and white jade glasses.

In 1937 Steuben Glass won a gold medal at the Paris Exposition; awards followed from the 1939 World Fairs in New York and San Francisco. In fact, a new star was born; Steuben Glass was embarked on a triumphant career of exhibitions that have continued to the present.[5]

Arthur Houghton believed that superlative glass required superb design in addition to the brilliant, colorless glass and flawless workmanship that his Corning predecessors had always striven for and frequently achieved. Steuben Glass has made its greatest contribution in the realm of design, striving for forms that embody the inherent properties of lead crystal. Paul Schulze, the present Director of Design at Steuben Glass, wrote recently that

> the shape and decoration should not be thought of as separate entities, but should become homogeneous, part of the whole object. All objects should be true to themselves and true to the material in which they are produced. Glass must be glass first. If it appears to be like something else it is then an impression.

By the late 1940s Steuben Glass was executing the first of many commissions for major presentation pieces. The *Merry-Go-Round Bowl*, which President Truman gave Princess Elizabeth of England in 1947, is one of the most famous. Other commissions have included the *United Nations Bowl*, given to Trygve Lie in 1950 (Ill. 737); the *Norway Cup*, presented to King Haakon in 1955; the *Papal Cup*,

729.   *The Lion Hunter* is a shallow crystal bowl 12 inches in diameter; designed for Steuben by Sidney Waugh. *Steuben Glass photograph*

730.   Sidney Waugh also designed the crystal *Europa Bowl* for Steuben; diam., 8 inches; engraved by copper wheel. *Steuben Glass photograph*

which Cardinal Spellman gave Pope Pius XII in 1956 (Ill. 738); the *Queen's Cup,* presented to Queen Elizabeth in 1957; an engraved vase that President Eisenhower gave Nikita Khrushchev in 1959; and the *Great Ring of Canada,* which commemorated that nation's centennial year of 1967. Even as these unique pieces were produced, museums in North America, Europe, and Asia were adding Steuben glass to their collections.

In 1951 Corning Glass Works moved Steuben Glass operations into its new Glass Center, where visitors could watch the process of manufacture. The move reinstated the custom of permitting onlookers, which had been discontinued about the turn of the century when crowds of the curious interfered with work. The Glass Center solved this problem by providing a grandstand for onlookers, who can watch the blowers, polishers, cutters, and engravers through a wall of glass.

As Plaut has pointed out, the 1950s brought recognition of Steuben glass "as a unique American art form." This by no means implies that it has been restricted to the designs of American artists. On the contrary, Steuben Glass has pioneered in the use of designs by artists in Europe and Asia. Steuben's commissions have resulted in exhibitions that included "Designs in Glass by Twenty-seven Contemporary Artists" (1940), "British Artists in Crystal" (1954), and "Asian Artists in Crystal" (1956). After a period in which the responsibility for design reverted to Steuben's own New York-based department, the company has again begun to embody in glass the designs of a few outside artists.

In 1969 the Steuben ideal of producing objects "true to the material in which they are produced" led the first Steuben designer to move to Corning. Paul Schulze made the move in 1974.

Arthur A. Houghton, Jr., Steuben Glass's founder and first president, retired at the end of 1972. Thomas S. Buechner, artist and author, succeeded him as president in January 1973. Under his leadership Steuben's ideal remains the same: to make the finest glass in the world. Its realization depends, as ever, on the ceaseless striving for artistry in glass.

731. *Ganymede,* a slender crystal vase with copper-wheel engraving; designed for Steuben by Sidney Waugh. Height, 11 inches. *Steuben Glass photograph*

732. *Trident Punch Bowl,* another Sidney Waugh design for Steuben.

733. *Whirlpool Vase,* designed by Samuel Ayres for the 1939 New York World's Fair. Its heavy cutting is used for shaping only. Height, 14½ inches. *Steuben Glass photograph*

734. The 1939 *World's Fair Cup,* designed by John M. Gates. The trylon and perisphere at top are cut, as are the apertures at top and bottom. Cutting by Floyd Manwarren and Nelson Doane; engraving by Joseph Libisch. Height, 28 inches. *Steuben Glass photograph*

735. *Left: The United Nations Bowl,* designed by George Thompson in 1950. Diam., 11 inches. *Steuben Glass photograph*

736. *The Papal Cup,* designed by George Thompson in 1956. Three rows of applied crystal on the stem symbolize the three crowns of the Papal Tiara. Height, 22 inches. *Steuben Glass photograph*

737. *Below, left: Lady in Waiting Vase,* designed by Cecil Beaton for Steuben Glass's "British Artists in Crystal" exhibit of 1954. Height, 14 inches. *Steuben Glass photograph*

738. *Below: The Temple Dance,* now in the permanent collection of the Government of Indonesia. Glass design by George Thompson; engraving design by Agus Djaya for Steuben's "Asian Artists in Crystal" exhibit of 1956. Height, 11½ inches. *Steuben Glass photograph*

739. *Arcus,* a recent example of Steuben Glass's geometric forms; designed by Peter Aldridge. Height, 3½ inches. *Steuben Glass photograph*

Much of Steuben's achievement since 1933 lies beyond the scope of this book. The company's bread-and-butter items, for example, are the heavy, undecorated tablewares, vases, and bowls that the United States recognizes on sight. They are as satisfying to use as they are to look at. Also untouched by cutting or engraving is the considerable Steuben menagerie. In this otherwise undecorated series, some objects combine glass and precious metals. The beguiling *Frog Prince* is an example.

During its early years Steuben Glass offered simple allover cuts on its tablewares; an example is the goblets cut with the St. Louis (or "hollow") diamond. The trend, however, has been toward carrying further Frederick Carder's pioneering use of cutting-as-shaping. The two pieces in Illustrations 733 and 734 are examples designed and executed for the 1939 New York World's Fair. Cutting-as-shaping is the only decoration of Samuel Ayres's bold *Whirlpool Vase.* The virtuosity of the cutting is scarcely noticeable in the New York World's Fair covered cup, designed by John M. Gates, engraved by Joseph Libisch, and cut by Floyd Manwarren and Nelson Doane, (who cut the seven pieces that Steuben made especially for the fair). The precision of Libisch's engraving of the stylized "Goddess Mithrana" is at once apparent. The trylon and perisphere that top the cup, however, appear to have been shaped from molten glass, as do the apertures at top and bottom. All are wheel-cut. Floyd Manwarren recalls the job as one of the most

difficult of his career. Cutting-as-shaping continues to evolve in Steuben's geometric shapes of the 1970s.

Steuben designers have also used cut motifs to accentuate engraving. One piece that has become a classic is Sidney Waugh's *Gazelle Bowl* of 1935, which has been commissioned more than 60 times. Its base is cut, and cut borders enclose 12 copperwheel-engraved gazelles. The cutting in Waugh's *Wine, Woman and Song* serves an artistic function midway between that of the cutting on the *Gazelle Bowl* and the cutting-as-shaping of the *Whirlpool Vase.*

The unity of shape, material, and decoration that Steuben Glass aims for has not always been achieved. The Goddess Mithrana is rather less appropriate to the World's Fair cup than is, for example, Jupiter's head on an H. P. Sinclaire & Co. amphora.[6] Yet when the aim is achieved, the result is breathtaking. An early example is Waugh's *Zodiac Bowl,* on which the 12 zodiacal symbols wheel around the central sun. More sophisticated by far is the recent piece shown in Illustration 743, a dreamlike vision in glass, gold, and gems limited to an edition of one. A massive rose is formed of five overlapping crystal petals, on each of which is engraved an episode from the *Roman de la Rose.* The rose's ruby pistils are surrounded by diamond stamens. Donald Pollard designed the rose, Howard Rogers the engraving, which Roland Erlacher executed. The jeweler's work is by Louis Feron.

Steuben Glass has occasionally departed from

Corning tradition by adding diamond-point detail to copper-wheel engraving. Such a piece is *Dandelions.*

In *The Hull,* Steuben Glass succeeded where its Corning predecessors failed. As already explained, the high-relief carving done at England's Webb company prompted Corning's cutting firms to import a steady stream of Bohemian engravers. Yet *Hochschnitt,* also called "glass carving," was never successfully transplanted. *The Hull* is an elliptical bowl engraved to suggest a Crusaders' ship. Some 70 figures are carved from the glass. They include helmeted soldiers, horsemen, and a king and his nobles. Steuben Glass says that the piece, designed by Zevi Blum and engraved by Roland Erlacher, "is the most ambitious example of high relief engraving ever executed by Steuben." The description is modest; we know of no comparable example of engraving virtuosity from any American manufacturer.

Steuben Glass continues to evolve; shapes and engraving designs of the 1970s bear little resemblance to those of the 1930s. Corning Glass Works's research continuously improves Steuben Glass's already brilliant crystal formula. New objects include jewelry: one of four pendants may be ordered in any of eight different engraving designs. A new series of Steuben "Classics" is inspired by the simple shapes of ancient China. Increasingly, Steuben designers are concentrating on the unusually high refractive and reflective qualities of their crystal, most apparent when it is cut and polished in prismatic form. Copper-wheel engraving, the most demanding technique for the decoration of crystal, is another area in which Steuben explores the limits of artistry in glass.

Paul Schulze writes of the future in words that echo Corning's past.

Our commitment is to produce the finest crystal glass in the world. By necessity, we must produce that which will ensure our survival. The ideal would be to combine those two goals. We are striving to reach that ideal. The present process is the combining of refinement and innovation, making better what we have...and creating for the future. It is no easy task to be a survivor and risk taker at the same time....

The future has already begun. We have in the past two years invited several artists to work with us. Peter Aldridge, Professor at the Royal College of Art and glass sculptor, brought us a series of forms, original and truly taking advantage of the prismatic reflective quality of our material. James Carpenter is presently working in Corning, producing forms developed from his own ability as a proven gaffer. These creative efforts are showing themselves in forms unknown to us in the past.

Our own designers are reaching toward their artist side to develop objects akin to their own personalities. I expect the objects that we produce to be forms incorporating decorative qualities and function; these will exist simultaneously, totally related one to the other, without ever being thought of as separate. In a word, the *total* form.

740. Sidney Waugh's *Gazelle Bowl* uses cutting sparingly. Diam., 6½ inches. *Steuben Glass photograph*

741. Sidney Waugh's *Wine, Woman and Song.* Diam., 10 inches. *Steuben Glass photograph*

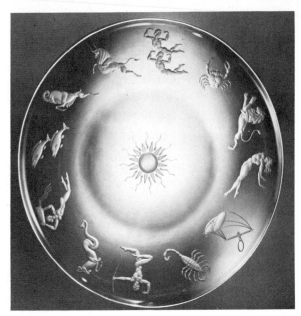

742. Sidney Waugh's *Zodiac Bowl* of 1935. Diam., 16 inches. *Steuben Glass photograph*

The design of early Steuben Glass was chiefly by Sidney Waugh. John Gates also designed for Steuben, as did John Dreves by the 1940s. Dreves resided in Corning; his duties included four-hour art lectures to Steuben engraving apprentices and the supervision of the experienced engravers. The late Robert Leavy, former vice-president and production manager, told us that

> Dreves would call the engravers up, and would explain what Waugh was trying to express and how to go about it so the piece would emotionally affect the viewer. He wanted the glass to express Sidney Waugh as much as Waugh did when he was present and speaking to you. The time was well worth while that we—especially Dreves—spent with the men.
>
> He would say to the engraver, "Lay it out and then bring it up to the studio and we'll discuss it." Then he'd begin to put refinements in. One hand he'd tell them to refine, and leave the other rough. "Then bring it back and we'll discuss it." And so on.

Outside artists invited to submit designs for Steuben crystal have been many and distinguished. Some of their names are listed in the summary below. Steuben's own designers, however, were usually responsible for the shapes on which the guest-artists' designs were engraved.

Present Steuben Glass designers are Paul Schulze, director; Donald Pollard, Lloyd Atkins, Bernard X. Wolff, and David Dowler. Others have included George Thompson *(Cathedral)* and James Houston *(Excalibur).*

Paul Schulze is a graduate of New York University and Parsons School of Design, where he later taught. He joined the Steuben Glass design department in 1961, becoming director of design in 1970. Among his major pieces are the *Cross* commissioned for St. Clement's Episcopal Church in New York; *Rotating Square,* in the collection of North Carolina State University; and the *Einstein Memorial,* in the collection of the National Air and Space Museum, Smithsonian Institution.

Designer and painter Donald Pollard is a graduate of the Rhode Island School of Design, who joined the Steuben Glass design staff in 1950. He is responsible for a large number of major works. Among them is *The Great Ring of Canada,* mentioned above. Pollard's designs have been included in every Steuben exhibition since 1955.

Lloyd Atkins is a graduate of Pratt Institute. His designs include *Ferdinand Magellan,* in Steuben's "Great Explorers" series; *Sea Chase,* and scores of representational and decorative figures, forms for engraving, and geometric designs. Many are represented in public and major private collections.

Graphic designer Bernard X. Wolff was educated at academic and art institutions in Southern California and at the Academy of Fine Arts in Rome. In 1965 he became chief designer for the Brooklyn Museum, leaving there to join Steuben Glass in 1973 as assistant director of design. In addition to designing the installations of Steuben exhibitions, he is responsible for the design of crystal objects, among them the cut and engraved *Ballooning.*

David Dowler is a graduate of the Syracuse University School of Art, where he was trained as an industrial designer and silversmith. He has received the Silver Guild of America award, and has exhibited at New York's Museum of Contemporary Crafts. He joined the design department of Steuben Glass in 1972. He is the designer of Steuben's *Eagle-base Bowl.*

Steuben Glass's cutting department has always been small in comparison with those of its predecessors. In the late 1930s it employed about a dozen roughers and smoothers. Robert Leavy recalled three great roughers, and two great smoothers. These were roughers Leonard Dow, Jack McGregor, and Floyd Manwarren, and smoothers Nelson Doane and Jemaine Kimball. "These men," Leavy has said, "were the best in the business. They were trained to do, and could do, work that would be impossible today."

As of 1977, Steuben Glass employed six design cutters, two smoothers, and nine polishers.

From 1933 to 1937 Steuben Glass sent all its engraving work to the home engraving shops that we have discussed in Chapter 8. In 1937 Master-engraver Joseph Libisch closed his home shop and began work in the Steuben factory, as did Clement Nitsche. Nitsche was to train apprentices, a task that foreman Libisch later shared. Other Corning en-

743. *The Romance of the Rose,* completed in 1977. Designed by Daniel Pollard; engraving design by Howard Rogers. Engraved by Max Roland Erlacher. Goldwork by Louis Feron. Height, 8 inches. *Steuben Glass photograph*

gravers followed them. Steuben Glass has continued to train young Americans in successive modifications of its apprenticeship program, but has also brought engravers from Europe.

In 1970 the Steuben engraving department included Master-engraver Max Roland Erlacher (Austria), Ladislav Havlik and Lubomir Richter (Czecho-slovakia), Peter Schelling (Germany), and Steuben-trained Paul Grieff, Roger Keagle, Roger Selander, and Kenneth Van Etten. Keagle has since died, and Erlacher has left to work in his own company. Since 1943 all Steuben craftsmen have been members of the AFGWU; relations between union and company have been cordial.

744. *The Hull,* an elliptical bowl in high-relief *(Hochschnitt)* copper-wheel engraving. 1975. Designed by Zevi Blum, engraved by Max Roland Erlacher. Height, 8⅛ inches; length, 13 inches. *Steuben Glass photograph*

746. *The End of the Trail,* engraved by the late Roger Keagle. Keagle occasionally executed private commissions such as this one. The blank is a Steuben vase. Height, 23.4 cm. *Coll. The Rockwell-Corning Museum*

745. Necklace with crystal pendant, designed by Eric Hilton. Width of crystal, 2 inches. *Steuben Glass photograph*

747. Floyd Manwarren cut this Steuben bowl about 1970 to match an older plate. Diam., 25.9 cm. *Coll. Mr. and Mrs. Thomas Dimitroff*

SUMMARY

Dates: 1933-to date

Address: Corning Glass Center

Blanks: Steuben Glass decorates only colorless lead crystal of its own manufacture.

Trademark: in early years a diamond-point S that is now used only rarely; usually a diamond-point script "Steuben"

Product: decoration on tablewares is now generally restricted to monograms and crests, but originally included simple cut designs; major engraved pieces, often made in limited editions or on special order, may be shaped by cutting and combined with precious metals and gems. Steuben Glass engraving is of superlative quality. The company accepts commissions for major presentation pieces.

Employees: designers in 1977 were Paul Schulze, director; Donald Pollard, Lloyd Atkins, Bernard X. Wolff, David Dowler, and—by invitation—Peter Aldridge, James Carpenter, Eric Hilton, and Laurence Whistler. Past designers included Sidney Waugh, Walter Dorwin Teague, George Thompson, John Gates, John Dreves, James Houston, Peter Yenawine, and Katherine de Sousa. Alexander Seidel has been a designer of engravings.

Outside artists who have designed for Steuben Glass include Henri Matisse, Cecil Beaton, Salvador Dali, Isamu Noguchi, Agus Djaya, Jean Cocteau, Thomas Hart Benton, Grant Wood, and other distinguished figures.

Earlier cutters included Larry Cahill, John Denson, George Lindstrom, Nelson Doane, Leonard Dow, Ed Hyland, Jemaine Kimball, Jack McGuire, Floyd Manwarren, and George Schoener. Today's design-cutters are Mario Gomes, Edward Smith, John Wheeler, Walter Biesada, William Frutchey, and Mack Witter.

In-factory engravers included Joseph Carroll, Frederick Dudley, Max Roland Erlacher, Fred Haselbauer, Roger Keagle, Anthony (Tony) Keller, Anton Krall, Joseph Libisch, Thomas Miller, Clement Nitsche, Joseph Oveszny, Edward Palme, Jr., and Reinhard Raabe. Recently the engraving department has included Kenneth Van Etten, Paul Grieff, Ladislav Havlik, Lubomir Richter, Roger Selander, and Peter Schelling.

Customers: Steuben Glass is available only at the company's own shops in New York City and Corning, and at a limited number of Steuben-designed rooms in selected department stores.

Floyd Manwarren
David Manwarren

"Jack" Manwarren's cutting career began in 1912 at the Ideal Cut Glass Co. of Canastota, New York. It continues today in the shop behind his house on Corning's Watkins Road, where he and his son David expertly repair fine old glass and Mr. Manwarren cuts orders from local firms and occasional private customers.[7]

Manwarren's first teacher was Corning-trained Ambrose Van Etten, Ideal's cutting foreman. Like most cutting firms, Ideal also had a shop of highly expert cutters, who had their own foreman. At Ideal this was Tom Burns, who gave Manwarren further instruction.

Manwarren left the Ideal Co. for army service in World War I. After the Armistice he worked for the Robertson Cut Glass Co., Catskill, New York, for four months. Next he worked briefly for the Tuthill company, with a view to learning more about his craft. He recalls roughing some of the company's fruit designs. His final brief training stint was with T. B. Clark of Honesdale, Pennsylvania.

About 1921 Manwarren returned to the Ideal company as foreman, and stayed until the company closed in 1933. His next employer was Steuben Glass, where, he recalls, he cut the World's Fair designs with smoother Nelson Doane. Some required cutting-as-shaping rather than decorative cutting. Mr. Manwarren says that cutting the "windows" in the top and bottom of the World's Fair cup was his most difficult job (Ill. 734).

During this period Manwarren and his wife, the former Thelma Wittman, lived in Beaver Dams, New York. Manwarren trained his wife as a smoother, and the two ran their own shop from 1939 to 1945. A chief customer was the Hunt Glass Works, but the Manwarrens also cut for the N. O. Phelps company of Rochester.[8]

During World War II Manwarren did war work for Corning Glass Works. He moved at war's end to Newark, New York, to cut for the Phelps company.

In the mid-1940s Manwarren returned to Corning and entered the employ of T. G. Hawkes & Co. Hawkes payroll records show him as consistently the highest-paid cutter. He again opened a home shop, in which he worked for Hunt Glass Works and private customers, before becoming Hunt's manager in 1957. When a heart attack forced him to reduce his workload during the winter of 1960/61, he worked only in his home shop. Again his wife worked with him.

In 1962 Mr. and Mrs. Manwarren were called to Hawkes & Co. "to finish up," as Manwarren put it. His last duty was a trip to Tiffin, Ohio, where Tiffin Glass was preparing to continue the Hawkes cutting designs. Manwarren showed the Ohio cutters how to cut them.

David Manwarren learned to cut glass from his father, beginning about 1970; he has become an expert repairman. Floyd Manwarren has cut for Corning's Vesta Glass in recent years, and also cuts a line of about a dozen exclusive designs for Erlacher Glass. Thus, in 1977, the Manwarren home cutting shop was running full speed.

SUMMARY

Dates: in Corning ca. 1946-to date
Address: Watkins Road
Blanks: supplied by customers
Trademark: none
Product: repairs, occasional special-order geometric cuts, light and pictorial cutting at this time
Employees: Thelma Wittman Manwarren smoothed glass for her husband until ca. 1962. David Manwarren has worked with his father since about 1970.
Customers: Vesta Glass, Erlacher Glass, and individuals

Peter Schelling

Peter Schelling was born in Neustadt, Germany (now Prudnik, Poland), in 1933.[9] His father was a painter and designer.

Schelling began his engraving studies in 1949, and received his certificate from the Staatliche Fachschule für Glasindustrie in Zwiesel, Germany. He stayed for an additional year to study designing and more advanced engraving, then came to the United States. Schelling has been a copper-wheel engraver for Steuben Glass since 1953.

Since 1970 Schelling has been teaching glass engraving at Corning Community College. At present the course can accommodate students at 14 lathes. Though the college catalog lists the course as a four-semester one, some students have stayed for six. They have come from all parts of the country, for this is the only course of its kind in the United States, and probably in the Americas.

Custom engraving in his home shop has been part of Schelling's artistic life almost since his arrival in Corning. Illustration 750 shows a Schelling portrait-plaque in the rare and time-consuming cameo technique; it is still unfinished. Schelling is also becoming known for his engraved crystal pendants, vases, and bowls.

Schelling's wife, who holds a Fine Arts and Industrial Arts degree from the Hochschule für Bildende Kunste, Berlin, is one of her husband's most promising engraving students.

SUMMARY

Dates: ca. 1954-to date
Address: Spencer Hill Road
Blanks: supplied by the Stromberghyttan, Orrefors, and Val St. Lambert companies, and by glass studio artists
Trademark: engraving often signed *P. Schelling* in diamond-point script
Product: chiefly engraved vases, bowls, pendants, and paperweights
Employees: none
Customers: eastern retailers and individuals

748. Unfinished portrait plaque engraved by Peter Schelling in the cameo technique. Height, 13.6 cm. *Coll. Peter Schelling*

749. Pale blue vase engraved by Peter Schelling. Height, 17.7 cm. *Coll. Robert Gamberi*

John Lentricchia

John Lentricchia, born in Italy, came to the United States in 1907.[10] His early life here included work on the railroad and helping to build a state road, but during most of his 50-year career he has worked for Steuben Glass Works and its successor, and for Corning Glass Works.

Because John's first boss found the name Lentricchia difficult, John was called John André for almost 30 years. His brother Luigi, who followed him to Corning in 1913, became Luigi André.

Lentricchia's first tasks at Steuben Glass Works were odd jobs such as sweeping, but he moved up to polishing punties and doing acid work. During the Great Depression, he cut glass lighting domes and made Pyrex brand glass. He also erased the occasional engraving errors on Steuben glass. The J. Hoare & Co. Bridge Street plant was another employer; there he polished glass and ground stoppers.

After retiring about 1957, Lentricchia opened a small cutting shop in the basement of his house at 163 West First Street, where he has employed an engraver from time to time. The shop repairs fine old glass, and also makes jewelry, which uses "jewels" cut from art glass and crystal in pendants, bracelets, and earrings.

SUMMARY

Dates: ca 1957-to date
Address: 163 West First Street
Blanks: none used
Trademark: none
Product: repair work and jewelry made from colored glass and crystal
Employees: none regularly
Customers: individuals

Max Roland Erlacher
Erlacher Glass

Max Roland Erlacher was born in Austria in 1933.[11] He wanted to become a sculptor, but when the only Austrian sculptor-teacher could accept no more apprentices, the boy entered a new Glasfachschule in Kramsach. Among its distinguished faculty, which had fled the Russian occupation of Czechoslovakia, was Master-engraver Hermann Schiller, who had long engraved for J. & L. Lobmeyr.

Erlacher stayed at the Glasfachschule for a fourth year of design and engraving studies with Schiller after completing his three-year journeyman's course. On Schiller's recommendation, J. & L. Lobmeyr hired Erlacher to engrave in Vienna. There Stefan

Rath supervised his continuing education and recommended him for Master's studies after the minimum three years. Erlacher received the degree a year later, his fourth year with Lobmeyr.

Erlacher's youth did not augur for rapid advancement at a firm that employed two older Masters. Rath's advanced age and Erlacher's desire to see more of the world also prompted him to emigrate. In 1957 he accepted an offer from Steuben Glass as more challenging than others from Sweden and Germany. Joseph Libisch had retired; Erlacher took over the engraving of first examples of the company's most difficult designs. He completed *The Hull* (Ill. 744) in 1975 and *Romance of the Rose* (Ill. 743) in 1977.

In the Mid-European tradition, Erlacher has engraved at home since 1952. In 1975 he and his wife Catherine opened Erlacher Glass, which now has two shops selling fine glass old and new. Corning-decorated glass includes several light-cut designs executed by Floyd Manwarren, which carry the company's "Shamroc" trademark. Lubomir Richter stone-engraves Bohemian-style scenes on pitchers and vases, as well as delicate floral designs on cased and crystal pendants.

In 1977 Erlacher left Steuben Glass to devote full time to his shop, where he accepts commissioned work for copper-wheel engravings. He has also engraved a limited edition of paperweights for the Paperweight Collectors' Association, and recently completed a presentation piece for the Baccarat company. Erlacher's mastery of anatomy and portraiture is evident in Illustrations 751 and 752; this special strength doubtless stems from his early interest in sculpture. The engraving of portraits is his preferred work.

SUMMARY

Dates: Erlacher has engraved at home since 1962. Erlacher Glass, 1975-to date
Addresses: 149 Walnut Street and Baron Steuben Place (northwest corner of Pine and Market streets)
Blanks: West Virginia Glass Specialty Co. blanks for the Shamroc and stone-engraved lines. Erlacher's engravings use fine lead crystal blanks such as Baccarat, or blanks supplied by customers
Trademarks: "Shamroc" label or signature on light-cut wares. Richter and Erlacher will sign their work on request.
Product: moderately priced tableware in *Vintage, Stars & Stripes,* and other cuttings that are chiefly pictorial; medium-priced stone-engraved pitchers, vases, pendants. Copper-wheel engraving of unsurpassed quality by Erlacher on objects selected by his clients
Customers: individuals for less-expensive wares; clients for Erlacher's engraving include the Paperweight Collector's Association and business concerns.

750. Pitcher stone-engraved by Lubomir Richter for Erlacher Glass in 1977. Height, 16.5 cm. *Coll. Mr. and Mrs. Lionel Mohr; Toronto Star photograph*

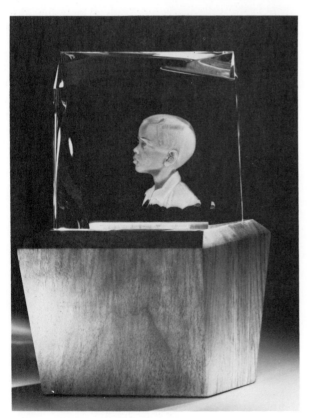

751. Portrait of Kenneth Michael Matthews, copper-wheel engraved by Max Roland Erlacher on a Baccarat blank. Ca. 1974. Height of glass, 12.2 cm. *Coll. Mrs. Kenneth Matthews*

752. *The Minute Man,* copper-wheel engraving by Erlacher on a Baccarat blank. 1977. Height, 18.8 cm. *Coll. Frederic Farrar; Frederic Farrar photograph*

Vesta Glass

In 1965 Richard L. Pope left the employ of Corning Glass Works and founded Vesta Glass on Goff Road in East Corning.[12] The company has prospered; it now supplies thousands of handmade glass items to gift shops and mail-order companies throughout the United States. Its products include paperweights, sand-carved glass objects, reproductions of hand-pressed early American glass, stained glass, and perhaps the world's largest selection of glass animals. In 1977 Vesta took over distribution of a major line of glass Christmas ornaments.

In 1973 Vesta Glass moved to a larger building on Watkins Road. Craftsmen across the country now supply its glassware. Among those who work in their homes or home shops are three from Corning: Floyd Manwarren has recently cut a map of Martha's Vineyard on plates and trays. Lorinda Freitas does pictorial cutting of birds and flowers. (A former cutter for the Hunt Glass Works, she works in her home on Halsted Street.) Harold Gross, a copper-wheel engraver, decorates a small line of pendants. Gross's training was at Steuben Glass and in a Corning Community College engraving course taught by Max Erlacher.[13]

In 1977 Mr. Pope bought the building at 37 East Market Street in Corning and opened a retail shop called "The Glass Menagerie."

SUMMARY

Dates: 1965-to date
Address: P.O. Box 1426, Watkins Road (company headquarters); 37 East Market Street (The Glass Mengarie)
Blanks: Federal Glass, West Virginia Glass Specialty Co., Owens-Illinois, Mid-Atlantic Glass, and Pittsburgh-Corning Corp. supply blanks for Vesta Glass's cut and engraved products.
Trademark: none
Product: Items made in Corning include barware, tableware, and pendants.
Employees: Corning craftsmen are cutters Floyd Manwarren and Lorinda Freitas and engraver Harold Gross.
Customers: gift shops and mail-order companies. Retail sales from The Glass Menagerie

Bacalles Glass Engravers

Bacalles Glass Engravers is a natural outgrowth of the Bacalles Glass Shop, a fixture at 10 West Market Street since shortly after World War II. The Bacalles Glass Shop has for many years ordered cut and engraved glass from Corning's home shops, chiefly those of cutter Floyd Manwarren and engravers Wilmot Putnam and Aiden Johnson. Bacalles's shop and his commissions to Corning craftsmen are of course well known.[14]

It was, thus, to George Bacalles, proprietor of the shop, that cutter Alberta Carl of Hunt Glass Works turned in 1968. Mrs. Carl, whom Corning cutters call "the girl whiz," was concerned. No blanks were coming in to the Hunt company, she said; the cutters knew that something was wrong. Mrs. Carl loved her work, and wanted to continue. Could Mr. Bacalles employ her?

"I probably have enough work for four to six months," Mr. Bacalles answered, "but we'll try to interest Tiffany." He spent $1,000 on blanks, and Mrs. Carl cut samples in her home in nearby Caton. Tiffany was not immediately interested. By November, however, the Tiffany buyer found herself short of stock, and ordered 8,000 pieces in the Bacalles *Wheat* and *Thistle* designs. Mrs. Carl cut them all.

When the Hunt company was sold about 1970, one after another of its cutters left to work for Bacalles. Two have since retired. At present Bacalles employs the five woman cutters named here in the summary. All are from glass-cutting families and had had long experience with the Hunt Glass Works. Mrs. Eleanor Mullen Downing had also cut for T. G. Hawkes & Co. The foreman is Donald Clarkson, who learned to cut glass at Bacalles's. His wife Diane is the company's "general factotum," Mr. Bacalles says; James Bacalles is also a member of the firm.

Though the company's name includes the word "engravers" in conformity with the loose terminology of recent years, Bacalles's products are in fact light pictorial cuttings. The company is a "stock house": one that stocks enough finished goods to ship any order within a day or two, and employs its cutters all year long. Alberta Carl's skill with the copper wheels makes fine engraving a possibility for the future.

Custom design in wholesale quantities is a company strength. "We can put any profile on glass," Mr. Bacalles says. "There are individuals who can do this, but no other companies." When a customer wanted Bicentennial eagles in 1976, Bacalles Glass Engravers shipped eight samples within a few days.

The company does not make stemware. Its best-selling products are hurricane shades, mugs, plates, barware, and bud vases. Most blanks come from Federal Glass; exceptions are listed below. The glass is unsigned, but George Bacalles hopes to introduce a high-quality engraved and signed line in the future.

Bacalles sells to retail customers through his glass shop. His glass is slowly becoming known to eastern shops, but sales of $250,000 in 1975 were just enough to keep the little company operating. People who own pieces in Bacalles *Federal Eagle* pattern include the members of the Nixon cabinet, to each of whom Robert Finch gave a dozen mugs, and Richard Nixon, to whom Senator Scott gave a dozen tumblers.

753. These pictorially cut objects illustrate four of Bacalles Glass Engravers' forty or more designs. Height of hurricane shade, 29.5 cm. *Coll. Bacalles Glass Engravers*

As of 1976, Bacalles Glass Engravers were making more than 40 pictorially cut designs.

SUMMARY

Dates: 1968-to date
Address: P.O. Box 1366; cutting shop at 413 Park Avenue
Blanks: mugs from Rumania; hurricane shades from Corning Glass Works; most other blanks supplied by Federal Glass.
Trademark: none
Product: moderately priced plates, mugs, bud vases, candy dishes, and other pictorially cut items in about 40 designs as of 1976
Employees: cutters are Alberta Phelps Carl, Eleanor Mullen Downing, Minnie Travis Holmes, Eva McNeil Travis, Lorene Hill Travis. The late Gust Eckstrom and Marjorie Wiles also cut for the company. Donald Clarkson, foreman; Diane Clarkson, "general factotum"
Customers: Corning Glass Center, Tiffany & Co., Bacalles Glass Shop, and eastern retailers

Roy Denson

Roy Denson retired from Steuben Glass as a gaffer in 1975 after four decades of service with the company.[15] He is the only operator of a Corning cutting shop that we know of who switched from blowing glass to cutting it. The change was doubtless facilitated by his familiarity with glass-cutting and cutting frames; his father, John Denson, was a cutter for many years. (See Chapter 9 for John Denson.)

Though Denson occasionally repairs old glass as a favor to a friend, his chief interest is the manufacture of jewelry from bits of old art glass or crystal. From a Steuben Aurene shade, for example, he may cut small square or heart-shaped pieces. He suspends these from gold-toned chains as pendants or bracelets, or fixes them to earring backs. Denson's home showroom is seldom without customers, and his driveway is packed with cars as Christmas approaches.

Denson's cutting shop is in the basement of his house. He used his father's equipment: a cutting frame equipped with a 16-foot belt and a polishing frame.

SUMMARY

Dates: 1975-to date
Address: 21 Glen Avenue
Blanks: none used
Trademark: none
Product: jewelry made from old crystal and art glass, both plain and engraved
Employees: none
Customers: individuals only

Chronological List of Cutting Companies and Home Shops In Corning and Immediate Vicinity*

HOARE & DAILEY, later
J. HOARE & CO.
1868-1920

JOSEPH F. HASELBAUER
Ca. 1876-1910

HAWKES RICH CUT-GLASS CO., later
T. G. HAWKES & CO.
1880-1962

HIERONIMUS WILLIAM FRITCHIE
Corning shop ca. 1888-1902 and 1904-16

JOSEPH NITSCHE, CLEMENT NITSCHE
Ca. 1894-1937

FRANK WILSON & SONS
1894-ca. 1897

CHARLES G. TUTHILL CUT GLASS SHOP
Ca. 1894-ca. 1898

HUNT & SULLIVAN, later HUNT GLASS WORKS; HUNT GLASS WORKS, INC.
Ca. 1895-ca. 1973

O. F. EGGINTON RICH CUT GLASS, later THE O. F. EGGINTON CO., INC.
1896-1918

BRONSON INKSTAND CO.
Ca. 1896-ca. 1899

GEORGE W. DRAKE & CO.
Ca. 1899-1908

CORNING GLASS WORKS
Ca. 1900-ca. 1929

JOSEPH BLACKBURN
1901-5

CORNING CUT GLASS CO.
1901-ca. 1911

ERNEST MULFORD
1901-ca. 1912

ARCADIAN CUT GLASS CO.
Reported in Corning, perhaps incorrectly, in 1902.

CRYSTAL MANUFACTURING CO.
1902-?

KNICKERBOCKER CUT GLASS CO.
1902-3

GIOMETTI BROTHERS
In Corning 1902-7, 1909-33

JOHN N. ILLIG, later JOHN N. ILLIG, MANUFACTURER OF ARTISTICALLY ENGRAVED GLASSWARE
Ca. 1902-ca. 1929

IDEAL CUT GLASS CO.
In Corning 1902-ca. 1904

ALMY & THOMAS
1903-7

ELMIRA GLASS CUTTING CO., later ELMIRA CUT GLASS CO.
Corning shop ca. 1903-ca. 1914

STEUBEN GLASS WORKS, later STEUBEN GLASS, CORNING GLASS WORKS (commonly referred to as "the Steuben Division"); STEUBEN GLASS
1903-to date

ERNEST L. BRADLEY
Ca. 1904-6

PAINTER CUT GLASS SHOP
1904-ca. 1905

H. P. SINCLAIRE & CO.
1904-28

EMILE WALTER
Ca. 1904-ca. 1942

J. J. BYRNE
Ca. 1905-ca. 1907

ANTHONY F. KELLER, ANTHONY J. KELLER
1905-ca. 1932

STANDARD CUT GLASS CO.
1905-ca. 1908

DELOS V. OLIN
1906-ca. 1908

NICHOLAS UNDREINER (later UNDERINER)
1906-ca. 1932

AMERICAN CUT GLASS CO.
Perhaps in Corning in 1906-?

PATRICK CALLAHAN
1907 or earlier-1916

AUGUSTUS K. ROSE
1907-?

MAJESTIC CUT GLASS CO.
Corning shop ca. 1907-ca. 1911

EDWARD PALME, SR., EDWARD PALME, JR.
1907 or 1909-66

EYGABROAT-RYON
Corning shop 1908-ca. 1911

ERNEST KAULFUSS
Ca. 1908-ca. 1948

HENRY KELLER
Ca. 1909-50

HIRAM ROUSE
1910 or earlier-ca. 1967

J. F. HASELBAUER & SONS, FRED HASELBAUER
1910-38

JOSEPH LIBISCH
Ca. 1911-37

CLIMAX CUT GLASS CO.
1911-ca. 1912

THOMAS SHOTTON CUT GLASS CO.
In Corning 1912

PETER A. EICK
1912-35

SIGNET GLASS CO.
1913-ca. 1916

HARRY M. JONES
Ca. 1915 or earlier-1930

WELLSBORO GLASS CO.
In Corning 1916-ca. 1917

FRED H. FULLER, CUT GLASS MANUFACTURER
Ca. 1916-ca. 1927

ADOLF KRETSCHMANN
Ca. 1918-55

PETER KAULFUSS
Ca. 1919-ca. 1926

LOUIS KLING
Ca. 1919-20

AMBROSE VAN ETTEN
Ca. 1920-53 (with interruptions)

BENJAMIN R. WATSON
Ca. 1921-ca. 1941

WILMOT PUTNAM
Ca. 1920-69

NATHANIEL O. PHELPS
Corning shop, ca. 1921-27

JOHN DENSON, DENSON & COSGROVE
Early 1920s-ca. 1930

CHARLES MAY
Ca. 1924-ca. 1926

HARRY GOODMAN
Ca. 1925-ca. 1932

JOSEPH HAHNE
Ca. 1930-ca. 1940

AIDEN JOHNSON
Ca. 1930-ca. 1968

FRANK KONIGSTEIN & EDWARD HAUPTMANN
1930-?

JOSEPH OVESZNY
Ca. 1935-ca. 1955

FLOYD MANWARREN, DAVID MANWARREN
In Corning ca. 1946-to date

PETER SCHELLING
Ca. 1954-to date

JOHN LENTRICCHIA
Ca. 1957-to date

MAX ROLAND ERLACHER, ERLACHER GLASS
Ca. 1962-to date

VESTA GLASS
1965-to date

BACALLES GLASS ENGRAVERS
1968-to date

ROY DENSON
1975-to date

* This list is based on the one in Spillman and Farrar's *Cut and Engraved Glass of Corning 1868-1940* (Corning, 1977), pp. 95-99, but includes the results of further research.

Reference Notes

CHAPTER 1

1. Editors of American Heritage, *American Heritage History of the Confident Years* (New York, 1969), p. 7. ©1969 American Heritage Publishing Company, Inc. Reprinted by permission from *The American Heritage History of the Confident Years* by Francis Russell.

2. Redrawn for *Brooklyn Eagle*, "Brooklyn *[Breukelen]*," for article Historic Brooklyn Series (Brooklyn [ca. 1948]), p. 15.

3. Dorflinger information from Kathryn Hait Dorflinger Manchee, "Dorflinger Glass," 3 parts (*Antiques*, April, May, July, 1972), I, p. 712. Hereafter, Manchee.

4. *The Corning Journal*, July 26, 1883, reported the arrival of a labor agitator who had been active in strikes at Brooklyn factories, "of one which...the father of the present Messrs. Houghton was proprietor." Hereafter, *Journal*.

5. Information about Brooklyn Flint Glass Works meetings is from an untitled, handwritten document in Corning Glass Works archives. It is a fragmentary minute book; the first entry dates from this reorganization meeting. We judge that the younger Houghton was elected president because correspondence shows him to have been in Brooklyn. Also, his father was the smaller stockholder and not present. Hereafter, BFGW minutes.

6. U.S. Design Patent 52, 854 of Feb. 27, 1866.

7. Uri Mulford, *Pioneer Days and Later Times in Corning and Vicinity: 1798-1920* (Corning [1922]), pp. 181-185 and passim. The book's coverage of the years with which we are concerned is a compilation of Corning newspaper reports. Hereafter, Mulford.

8. *Papers on Appeal*, p. 304, Record, *Corning Glass Works* v. *Corning Cut Glass Company et al.*, 126 A.D. 919, 75 A.D. 629 (Fourth Dept., 1902). p. 140. Hereafter, CGW suit.

9. CGW suit, pp. 157, 284-85, and others.

10. Mulford, pp. 254-55.

11. William F. Dorflinger, "The Development of the Cut Glass Business in the United States." Paper read before the American Association of Flint and Lime Glass Manufacturers at the Annual Meeting, July 25, 1902. Unpaged. Hereafter, Dorflinger speech.

12. Manchee I, p. 714.

13. Harlo Hakes, ed., *Landmarks of Steuben County* (Syracuse, 1896), Part II, p. 61. Hereafter, Hakes.

14. Mulford, pp. 224-25.

15. Stan Gores, *1879 Centennial Collectibles and Price Guide* (Fond du Lac, Wis., 1974), p. 30.

16. Jonathan Arlow, "Two Hundred Years of Crazy Health Kicks," *Mainliner* (Oct., 1976), p. 52. The effect of light filtered through glass of various colors had been the subject of experiments for some decades. (A blue glass pane may be seen in the Southold, L.I., Historical Society's Hallock-Currie-Bell House, which dates from 1899. At that time, a Society spokesman says, blue glass was believed to counteract tuberculosis germs.)

17. Stefan Lorant, *The Presidency: A Pictorial History of Presidential Elections from Washington to Truman* (New York, 1952), pp. 339-62.

18. This information comes from Mrs. Alvin Haar, Mrs. Virginia Illig Driscoll, and others.

19. Robert F. McNamara, *A Century of Grace: The History of St. Mary's Roman Catholic Parish, Corning, N.Y., 1848-1948* (Corning, 1948), p. 117.

20. CGW suit, p. 142 and passim.

21. CGW suit, p. 200.

22. Sons and daughters of several glassworkers have reported a Corning Glass Works-Dorflinger agreement not to hire each other's workers without a three-month lapse between employers. Hawkes & Co. and Sinclaire & Co. had a similar agreement that specified six months' notice. There seems to have been no comparable one between the Hawkes and Dorflinger companies.

CHAPTER 2

1. CGW suit, pp. 151-52.

2. Pearce Davis, *Development of the American Glass Industry* (New York, 1970), p. 275.

3. Hiram Rouse, "Jobs with Time, Etc.," unpublished work notebooks ([Corning], 1902-10), passim. Corning–Painted Post Historical Society. Hereafter, Rouse.

4. T. G. Hawkes & Co., Cash Book, 7 vols., unpublished ([Corning], 1900-1910), passim. Corning Museum of Glass. Hereafter, Cash Book.

5. *China, Glass and Lamps, a Weekly Journal for the Buyer*, fall, 1907-spring, 1908, passim. Hereafter, *China, Glass and Lamps*.

6. Manchee II, p. 1011. Trade directories continued to list the company for several years, but the 1921 closing date has been confirmed by interviews with Joseph Falk and the late Eric Liljeqvist, former Dorflinger glass blowers. Hereafter, Falk, Liljeqvist.

7. McNamara, p. 83. Corning newspapers also covered the strike.

8. American Flint Glass Workers Union, *Proceedings of the...Annual Convention...* (Pittsburgh, 1893, 1896, 1897, passim. Hereafter, the union convention proceedings will be cited as *AFGWU Proceedings* plus the year.

9. *AFGWU Proceedings*, 1904, pp. 24-29.

10. Manchee II, p. 1007, and "Hawley 1900: J. S. O'Connor—Rich Cut Glass." The latter is an unpaged facsimile of two pages of a work given as *Illustrated Wayne Co.*, 1900. No publisher is given for either the facsimile or the original. Hereafter, O'Conner biography.

11. CGW suit, p. 158.

12. CGW suit, p. 142.

13. CGW suit, p. 144.

14. We are indebted to Floyd Manwarren for this and much other information about glass cutting and cutters. Mr. Manwarren's career is one of the subjects of Chapter 20. Hereafter, Manwarren.

15. The patent drawing for this design is pictured in A. C. Revi, *American Cut and Engraved Glass* (Camden, N.J., and New York, 1970), p. 348. Hereafter, Revi.

16. Interviews with Clement Nitsche and Leon Swope. Rouse, passim, recorded designs by a number of engravers. Hereafter, Nitsche, Swope.

17. CGW suit, pp. 153, 193. Here too there was an occasional exception. The Hawkes company's use of two Dorflinger blanks in 1889 has been mentioned above.

18. CGW suit, p. 153.

19. Corning Glass Works's records of Best Metal sales end in 1910; class of product records show it made through 1912. The discrepancy may be ascribable to frequent flooding of the company's records.

20. CGW suit, p. 157; Liljeqvist.

21. Op. cit., p. 153.

22. CGW suit, p. 159.

23. BFGW minutes.

24. Mulford, p. 256.

25. State of New York, Supreme Court, Appellate Division, Fourth Judicial Dept., H. P. Sinclaire, appellant, v. T. G. Hawkes & Company, et al., respondents (1906), pp. 5 ff. Hereafter, Sinclaire suit.

26. CGW suit, p. 277.

CHAPTER 3

1. CGW suit, pp. 142-44. We have corrected punctuation and added paragraphing and subtitles.

2. The Dorflinger speech of 1902 placed the beginning of acid polishing about ten years earlier i.e., about 1892.

3. CGW suit, pp. 292-93.

4. T. G. Hawkes & Co., *Glass, Silver, Etc.*, an unpublished record of the company's suppliers (Corning [ca. 1893-1903]), unpaged. Corning Museum of Glass. Hereafter, *Glass, Silver, Etc.*

5. J. S. Ingram, *The Centennial Exposition, Described and Illustrated...* (Philadelphia, etc., 1876), p. 284.

6. James Plaut, *Steuben Glass: A Monograph*, 3d rev. and enlarged ed. (New York, 1972), p. 17.

7. Paul Perrot, *Short History of Glass Engraving* (New York, 1973), pp. 11-12.

8. T. G. Hawkes & Co., *Factory Pay Roll*, 2 vols., unpublished (Corning, 1943-62), unpaged, passim. Hereafter, Pay Roll.

9. Master engraver Max Roland Erlacher supplied this information about engraving apprenticeships. Hereafter, Erlacher.

10. Zuzana Pešatová, *Bohemian Engraved Glass* (Feltham, England, 1968), p. 20. Hereafter, Pešatová.

11. Because successful completion of a prescribed course of studies earns a degree, usually Master of Fine Arts, we capitalize the words "Master" and "Masterpiece" to indicate such training.

CHAPTER 4

1. Hakes.

2. CGW suit, p. 41.

3. *Journal*, Aug. 18, 1903.

4. *Journal*, Aug. 1, 1873; Oct. 31, 1873.

5. *Journal*, page 90.

6. CGW suit, page 149.

7. *Journal*, June 26, 1884.

8. *Journal*, Aug. 6, 1902.

9. *Daily Journal*, May 15, 1906.

10. *Corning Evening Leader*, Jan. 13, 1914.

11. Corning Glass Works Archives, Corning.

12. George S. and Helen McKearin, *American Glass* (1941), Pl. 57A; also shown in their *Two Hundred Years of American Blown Glass* (1949), Pl. 88; and in J. S. Spillman, and E. S. Farrar, *The Cut and Engraved Glass of Corning, 1868-1940* (1977), Fig. 33.

13. CGW suit, p. 174.

14. CGW suit, p. 194.

15. Ibid.

16. CGW suit, p. 208.

CHAPTER 5

1. Obituary, T. G. Hawkes, *Corning Evening Leader*, July 17, 1913.

2. CGW suit, p. 41.

3. Obituary, Samuel Hawkes, *Corning Leader*, June 26, 1959.

4. Sinclaire suit, p. 14; CGW suit, p. 158.

5. T. G. Hawkes & Co., Stock Ledger, Corning, 1890-1922, Corning Museum of Glass. Hereafter, Stock Ledger.

6. *Journal*, Sept. 3, 1886.

7. AFGWU Proceedings, 1904.

8. *Journal*, July 16, 1902. See Chapter 18, Steuben Glass Works, for further history of this property.

9. *Journal*, March 27, 1901.

10. Cash Book.

11. *Corning Evening Leader*, Dec. 14, 1912.

12. Paul V. Gardner, *The Glass of Frederick Carder* (New York: Crown Publishers, 1971), pp. 41-42.

13. Correspondence from White House to CMG, 1977.

14. *Jewelers' Circular*, Dec. 8, 1926.

15. Correspondence from White House to CMG, Oct., 1977.

16. Correspondence, Samuel Hawkes to Fostoria Glass Company, Moundsville, W. Va., 1916.

17. Boggess, Bill and Louise, *American Brilliant Cut Glass* (New York: Crown Publishers, 1977), *Ill. 175C*.

18. Rouse.

19. CGW suit, p. 139.

20. *"Glass, Silver, etc."*

21. C. Dorflinger & Sons *Factory Office Price List.* Hereafter, Dorfl. l.

22. Interview, Betty Schaefer and E. S. F., Corning, July 26, 1976.

23. Interview, Hazel Smith and E. S. F., Corning, April 14, 1977.

24. Boggess, op. cit., Ill. 17A.

25. Interview, Floyd Manwarren with E. S. F.

26. Interview, Mrs. R. Webster, Corning, June 26, 1976.

CHAPTER 6

1. Information not otherwise footnoted has been provided by Mrs. Walter (Dorothy Hunt) Sullivan, Thomas Sullivan, Mary Krebs, and Floyd Manwarren.

2. Frank Wilson & Sons, founded a year earlier, was short-lived and probably a subcontractor only.

3. Corning Glass Works's agreement of exclusivity with Hoare and Hawkes has been discussed. No sales to Hunt appear in Dorflinger 1.

4. 1889 Paris Exposition Catalog.

5. *China, Glass & Lamps*, Sept. 12 and 26, 1903.

6. See Revi, p. 197.

7. *China, Glass & Lamps*, Apr. 27, 1907.

8. Revi shows the patent drawing on p. 198.

9. *Focus on Corning: the Crystal City of the World*...(Corning, 1948). It is possible that the authors may have mistaken the administration. The White House Registrar writes that "our records are not complete to every administration but we do have official orders.... None of our records mention the Hunt Glass Works supplying glass to the White House in the early 20th century." (White House orders, however, were customarily placed through a retailer.) Further, the Harding home in Marion, Ohio, shows a set of gold-encrusted stemware that The Hardings used in the White House, and remnants of two H. P. Sinclaire & Co. sets that the Hardings personally owned. Trade journals mention the gift of the gold-encrusted set to President Harding.

10. Mrs. Ethel Travis Barnes supplied this information. The fifteen woman cutters reported in the 1948 newspaper article may have included trainees.

CHAPTER 7

1. Most of the information in this chapter is taken from interviews with Susan Egginton Altonen and Lucille Egginton of Corning, July 1974, both daughters of Walter Egginton.

2. *New York Journal of Commerce*, Sept. 27, 1898.

CHAPTER 8

1. Two engraving companies, J. F. Haselbauer & Sons and John N. Illig, Manufacturer of Artistically Engraved Glassware, are the subjects of later chapters.

2. "The Fritsche Ewer" ([New York], 1886), unpaged. Meistersdorf, also spelled without the second *s*, is now Mistrovice, Czechoslovakia.

3. H. P. Sinclaire would report this to the *New York Tribune* in 1888. The *Journal* reprinted the story Aug. 20.

4. Except for deductions from known facts, or where another source is noted, Mrs. Catherine Haselbauer Dencenburg, daughter of George Haselbauer, is the source of information about her father, uncle, and grandfather. Hereafter, Dencenburg.

5. Ignatius Haselbauer's work cannot be identified. He came to Corning from Scotland about 1888, and died about 1898.

6. Mrs. Helen Fritchie Arnoldy is the source of information about her father except where another source is noted. She has provided his passport, marriage license, and 1885 medal. Hereafter, Arnoldy.

7. Clement Nitsche identifies this "older Kretschmann" as the Webb engraver who summoned his compatriots to Corning. The dates when he worked in Corning and when he left, however, are as indicated by Corning directories.

8. Unpublished photo-postcard showing four engravers. Mailed in an envelope that is now missing, it is dated only "Toledo, 1910," and is written in German. It identifies two engravers as Keller and Gunther. A third name is illegible. Emil, the signer, does not give his last name.

9. Haselbauer gave his birthplace as Bohemia in the 1880 census. Meistersdorf is suggested by the family tradition that he "had a hand in" bringing to Corning other Meistersdorf engravers.

10. The 1880 census established his age. The fact that Joseph's sons had cousins other than the sons of Ignatius Haselbauer indicates that they were the children of Augustus.

11. Manchee II, p. 1009, says of this order that "in 1906 Theodore Roosevelt added 170 pieces to the [Benjamin Harrison] set, including the first highball glasses bought for the White House..." The cutting was T. G. Hawkes & Co.'s patented *Russian* design.

12. Fritchie may have been in Corning by 1887. No directory is extant for that year.

13. Payments began April 27, 1901. Some marked "add'l" may have been for work in Nitsche's home shop.

14. The Hawkes Cash Book shows that Clem Nitsche was "paid in full" August 6, 1904.

15. Information about Illig is from his daughter, Mrs. Virginia Illig Driscoll; and his daughter-in-law, Mrs. John D. Illig, except where another source is noted.

16. Richard D. Mandell, *Paris 1900: the Great World's Fair*, copyright Canada 1967 by University of Toronto Press, p. 82.

17. Clyde Hauff, who worked at the Sinclaire company from about 1909 to about 1916, placed Illig at the company during that period. Hereafter, Hauff.

18. *Pottery & Glass* reported in its August, 1910 issue on Upham, "the energetic representative of... H. C. Fry...the Empire Cut Glass Company, and John N. Illig."

19. Except where another source is noted, information about Emile Walter comes from his daughter, Mrs. Edward Dailey; and from his grand-

daughters, Mrs. Vincent Welch and Mrs. Lawrence Hausheer.

20. Information that is not otherwise attributed is from Robert Keller, Mrs. Richard Keller, Mrs. Dorothy Keller Mahoney, and from the late Anthony J. (Tony) Keller.

21. Information not otherwise footnoted is from Underiner's departure and birth certificates *(Entlassungs-Urkunde, Geburtsurkunde)*, and Certificate of Naturalization, supplied by his grandson, Nicholas Williams of The Corning Museum of Glass.

22. Information about Edward Palme, Sr., has been compiled from family records and memories by Mrs. Edward Palme, Jr., except where another source is noted. Hereafter, Palme.

23. *Corning Glass Works Gaffer*, May, 1948, p. 16, quoting a son, gives 1905; a Palme daughter gives 1907.

24. Information about Ernest Kaulfuss and his brother has been supplied by his daughters, Mrs. Dorothy Kaulfuss Coats, Mrs. Ruth Stewart, and Mrs. Tessie Kaulfuss LaMonica, except where another source is noted.

25. Information about Henry Keller has come from Mrs. Richard V. Keller, Clement Nitsche, Mrs. William Rotsell, Thomas Miller, Clyde Hauff, Mrs. Harold Allison, and Steuben engravers Peter Schelling and Max Erlacher. Keller's birth date is from his headstone.

26. The judgment is that of Peter Schelling and Max Erlacher.

27. Information about Hiram Rouse has been compiled from family records and memories by Mrs. Evelyn Rouse HoganCamp, Hiram Rouse's cousin, except where another source is noted.

28. Hauff; directories.

29. Steuben Glass (reorganized 1933) has never manufactured or sold cutting blanks. Many purchasers of Steuben pieces, however, have had them engraved or cut in Corning's home shops.

30. Information about Joseph Libisch has been supplied by his daughter in consultation with her uncle, Anton Libisch, except where another source is noted.

31. The date is from Miroslava Despot, "Josef Lobmeyr and His Glassworks in Slavonia," *Journal of Glass Studies*, IV (Corning, 1962), p. 105. Hereafter, Despot.

32. Despot, p. 107.

33. This was a man named Ostermeyr. The works burned in 1912 according to Anton Libisch, who watched the fire from a hill where he was gathering wood for its furnaces.

34. Except where another source is noted, Mrs. Esther Kretschmann Patch has supplied information about her father.

35. The closing dates of the Dorflinger and Hoare companies (1921, 1920) is the basis for our estimate of 1918 as the opening date of Kretschmann's home shop. In fact, it may have been far earlier.

36. Information about Kaulfuss has been supplied by his grandson, C. H. Kaulfuss, and his great-grandson, the Reverend C. H. Kaulfuss, except where another source is given.

37. Wilmot Putnam, Jr., has provided information about his father except where another source is noted.

38. This was reprinted in John F. Hotchkiss, *Cut Glass Handbook and Price Guide* (Rochester, 1970), p. 109.

39. Putnam's teaching years can be dated approximately as those when H. W. Fritchie was in Toledo (1902-4) by a Cash Book entry. Sturtevant was "pd in full" August 31, 1905, presumably the date when he left the company.

40. Information about Nathaniel Phelps has been

provided by his son, Donald Phelps, except where another source is noted.

41. Mrs. William Rotsell, who worked with Lena Flaspheler Phelps at H. P. Sinclaire & Co., says that Mrs. Phelps's duties included entering drawings of new blanks in the company's number books.

42. Information about the May family's birthplace comes from Mrs. Joseph Hopper, engraver Frank Konigstein's daughter (see below). Hereafter, Hopper.

43. Information about Goodman is from his daughter, Mrs. Arthur Kantz, except where another source is noted.

44. Information about Hahne has been supplied by Mrs. Matthew Cammen, Mrs. Hahne's niece; and by Hopper.

45. Information about Aiden Johnson has been supplied by his widow, Mrs. Mary Johnson, except where another source is noted.

46. Information is from Mrs. Hopper and Mrs. Frank Konigstein except where another source is noted.

47. This information comes from former Corning Glass Works gaffer Joseph Fox, who knew the Keller-Hauptmann-Konigstein family of engravers well. Hereafter, Fox.

48. Information about Edward Palme, Jr., has been supplied by Mrs. Palme except where another source is noted.

49. Palme supplied this information to Bob Gill for Gill's privately mimeographed "Corning's Crystal" (Corning, n.d.), p. 3.

50. CGW records disagree with Mrs. Palme's memory of the years when Palme worked for Steuben Glass. CGW gives 1938-60; Mrs. Palme remembers 1938-57.

51. The spelling of Oveszny's name, and his birth and death years, are as they appear on his headstone.

52. Information about the Ovesznys in Europe and Pennsylvania is from Mrs. Johanna Schaffer of Jeannette, Pennsylvania, a family friend.

CHAPTER 9

1. Chapter 20 discusses cutting companies and home shops presently operating in Corning.

2. CGW suit, pp. 152-53.

3. Information about Michael Moore has been provided by his son Robert, courtesy of Miss A. E. McCloskey.

4. Steuben Glass Works–Steuben Division sold blanks until Corning Glass Works reorganized it as the modern Steuben Glass in 1933. Sinclaire & Co. made free-blown blanks in a small factory in Bath, New York, and later in Dunkirk, New York, 1920-27.

5. Information about the Wilsons has been provided by Mrs. Thelma Wilson Grover, C. Frank Wilson's granddaughter, except where another source is noted.

6. We are indebted to George Parker of the AFGWU, Toledo, for information about LU 28.

7. CGW suit, p. 149. The second name is incorrectly spelled Dotten.

8. Op. cit., p. 169.

9. Revi, p. 340.

10. *Corning–Painted Post Historical Society Bulletin*, vol. 1, no. 3 (Corning, May 1963), p. 3. Hereafter, *Bulletin*.

11. CGW suit, pp. 80-81, 88.

12. The rare "Corning Cut Glass Co." trademark is not that of Corning Glass Works. Its owner is the subject of Chapter 11.

13. Though Mulford's name does not appear in the 1880 census, he was among the Hoare & Dailey workmen who signed a letter printed in the *Journal* October 14, 1880.

14. A Corning Museum of Glass taped interview with the late Mrs. T. E. O'Brien, a former Corning Cut Glass Company employee, gave his employees as four or five and also described his product.

15. Hosea Clark, manager of Pittston Cut Glass, testified in CGW suit, p. 289, that "I have seen him when he had six frames and when he had ten."

16. Percy Johnson, Blackburn's grandson, has provided the information about his grandfather's background and cutting shop.

17. Information for which no other source is noted is from a copy of Knickerbocker's incorporation papers.

18. Mulford, p. 387.

19. "Blank Negatives" ([New Bedford, Mass.], 1905-9), unpublished. Hereafter, Blank Negs.

20. Joe Hayes, "A Man of All Trades," Elmira, N.Y., *Sunday Telegram*, Sept. 19, 1976.

21. Glenn Thomas reports trips to Tiffin with his father to select blanks. Also Blank Negs.

22. Hawkes's testimony in CGW suit, p. 150.

23. As indicated in Blank Negs.

24. Dorfl. I. Also Blank Negs.

25. This clipping reached us without identification. Its title is "Flames Put Ferris Cut Glass Co. Out of Business." Mulford, p. 444, gives the fire date as April 18, 1913, and the damage to the "Ferris Glass Company" as $2,000.

26. "Johnny Knew His Glass," *Elmira Sunday Telegram*, Apr. 20, 1975.

27. Our only information about Bradley is from Corning directories.

28. Mrs. Louise Painter Hallahan, daughter of Ernest Painter, is the source of information about the brothers' later careers.

29. Except for the Byrnes listing in Blank Negs., information is from Corning city directories.

30. We have found no evidence that Corning's Standard Cut Glass Co. was connected with either of the two firms of that name discussed in Revi, pp. 142-44, 448.

31. Information about the Share family comes from Mrs. Roswell Webster and John Share, granddaughter and great-grandson of Samuel Jabez Share.

32. Rose is listed as a cutter in the 1899 directory, but not in 1891 and 1893; between these years no directories are extant.

33. Information about Callahan comes from his *Journal* obituary, which reached us without a date, from Corning directories, and from R. H. McElroy.

34. This deduction is supported by the *Journal*, Oct. 14, 1880. A letter in this issue, signed by Hoare & Dailey workmen, does not include Patrick Callahan's name, but does include his brother's.

35. Information is from former cutter Gerald Davis. Hereafter, Davis. The 1921 Corning directory also lists Jones as employed at the Sinclaire company. Mr. Davis says that Jones did puntying.

36. Peter Eick's daughters, Florence and Evelyn Eick, have provided all information about their father that is not otherwise footnoted.

37. Eick's work for Illig has been reported by Mrs. Virginia Illig Driscoll, Illig's daughter; and Joseph Fox, Illig's financial backer.

38. Fox says that Eick was Illig's only remaining employee when the company closed. This suggests a final date of 1924 to 1927 (see Chapter 17).

39. Holland B. Williams has reported these relationships. His inability to remember the company suggests that he and Miss Haradon were inactive associates.

40. Information about Signet's customers and products is from this sales book.

41. Information about Harry Jones comes from his nephew, Fred Gillard, and Mrs. Gillard, and from his wife's niece, Mrs. Frances Hanley, except where another source is noted.

42. Carrie Ellison of Corning called the Jones cutting shop to our attention.

43. Jones's Corning Glass Works employment record is incomplete. Additional information has been assembled by Otto Hilbert of Corning Glass Works from conversations with other employees who knew Jones.

44. Reports about Wellsboro Glass Co. antedate by a few months John (Jack) Hoare's return from Wellsboro to J. Hoare & Co. in Corning, and seemed for that reason to be advance rumors of the change.

45. CGW suit, p. 275.

46. Former cutter Leon Swope of Wellsboro, still active in his nineties, remembers this company. Mr. Swope has also provided unerringly accurate information about his own employers in Wellsboro and Middletown, N.Y. Hereafter, Swope.

47. Information about the company is from Mrs. Evelyn Rouse HoganCamp except where another source is noted. Mrs. HoganCamp, who often worked in the Fuller factory, is related to Nell Fuller's adoptive parents, the Allens.

48. This information is from Mrs. Emil Schrickel, a childhood friend of the Fuller-Allen family. Mrs. Schrickel recalls sitting with Nell Fuller's adoptive mother in her later years, when she loved to light up a corncob pipe.

49. Except where another source is noted, information about Ambrose Van Etten has been supplied by his widow, Mrs. Elizabeth Van Etten; his son, Bernard, and cousin, Douglas Van Etten; by Mrs. Maynard Van Etten, Gerald Davis, and Floyd Manwarren.

50. Mr. Manwarren is one of the subjects of Chapter 20.

51. Information about Watson has been supplied by his son-in-law, the late Ranald McMullin, and Mrs. McMullin, except where another source is noted.

52. This information comes from Fred Gillard, one of the boys who supplied Watson with bottles.

53. John Denson's son, Roy, has supplied information about his father except where another source is noted. Roy Denson's cutting shop is one of the subjects of Chapter 20.

CHAPTER 10

1. Information about G. W. Drake and the Drake family has been compiled from Hakes, Mulford, and the Corning directories. Leslie Clute, son of Drake's bookstore partner, was our informant about Clute & Drake and the purchase of the Bronson Inkstand Co.

2. This fact seems to be common knowledge in Corning. It has been reported by R. O. Sinclaire, the late Dr. Henry Elwell, and others.

3. *China, Glass & Lamps*, May 31, 1902.

4. Dorfl. I.; also Blank Negs.

5. Vases 836 and 1090 and the celery appear in *C. Dorflinger & Sons Catalog* (reprint) (Hanover, Pennsylvania, 1970), Plates 6, 56, 76. Part of stemware set 520 is pictured in Manchee III, p. 97.

CHAPTER 11

1. Hakes, II, 272.

2. *Journal*, Aug. 6, 1902; also Mulford, p. 416.

3. CGW Suit, p. 271.

4. This information is from the late Francis Conroy.

5. CGW suit, pp. 289-90.

6. CGW suit, p. 243.

7. National Reporter System, *The New York Supplement* (St. Paul, 1903), vol. 78, p. 1112.

8. Letter dated June 25, 1906, in CGW suit, p. 361.

9. The 1903 Corning directory showed that a number of cutters had moved to Painted Post, which would have been convenient to the Corning Cut Glass Co. but also to the Crystal Manufacturing Co. until World War II. Three of them have been identified above as Sebring employees. The others were Bert Abbey, George Abbey, Fred Balcom, Frank Drake, James Gurnsey, Ross Hammond, Rutherford Harrington, Ned Hicks, Walter Hicks, Charles B. Howell, Ransom Libbey, Willard Lockwood, Edward Maine, Eugene Maine, William Osterhout, and Clarence Rowe. In 1911/12 cutters Sylvia T. Davis and Mary E. Morse lived in Painted Post, but had left (or married) before the 1913/14 directory was printed.

CHAPTER 12

1. Information about the company is from Charles and Clarence Giometti, sons of L. C. Giometti, and Mary Giometti Smith, their sister, except where another source is noted.

2. Information about Stowell is from his daughter, Mrs. Matthew Cammen.

CHAPTER 13

1. Mrs. Penrose Hawkes reports that the visit interrupted Samuel Hawkes's wedding trip; Mrs. Sally Hawkes Thornton, Samuel's daughter, reports a mention of it in her mother's diary. The Cash Book reflects it in a May 8, 1902, entry: "Exp for Sam. Hawkes in England. Business of T. G. Hawkes & Co. 100."

2. Gardner's 373-page monograph is required reading for every admirer of Frederick Carder's glass. The author worked with Carder from the 1920s until World War II. He shows line drawings of Steuben blanks, and photographs of Steuben pieces of all kinds, many of them in color. The information he gives goes beyond the scope of our single chapter.

3. Carder seems also to have visited the Paris Exposition of 1900. His signed copy of the Exposition catalog is in the library of The Corning Museum of Glass.

4. "March" is clearly an error. Gardner reports that Carder visited Pittsburgh and Washington before coming to Corning (p. 23). We will show that he reached Corning by March 7; hence he must have left England in February.

5. Information about the friendship comes from Sinclaire's youngest son, Reginald. Sinclaire's death in November 1902 may have helped Hawkes overcome his reluctance to admit that he planned to open a rival glass factory.

6. Estate Inventory for T. G. Hawkes, unpublished (Corning, [1913]), p. 28.

7. Op. Cit., p. 8.

8. Cash Book: reimbursement to Hawkes for payment of Carder's June salary.

9. Manchee writes (II, p. 1011) that the dispute was "over inventory." Chapter 14 will show that Sinclaire continued a close relationship with the Dorflinger company.

10. The AFGWU's side of this struggle is told in detail in *Proceedings*, 1904. The Hawkes side is documented in the Cash Book, which shows Steuben Glass Works payments to Thomas Hawkes

and lawyer Willis S. Reed "for men at Ellis Isl.", and to Hawkes for "exps to Washington D.C." between November 2 and December 18, 1903.

11. Interview with Joseph Falk.

12. Revi, p. 175.

13. Unpublished letters of June 1, 1914, and January 30, 1915, from T. G. Hawkes & Co. (initialed by Townsend deM. Hawkes) to Steuben Glass Works.

14. Hawkes Estate Inventory, p. 28.

15. Mulford, p. 436.

16. The late Robert Leavy, long production manager of Steuben Glass.

17. Gardner, p. 32, Ill. 57.

18. The Lentricchia brothers' surname is given as "André" in Corning directories of the 1920s because their boss thought Lentricchia was too difficult.

CHAPTER 14

1. Estelle Farrar's two-volume *H. P. Sinclaire, Jr., Glassmaker* is a detailed history of the Sinclaire company and identification guide to its products. Though later research has yielded some additional information, the earlier work supplies the basis of this chapter.

2. Unpublished letter of January 5, 1883.

3. Unpublished letter of February 16, 1883.

4. Allen's grandson, Walter M. Allen, is the source of this information.

5. *Glass, Silver, Etc.* is in Sinclaire's handwriting.

6. Dencenburg.

7. Baccarat showed some of its 1889 Exposition pieces in a Neiman-Marcus "French Fortnight" promotion in Dallas during the spring of 1970.

8. Stock Ledger. Also, Sinclaire suit, passim, confirms that Sinclaire purchased the stock. It is the source of information in the paragraph that follows.

9. Letter from Murray Sinclaire to Douglas Sinclaire, unpublished (Aug. 7, 1927). The Stock Ledger shows that Sinclaire held his Hawkes stock through a 1922 reorganization.

10. The opening and closing dates of this little company are unknown. Mrs. Edna Hanley Rotsell, Sinclaire & Co. saleswoman, recalls that production seemed to have stopped by 1920, but that there were still Ravenwood pieces in the stockroom.

11. Lucy Egginton.

12. H. P. Sinclaire & Co. Private Ledger No. 1, unpublished (Corning, Jan. 25, 1904-Dec. 31, 1920), unpaged. Hereafter, Ledger.

13. *National Glass Budget*, Apr. 22, 1922, quoting "a recent issue" of the *Elmira Telegraph*.

14. Mulford, p. 393.

15. Stock Ledger.

16. Sinclaire suit, p. 6. The suit, passim, is also the source of information in the paragraph that follows.

17. Cash Book.

18. Robert Sinclaire remembers this order, and thinks that the goblets' wholesale price was $1,800 a dozen.

19. We have verified this information with the curator of the Harding home in Marion, Ohio, where *Adam* decanters could still be seen in 1974. The rest of the two sets was sold by Mrs. Harding's heir.

20. Dorfl. I

21. Liljeqvist.

22. Dorfl. I.

23. Liljeqvist.

24. Blank Negs.

25. Liljeqvist.

26. This design, popular with collectors, is often called *Greek Key & Laurel*. This has led to confusion between *Flutes & Panel Border* and the

cheaper *Panel Border*, in which the fluting was omitted.

27. The Corning Museum of Glass has a Steuben-signed goblet in a Sinclaire & Co. design of the 1920s.

28. We have shown that small companies were often unlisted in directories. The 1905 directory listed twelve cutting companies, but the Elmira Cut Glass Co., the Painter cutting shop, and perhaps others were operating but unlisted.

29. Rouse names only those engravers in the downstairs shop. The upstairs one is known from interviews with Nitsche, Davis, and others.

30. Cutter-designer James Clark worked for the Sinclaire company during all of its life. His son, Howard Clark, says that his father once briefly left the company, but "Mr. Sinclaire sent a man to get him."

31. Manwarren and the late Mary Dow Canfield were in agreement about the identity of these men.

32. Information about Sinclaire & Co. craftsmen comes from Clyde Hauff, who worked at the company for six years; from Manwarren; Davis, from a dozen or more additional interviews; and from Corning directories.

33. Salesmen's names from Private Ledger. Agents from letters of K. P. Lockitt and Murray Sinclaire to Douglas Sinclaire, 1927.

CHAPTER 15

1. See also Chapter 8, introductory section and "Joseph F. Haselbauer."

2. Chapter 8 has cited a newpaper story of 1906, connecting the Haselbauers with White House orders, some of which were made by C. Dorflinger & Sons.

3. Krebs.

CHAPTER 16

1. Except where another source is noted, information about the Shotton company is from *Leader* stories of July 19, July 26, Aug. 2, Aug. 7, and Oct. 1, 1912.

2. The late Ranald McMullin provided this information; his wife's grandfather was with the group.

3. A total of 766 employees producing $600,000 worth of glass annually seems unlikely: output would be less than $800 per employee.

4. This information comes from Gerald Hazelbauer and Mrs. Thomas Hazelbauer.

5. These agreements are known from the 1927 Sinclaire correspondence cited in Chapter 14, and from the children of Dorflinger craftsmen who left White Mills to work for Corning Glass Works.

6. Gerald Hazelbauer.

CHAPTER 17

1. Sources of information are cited in Chapter 8.

2. Mrs. William Sinclaire, wife of a Sinclaire & Co. silent partner, gave two Illig-engraved Sinclaire plates as a wedding present to Mrs. Douglas Sinclaire in 1918, with the information that such designs had been discontinued before the war.

3. The gang-cut wheel, introduced about 1913, was exploited in Corning almost at once by the Hawkes & Sinclaire companies also. It made several parallel incisions at one time.

4. The *Leader* article of May 2 identified the owners as James Sebring, former president of Corning Cut Glass Co., and Justin Purcell, later active in T. G. Hawkes & Co.

5. Fox.

CHAPTER 18

1. *Glass Trade Directory,* 1902; *China, Glass & Lamps,* May 3, 1902.
2. Revi, p. 210.
3. *Bulletin,* May 1963, p. 2.
4. CGW suit, pp. 218-19, 258.
5. P. 354.

CHAPTER 19

1. Information about John S. Earl and his sons has been supplied by Dorothy Earl Barbera, daughter of John Earl, Jr., except where another source is given.
2. Lillian Pattinson, "Glass Gathering by a New England School Ma'am," mimeographed, p. 22.
3. An interesting sidelight suggests that Union Co. specialized in giant punch bowls. The late Eric Liljeqvist told us in 1971 that his brother David was gatherer of a Union Co. shop that made a punch bowl for the Libbey company. Libbey cut the bowl for the 1904 St. Louis World's Fair. "Seems to me it was ninety-three pounds in weight," Liljeqvist said. "Now, I don't know what they used to call that factory, but it was in Somerville." This bowl was, of course, surpassed by the one Earl's company cut.
4. Blank Negs.
5. Dorfl. I.
6. This information comes from Mrs. Thomas Hazelbauer, daughter-in-law of the Shotton foreman, who owns matching glasses. They are shown in Chapter 9.
7. The *Leader* reported Nov. 11, 1907, that the factory had "stood over the creek" in Addison "for the past 17 years."
8. Information about Erhardt and Schaeffer is from Mrs. Gerald Donegan, Erhardt's daughter, except where another source is noted.
9. Revi reports also on this company (pp. 149-51). Mrs. Martin Rosenblum, "The Tuthill Cut Glass Company," *The Historical Society of Middletown and the Walkill Precinct, Inc., Sixth Annual Yearbook* ([Middletown], 1958), gives a more complete report. The statement in this report that the Tuthill company exhibited at the St. Louis Exposition of 1903, however, is not verified by the Exposition catalog.
10. Dorfl. I.
11. Blank Negs.
12. Cutters' names are from Rosenblum, as are the company addresses.
13. Information about the Majestic company comes from Mrs. Beatrice Perling, daughter of the founder, except where another source is noted.
14. Blank Negs.
15. *China, Glass & Lamps,* May 10, 1902. The name given in the article is incorrect, however.

16. Information about Charles Rose is from his son, Clayton Rose, except where another source is noted.
17. Information about Ideal Cut Glass Co.'s workmen and building are from Manwarren.
18. Blank Negs.
19. This information comes from Mrs. Francis Taylor, daughter of Charles Carroll and niece of John Vallely, who also supplied the latter's obituary.
20. *Leader,* July 19, 1912.
21. Information in this paragraph is from a *China, Glass & Lamps* story of June 9, 1906.
22. Dorfl. I. Also Blanks Negs.
23. Information about the Phelps companies has been provided by Donald Phelps, Mrs. Phelps, and Floyd Manwarren.
24. Dorfl. I. Also Blank Negs.
25. Revi, p. 382, gives information about later owners of this company.
26. Vallely's obituary has reached us undated, and without the newspaper's name. His niece gives the year of his death as 1955.
27. Information about Fred Eygabroat comes from his sister, Mrs. Sara Eygabroat Knowles, and his nephew, Fred Eygabroat Balcom, except where another source is noted.
28. Information about Everett Stage in this and the following section has been provided by his daughter, Mrs. Adeliene Stage Butla, except where another source is noted.
29. Blank Negs. Also Dorfl. I.
30. Thomas.
31. This information comes from the late Mr. Dillon and from Lawrence Holton, son of William Holton, who also supplied information about his father in the section that follows. Hereafter, Holton.
32. Information not otherwise footnoted is from Mrs. Adeliene Stage Butla.
33. Holton.
34. Copy of "Certificate of Election to Dissolve," Stage-Kashins Cut Glass Co., filed Aug. 17, 1949; approved March 27, 1950.
35. Holton.
36. Information is from Walter M. Allen except where another source is noted. Mr. Allen has researched his father's company for several years. His sources include *American Glass Trade Directory,* 1919-22; *Pennsylvania Industrial Directory,* 1913, 1916, 1919, 1922; *Charters of Corporation, Pennsylvania,* 1911-13; Johnstown city directories, local newspapers, and interviews with family members and former employees, particularly Phillip Boyer, Earla Lint, and Mary Kidd Hite. Hereafter, Allen.
37. See Revi, p. 348.
38. This was probably in 1910 or 1912, when Corning Glass Works records indicate the last sales of cutting blanks.

39. Information about Berleue Cut Glass from Allen.
40. Our information about this company comes from Hosea Clark's testimony in CGW suit, pp. 279-81.
41. *Glass Trade Directory.*
42. Leon Swope has provided information about Hoare & Millspaugh workmen and products in a number of interviews and letters. Material not otherwise footnoted is from this source.

CHAPTER 20

1. We are indebted to the two books named above, and to several members of the Steuben company, for our information about Steuben Glass. Arthur A. Houghton, Jr., Thomas Buechner, and Paul Schulze have discussed Steuben's goals with us. We have consulted the late Robert Leavy, Max Roland Erlacher, the late Thomas Miller, Peter Schelling, and Kenneth Van Etten for information about Steuben craftsmen. Information about employment records and Steuben Glass's early days has been made available through Otto Hilbert of Corning Glass Works. Mrs. Jane Kaufmann and Mrs. Isobel Lee Beers have provided detailed information about Steuben designs and designers.
2. An extant formula for C. Dorflinger & Sons crystal also includes no decolorizer; a side-by-side comparison of this crystal with that of Steuben shows them to be of equal brilliance.
3. Plaut, p. 3.
4. We have been unable to determine whether the Carder glasses included in the Fine Arts Society show—Intarsia, for example—were for purposes of comparison only, or whether they were still in production.
5. See Plaut, pp. 107-8, for a list of exhibitions of Steuben glass.
6. Cf. Farrar I, p. 21.
7. Information in this section is from Manwarren.
8. The Phelps company is discussed in Chapter 19.
9. Information in this section comes from Mr. and Mrs. Peter Schelling.
10. Information about John Lentricchia comes from Mr. Lentricchia, his brother Louis, and his daughter, Mrs. Joseph Gargano.
11. Information about Max Erlacher and Erlacher Glass comes from Erlacher.
12. Information about Vesta Glass comes from Richard L. Pope except where another source is noted.
13. Information about Lorinda Freitas and Harold Gross comes from Erlacher.
14. Information about Bacalles Glass Engravers has been supplied by George Bacalles.
15. CGW records. Other information in this section is from Denson himself.

Bibliography

American Flint Glass Workers' Union *Proceedings of (Various) Convention(s) of The American Flint Glass Workers Union held in various cities, 1893-1904.*

[Atkinson, Carlotta Dorflinger or Suydam, Frederick Dorflinger] *Christian Dorflinger: A Miracle in Glass.* White Mills, Pa., 1950.

Boggess, Bill and Louise. *American Brilliant Cut Glass.* New York, 1977.

"Bohemia," *Encyclopaedia Britannica.* 11th ed. vol. 4, Cambridge, England, 1910.

Brooklyn Eagle. "Brooklyn [Breukelen]," in Historic Brooklyn Series, Brooklyn, [ca. 1947].

China, Glass and Lamps, A Weekly Journal for the Buyer, 1904-12.

Commoner and Glassworker, vols. 20-23, 1898-1902.

Corning City Directories, various titles, 1868 to date.

Corning Daily Journal, 1892-1910.

Corning Democrat, 1886.

Corning Evening Leader, 1908-68.

Corning Glass Works. *Cullet,* vol. 2, no. 10, Sept. 1920.

Corning Journal, 1870-1905.

Corning Junior Chamber of Commerce Publications Committee. *Focus on Corning: The "Crystal City" of the World.* Corning, 1948.

Corning-Painted Post Historical Society *Bulletin.* vol. 1, nos. 3, 4, 5. Corning, May-July & Sept. 1963.

Davis, Pearce. *The Development of the American Glass Industry.* New York, 1970.

Despot, Miroslava. "Joseph Lobmeyr and His Glassworks in Slavonia," *The Journal of Glass Studies.* vol. 4. 1962.

Dorflinger, C. & Sons. *Blank Prices 1920/21.* Unpublished. White Mills, Pa., 1920-21.

——. *Factory Office Price List.* Unpublished. White Mills, Pa., n.d.

Dorflinger, William. "The Development of the Glass Business in the United States." Paper read before the American Association of Flint and Lime Glass Manufacturers at the Annual Meeting at Atlantic City, N.J., July 25, 1902.

Drake, Franklin N., In Memory of. Corning, 1893.

Duthie, Arthur Louis. *Decorative Glass Processes.* "The Westminster Series." London, 1908.

Editors of American Heritage. *American Heritage History of The Confident Years.* New York, 1969.

Farrar, Estelle Sinclaire. *H. P. Sinclaire Jr. Glassmaker.* 2 vols. Garden City, N.Y., 1974, 1975.

Gardner, Paul V. *The Glass of Frederick Carder.* New York, 1971.

Gill, Bob. "Corning Crystal." Mimeographed. Corn-ing, 1962, 1963.

Gores, Stan. *1876 Centennial Collectibles and Price Guide.* Wisconsin, 1974.

Guttery, D. R. *From Broad-Glass to Cut Crystal. A History of the Stourbridge Glass Industry.* London, 1956.

Hakes, Hon. Harlo, ed. *Landmarks of Steuben County.* Syracuse, 1896.

Hawkes, T. G. & Co. *Cash Book.* 7 vols. Unpublished. Corning, 12/1/00-12/31/10.

——. *Day Book.* 2 vols. Unpublished. Corning, 1904-10.

——. *Factory Pay Roll.* 2 vols. Unpublished. Corning, 1/43-12/62.

——. *Glass, Silver, etc.* Unpublished. Corning, n.d.

——. Number books of Steuben Glass 1, 2 & 3. Corning, n.d.

——. Unpublished correspondence with Steuben Glassworks, 1914-22.

——. Unpublished correspondence with Fostoria Glass Co., 1916.

Jewelers' Circular, Dec. 8, 1926.

Johnston, Alfred S. "The Fritsche Ewer." New York, 1886.

Kearne, C. P., & H. J. Emmerich, eds. *The Marion Scudder Manual of Extinct or Obsolete Companies.* vol. 1. New York, 1926.

Lorant, Stefan. *The Presidency: A Pictorial History of Presidential Elections from Washington to Truman.* New York, 1952.

Louisiana Purchase Exposition 1904. *Official Catalogue of Exhibitors.* St. Louis, 1904.

McKearin, Helen & George. *Two Hundred Years of American Blown Glass.* Garden City, N.Y., 1950.

McNamara, Robert F. *A Century of Grace: The History of St. Mary's Roman Catholic Parish, Corning.* Corning, 1948.

National Glass Budget. Pittsburgh, 1909.

——. *Glass Factory Directory.* Pittsburgh, 1912-36.

New York Exhibition. *New York Catalogue of the New York Edition of the Industry of All Nations, 1853.* New York, 1853.

New York Journal of Commerce, Sept. 27, 1898.

New York Reports, 1902-11.

New York Supplement and State Reporter, 1902-11.

Pairpoint Corporation. *Blank Negatives.* New Bedford, Mass., 1905-8.

Papers on Appeal, Record, p. 304, Corning Glass Works v. Corning Cut Glass Company et al. 126AD919, 75 A.D. 629 (Fourth Dept., 1902).

Paris Universal Exposition 1889. *Official Catalogue of the United States Exhibit.* Paris, 1889.

Pattinson, Lillian G. "Glass Gathering by a New England Schoolmarm." Unpublished ms. of a talk given to the Somerville, Mass., Historical Society. Dorchester, Mass., 1950.

Pearson, J. Michael. *Encyclopaedia of American Cut & Engraved Glass 1880-1917.* 2 vols. Miami Beach, 1975-77.

Perrot, Paul. *Short History of Glass Engraving.* New York, 1973.

——. et al. *Steuben: Seventy Years of American Glassmaking.* New York, 1974.

Plaut, James S. *Steuben Glass.* 3rd rev. & enlarged ed. New York, 1972.

Pottery & Glass, Aug. 1910.

Pottery & Glass Salesman, Oct. 6, 1910, vol. 2, no. 10.

The Pottery & Glass & Brass Salesman, Oct. 6, 1910, vol. 3, no. 10.

Record on Appeal, Henry P. Sinclaire, Appellant, v. T. G. Hawkes & Company, et al., Respondents, Supreme Court, Appellate Division, Fourth Department, 1906.

Revi, Albert Christian. *American Cut & Engraved Glass.* New York, 1965.

——. *Nineteenth Century Glass Its Genesis & Development.* Rev. & enlarged. New York & Camden, 1967.

Rouse, Hiram. "Jobs with Time." Unpublished notebooks. Corning, 1905-10.

Signet Glass Co. Inc. *Sales, Transfers,* Corning, Feb. 18, 1914-Dec. 31, 1915.

Sinclaire, H. P. & Co. *Private Ledger No. 1.* Unpublished. Corning, 1904-21.

——. Unpublished correspondence.

H. P. Sinclaire, Sr., to H. P. Sinclaire, Jr., 1883.

K. P. Lockett to Douglas Sinclaire, 1927.

Murray Sinclaire to Douglas Sinclaire, 1927.

Societe Anonyme des Cristalleries du Val St. Lambert (Belgique). Directeur General Georges Deprez. Undated catalog. Liège, n.d.

Spillman, Jane, & E. S. Farrar, *The Cut and Engraved Glass of Corning, 1868-1940.* Corning, 1977.

Steuben Glass. Various catalogs and exhibit catalogs. New York, 1956-77.

Union Glass Works. *Houghton Batch Book.* Unpublished. 1859.

Weiss, Gustav. *The Book of Glass.* Translated by Janet Seligman. New York, 1971.

World's Columbian Exposition 1893. *Official Catalogue,* Part VIII. Chicago, 1893.

Zuzana Pešatová. *Bohemian Engraved Glass.* Translated by Arnošt Jappel. Photographs: Jindrich Brok. Feltham, Middx., England, ca. 1968.

Index

Page numbers in italics refer to material in illustrations or captions. Patterns and designs identified only by number designations are not indexed.